THE FALSE PRISON

VOLUME II

THE FALSE PRISON

A Study of the Development of
Wittgenstein's Philosophy

VOLUME II

DAVID PEARS

CLARENDON PRESS · OXFORD
1988

Oxford University Press, Walton Street, Oxford OX2 6DP

Oxford New York Toronto
Delhi Bombay Calcutta Madras Karachi
Petaling Jaya Singapore Hong Kong Tokyo
Nairobi Dar es Salaam Cape Town
Melbourne Auckland

and associated companies in
Berlin Ibadan

Oxford is a trade mark of Oxford University Press

Published in the United States
by Oxford University Press, New York

British Library Cataloguing in Publication Data
Pears, David, 1921–
The false prison : a study of the
development of Wittgenstein's philosophy.—
Vol. 2
1. English philosophy. Wittgenstein,
Ludwig, 1889–1951 – Critical studies
I. Title
192
ISBN 0–19–824487–8
ISBN 0–19–824486–X Pbk

Library of Congress Cataloging-in-Publication Data
Pears, David Francis.
The false prison.
(Revised for vol. 2)
Includes bibliographies and indexes.
1. Wittgenstein, Ludwig, 1889–1951.
I. Title
B3376.W564P35 1987   192   87–5566
ISBN 0–19–824487–8
ISBN 0–19–824486–X Pbk

Printed in Great Britain
at the University Printing House, Oxford
by David Stanford
Printer to the University

PREFACE

THIS is the second of two volumes of a continuous study of the development of Wittgenstein's philosophy. It deals with the work that he did after 1929 even more selectively than the first volume dealt with the system of the *Tractatus*. No attempt has been made to cover the rich variety of this *œuvre* and, in particular, very little is said about his later philosophy of logic and mathematics. The structure of the volume is extremely simple: two lines of thought are traced in full detail, one starting from the treatment of solipsism in the *Tractatus*, and the other developing out of the early theory of language proposed in that book.

The frequent references to the first volume speak for my conviction that a full understanding of Wittgenstein's later thought can hardly be achieved in isolation from his earlier thought. However, it is quite possible to read this volume without the first one just as it is quite possible to read *Philosophical Investigations* without the *Tractatus*.

The attention devoted to Wittgenstein's first attempt, in and immediately after 1929, to work out an application of the theory of language of the *Tractatus* may strike some people as excessive. My view is, of course, the opposite. Many misunderstandings of *Philosophical Investigations* come from neglecting his early attempts to formulate a phenomenalism which would not have the usual absurd consequences and to master the problem of other minds. If anything, that part of this book should have been longer.

I am grateful to Philippa Foot and Gavin Lawrence for suggesting improvements to a draft of the first seven chapters of this volume and to Elsie Hinkes for her sympathetic typing of a very inscrutable manuscript.

CONTENTS

Abbreviations   viii

PART III · INSIDE THE LATER SYSTEM

9. Transition   199

10. The Exemplary Treatment of the Ego   226

11. The First Attempt to Extend the Treatment of the Ego to   270
    Sensations and their Types: Reactions to Phenomenalism

12. The First Attempt to Extend the Treatment of the Ego to   296
    Sensations and their Types: Other Minds

13. The Private Language Argument of *Philosophical*   328
    Investigations

14. The Disabling Defect of a Private Language   361

15. The Structure of the Private Language Argument   389

16. Rule-following: the Rejection of the Platonic Theory in   423

17. Rule-following: The Rejection of the Platonic Theory in   460
    Philosophical Investigations

18. The Next Problem   502

Bibliography   535

Index   539

ABBREVIATIONS

A. Works originating from Wittgenstein

BLBK   *The Blue Book*, in L. Wittgenstein: *The Blue and Brown Books*, Blackwell, 1958.

BRBK   *The Brown Book*, in L. Wittgenstein: *The Blue and Brown Books*, Blackwell, 1958.

CLI   *Wittgenstein's Lectures, Cambridge*, 1930–32, ed. D. Lee, Blackwell, 1980.

CLII   *Wittgenstein's Lectures, Cambridge, 1932–35*, ed. Alice Ambrose, Blackwell, 1979.

LFM   *Wittgenstein's Lectures on the Foundations of Mathematics*, ed. C. Diamond, Harvester Press, 1975.

LWVC   *Ludwig Wittgenstein and the Vienna Circle: Conversations Recorded by Friedrich Waismann*, ed. B. McGuinness, tr. J. Schulte and B. McGuinness, Blackwell, 1979.

B. Works by Wittgenstein

NB   *Notebooks 1914–1916*, ed. G. H. von Wright and G. E. M. Anscombe, tr. G. E. M. Anscombe, Blackwell, 1961.

NLPESD   'Notes for Lectures on "Private Experience" and "Sense Data" ', *Philosophical Review*, Vol. 77, No. 3, 1968.

PG   *Philosophical Grammar*, ed. R. Rhees, tr. A. Kenny, Blackwell, 1974.

PI   *Philosophical Investigations*, tr. G. E. M. Anscombe, Blackwell, 1953; 3rd edn., Macmillan, 1958.

PR   *Philosophical Remarks*, ed. R. Rhees, tr. R. Hargreaves and R. White, Blackwell, 1975.

RFM   *Remarks on the Foundations of Mathematics*, ed. G. H. von Wright, R. Rhees and G. E. M. Anscombe, tr. G. E. M. Anscombe, Blackwell, 3rd edn., 1978.

RPPI   *Remarks on the Philosophy of Psychology*, Vol. I, ed. G. E. M. Anscombe and G. H. von Wright, tr. G. E. M. Anscombe, Blackwell, 1980.

RPPII   *Remarks on the Philosophy of Psychology*, Vol. II, ed. G. H. von
         Wright and Heikki Nyman, tr. C. G. Luckhardt and M. A. E.
         Aue, Blackwell, 1980.

TLP   *Tractatus Logico-Philosophicus*, tr. C. K. Ogden, Routledge,
         1922, and tr. D. F. Pears and B. McGuinness, Routledge,
         1961.

PART III

INSIDE THE LATER SYSTEM

9
Transition

M OST philosophers change the character of their thoughts at some time in their lives. If they begin by driving straight paths through the dense manifold of the world, they are likely to end by accepting all its tortuous intricacies. *La force de l'âge* yields to *la force des choses* and their inquiries take a different course, more circuitous but also more perceptive. Wittgenstein made this transition, but in his case there was something special about it, because it was not just the effect of maturity. He was following a new conception of the nature of philosophy.

His early system had been constructed under the guidance of the old idea, that philosophy penetrates phenomena and reveals their underlying structure. Its results were, therefore, theories. At the centre stood the theory that factual sentences are pictures, produced by putting together the names of simple objects; then there was the theory that these sentences can be combined with one another in only one way, truth-functionally, so that the senses of the combinations will depend entirely on the senses of the sentences that went into them; and, finally, the theory that anything else that we tried to say in sentences would lack factual sense. From this it followed that all philosophical theories, including these three, themselves lacked factual sense, and that was a paradox which could not be left unexplained.

His explanation was that philosophical theories are unlike scientific theories not only in their content—that was obvious enough—but also in the kind of thinking and experience that leads to their adoption. They are not hypotheses established by experiment but expressions of a different kind of knowledge. They are insights into the structure of our own thoughts: we think about the world and our life in it, and the essential features of our thoughts are revealed in the essential features of the language that clothes them.

This was the position that he adopted in the *Tractatus*, but it was not a stable position. If philosophical results, like the picture theory of sentences or the theory of the limits of factual sense, are not hypotheses established by experiment, it may be an understatement to say that they are unlike scientific theories. The truth may be that they are insights which cannot find their proper expression in any kind of theory. The *Tractatus* already contained hints that this is indeed the truth and that philosophy is so different from science that its results cannot be regarded as theories of any kind.

Philosophy is not one of the natural sciences.
(The word 'philosophy' must mean something whose place is above or below the natural sciences, not beside them.)[1]

So far, this is consistent with the idea that philosophers can theorize, provided that their theories are not supposed to be scientific and are not even offered in a scientific spirit. But his next remarks hint at the bigger difference:

Philosophy aims at the logical clarification of thoughts.
Philosophy is not a body of doctrine but an activity.
A philosophical work consists essentially of elucidations.
Philosophy does not result in 'philosophical propositions', but rather in the clarification of propositions.
Without philosophy, thoughts are, as it were, cloudy and indistinct: its task is to make them clear and give them sharp boundaries.[2]

In his second book, *Philosophical Investigations*, his rejection of all philosophical theorizing is explicit and total:

It was true to say that our considerations could not be scientific ones. It was not of any possible interest to us to find out empirically 'that contrary to our preconceived ideas, it is possible to think such-and-such'—whatever that may mean. (The conception of thought as a gaseous medium.) And we may not advance any kind of theory. There must not be anything hypothetical in our considerations. We must do away with all *explanation*, and description alone must take its place. . . .[3]

Here we have his new, more extreme conception of philosophy: it must not try for theories of any kind. Evidently, this is more than the usual shift from the selective, organizing vision of youth to the more open receptivity of maturity.

A philosopher who avoids all theorizing is really giving up a number of different things. It is science that has provided the dominant model

---

[1] L. Wittgenstein: *Tractatus Logico-Philosophicus*, tr. C. K. Ogden, Routledge, 1922, and tr. D. F. Pears and B. McGuinness, Routledge, 1961 (henceforth *TLP*), 4.111.
[2] Ibid., 4.112.
[3] L. Wittgenstein: *Philosophical Investigations*, tr. G. E. M. Anscombe, Blackwell, 1953; 3rd edn., Macmillan, 1958 (henceforth *PI*), I § 109.

for theories in the last five hundred years, and so he is severing the old connection between philosophy and science. The severance is complete, because philosophy neither is, nor is like, a science. That is the point made in the *Tractatus*. But in how many ways is it unlike a science? There seem to be two main differences, both emphasized in *Philosophical Investigations* and together pushing his new conception of philosophy far beyond the point reached in the *Tractatus*.

One difference is that anyone who offers a scientific theory must have started by collecting the phenomena to be explained. Even at that early stage he will necessarily be ignoring some of the differences between the items in his collection, because he will believe them to be irrelevant to his inquiry. Also, if the theory eventually adopted by him is successful, it will probably explain further phenomena that had not originally struck him as connected. Evidently, this is an undertaking which depends on turning a blind eye to certain differences within the set of phenomena to be explained, and that is one of the things that should never be done by philosophy, if Wittgenstein's later conception of it is right. Like art, and unlike science, it should never ignore idiosyncrasies.

There is a passage in *The Blue Book* which explains the importance of never ignoring the differences between cases which we start, quite correctly, by grouping together:

... I shall in the future again and again draw your attention to what I shall call language-games. These are ways of using signs simpler than those in which we use the signs of our highly complicated everyday language. Language-games are the forms of language with which a child begins to make use of words.

... When we look at such simple forms of language, the mental mist which seems to enshroud our ordinary use of language disappears. We see activities, reactions, which are clear-cut and transparent ...

Now what makes it difficult for us to take this line of investigation is our craving for generality.

This craving for generality is the resultant of a number of tendencies connected with philosphical confusions. There is—

(*a*) The tendency to look for something in common to all the entities which we commonly subsume under a general term.—We are inclined to think that there must be something in common to all games, say, and that this common property is the justification for applying the general term 'game' to the various games; whereas games form a *family* the members of which have family likenesses.[4]

---

[4] *The Blue Book* (henceforth *BLBK*), in L. Wittgenstein: *The Blue and Brown Books*, Blackwell, 1958, p. 17.

A little later he mentions another tendency, which reinforces our predilection for generality:

(*d*) Our craving for generality has another main source: our preoccupation with the method of science. I mean the method of reducing the explanation of natural phenomena to the smallest possible number of primitive natural laws; and, in mathematics, of unifying the treatment of different topics by using a generalization. Philosophers constantly see the method of science before their eyes, and are irresistibly tempted to ask and answer questions in the way that science does. This tendency is the real source of metaphysics, and leads the philosopher into complete darkness. I want to say here that it can never be our job to reduce anything to anything, or to explain anything. Philosophy really *is* 'purely descriptive'. (Think of such questions as 'Are there sense data?' And ask: What method is there of determining this? Introspection?)

Instead of 'craving for generality' I could also have said 'the contemptuous attitude towards the particular case'.[5]

Near the end of this passage he introduces the other distinctive feature of his later philosophy, which is that, in any case, it does not seek explanations. This is surprising, because it does seek understanding, and anyone who gets to the bottom of anything that he originally found hard to understand might reasonably be expected to give an explanation of it. This is what happens in other subjects, so why should it be different in philosophy? Isn't the non-theorizing philosopher now giving up too much?

These questions must not be answered in a hurry, because they presuppose the distinction between description and explanation. That is a distinction that can be drawn in more than one way, and a lot depends on the way in which Wittgenstein is drawing it. What exactly does he mean when he says that 'we must do away with all *explanation* and description alone must take its place'?

Part of his meaning is that philosophers must not try to explain things in the same kind of way as scientists. This takes him further than the main point made in the *Tractatus*, that philosophy is not another science. He is now implying that it does not even operate in the same kind of way as science. It is characteristic of scientists not only to observe and record the phenomena but also to go beneath them and discover the deeper facts that explain them. For example, observation establishes that gases expand when they are heated, but the explanation of this result comes from a deeper level: gases are

[5] *BLBK*., p. 18.

composed of particles which require more space when heat puts them in rapid motion. Wittgenstein's point is that philosophy does not operate in anything like that way.

The point needs to be put guardedly, because, though this kind of explanation is characteristic of science, it is not universal. Scientific theories do not always invoke new things discovered at a deeper level. A newly discovered pattern in the behaviour of familiar things can be just as explanatory. This alternative was discussed by Wittgenstein in the *Tractatus*,[6] and he used Newton's treatment of gravity to illustrate it, but perhaps the example that would occur to most people today is Einstein's special theory of relativity, which simplified our picture of familiar phenomena by redefining simultaneity. So the point made above must be put in a more restricted way: philosophy does not operate in anything like *one of the ways*, perhaps the most spectacular way, in which science operates.

The point would not be worth making if nobody had ever supposed that philosophy did operate in that way. So we need to know who had supposed this, and whose philosophical theories would have struck Wittgenstein as examples of this error.

One obvious example was his own earlier work, especially the dogmatic presentation of it in the *Tractatus*,[7] where he claimed to have discovered the structure of all factual language: it had to be a truth-functional development of elementary sentences, each of which had to be produced by putting together the names of simple objects. This structure was not our invention but something imposed on us by the nature of things. So the familiar phenomena—in this case our own language and thought—could be explained only if we went beneath them and discovered their underlying structure and its basis in reality.[8]

These claims were evidently inspired by the achievements of science. If the kinetic theory of gases could explain such a wide range of physical phenomena by moving to a deeper level, why should not philosophy do the same for all language and thought? The point to notice here is not just that logical atomism is modelled on physical atomism. It is that this whole way of doing philosophy is modelled on the methods of science, even if its results are firmly distinguished from scientific results, as they were in the *Tractatus*.

---

[6] *TLP* 6.32–6.35.
[7] The treatment is more tentative and exploratory in *Notebooks, 1914–1916*, ed. G. H. von Wright and G. E. M Anscombe, tr. G. E. M. Anscombe, Blackwell, 1961 (henceforth *NB*).   [8] See *TLP* 6.124.

Now it is a striking feature of the philosophical theory put forward in that book that it lacked something which is indispensable for scientific theories, namely verification or at least, confirmation. For Wittgenstein was not in a position to give any examples of elementary sentences or simple objects.[9] However, he did not regard this as a weakness in his system. He believed that his a priori argument showed that simple objects must serve as the basis of any factual language, and so it did not seem to him to matter if confirmation of his conclusion was delayed. His attitude was a curious mixture of dogmatism about the truth of his general theory and insouciance about its detailed application, which, he believed, would be discovered later.

His later criticism of this mixture of dogmatism and insouciance in the *Tractatus* is developed in a conversation with Waismann in 1931:

> One fault you can find with a dogmatic account is, first, that it is, as it were, arrogant. But that is not the worst thing about it. There is another mistake, which is much more dangerous and also pervades my whole book [sc. the *Tractatus*], and that is the conception that there are questions the answers to which will be found at a later date. It is held that, although a result is not known, there is a way of finding it. Thus I used to believe, for example, that it is the task of logical analysis to discover the elementary propositions. I wrote, We are unable to specify the form of elementary propositions,[10] and that was quite correct too. It was clear to me that here at any rate there are hypotheses and that regarding these questions we cannot proceed by assuming from the very beginning, as Carnap does, that the elementary propositions consist of two-place relations, etc. Yet I did think that the elementary propositions could be specified at a later date.[11]

He is accusing himself of dogmatism, but pointing out that he did, at least, avoid dogmatizing about the details. However, that still left him with the question how the details would be discovered, and here he made his second mistake: he believed that they would be discovered only after a deep investigation, when in fact they lay open to view on the surface. He was like a prospector who cannot believe that he does not have to dig for gold:

---

[9] See Vol. I pp. 67–9.
[10] See *TLP* 5.55 ff., discussed in Vol. I pp. 124–8 and 162.
[11] *Ludwig Wittgenstein and the Vienna Circle: Conversations Recorded by Friedrich Waismann*, ed. B. McGuinness, tr. J. Schulte and B. McGuinness, Blackwell, 1979 (henceforth *LWVC*), p. 182. The reference, given by the editor, is to R. Carnap: *Der Logische Aufbau der Welt*, Berlin, 1928 (tr. R. A. George, *The Logical Structure of the World*, Routledge, 1967).

. . . Only in recent years have I broken away from that mistake. At the time I wrote in a manuscript of my book (this is not printed in the *Tractatus*),[12] The answers to philosophical questions must never be surprising. In philosophy you cannot discover anything. I, myself, however, had not clearly enough understood this and offended against it.

The wrong conception which I want to object to in this connection is the following, that we can hit upon something that we today cannot yet see, that we can *discover* something wholly new. That is a mistake. The truth of the matter is that we have already got everything, and we have got it actually *present*; we need not wait for anything. We make our moves in the realm of the grammar of our ordinary language, and this grammar is already there. Thus we have already got everything and need not wait for the future.[13]

He is criticizing a particular example of the error of modelling philosophy on science, the logical atomism of the *Tractatus*. His point is that it is a mistake to hold up science as an example for philosophy, and, in particular, a mistake to assume that the task of philosophy is to discover a deep structure hidden beneath the surface of language and thought. Solutions to philosphical problems can be gathered from aspects of our thought and language that are already familiar to us. We have internalized the rules that govern our thought and speech, and philosophy has to elicit them from our minds by a special kind of self-examination and not by focusing an analytical microscope on the products.

Does this mean that philosophy is not an empirical investigation but an a priori one? If this question is asking whether philosophers examine the intellectual apparatus that we bring to bear on the world rather than the world on which we bring it to bear, Wittgenstein's answer was affirmative. Philosophical results are prior to scientific results because philosophy checks the tools while science actually uses them on the world.

But what if the question is taken to be asking whether philosophy's method of checking the tools is itself a priori or empirical? That is not so easy to answer. For though language is, of course, a phenomenon to be investigated empirically, like any other, philosophers are evidently

---

[12] The editor's note is: 'This remark (or, these remarks, if the two following remarks are meant) do not occur in the *Prototractatus*. In 6.1251 Wittgenstein says, "Darum kann es in der Logik auch nie Überraschungen geben" ("Hence there can *never* be surprises in logic either")—cf. 6.1261. "Auch" was added in MS and is much easier to understand if we assume that Wittgenstein intended to precede 6.1251 of *TLP* by the remark here quoted.'

[13] *LWVC* pp. 182–3.

interested in the thoughts expressed by the words rather than in the contingent features of the words that clothe them. They want to know whether our thoughts necessarily have the structure that they actually have, because it is imposed on them from outside by the world, or whether necessity is always internal to a particular way of thinking—a particular language-game—which we have adopted without having been forced to do so. In the *Tractatus* he favoured the first of these two suggestions,[14] and later, when he found the second one more convincing, it seemed to him that his earlier mistake had been typical of metaphysical thinking.

First, he had argued dogmatically and a priori that all language and thought must have an atomic structure imposed on it by the world. Then when he failed to find this structure either on the surface or on any level of analysis that he had actually explored, he still insisted that it must be discoverable on some deeper level of analysis. That gave his early theory of language a curiously ambiguous status. On the one hand, it was established a priori and so it did not seem to need experiential verification. But on the other hand, it was supposed to have some sort of experiential status, if only on a very deep level of analysis, and that seemed to give it the explanatory power of a scientific theory. In short, it lay in a kind of limbo, semi-detached from experience, actually relying on an a priori argument, but concealing the nature of its support in order to be able to claim the explanatory power of a genuinely predictive theory.

The effects of putting philosophical theories in a quasi-scientific limbo are worth scrutinizing more closely. So far, we have only one example of a theory with this ambiguous status, the logical atomism of the *Tractatus*. But it would be a mistake to think that, when Wittgenstein says that 'we may not advance any kind of theory',[15] he is merely reacting against his own earlier procedure. The theory advanced in the *Tractatus* belongs to a type that has had a long vogue. The general mark of the type is the idea that the world imposes a fixed structure on our thought. This is compatible with a great deal of superficial variation between one conceptual system and another and so between one natural language and another. All that is required is that the different languages express thoughts with the same deep structure matching the unique structure of reality. Plato's philosophy

---

[14] See Vol. I pp. 10–16.
[15] *PI* I § 109, quoted above, p. 200.

belongs to this type and there have been many other examples of it since his day.

The peculiarity of its exemplification in the *Tractatus* is that the medium to which the general idea is directly applied is language. The idea is that we confront the world with a language whose appropriateness is guaranteed by the fact that its deep structure matches that of the world. This gives the deep structure of language a crucial role to play: naturally, it does not guarantee the truth of everything that we say, but it does guarantee that it is the kind of thing that might be true—indeed, perfectly true—of the world. It is a weakness in this theory that it lies in a limbo in which confirmation has not been achieved, and, what is more disturbing, may even be thought to be something that is not really needed. Certainly, there is none of the careful deduction of testable consequences that is characteristic of science.

If we summed up Wittgenstein's case against philosophical theories at this point, it would be that they are postulates of reason rather than the experiential discoveries that they claim to be. It might be argued in their defence that they are only postulates that run ahead of immediate verification in the manner of certain scientific theories. But that is not really so. They are postulates that can never be verified, because their a priori status leaves no room for verification, and because, in any case, their implications are not determinate, so that we really would not know exactly what would have to be the case if they were true. Nevertheless, they do have an effect on the way we see things, because they bring out certain favoured aspects of our view of the world and our position in it, and they suppress other, less favoured aspects. Indeed, this loading of features, or caricaturing, is done all the more effectively because it is done from its own special limbo. These philosophical statements are powerful and privileged.

However, Wittgenstein's case against philosophical theories goes beyond this point in two distinct ways, each of which introduces a major theme in *Philosophical Investigations*.

First, he argues that the structure of factual language postulated as essential in the *Tractatus* was required to play an impossible role. It is an important part of his argument that he had failed to notice the impossibility because he did not treat the theory with the seriousness and rigour with which he would have treated a scientific theory, but left it in the limbo. To put his self-criticism in another way, his early theory of meaning postulated something which was, in fact, impossible, but which passed the superficial scrutiny normally given to speculations which hover equivocally on the fringe of science.

That puts it very briefly. In order to appreciate this criticism, we must look again at the *Tractatus*. The early system was centred on the pure essence of language. This essence was supposed to be embodied in a structure which acted as a kind of intermediary between language and the world. It was the pre-existing grid through which senses were conducted to each sentence in a natural language. We only needed to attach names to objects, and then, without more ado, an entire language would spring into existence. Each sentence would occupy its place in the pre-ordained structure, and the logical connections between one sentence and another would be fixed once and for all.[16]

He realized later that this theory of language greatly underestimated our continuing contribution to fixity of meaning and so represented the whole enterprise in a way that made it impossible. One of the recurrent themes of *Philosophical Investigations* is that we cannot give a word a meaning merely by giving it a one-off attachment to a thing. What is needed is a sustained contribution from us as we continue to use the word, an established practice of applying it in a way that we all take to be the same. So when he overlooked this contribution in the *Tractatus*, the result was a theory which was not merely wrong by omission, but, as a result of the omission, impossible. However, the impossibility was not noticed, because the theory was kept in the limbo where implications are not worked out in detail and testability is not taken seriously.

In *Philosophical Investigations* he demonstrates the impossibility very elegantly. The first step is to point out that the indefinitely prolonged sequence of correct applications of a word cannot be fixed unequivocally by any example or set of examples. It will always be possible to continue the sequence in more than one way. Nor can we eliminate this latitude by falling back on something in our minds, like a picture or a rule or a mental act. For a picture too can always be applied in more than one way, and the same is true of any words that may be used in the formulation of a rule, and a mental act may have more than one sequel. The correct continuation of a series can be determined only by what we, who continue it, find it natural to do. So if our contribution is ignored, it will not be possible to pick out the right continuation from the others. Anything will pass as correct, and the distinction between

---

[16] See *TLP* 6.124, discussed in Vol. I pp. 23–5.

obeying the rule and disobeying it will collapse. This distinction must be based on our practice, which cannot be completely anticipated by any self-contained thing. We do not, and cannot, rely on any instant talisman.

The theory of meaning offered in the *Tractatus* is not the only target of this later criticism. It is directed against any theory that tries to put meaning on a static basis.[17] The point is a general one: all theories of this kind make an impossible demand on the thing that they choose for the key role in the speaker's mind, whether it be a picture or a rule or the flash of understanding produced by an example. It is not that we fail to find the right instant talisman through lack of philosophical ingenuity: we cannot find an instant talisman, because there could not be such a thing. However, philosophers paper over its impossibility with vague words, because their theory is not really intended for verification, like a scientific theory, and its implications are not worked out in detail.

This part of Wittgenstein's later philosophy is not easy to understand, because he deploys his forces on such a wide front. People find it hard to see how a single argument, or battery of arguments, can be directed both against the abstract, hidden structure postulated in the *Tractatus* and against the appeal to something familiar, like a picture in the word-user's mind. How can the same considerations be marshalled against these two very different suggestions? The short answer to this is that there are two equally slippery paths leading to the limbo in which so many philosophical theories terminate: one is to postulate something remote and recondite to play an impossible role, and the other is to give an equally impossible role to some perfectly familiar kind of thing. In this particular case, the impossible role is the anticipation of the whole series of correct applications of a word. The first kind of theory imagines that they are all laid out in advance waiting for us to come along and pick them up, while the second kind of theory chooses something familiar, like a picture in the word-user's mind, and treats it, in an equally fantastic way, as a guide which has already picked them all up.

When the two kinds of theory are put like this, we can see that they are closely connected with one another. They both make the same impossible demand: when a word is attached to a thing, it must immediately slot into a pre-existing grid or lock on to rails extending

---

[17] See *Wittgenstein's Lectures on the Foundations of Mathematics*, ed. C. Diamond, Harvester Press, 1975 (henceforth *LFM*), p. 184.

indefinitely into the future. [18] The theory put forward in the *Tractatus* is almost exclusively concerned with this pre-ordained structure and says very little about the obvious need for something in the word-user's mind to fasten on to it. The later theory, directly attacked in *Philosophical Investigations*, concentrates on what is in his mind, and says less about the supposed external counterpart in reality. But, of course, both parts of the theory are needed if it is going to have any hope of providing a complete explanation of the kind that was thought to be required.

There is a passage in *The Blue Book* which describes the development of the mental part of this theory, and explains the origin of our illusion that we need, and can rely on, an instant talisman:

... If you are puzzled about the nature of thought, belief, knowledge, and the like, substitute for the thought the expression of the thought, etc. The difficulty which lies in this substitution, and at the same time the whole point of it, is this: the expression of belief, thought, etc. is just a sentence;—and a sentence has sense only as a member of a system of language; as one expression within a calculus. Now we are tempted to imagine this calculus, as it were, as a permanent background to every sentence which we say, and to think that, although the sentence as written on a piece of paper or spoken stands isolated, in the mental act of thinking the calculus is there—all in a lump. The mental act seems to perform in a miraculous way what could not be performed by any act of manipulating symbols. Now when the temptation to think that in some sense the whole calculus must be present vanishes, there is no more point in *postulating* the existence of a peculiar kind of mental act alongside of our expression. This, of course, doesn't mean that we have shown that peculiar acts of consciousness do not accompany the expressions of our thoughts! Only we no longer say that they *must* accompany them. [19]

This part of the theory grows very naturally out of the other part. There would be no point in giving meaning a fixed paradigm in reality unless there were something in our minds to put us in touch with it,

[18] See *TLP* 6.124 and *PI* I § 218. The grid described in the *Tractatus* is entirely general, while the fixed rails rejected in *Philosophical Investigations* are peculiar to particular words, but the mistake made in both cases is the same.

[19] Sc. in order to explain them. *BLBK* p. 42. Cf. R. Rhees's notes of the lectures given by Wittgenstein in 1936, of which Wittgenstein's own notes were published as 'Notes for Lectures on "Private Experience" and "Sense Data"' in *Philosophical Review*, Vol. 77 No. 3, 1968 (henceforth *NLPESD*): 'We assume that he must have an "interpretation" in his mind, as something which can't be further interpreted, so we have the idea that he would have the *use* of a symbol as something given in a lump.' (*Philosophical Investigations* (the periodical), Vol. 7 No. 1, Jan. 1984, p. 22.)

mind /world

and, equally, this mental talisman would be pointless if it did not put us in touch with a paradigm outside our minds.

The second development of Wittgenstein's case against philosophical theories is closely connected with the first one. It too is a criticism of the sketchiness of explanations offered in a quasi-scientific spirit and not worked out with the rigour and seriousness of science, and it too introduces a major theme of *Philosophical Investigations*. But this time the insouciance that is criticized has a different origin. For the philosophical theory that is under attack is not a technical one, but, rather, one that is derived from ordinary, everyday experience. This creates the illusion that it is already a fully developed and firmly established theory, needing no special attention and no particular care in its interpretation and application.

We all know that we can keep our thoughts to ourselves, that nobody can feel his friend's pain, and so on. This suggests the easy generalization that the mind is a private place in which all thinking and all sensing occurs. So when I write this sentence, there are the inky, visible words on the paper and in my mind the thought and the visual impression of its externalization. Now who could possibly object to these innocuous reflections on a small part of my everyday life? We must, of course, realize that the mind is only metaphorically 'a place', but civilized people hardly need to be warned about that.

But now suppose that these platitudes are treated as a theory. Imagine that you watch me writing these words through utterly naïve eyes. You expel from your mind everything that you know about such performances, our whole literary tradition, all the paintings which show the Evangelists writing the Gospels, and so on. Then you ask how I manage it, putting this question to yourself in the spirit of someone who chops down a tree and finds Pythagoras' Theorem inscribed in the grain of the trunk. Would the answer be that my written words express my hidden thought? Would that explain my achievement?

We might well doubt whether the inner process can be used so simply and so universally to explain the outer one, because there are a lot of difficulties here for anyone who elevates the familiar platitudes to the status of a theory. First, it is not easy to see how to get independent verification of the occurrence of the inner process. One can appreciate this difficulty without becoming a behaviourist. The trouble is that if the inner process, which is supposed to occur in the 'private place' of the mind, is going to yield an explanation, it must be introduced and tied down with scientific rigour. But how can that be done independently of the outer process which it is supposed to explain? It seems that the extended development of this natural metaphor will never produce a theory like the kinetic theory of gases. In any case, why should anyone think that the inner process stands in any less need of explanation than the outer one? If the regress of explanations must stop somewhere, why should it not sometimes stop where it starts, with the outer process? This, of course, doesn't mean that we have shown that peculiar acts of consciousness do not accompany the expressions of our thoughts! Only we no longer say that they *must* accompany them.'[20]

That remark comes from the passage already quoted from *The Blue Book* in which Wittgenstein is explaining the first of the two further developments of his case against philosophical theories. It is not in the least surprising that the two lines cross at this point. For though his main criticism of theories of meaning that rely on an instant talisman is that they are postulating something impossible, he follows this up with the objection that their postulate is anyway unnecessary. This line of argument then forms part of his general critique of the attempt to extract a theory from our ordinary ideas about the inner processes of perception and thought. We may trace his lines of argument separately—indeed, that is the only way to understand them—but we must remember that in his writings they are always intersecting with one another, and that it is at these interactions that we are able to get a commanding view of his later philosophy.[21]

In *Philosophical Investigations*, when he criticizes the so-called 'theory' of the inner performances of the mind, he emphasizes its lack of rigour and its failure to introduce mental processes and states in a way that would give them real explanatory power:

How does the philosophical problem about mental processes and states and about behaviourism arise?—The first step is the one that altogether escapes

[20] There is a neat example of this rejection of the need for any kind of inner process in a passage in *BLBK*, where he argues that in order to understand the word 'yellow', it cannot be necessary to get an image of the colour (*BLBK* p. 3, see below, pp. 522–3).

[21] So in his Preface to *PI* he says: 'The best that I could write would never be more than philosophical remarks; my thoughts were soon crippled if I tried to force them on in any single direction against their natural inclination.—And this was, of course, connected with the very nature of the investigation. For this compels us to travel over a wide field of thought criss-cross in every direction.—The philosophical remarks in this book are, as it were, a number of sketches of landscapes which were made in the course of these long and involved journeyings.' (*PI* p. ix e.)

notice. We talk of processes and states and leave their nature undecided. Sometime perhaps we shall know more about them—we think. But that is just what commits us to a particular way of looking at the matter. For we have a definite concept of what it means to learn to know a process better. (The decisive movement in the conjuring trick has been made, and it was the very one that we thought quite innocent.)—And now the analogy which was to make us understand our thoughts falls to pieces. So we have to deny the yet uncomprehended process in the yet unexplored medium. And now it looks as if we had denied mental processes. And naturally we don't want to deny them.[22]

So in his long critique of sensation-language he never denies that we have sensations with phenomenal properties. The denial would be absurd. He even allows that our natural tendency to model the inner world on the outer one is harmless when we are actually using language to report our sensations. He criticizes it only when it makes us theorize about them in a way that deprives them of any criterion of identity. The criticism is very clear in his 'Notes for Lectures on "Private Experience" and "Sense-data" ':

> 'But aren't you neglecting something—the experience or whatever you might call it—? Almost *the world* behind the mere words?'
> . . . But what more can I do than *distinguish* the case of saying 'I have toothache' when I really have toothache, and the case of saying the words without having toothache? I am also (further) ready to talk of any x behind my words so long as it keeps its identity.[23]

But how does this theory deprive our sensations of their criteria of identity? The answer is given in *Philosophical Investigations*. If the normal connections between sensation and stimulus and between sensation and response are severed, we cannot just assume that it would still be possible for me to give myself a kind of ostensive definition of a sensation-type. For how, in that extremity, would I do it?

. . . How? Can I point to the sensation? Not in the ordinary sense. But I speak, or write the sign down, and at the same time I concentrate my attention on the sensation—and so, as it were, point to it inwardly.—But what is this ceremony for? For that is all it seems to be! A definition surely serves to establish the meaning of a sign.—Well, that is done precisely by the concentration of my attention: for in this way I impress on myself the connection between the sign and the sensation.—But 'I impress it on myself' can only mean: this process brings it about that I remember the connection *right* in the future. But in the

[22] Ibid., I § 308.
[23] *NLPESD* pp. 296–7.

present case I have no criterion of correctness. One would like to say: whatever is going to seem right to me is right. And that only means that here we can't talk about 'right'.[24]

This is his main argument against the possibility of a 'private language'.

The details of this argument will be given later. The point to be made now is a general one about the structure of his later philosophy: he evidently believed that, if an argument like this one succeeds in refuting a so-called 'theory', it does not inflict any real loss on us. It is not easy to appreciate this. Even when the rejected theory postulates something recondite, like the essential structure of language specified in the *Tractatus*, we are apt to feel that the loss is substantial. But when the rejected theory takes something quite ordinary and familiar, like our sensations, and tells an impossible story about them, our feeling of loss is apt to be much greater. For we allow the story to permeate the things that figure in it—it is, after all, the development of quite ordinary ideas—and so, when we are deprived of the story, we feel that we are also deprived of the things. However,

. . . What we are destroying is nothing but houses of cards and we are clearing up the ground of language on which they stand.[25]

The philosophical theories that are swept away had neither substance nor foundation, and we are no worse off without them. Whether we remain in the business of philosophizing is another question, the answer to which will depend on what there is to take the place of traditional theorizing.

Perhaps the best way to appreciate Wittgenstein's later conception of philosophy is to start from the *Tractatus* and to assess the effects of the subsequent change in his method. He began by taking over the traditional idea that philosophy explains the whole range of phenomena—'the world as we find it'[26]—by revealing the deep structure of things. What had to be explained was the appropriateness of language to the world—not its truth, of course, but its capacity for truth. The proposed explanation was that language can be deduced to be, at the ultimate level of analysis, a system exhibiting the same structure as the world.

That was a theory, but not a scientific one. It could not be a scientific theory, because there was nothing outside the partnership of language and the world which could possibly be brought in to explain

---

[24] *PI* I § 258.   [25] Ibid., I § 118.   [26] Cf. *TLP* 5.631.

it. Everything was necessarily seen through the same pervasive medium, which would immediately frustrate any attempt to get outside it and treat it as an object of scientific inquiry. The common structure of language and the world was something that could only be shown, not described.[27] Any description would have to rely on it and the only way to apprehend it was through a special kind of insight, which borrowed the language of science in default of any more appropriate mode of expression, but did not mean it in the usual way.

This tense conception of philosophy is well conveyed by Wittgenstein's own retrospective account of it:

> Thought is surrounded by a halo.—Its essence, logic, presents an order, in fact the a priori order of the world: that is, the order of *possibilities*, which must be common to both world and thought. But this order, it seems, must be *utterly simple*. It is *prior* to all experience, must run through all experience; no empirical cloudiness or uncertainty can be allowed to affect it—It must rather be of the purest crystal.[28]

> The ideal, as we think of it, is unshakeable. You can never get outside it; you must always turn back. There is no outside; outside you cannot breath. . . .[29]

The tension in this conception of philosophy was produced by the opposition of two forces. On one side stood philosophy demanding some way of expressing its insights. They evidently could not be presented as scientific theories, and it looked as if the demand could only be met by a concession: theories might be constructed but only theories of a unique kind, specially adapted to convey philosophical understanding. But this underestimated the obstacle standing on the other side. When theories were deprived of their scientific character, they lost all the features that gave them their explanatory power. The compromise that was required of them was an impossible one, and the adaptation involved weaknesses which proved to be fatal.

Wittgenstein's rejection of quasi-scientific theorizing in philosophy is a direct development of the way in which he set up his early system, something which merely emerges more clearly in his later philosophy. The theory of language of the *Tractatus* indicates how sentences get their senses by being connected with possibilities. Now we may ask in science why some of these possibilities are realized as facts, while others are not. That is because we can identify particular possibilities in the zone surrounding the world of facts and trace their vicissitudes. But outside that zone there is no further zone containing identifiable

[27] See Vol. I pp. 142–52.   [28] *PI* I § 97.   [29] Ibid., I § 103.

candidates for possibility, about which we can ask in metaphysics why some of them achieve real possibility, while others do not. The outer zone is just an undifferentiated void.

But what then took the place of philosophical theorizing in Wittgenstein's later work? It is easy to get a short answer from him, but much less easy to achieve a real understanding of the transition. The short answer is that theories had to be cut off at the roots by a scrupulous refusal to generalize. The idiosyncrasies of each case had to be respected and there were to be no forced assimilations of one thing to another. The very desire for explanation had to be eradicated because it always brought on 'the contemptuous attitude towards the particular case'.[30]

However, that is an extremely negative account of the transition and it might well be taken as the characterization of a refusal to philosophize. It is all very well for Wittgenstein to say that 'we must do away with all *explanation* and description alone must take its place'.[31] He ought also to give us some reason for regarding the description as a contribution to philosophy. If it does not explain what we find puzzling, there must be something else that it does, some special effect that it produces. But what is it?

He identifies the special effect at which his descriptions aim in the continuation of § 109 of *Philosophical Investigations*:

. . . And this description gets its light, that is to say its purpose, from the philosophical problems. These are, of course, not empirical problems; they are solved, rather, by looking into the workings of our language, and that in such a way as to make us recognize those workings: *in despite of* an urge to misunderstand them. The problems are solved not by giving new information, but by arranging what we have always known. Philosophy is a battle against the bewitchment of our intelligence by means of language.[32]

This new characterization of philosophy is centred on our natural tendency to fall into certain kinds of error. Philosophy can only be understood as part of the pathology of the intellect. There is, of course, no suggestion that the error is wilful: the point is that our minds have natural biases which philosophers must show us how to resist. But is there, perhaps, the further suggestion, that it is only these biases that create the need for philosophy, just as it is only mental illness that creates the need for psychotherapy?

---

[30] See *BLBK* pp. 17–18, quoted above, pp. 201–2.
[31] *PI* § 109, quoted above, p. 200.   [32] Loc. cit., continuation.

It is not obvious how this question should be answered. If we had only this passage to guide us, we would take Wittgenstein to mean that what sets philosophy going is a special kind of problem and not a perversion of reason. His idea would be that the problem is always posed by some baffling feature of our own thought. Even if we are able to use our conceptual devices without any trouble, we are often nonplussed by them when we step back and try to see how they work. One remedy is simply to use them without trying to understand them, as most of us do all the time and the rest of us do most of the time. However, the desire for philosophical understanding is just as natural as the activities which occasion it, just as much part of our lives. If the search for the abstract insights of philosophy is biased by the intellect's tendency to lead us into error, that is something that happens when the search is on. It is not what starts it.

That would be one interpretation of his new view about the nature of philosophy. However, there are passages which support a more extreme view. For example, earlier in *Philosophical Investigations* we find this:

. . . the conception of naming as, so to speak, an occult process. Naming appears as a *queer* connection of a word with an object.—And you really get such a queer connection when the philosopher tries to bring out *the* relation between name and thing by staring at an object in front of him and repeating a name or even the word 'this' innumerable times. For philosophical problems arise when language *goes on holiday*. . . .[33]

This seems to go further than what he says in § 109, because it apparently implies that philosophical problems *originate* in misunderstandings. Nor was this a new idea in *Philosophical Investigations*. For in the Preface to the *Tractatus* he had said:

The book deals with the problems of philosophy, and shows, I believe, that the reason why these problems are posed is that the logic of our language is misunderstood.[34]

The two passages in *Philosophical Investigations* are not irreconcilable. We could take him to mean that the problems of philosophy become intractable when a misunderstanding intervenes, and that, though language goes on holiday as soon as we step back from our use of it and

---

[33] Ibid., I § 38.
[34] *TLP* p. 3. the same extreme view can be found in R. Rhees's notes of the lectures given by Wittgenstein in 1936. See the periodical *Philosophical Investigations*, Vol. 7 No. 2, Apr. 1984, p. 139.

ask how it works, the holiday does not have to start as an intellectual
Saturnalia. We certainly do not want to saddle him with the thesis that
someone who asks, 'What is a number?' must already be confusing the
abstract with the concrete. True, he does think that certain philosophical
problems arise only because a mistaken assumption has been made; for
example, that a child who asks his mother how she knows that her
visual impressions of red are not like his of blue, is assuming
mistakenly that visual impressions are like objects. But it is obvious
that this kind of aetiology cannot be extended to all philosophical
problems.

We must allow for the fact that his later philosophy is very self-
deprecating. He is painfully aware that it is a unique and very marginal
way of thinking, an alternative to living, not just because it is not
practical, but because it detaches the mind from its normal engagement
with the world, without finding any new point of attachment for it. It is
the least adventurous of all adventures among ideas, because it circles
back to its starting-point. But, once undertaken, it is the most
interminable, because there is really no end to the loops traced by
these inward-looking searches for understanding.

. . . The real discovery is the one that makes me capable of stopping doing
philosophy when I want to.—The one that gives philosophy peace, so that it is
no longer tormented by questions which bring *itself* in question.—Instead, we
now demonstrate a method, by examples; and the series of examples can be
broken off.—Problems are solved (difficulties eliminated), not a *single* problem.

There is not *a* philosophical method, though there are indeed methods, like
different therapies.[35]

This does not mean that the desire for this kind of understanding is
unnatural, but it does raise the question how far it should be indulged.
One way to answer this question is to emphasize the turning-points
where satisfaction has been most noticeably achieved, and those are
undoubtedly the points at which perennial misunderstandings have
been removed. This tends to create the impression that those
misunderstandings were themselves the origins of the problems.

There is really no need to settle precisely how far Wittgenstein
pushes his new conception of philosophy. The important thing is that
he is moving it away from theorizing and towards plain description of
the phenomenon of language. The description is intended to make us
see how our own linguistic devices work, simply by putting them in

[35] *PI* I § 133.

their place in our lives without using any technical terms. If we object, that nothing so familiar or banal can possibly yield philosophical understanding, he will reply that, on the contrary, it gives us all the insight that we need, and that the attempt to go beyond it and theorize can only produce misunderstanding. We think that we need nourishment when what we really need is clear water.

If he is right about this, philosophical problems are generated by a failure to understand something which we have already internalized, the use of our own language. So in order to solve them, we can only look more closely at what we already know how to do. This is all that he offers by way of positive precept and, if it seems too little, that is probably because we are forgetting the contribution made by the negative precept which lies behind it: 'Do not theorize.'

What we have to realize is that this prohibition is tempered by a concession: 'Allow yourself to be tempted to theorize.' For though it is a mistake to yield to the temptation, it is necessary to feel it, because *that degree* of misunderstanding is an unavoidable stage on the way to understanding. We have to be able to feel the attractions of philosophical theories, which we must resist, and only then return to our familiar linguistic practices and see them as they are.

But why should understanding be possible only after a narrow escape from misunderstanding? People can achieve virtue without having to overcome the temptations of vice. So why should it be any different with the intellect? It is not sufficient to point out that this was, in fact, Wittgenstein's own intellectual history, because it can always be objected that it would have been better if he had moved directly to his final destination. The question is a difficult one, because his later philosophy really is much less self-revealing than it seems to be on first reading. He tells us that he is now working on the surface of language, and that is evidently so. He also tells us that his descriptions of what happens on the surface get their point from deep illusions, but, though that it is often so, it does not seem to be always so, and, even when it is so, it is not entirely clear why it is so.

It might be helpful at this point to look again at the two things that are given up by a philosopher who refuses to theorize. One is the neglect of fine differences between the various phenomena that are collected together for explanation, and the other is the whole enterprise of explaining the phenomena. Now it would be absurd to suggest that you cannot appreciate the point of a fine distinction between two things unless you begin by overlooking it and lumping them together. So though Wittgenstein often criticizes 'the craving for generality',[36] that cannot be the source of his idea, that understanding can be achieved only by a philosopher who has been drawn towards a misunderstanding and felt its charm. So it looks as if the key to this puzzling aspect of his later philosophy is to be found in his ideas about explanation.

If his leading idea was the simple one, that philosophy neither is, nor is like, a science, the subtlety and complexities come from his realization that this is not something which we can accept once and for all and then go on to philosophize in a more appropriate way. One reason why we cannot immediately accept this categorization of disciplines and put it behind us is that it leaves philosophy with no clear status of its own, and so the temptation to construe it as a variant of science is constantly renewed. Every philosophical inquiry, whatever its particular object, leads us through this general temptation and out to a flat acceptance of the familiar features of language in its place in our lives.

But why should a general enlightenment have to be repeated again and again in each particular instance? There is a reason for this too. If philosophy exists on the edge of science, it will never be immediately clear where the line that separates them runs. So we will have to discover that a particular problem is philosophical by trying and failing to give it a scientific solution:

> The results of philosophy are the uncovering of one or another piece of plain nonsense and of bumps that the understanding has got by running its head up against the limits of language. These bumps make us see the value of the discovery.[37]

If we had a general theory about the limits of factual language, like the one offered in the *Tractatus*, there would be no need for the constant repetition of this painful experience. But we have no such theory. Therefore, a continual probing of the limits is an essential feature of philosophy.[38]

If Wittgenstein's later work depends so heavily on the contrast between philosophy and science, it may seem surprising that he is not

---

[36] *BLBK* p. 17, quoted above, p. 201.

[37] *PI* I § 119. Of course, not all these misadventures on the limits of language come from confusing philosophy with science. In *Philosophical Investigations* the limits of language are no longer simply the limits of factual language.

[38] The need for this continual probing is recognized in *TLP* 6.53, a passage which anticipated later developments.

very explicit about the quasi-scientific character of the theorizing that he criticizes in *Philosophical Investigations*. But there is a reason for this too. When we look back on his gradual progress to his later method, we can see that much of the ground had been covered by the time that he compiled the *Tractatus*. For the explicit thesis of that book is that philosophy is not a science, and there was also a hint that its goal is not the construction of theories of any kind. However, this methodological advance is not accompanied by a clear commentary. For the account that he actually gives of his method in the *Tractatus* is full of tension and very deficient in detail. Later, when he gives an account of his completely developed method, it is much more relaxed and informative, but, naturally, it is concerned with the continuation of his journey beyond the point reached in the *Tractatus*. So the gap between philosophy and science is, for the most part, taken for granted in *Philosophical Investigations*, and attention is focused on consequential developments. For example, in his later writings he often observes that philosophical theories are like pictures without any definite application: if he seldom makes the connected point, that they are trying but failing to imitate science, that is because it is an obvious one, worth emphasizing only when he was first establishing the gap between philosophy and science.

There are also other things that help to explain the emphasis in his account of his later method. His contempt for scientism must have made frequent references to the gap between science and philosophy seem unnecessary, and there is also the obvious fact that he was not a man given to self-revelation. Our remedy is, of course, to turn from his description of his method to his practice of it. Then we can immediately see the importance of the shadow that science casts over philosophy. For all the deficiencies of philosophical theorizing evidently come from a single source, the necessarily unsuccessful attempt to match scientific achievements. The trouble is that there is nowhere for philosophy to go for the verification of its theories, because 'there is no outside; outside you cannot breathe'.[39] Consequently, the detailed implications that we expect of a scientific theory are lacking, and all that is left is an evasive picture, uncommitted to any particular application and so never facing the test of truth. Philosophical theories put themselves in limbo.

If we look at Wittgenstein's practice of his later method, we may be

---

[39] *PI* I § 103, quoted above, p. 215.

able to get a more detailed answer to a question that was raised earlier:[40] 'Is philosophy an empirical discipline?' We may start from the fact that the manœuvres on any page of his later writings are complex and often difficult to follow. It is not the individual remarks that are inscrutable, but their point and their drift. However, things often become much clearer when we see that his remarks are responses to the counter-moves suggested by some would-be theory with which he never loses contact. One does not need to have read far into *Philosophical Investigations* to realize that this is what is going on. His thoughts are 'marking' shadowy adversaries moving behind the front. But is this really philosophy? Ought not his response to have been the production of alternative theories? This is like asking whether it is really warfare when there is no battle. However, his strategy does produce a curious effect. His actual manœuvres are all in the zone of contingent linguistic facts, but their point lies elsewhere. So his writing is both baffling and fascinating, like a dialogue with two quite different levels of significance.[41]

It is impossible to anticipate all the things that might make his later method hard to understand. However, there is one difficulty, already mentioned, which does deserve more discussion before the detailed examination of his later work begins. There are, as already observed, two different kinds of theorizing rejected in *Philosophical Investigations*, and his critique makes a somewhat different impact on each of them. This can make it difficult to see exactly what is going on, and so it may be worth saying a little more about the origins of the two kinds of philosophical theory, and about their vicissitudes in the hostile atmosphere of his later thought.

The first of the two kinds of theory reaches beyond the phenomena and postulates something transcendent to explain them, while the second kind ascribes a transcendent function to something ordinary and familiar. The *Tractatus*, which contains a clear example of the first kind of theory, is reviewed and criticized at the beginning of *Philosophical Investigations*. Then follows a long critique of the general

---

[40] See above, p. 205.

[41] Fania Pascal once asked him: ' "Why are you so sure your work is no earthly good to me?" He said, as far as I can remember: "Suppose you were trying to draw a chart of the progress of a hospital sister walking round her ward, then of another doing likewise on another floor, and finally, to produce *one* chart which would combine and illustrate their joint progress . . .?" I cried out: "Oh, I could never grasp it!" ' (Fania Pascal: 'Wittgenstein: A Personal Memoir', in *Recollections of Wittgenstein*, ed. R. Rhees, Oxford, 1984, p. 13.)

pattern of thought under attack, which includes not only the theory of meaning of the *Tractatus* but also all similar theories. All these theories start from the same point: they assume that our practice is not a sufficiently firm basis for meaning, which must, therefore, be guided by some fixed paradigm outside our minds. However, such a paradigm would not help us, unless we had something within our minds to register it. The second kind of theory begins to emerge when philosophers ask themselves what this thing in our minds can possibly be. It is, they suggest, a picture, a rule, or a flash of understanding produced by an example. But though all these things are familiar elements in our experience, the function ascribed to them is transcendent, because it always reaches beyond the horizon set by the applications of the vocabulary to date. But Wittgenstein's objection is that these theories are in much worse trouble than that. For even if all the correct applications of a word really were somehow laid out in advance, no instant mental talisman could serve as our guide to them.[42]

All these theories may be grouped with the theory of meaning of the *Tractatus*, and that was how they were presented earlier. They all make the a priori postulate, that something static must serve as the basis of meaning. Wittgenstein's response is that what they all postulate is impossible, and that we fail to notice the impossibility only because we do not work out the details.

However, the theories criticized in this part of *Philosophical Investigations* are in two ways unlike the theory of meaning of the *Tractatus*. First, there is the difference that has already been mentioned: the idea developed in the *Tractatus* is that outside our minds there is a fixed grid determining the general structure of our language, whereas the fixed rails rejected in *Philosophical Investigations* are peculiar to particular words. Second, the *Tractatus* has almost nothing to say about what goes on in the mind of a speaker, but the theories criticized in the later book do identify something in his mind which is supposed to serve as his guide to the fixed meaning of a word—maybe, a picture, or a rule, or a flash of understanding. This mitigates the transcendent character of these theories: the instant mental talisman is empirically identified and it is only its function that remains transcendent.

The effect is to bring these theories closer to those criticized by Wittgenstein in the second of the two phases of his thought that were

---

[42] See *PI* I § 219, discussed below, pp. 441, 465–6 and 489–90.

distinguished above.[43] They are theories which seem to draw the line between the phenomena to be explained and the explanation within experience, just like the theory that my writing that sentence could be completely explained by what occurred in the 'private place' of my mind. So they do, at least, talk about familiar things. However, he still criticizes them on the ground that they are really only pseudo-scientific. What may be difficult to see at this point is how the same criticism can be made of two such different types of theory.[44]

The criticism is appropriate to both types of theory, because it is just as unscientific to give some ordinary thing powers which transcend possibility as it is to postulate something whose existence transcends experience. Both procedures result in a theory confined to the limbo of pseudo-science. In both cases the remedy is the same: take the words used to identify the transcendent thing, or to characterize the empirical thing in a way that transcends possibility, and bring them back to their ordinary use as parts of our language in its place in our lives. That will give us at home the understanding that we went so far afield to seek.

When Wittgenstein's later philosophy is interpreted in this way, many of its puzzling features fall into an intelligible pattern. For example, people sometimes ask how he can claim to avoid theories, when he himself argues that meaning cannot be put on a static basis, or that there cannot be a 'private language'. The answer is that his reductive arguments remove pseudo-theories, but not in order to make room for genuine ones. He makes no theoretical assumptions because he is in a different line of business—'clearing up the ground of language'.[45]

Another puzzling feature of his later philosophy is his attitude to things in the mind, such as sense-impressions, images, and thoughts. He seems to treat these things dismissively and yet he claims that he is not a behaviourist.[46] How can he have it both ways? The explanation is not that he regards these things as transcendent fantasies, like the deep structure of language postulated in the *Tractatus*. They are real enough, and a perfectly familiar part of our lives, and he is only blocking the attempt to give them an independent status and complete explanatory power.

[43] See above, pp. 211–14.
[44] Another example of this difficulty was mentioned in Vol. I pp. 42–3. The ego is transcendent, but sense-data are not transcendent. So how could Wittgenstein take the successful treatment of the ego and extend it to sense-data?
[45] *PI* I § 118, quoted above, p. 214.
[46] Ibid., I § 308, quoted above, pp. 212–13.

But the best way to appreciate his later method is to see it in action, and the next chapter will take up the discussion of solipsism at the point where it was left at the end of Volume I and follow the road leading from that point into his later philosophy. However, there are two warnings that need to be given first.

One is a warning about the pace and pattern of change in his philosophy. The impression may have been given that in 1929, or perhaps in the immediately preceding years, there was a sudden and complete volte-face. People are always ready to mythologize an individual's intellectual development in this way. It is so quiet that it seems almost to demand something analogous to the idea that the history of the world is determined by the actions of great men. Wittgenstein's strange, dedicated life makes his intellectual history especially vulnerable to this kind of treatment. But no such impression was intended. What has been described here is the fully developed later method, and there has been no suggestion that it was attained by a single inspired bound. In fact, it will appear later that it evolved gradually through the overlapping stages of parallel developments.

The other warning is against over-simplification, which is something in which this chapter really has indulged, and deliberately. The excuse is that the structure of Wittgenstein's later thought is not immediately clear and his method not entirely self-revealing. It was, therefore, necessary to drive one or two straight paths through his later work, leaving the complications until later. If this strategy has given the impression that he had a single method, or that, confronted by a problem, he would seek a single argument to solve it, now is the time to relinquish it.

IO

The Exemplary Treatment of the Ego

TRAVELLERS lost on a wide plain are sometimes lucky enough to find some feature, a pinnacle, perhaps, or a mesa, visible from afar, which will guide them even when they are walking away from it. If you pick up *Philosophical Investigations* not knowing what sort of book it is going to turn out to be, you may look for a theory to serve as the point on which all Wittgenstein's manœuvres converge. Even those who know that there is no such destination often suppose that at least he must be moving away from a single point, which is usually identified as the theory that it would be possible to set up a sensation-language that was completely detached from anything in the physical world.[1] Alternatively, his single point of departure, the idea on which he is turning his back, is taken to be the theory that a language used to describe physical objects as well as sensations might be sustained by the solitary efforts of one person.[2]

However, there is no need to look for a single theory to give *Philosophical Investigations* the unity of a conventional book, not even a single theory which achieves this result in a negative way by serving as its point of departure. On the contrary, the preparatory studies for the work contain many distinct lines of thought which do not even look as if they all radiated outwards from the destruction of a single theory. It is hardly likely that, when they appeared in *Philosophical Investigations*, they suddenly achieved a simple unification which had never even been in sight before.

On the other hand, many of them do exhibit interconnections on a high level of generality, and, no doubt, he intended to indicate these links by the arrangement of his remarks in the book. For example, although the two critiques of other philosophers' theories of language

[1] The sense-datum language which, according to Russell, is the independent basis of all descriptive language. See Vol. I pp. 42–8, and *PI* I §§ 243 ff.

[2] This is S. A. Kripke's suggestion, supported, he claims, by *PI* I §§ 201–2. See his *Wittgenstein on Rules and Private Language*, Blackwell, 1982. A different interpretation of this part of *PI* was proposed in Vol. I pp. 10–11 and 58–60. The issue will be discussed in Chs. 17 and 18.

which he develops in the middle of the book are aimed at different targets,[3] they are evidently connected with one another at several points. The precise identification of the two targets is controversial, but it seems that in each case the move that is being attacked is the adoption of a definition or criterion which clamps together two things which are, and must be, logically independent of one another. First, the correct use of a word can never be tied by definition to the user's impression of correctness, and, second—the reverse direction of fit— whatever it is in his mind that guides his use of a word, it can never be tied by definition to a fantasized string of correct applications stretching out indefinitely into the future.[4]

The connection between these two critiques is close. When a philosopher treats a word-user's mental equipment as a guide which tells him exactly how to apply the word on all future occasions, he puts it in a position very like that of sensation-types when their correct descriptions have been detached from the physical world and attached to their owner's impression that he is describing them correctly. In both cases alike something which in fact rests on a flexible web of supporting criteria is given a single definition which fixes it rigidly but, unfortunately, in a way that puts an end to the essential give and take between language and the world. However, these are connections which hold on a high level of generality, and they provide no support for interpretations which try to connect all Wittgenstein's main lines of thought with the rejection of a single, specific theory. On the contrary, the unifying structure on the higher level of generality is evidently superimposed on diversification on the lower, more specific level.

In any case, the best policy must surely be to start with one of his main lines of thought and to follow it without any preconceived idea about its final integration into the structure of *Philosophical Investigations*. It may or may not be woven into a tight plait with his other leading ideas—that can be left open for the time being. There is also another prejudice to be resisted: the book must not be treated as the definitive pronouncement which supersedes everything that led up to it. That treatment is wholly inappropriate to the way in which he worked. He would record an idea when it first occurred to him, develop it, drop it, come back to it, alter it, and add to it, and finally, perhaps, harvest part of the product—not necessarily the growth of the final years—for

---

[3] They occur in two consecutive blocks of remarks in *PI* §§ 138–242 and 243 ff.

[4] This interpretation of his two lines of attack was suggested in Vol. I pp. 59–60. It will be supported in detail in Chs. 13–18.

inclusion in the book. So it really is essential to go back to the point of origin of each of his ideas and to trace all its subsequent vicissitudes. To say that they are their history would be nearer the truth than to identify them with their final manifestations in *Philosophical Investigations*.

The line of thought chosen as the topic of this chapter and the next five starts from the treatment of solipsism in the *Tractatus*, leads to the argument against the possibility of a sensation-language completely detached from everything in the physical world, and then opens up a whole new philosophy of mind. This new philosophy does not offer any theory of the mental. On the contrary, it is a sustained attempt to retrieve us from the errors of the two extreme theories which, between them, polarize the neutral truth, introspectionism and behaviourism.[5] However, that is the end of this particular line of thought; it begins with the problem of the self.

There are several rejected theories which may serve as landmarks along this route, and there is no harm in using them for orientation, provided that we do not treat any one of them as the unique point of departure for the whole of Wittgenstein's later philosophy. The first of these theories was the theory of the ego. His early critique of this theory looked as if it was on the right lines and in 1929, when he had reinforced it by adding a further argument against solipsism and an alternative account of the ownership of sensations, it could serve as a model for his treatment of the much more difficult problem of the status of the sensations themselves.[6] So the first thing to be done now is to recapitulate the argument used aginst solipsism in the *Tractatus*, and to show how he strengthened it in 1929 by adding another argument backed up by a full description of the language-game of ascribing sensations to people. Then the next task will be to demonstrate exactly how these achievements served as model for the long inquiry into the status of sensations which ended, in *Philosophical Investigations*, with the rejection of the possibility of a sensation-language detached from everything in the physical world. That part of the book is notoriously difficult to understand when it is cut off from the work that preceded it and read in isolation. So it ought to be illuminating to approach it along Wittgenstein's actual line of inquiry, starting from that conspicuous landmark, the exemplary treatment of the ego.

In the *Tractatus* he offered the solipsist a dilemma.[7] Either this ego

[5] See above, p. 214, and Vol. I pp. 44–5.
[6] See Vol. I pp. 48 ff.   [7] *TLP* 5.6–5.641. See Vol. I Ch. 7.

to which the only objects that exist are presented is identified independently of those objects, or else its identification is not independent of them. If its identification is not independent of them, the solipsist's claim will be empty, because, when he points out 'the only objects that exist', he will stand identified merely as the subject to which these objects are presented. As he says later in *The Blue Book*,[8] if the solipsist accepts this horn of the dilemma, he will be like someone who constructs a clock with the dial attached to the hand, so that they both go round together. Alternatively, if the identification of this ego is independent of the objects presented to it, his claim will be self-refuting. For the only way in which it can get independent identification is through his body, which is one body among others in the physical world.

The principle on which this argument relies is that the identification of a set of objects can be achieved only when it is done from a base which is independent of those objects. If the solipsist's ego is clamped by definition to its own objects—according to him, the only ones that exist—it cannot possibly be used as the point of origin of a system which will serve to identify that privileged set. That would be like producing a map with a grid-system originating at a point which could be identified only as 'the point of origin of these numbered lines'— imagine that it was a map of part of the floor of an ocean. This principle is derived from the more general principle mentioned above: if two things are in fact independent of one another, it is a mistake to clamp them together by definition in some philosophical theory so that there is rigid immobility where there ought to have been movement and interaction.[9]

That is a slightly tendentious formulation of the two connected principles on which Wittgenstein's early critique of solipsism had relied. For if a philosopher is trying to describe things as they are, it must be a mistake to say that there is a definitional connection between two of them when in reality there is no such connection. But the solipsist certainly will not accept this simple refutation. He will say that he is not trying to describe things exactly as they are. His thesis is intentionally innovative, and he will argue that, though it fails to score as a literal truth, at a deeper level it succeeds in giving a truer picture of our situation. So he will demand to be told what he loses by his innovation. What is it that he wants to do, but can no longer do, after

[8] *BLBK* p. 71.
[9] See Vol. I p. 58.

he has cut his private world out of the original common world? What are the sanctions that are supposed to be operating against him?

Wittgenstein's response is given very clearly in the *Tractatus*. The solipsist wants to say something informative.[10] But after he has cut his private world out of the common world in which he started—or, at least, seemed to start—he cannot get any factual content into what he says. 'The only objects that exist are . . .'—what can he say next? If he says '. . . those that are presented to this ego', he will be standing back from a situation in which a certain ego is aware of a certain set of objects, and he will have to say which ego he means, just as a map-maker has to identify the point of origin of his grid-system. So he had better say, 'The only objects that exist are *these*', simultaneously performing the mental analogue of pointing at them. This is clearly his best option, because it allows him, or, at least, seems to allow him, to use his own identity as the one who points, without mentioning himself and so without getting entangled in the problem of identifying himself. But, according to Wittgenstein, this too lacks factual content: the hand is still strapped to the dial, not so openly this time, it is true, but just as tightly and with the same frustrating outcome.

But is this further development of the early critique of solipsism valid? That is the question that had to be settled in 1929. Was it really impossible for the solipsist to evade the dilemma put to him in the *Tractatus* by mentally pointing to 'the only objects that exist', instead of trying to identify them by relating them to an ego which would itself need to be identified? When Wittgenstein took up this problem again in 1929, his intention was to close this escape-route. His detailed examination of the language-game of ascribing sensations to people was designed to show that, when the solipsist retreats into his private world, the ability to make discriminating references to individuals is something which he is unable to take with him.

One of the recurrent difficulties in the interpretation of Wittgenstein's writings is to appreciate the details and, at the same time, to see their place in the larger scheme of his philosophy. The *Tractatus* gives the abstract pattern without the details—indeed, its lack of any account of the conditions of successful reference, which is what leaves the solipsist with an apparent line of escape from the dilemma, is hardly an omission of detail—and the later writings are always concerned with details but seldom explain how they fit into the overall composition. So

---

[10] See *TLP* 5.62.

in this case, as in many others, it is best to begin by filling in the general background. That will be a fairly lengthy business, but it is worth completing it before starting to analyse Wittgenstein's exemplary treatment of the ego.

The first point that needs to be made is an obvious one: he is not criticizing the solipsist for failing to convey information to other people. That would hardly be likely to worry a philosopher who denied their existence. The argument is that, even if there were other people around, they would not get any information out of the solipsist's declaration, because he has not put any into it. Now he may think that he at least knows what he means because he is in the middle of what it is all about. But if his new formulation, 'The only objects that exist are *these*,' really did succeed in avoiding emptiness, that could only be because he had put some content into it, and it would not be possible for it to have content only for him. He, of course, will feel that he has some inkling of the content that he would like to extract from his situation and project into his communiqué, but that is not enough. An impression of a possible content is not an actual content and a velleity is not an act.

Anyone who is familiar with Wittgenstein's later argument against the possibility of a completely detached sensation-language will see immediately that it is related to this early criticism of solipsism. The later argument is an application of the same general embargo on faulty definitional connections deep within a system intended for communication, even if only with oneself.[11] The difference between the two applications of the general principle is that in this treatment of the ownership of sensations the criticism is that the identification of a set of particulars is frustrated when the subject is not independently fixed, while in *Philosophical Investigations* the criticism is that the identification of types is frustrated when the criteria for their correct description are not independently fixed.

There is a passage in *The Brown Book* which gives some indication of the similarity between these two applications of the general principle.

... Looking at a uniformly coloured wall I might say 'I don't just see that it has the same colour all over, but I see a particular colour.' But in saying this I am mistaking the function of a sentence.—It seems that you wish to specify the colour that you see, but not by saying anything about it, nor by comparing it with a sample,—but by pointing to it; using it at the same time as the sample and that which the sample is compared with.

[11] Cf. Vol. I pp. 58–60.

. . . the sentence, 'I see this', as it is sometimes contemplated by us when we are brooding over certain philosophical problems. We are then, say, holding on to a particular visual impression by staring at some object, and we feel it is most natural to say to ourselves 'I see this', though we know of no further use we can make of this sentence.

It is as though the sentence was singling out the particular colour I saw; as if it presented it to me.

It seems as though the colour which I see was its own description.

For the pointing with my finger was ineffectual. (And the looking is no pointing, it does not, for me, indicate a direction, which would mean contrasting a direction with other directions.)

What I see, or feel, enters my sentence as a sample does; but no use is made of this sample; the words of my sentence don't seem to matter, they only serve to present the sample to me.

I don't really speak *about* what I see, but *to* it.

I am in fact going through the acts of attending which could accompany the use of a sample. And this is what makes it seem as though I was making use of a sample. This error is akin to that of believing that an ostensive definition says something about the object to which it directs our attention.

When I said 'I am mistaking the function of a sentence' it was because by its help I seemed to be pointing out to myself which colour it is I see, whereas I was just contemplating a sample of colour. It seemed to me that the sample was the description of its own colour.[12]

This is a clear case of language going on holiday: 'the pointing with my finger was ineffectual. (And the looking is no pointing, it does not, for me, indicate a direction, which would mean contrasting a direction with other directions.)' No doubt, I have a vestigial feeling that I am pointing successfully to a colour, but I am not really doing so. This, of course, is a case of failed pointing to a type, but it looks as if it is much the same with particulars: when the solipsist says '*These* objects', he may focus his attention on to them, but that does not count as picking them out, because it fails to satisfy the conditions of discriminating reference.

But what exactly are the conditions of discriminating reference to particulars? The phrase is a vague one, and, if this new criticism of solipsism is going to be effective, it needs to be made more precise and

---

[12] L. Wittgenstein: *The Brown Book* (henceforth *BRBK*), in *The Blue and Brown Books*, Blackwell, 1958 (dictated in 1934–5), pp. 174–5. Cf. R. Rhees's notes of the lectures that Wittgenstein gave in 1936, published in *Philosophical Investigations* (the periodical), Vol. 7 No. 2, Apr. 1984, p. 113. Cf. p. 131.: 'What we have here is: taking the same thing as a sample and as what is described by the sample. Like trying to catch your own thumb.'

it must be established by detailed argument. In the case of particulars the failure and the conditions themselves are not so obvious as they are in the case of pointing to a type like a colour. But what can be said immediately in this introductory sketch of the background is that, if the solipsist does fail in his attempt to internalize discriminating reference to individuals, his failure will be very like the failure to pick out the colour that is the topic of this passage.

It is worth going back once more to the *Notebooks* and the *Tractatus*, in order to put the 1929 treatment of the ego in its proper setting. The really illuminating part of the early discussion was concerned with the competition for the ego by the bodies that strive to appropriate it.[13] The solipsist proclaims his egocentric thesis, but he is reticent about the placing of the ego. Wittgenstein argues he will arrive at solipsism if he tries to seat it in his own body, and that he will arrive at idealism if he tries to 'spread' it among all human bodies.[14] Either way, his theory will be self-refuting, because, of course, his body is one among others, and the set of all human bodies is one set among others in the physical world. So, naturally, he chooses a third option: the ego is not attached to any body—not even to his body—and yet it is identifiably his.

There are several lines of thought in the early discussion which surface again in 1929. First, the solipsist is obviously going for a personal form of egocentrism, but nobody expects him to opt for the version which explicitly seats the ego in his own body—still less to opt for the idealist version which spreads it over all human bodies— because these versions are obviously self-refuting. So he is really forced to choose a third option, which may be called 'sliding-peg egocentrism'.[15] It is, of course, questionable whether this third version really ought to count as a form of solipsism. If the ego is not pegged down, with what justification can he call it 'mine'? He may reply that the fact that he can refer to it immediately shows that his references to it must be self-references. But does that really follow? How does he know that he alone can refer to it immediately? On what does he base this essential restriction? Might it not be the collective subject of all human consciousness? These questions lead straight into the 1929 investigation of the ascription of sensations to people. The word

---

[13] This part of the discussion is developed more fully in *NB* than in *TLP*. See Vol. I pp. 167–72.

[14] See *NLPESD* p. 281, and *NB* 15 Oct. 1916, discussed in Vol. I pp. 169–70.

[15] The ego is not fixed, just as the value of a currency is not fixed when the sliding-peg system of exchange-rates is adopted.

'person' is a count-noun and the solipsist has to 'make a connection with a person',[16] but how will he do that?

In the *Notebooks* and the *Tractatus*, when Wittgenstein drives the solipsist into sliding-peg egocentrism, the argument that he uses throws a strong light on the development of his philosophy. It is a simple argument: if the solipsist pegs down the ego in his own body, his thesis will be self-refuting, but it will be empty if he does not peg it down at all. In spite of its simplicity this is an argument with an interesting structure. In the *Tractatus* the context in which solipsism was introduced was the question how factual language is limited. The solipsist suggested that in addition to the general limit—it only contained truth-functions of elementary sentences mentioning simple objects—there was also a personal restriction—they had to be simple objects presented to him.[17] He then tried to cut his miniature, private world out of the enveloping common world by limiting language to sentences that he could understand, because they named objects that he had encountered. Now one of the main themes of the *Tractatus* is that language can be limited only from the inside, because it is not possible to cross the limit in thought and identify particular non-objects and particular pieces of non-sense on the far side of it.[18] It follows that the solipsist cannot start by placing his ego in the common world and then go on to claim that nothing exists outside his private world. That would be an incoherent procedure, and thus he is driven into sliding-peg egocentrism.

What makes this argument especially interesting is that from 1929 onwards Wittgenstein took it for granted that it also applied to the objects presented to the ego. Just as the solipsist was forced to abandon the naïve version of his theory, which started by giving his ego an empirical fix in the common world, so too it was impossible for a phenomenalist to start by identifying his sense-data empirically within the common world, and then go on to claim that language was limited to sentences about his sense-data. In both cases alike the destination was incompatible with the starting-point. If language really was limited by the identity of the subject or by the line of objects presented to the subject, then any attempt to give an empirical fix either to the point of origin of the world that could be described in language or to its base-line would necessarily lack sense. So when a phenomenalist tried to use mental sense-data both as an empirically identified base-line and

---

[16] See *NLPESD* p. 297.   [17] See Vol. I p. 153.
[18] See Vol. I pp. 148–51 and 157.

as the limit of language, the result was plainly incoherent. Incidentally, it would be even more incoherent if the phenomenalist added other people's mental sense-data to the base-line like the egocentrist who arrives at idealism by 'spreading the ego'. The only tenable form of phenomenalism was sliding-peg phenomenalism.[19] Anyone who could understand the *mise-en-scène* of British Empiricism would see that it stopped the act before it could really begin. The argument is entirely general: it is always incoherent to try to draw the limits of language and its correlate, the phenomenal world, with its point of origin or its base-line empirically fixed on a more extensive map.

This yields a strikingly symmetrical picture of the development of this part of Wittgenstein's philosophy. He was following two parallel lines of investigation, one a critique of attempts to use the ego as the point of origin of a private world or microcosm, and the other a critique of attempts to use sense-data as the limiting base-line of such a world. Each of these two critiques had two distinct parts. First, he argued that it was incoherent to suggest that the point of origin or, in the other case, the limiting base-line, of a private world, could be identified empirically within the original common world or macrocosm. Then he argued that, even if this could be done, the solipsist would find that there were certain essential linguistic devices that he was unable to take with him on his retreat into his private world. When he tried to set himself up in a private world based on his ego, he would lose the discriminating references to individuals on which his theory depended;[20] and when he tried to set himself up in a private world limited by the line of his own mental sense-data, he would lose the capacity to register their different types, and so he would not have any private language left to speak.[21] Of course, it is usually the same philosopher who disables himself in these two ways, but they need to be investigated separately.

That slightly exaggerates the parallelism between his two lines of inquiry. There is not much development of the argument against ordinary phenomenalism with an empirically identified base-line, because he tended to take its incoherence for granted. There are also

---

[19] This interpretation of the work that Wittgenstein started in 1929 will be defended in the next chapter.

[20] This might be called 'the first private language argument', because it is, on its own line of investigation, the exact counterpart of the private language argument of *PI* I §§ 243 ff.

[21] This is the argument of *PI* I §§ 243 ff., and it might be called 'the second private language argument'.

other differences between his two critiques, but they can be left to
emerge in the rest of this chapter and in the next five, as this
interpretation moves forward step by step. The first step in the detailed
exposition will be to explain his 1929 account of the ascription of
sensations to persons. But before that is begun, there is one more link
with the earlier critique of solipsism that needs to be mentioned.

The sketch, now almost completed, of the lines of thought
connecting the early critique of solipsism with the 1929 account of the
ownership of sensations will have indicated how Wittgenstein saw the
strategic situation. The solipsist wants to treat the ego as his own, but if
he explicitly seats it in his body, he is in trouble. However, he does
have, or, at least, it seems to him that he has, another resource: he can
rely on a fact, which, if he allowed himself to speak in popular terms,
he would put like this: 'In real life I can point out objects in my physical
environment without needing to establish my own identity every time.'
His idea is that in his daily life in the common world he knows who he
is 'from the inside', and he thinks that he can simply retain this
knowledge and exploit it when he retreats into his private world and
points out the different objects that make their appearance in it.

There are two ways in which his critic can respond to the careless
assumption that the resources available in the common world can be
internalized without significant loss. One response is to use 'the first
private language argument' and to insist that, on the contrary,
something really essential is lost, namely the capacity to make
discriminating references to individuals. The other response is to
explain to the solipsist how he came to be under the illusion that he
could internalize this capacity without any trouble.

The explanation would be intended to be therapeutic. The solipsist
needs to be brought to see that he began to go wrong after he noticed
that he could exercise the capacity to make discriminating references
to individuals without even having to ask himself who he was. This
independence of the identity of the mind is really impressive. He
wakes up in a plane and knows that this half-written page belongs to
the manuscript of his book, and that that piece of coast below is part of
Ireland, but his own identity, on which these references are based, is
something vouched for by his memories. So he has a clear sense of his
own identity within his mind and he does not even ask himself
whether, perhaps, his body helps to sustain it. If he did suffer from a
momentary blank when he woke up, he certainly would not look for
identifying marks on his body. Isn't it obvious that the physical

examination would be irrelevant if he did not already know the identity of the examiner within? And isn't it equally obvious that it would be no good searching the present field of his consciousness for the elusive subject of all his experiences? So, step by step, he is driven to the conclusion that he can easily retreat into his private world and still go on making discriminating references to individuals based on his own inner, but nevertheless perfectly secure identity.

When the solipsist retraces his steps, he must feel and resist the force of the considerations that led him astray. The fact is that he could not preserve his own identity in complete detachment from everything in the physical world. If he really were in that predicament, the very idea of picking himself out as subject would never occur to him, and, even if it did occur to him, it would be something that he could not possibly achieve.[22] However, it is never enough to confront the solipsist head-on with this kind of objection. He must also be brought to see why he found the path to his illusion so inviting. Each step made the next one harder to resist and yet, when he had taken the last one, he had gone completely astray. The cure can only be to make him retrace his steps and to teach him to resist, one by one, the slight pressures which cumulatively led him so far from the truth. This lesson can be learned only from a detailed, well-aimed description of the actual language-game of ascribing sensations to people.

These two reactions to solipsism evidently originated in the *Notebooks* and the *Tractatus*. The first one, the direct rebuttal, has already been explained as a development of the early critique: the solipsist introduced his thesis in an incoherent way, and, when he tried to evade this charge by basing his references on the assumed identity of a subject that is used but not mentioned, he could not get away with it. The second reaction, the therapeutic one, is a development of the appreciative side of the early discussion: the solipsist really had got hold of something important—all experience really is had from a point of view not represented in the experience itself—but it was not something that could be used to support his theory.

That completes the sketch of the background to the investigation, begun in 1929, of the ascription of sensations to their owners. The remainder of this chapter will be concerned with the owners

---

[22] The reasons why he could never achieve it were explained in the earlier discussion of Hume's second, and more interesting thesis, that the very idea of an impression of an inner subject is a 'manifest contradiction of absurdity'. See Vol. I pp. 158–60.

themselves and the next five will deal with what they own, sensations of various types.

The first point that needs to be made is one about Wittgenstein's account of the concept of the ownership of sensations, or, more generally, experiences. The most striking thing that he says on this topic is that it would be possible to dispense with the first-person pronoun. The word 'I' can be eliminated because, when I use it to report that I have toothache, it is not a feature of my experience that this toothache that I feel is owned by me rather than by someone else. This part of his 1929 treatment of the ego led Sir Peter Strawson to call it 'the no-ownership theory'.[23] That is too dramatic a characterization of Wittgenstein's manœuvre, because he is only drawing attention to the fact that there is no inner subject for the word 'I' to denote. It would be more appropriate to call it 'the theory of ownership without any internal mark'.[24]

Let us assume that someone is in pain, and the question is not about the type of the sensation—'Is it really pain?'—but about the owner—'Who is in pain?' Now it is a striking fact that the person who answers 'I am' does not have to work out whether to say this or to say that it is someone else.

We might also put the question like this: What in my experience justifies the 'my' in 'I feel *my* pain'? Where is the multiplicity in the feeling that justifies this word? And it can only be justified if we could also replace it by another word.[25]

The experience of feeling pain is not that a person 'I' has something.

I distinguish an intensity, a location, etc. in the pain, but not an owner.[26]

The phenomenon of feeling toothache I am familiar with is represented in the idioms of ordinary language by 'I *have* a pain in such and such a tooth'. Not by an expression of the kind 'In this place there is a feeling of pain'. The *whole*

---

[23] P. F. Strawson: *Individuals: An Essay in Descriptive Metaphysics*, Methuen, 1959, pp. 95–9. His attribution of the theory to Wittgenstein is based on G. E. Moore's notes of Wittgenstein's lectures in 1930–3 (*Mind*, Vol. 64 No. 253, Jan. 1955, pp. 13–14). When Strawson wrote his book the later works of Wittgenstein, in which he developed his ideas about the ownership of sensations, had not yet been published. The only other available source for them was M. Schlick's article, 'Meaning and Verification', *Philosophical Review*, Vol. 45, 1936, reprinted in *Readings in Philosophical Analysis*, ed. H. Feigl and W. Sellars, Appleton-Century-Crofts, 1949.

[24] See Vol. I pp. 179–87. The loss of the ego is no real loss. However, there might still be some other real deprivation entailed by Wittgenstein's thesis. The question, whether this is so, will be discussed at the end of this chapter.

[25] *Philosophical Remarks*, ed. R. Rhees, tr. R. Hargreaves and R. White, Blackwell, 1975 (henceforth *PR*), § 63.

[26] Ibid., § 65.

field of this experience is described in this language by expressions of the form 'I have . . .'.[27]

To put the point linguistically, the sufferer does not have a space next to the word 'pain' into which he might have slotted a different pronoun. So there is a sharp contrast with the case in which he has to slot into his report of a sensation that he feels the right word for its type. There is, therefore, no valid inference from the incorrigibility of his identification of the owner, when he is the owner, to the incorrigibility of his identification of the type. It is a separate question whether sensation-types are always unmistakable to their owners.[28]

These passages show very clearly what Wittgenstein is excluding. When I feel toothache I do not have to pick out myself as the owner from a range of candidates for owning it. The point can be illustrated by the example used in Part I: the predicament of a schoolboy with a headache should not be assimilated to the predicament of the schoolmaster who wants to identify the sufferer and asks him to put up his hand. The boy need not, and cannot ask himself to which subject the headache that he feels belongs.[29]

This is a phenomenological point, but it produces two distinct effects on the language-game of ascribing sensations to people. First, in my own case, when I use the word 'I', its reference is not problematical to me, as it would be if I heard, but could not identify, another person using it, and so there is really no need for me to use the word to make this non-problematical reference:

. . . The word 'I' does not refer to a possessor in sentences about having an experience, unlike its use in 'I have a cigar'. We could have a language from which 'I' is omitted from sentences describing a personal experience. Instead of saying 'I think' or 'I have an ache' one might say 'It thinks' (like 'It rains'), and in place of 'I have an ache', 'There is an ache here'.

. . . Acceptance of such a change is tempting, because the description of a sensation does not contain a reference to either a person or a sense organ.[30]

The proposed elimination of the first-person pronoun has already been mentioned, and it will be discussed later in this chapter.

The second linguistic effect of the phenomenological point is an effect produced on other people's self-ascriptions of sensations:

'I have a pain' is a sign of a completely different kind when I am using the

---

[27] Ibid., § 66.   [28] See Vol. I pp. 57–8.   [29] See Vol. I p. 40.
[30] *Wittgenstein's Lectures, Cambridge, 1932–35*, ed. Alice Ambrose, Blackwell, 1979 (henceforth *CLII*), pp. 21–2. Cf. *PR* § 57.

proposition, from what it is to me on the lips of another; the reason being that it is senseless, as far as I am concerned, on the lips of another, until I know through which mouth it was expressed. The propositional sign in this case doesn't consist in the sound alone, but in the fact that the sound came out of this mouth. Whereas in the case in which I say or think it, the sign is the sound itself.[31]

So when I say 'I am in pain' my thought changes its clothing on the way out into the physical world in which it is expressed, and it does this without any extra help from me.

The two points made in these two passages may be combined in the following way. The personal part of my message is automatic for me, and so I do not need to use the first-person pronoun to contribute what is evidently a necessary element to its sense. On the other hand, it is not automatic for those who hear me—it might have been someone other than me who was in pain—but they are not baffled by the absence of the first-person pronoun, because my mouth makes the necessary contribution to the sense of my message. It signifies me because it is part of me.

This point is going to be an important part of the therapy offered by Wittgenstein. The solipsist starts from the true thesis that all experience is had from a point of view not represented in the experience itself, but he goes wrong when he infers that he can make a discriminating reference to himself in complete detachment from his body. The inference is tempting because the reference to himself really is made without the use of any physical criteria. However, according to Wittgenstein, it achieves the status of a genuinely discriminating reference to an individual only because his mouth is a proper part of its expression. This does not mean that, to use Quine's phrase, he 'makes an honest proposition' of 'I am in pain' by expressing it. It means that the possibility of expressing it in a way that uses the speaker's mouth as a proper part of the propositional sign is a necessary condition of its sense.

But that, of course, is just what remains to be established. It may be true that, when the solipsist retreats into his private world, he cannot take with him the capacity to make discriminating references to individuals. But what argument did Wittgenstein use to show that it is true?[32] And what kind of connection between mind and body did he

---

[31] *PR* § 64.

[32] Whatever his argument, it will have a good claim to the title 'the first private language argument'. For it will have to demonstrate that the solipsist loses the capacity to

think was required to sustain the language-game of ascribing sensations to people?

There are two kinds of discriminating reference to individuals that the solipsist has to be able to make in his private world: he must be able to refer both to his own sensations and to himself. The objection, that he loses the second of these two capacities when he retreats into his private world is made in *The Blue Book* in the passage in which Wittgenstein introduces the concept of 'the geometrical eye'. This concept was mentioned in Volume I,[33] but there was not much discussion of it, and his explanation of it must now be analysed and sifted for his first private language argument, which will be an argument designed to show that there is no possibility of discriminating self-reference in the solipsist's private world.

The idea is an elegant one. When we reflect on the way in which sight works, we seem to find two different points on which everything converges. There is the eye, a physical object, which collects the light-rays and there is the focal point at the back of the visual field. If you are asked to indicate your right eye with the index finger of your right hand, you can do it with both eyes shut. But if you are asked to indicate the focal point at the back of your visual field, you need to open one eye at least, in order to be able to see your finger align itself on the axis of your visual field and make its central approach. Now since people see with their eyes, you will make the same hand movement whichever of these two requests you are obeying. But that is only contingently so. For people might have seen with their navels and used their eyes only to express their feelings, and in that case the two requests would have elicited different responses.

The point of this is that the solipsist's misunderstanding of the self-ascription of sensations is, according to Wittgenstein's diagnosis, very like a failure to understand what kind of thing the focal point at the back of his visual field really is. Self-ascriptions of sensations enjoy a certain immediacy and independence in practice, and the solipsist thinks that this is because the true subject really is an independent reference-point behind the mind, like the body, on the ordinary view,

---

make discriminating references to individuals, so that his 'private language' will go lame on that leg, just as the private language argument developed in *PI* I § 243 ff. ('the second private language argument') demonstrates that he loses the capacity to make discriminating references to sensation-types and so his 'private language' goes lame on its other leg.

[33] See Vol. I pp. 156–7 and 181.

behind the cone of physical space that is seen. The diagnosis is that this is a mistake analogous to the mistake of treating the focal point at the back of the visual field in the same way as the eye.

But where is the argument to prove that the solipsist really has made a mistake at this point? After all, he does not have to lay himself open to Hume's criticism, that he is naïvely assuming that the true subject is a thing, or, at least, that it ought to show up in a separate impression. He might even take over Hume's theory of personal identity and claim that his past impressions and ideas, remembered now, give him all that he needs for genuinely discriminating self-reference. So where is Wittgenstein's argument?

This is what he says in the passage in which he introduces the concept of 'the geometrical eye':

Now let us ask ourselves what sort of identity of personality it is we are referring to when we say 'when anything is seen, it is always I who see'.

. . . what I wished to say was: 'Always when anything is seen, something is seen'. I.e. that of which I said it continued during all the experiences of seeing was not any particular entity 'I', but the experience of seeing itself. This may become clearer if we imagine the man who makes our solipsistic statement to point to his eyes while he says 'I'. . . . But what is he pointing to? These particular eyes with the identity of physical objects? (To understand this sentence, you must remember that the grammar of words of which we say that they stand for physical objects is characterized by the way in which we use the phrase 'the *same* so-and-so', or 'the identical so-and-so', where 'so-and-so' designates the physical object.) We said before that he did not wish to point to a particular physical object at all. The idea that he had made a significant statement arose from a confusion corresponding to the confusion between what we shall call 'the geometrical eye' and 'the physical eye'. I will indicate the use of these terms: If a man tries to obey the order 'Point to your eye', he may do many different things, and there are many different criteria which he will accept for having pointed to his eye. If these criteria, as they usually do, coincide, I may use them alternately and in different combinations to show me that I have touched my eye. If they don't coincide, I shall have to distinguish between different sense of the phrase 'I touch my eye' or 'I move my finger towards my eye'. If, e.g., my eyes are shut, I can still have the characteristic kinaesthetic experience in my arm which I should call the kinaesthetic experience of raising my hand to my eye. That I had succeeded in doing so, I shall recognize by the peculiar tactile sensation of touching my eye. . . . As to visual criteria, there are two I can adopt. There is the ordinary experience of seeing my hand rise and come towards my eye, and this experience, of course, is different from seeing two things meet, say, two finger tips. On the other hand, I can use as a criterion for my finger moving towards my eye what I see when I look into a mirror and see my finger nearing my eye. If that place on my body which, we say, 'sees' is to be determined by moving my finger towards my eye, according to the second criterion, then it is conceivable that I may see with what according to other criteria is the tip of my nose, or places on my forehead; or I might in this way point to a place lying outside my body. If I wish a person to point to his eye (or his eyes) according to the second criterion *alone*, I shall express my wish by saying: 'Point to your geometrical eye (or eyes).'[34]

The diagnosis of the solipsist's mistake is offered in the middle of this passage: 'The idea that he had made a significant statement arose from a confusion corresponding to the confusion between what we shall call "the geometrical eye" and "the physical eye".' The point is not just that two different things are confused, but that there is a confusion between two things belonging to different types. The identity of 'the geometrical eye' is of a totally different type from the identity of 'the physical eye', and similarly the identity of the solipsist's ego is of a totally different type from the identity of a person.

But though this is an elegant diagnosis of the solipsist's mistake, if he has made one, it is not entirely clear that he really has made one. This looks like a case where the therapy has begun before the malady has been confirmed. Or is Wittgenstein relying on something that he takes to be too obvious to need explicit statement?

There is a passage in his slightly later 'Notes for Lectures on "Private Experience" and "Sense data" ' which may throw some light on the structure of his argument:

'What is seen *I* see (pointing to my body). I point at my geometrical eye, saying this. Or I point with closed eyes and touch my breast and feel it. In no case do I make a connection between what is seen and a person.

I am tempted to say: 'It seems at least a fact of experience that at the source of *the visual field* there is mostly a small man with grey flannel trousers, in fact L.W.'—Someone might answer to this: It is true you almost always wear grey flannel trousers and often look at them.

'But I *am* in a favoured position. I am the centre of the world.' Suppose I

---

[34] *BLBK* pp. 63–4. The two visual criteria are specified in a rather confusing way. He appears to be saying that if I use the first one, I will be relying on my knowledge of the location of my 'physical eye' and watching my finger approach the place where I know that it is, and that if I use the second one, I will watch my finger approach the place which 'sees', wherever it is, and then look in a mirror to discover where that place is. But unfortunately the descriptions of the two visual criteria do not make it entirely clear which of them involves seeing your finger align itself on the axis of your visual field and make its central approach.

saw myself in the mirror saying this and pointing to myself. Would it still be all right?

When I say I play a unique role I really mean the geometrical eye.

But the point is that I don't establish a relation between a person and what is seen. All I do is that alternately I point in front of me and to myself.[35]

When I point at my geometrical eye, I do not 'make a connection between what is seen and a person'. This must be the clue to his reason for insisting in *The Blue Book* that the geometrical eye has a totally different type of identity from the physical eye. So perhaps he is taking it as obvious that the 'geometrical ego' is not the kind of thing that could possibly count as a person. But why not? Isn't it a bit arbitrary to reject the solipsist's concept of a person just because it is minimal? It is, of course, a scaled-down model, but it is hardly what Berkeley would have called 'a killing blow' to point out that it lacks a body. Why should it have a body?

There must be a further assumption underlying Wittgenstein's argument, not explicitly stated, but left, as it were, to introduce itself between the lines. Most probably he was assuming that a discriminating reference to oneself must be a reference to something of the same general type, or, at least, in part, of the same general type as the objects presented to oneself.

This would be a plausible assumption, because it certainly identifies a necessary condition of discriminating references to individuals in the physical world. It is because my body is one object among others that I can refer to the others and know what I am doing when I refer to them: I am exploiting temporary relations between one object and others that it passes in space. Naturally, I would not be able to learn how to do this if my body were as ephemeral as its spatial relations to other bodies, and there would be no point in doing it if I could not record its travels. But when I succeed in doing it, I am doing something definite and I know what it is that I am doing, only because I can also refer reflexively to my own body.

The assumption is not very demanding. I might be the only person around just as I might be the only person around in the other case—describing different types of objects.[36] Nevertheless, it is sufficiently demanding to block the solipsist's internalization of discriminating

---

[35] *NLPESD* pp. 297–9.
[36] See Ch. 14 for a defence of this interpretation of Wittgenstein's (second) private language argument.

references to individuals. This is not simply because such references necessarily depend on a body. That would be too narrow a requirement. The real reason is more general: they must be references to objects of the same general type as oneself or, at least, of the same general type as part of oneself. We must not rule out by stipulation the possibility that the requirement might be met within the mind. Even if it looks highly unlikely, we must at least ask whether the mind contains resources for meeting it in some parallel way. But how could it do that? Would the idea be that there might be an impression of the subject within the mind? Now the absence of any such impression is only the beginning of the obstacle that confronts the solipsist at this point. The deeper difficulty is that there could not possibly be an internal impression that would count as an impression of the self, because the primitive experiments that identify my body for me in infancy could not conceivably be matched by any similar manœuvres within my mind.[37] So the solipsist has to move even further back and claim that the true subject is the 'geometrical ego' which holds itself aloof from such mundane contacts. But that makes it a non-starter rather than a mere loser, because it belongs to a type that is not only wrong, but radically and totally wrong for its function.

If this was Wittgenstein's objection to the solipsist's attempt to internalize self-reference, it is understandable that his direct criticism had hardly started before it was merged into diagnosis and therapy. This was partly because the requirement of sameness of general type is so obviously correct, but there was also another reason: the solipsist was in such rapid flight that he did not make any serious attempt to find a mental counterpart of the physical conditions of genuinely discriminating references to individuals but retreated immediately to the 'geometrical ego'. If Wittgenstein is right, though the solipsist was then left with a vestigial feeling that he was pointing to himself, there was nothing else surviving from the real performance.

If this argument from the requirement of sameness of type establishes that the solipsist cannot make discriminating references to himself after he has retreated into his private world, it also establishes that he cannot make discriminating references to anything else. So his would-be references to his sensations are blocked, not because they are elusive, like his ego, but because he lacks the kind of base that he

---

[37] This argument was presented above as a development of Hume's second and more interesting reason for rejecting the impression of the self. See above, p. 237 and Vol. I pp. 158–60.

needs to support his references to them. This is a direct consequence of the failure of his internalized self-references, but it is also connected with another fault which Wittgenstein explains in the passage in *The Blue Book* in which he introduces the analogy of the self-frustrating clock-maker:

> Now we can make use of such an expression as 'pointing to the *appearance* of a body' or 'pointing to a visual sense datum'. Roughly speaking, this sort of pointing comes to the same as sighting, say, along the barrel of a gun. Thus we may point and say: 'This is the direction in which I see my image in the mirror'. One can also use such an expression as 'the appearance, or sense datum, of my finger points to the sense datum of the tree' and similar ones.
>
> Now when in the solipsistic way I say '*This* is what's really seen', I point before me and it is essential that I point *visually*. If I pointed sideways or behind me—as it were, to things that I don't see—the pointing would in this case be meaningless to me; it would not be pointing in the sense in which I wish to point. But this means that when I point before me saying 'this is what's really seen', although I make the gesture of pointing, I don't point to one thing as opposed to another. This is as when travelling in a car and feeling in a hurry, I instinctively press against something in front of me as though I could push the car from the inside.
>
> When it makes sense to say 'I see this', or 'this is seen', pointing to what I see, it also makes *sense* to say 'I see this', or 'this is seen', pointing to something I *don't* see. When I made my solipsist statement, I pointed, but I robbed the pointing of its sense by inseparably connecting that which points and that to which it points. I constructed a clock with all its wheels, etc., and in the end fastened the dial to the pointer and made it go round with it. And in this way the solipsist's 'Only this is really seen' reminds us of a tautology.[38]

We have to suppose that the solipsist is not picking out one object from an array, but picking out the whole array in his visual field at the moment. Wittgenstein's criticism is that this is not really a case of picking out at all, because there is no larger field from which he is making a selection, and no possibility of pointing mistakenly to something that is not in his visual field, because his visual field has no neighbours.[39]

This is another phase of the first private language argument. It demonstrates a further deficiency in the solipsist's internalized references to individuals. In his private world the subject and the contemporary array are clamped together and this produces two related effects. First, the subject loses the independence that it must

<hr />

[38] *BLBK* p. 71.   [39] See Vol. I pp. 39, 155, and 181.

have if it is to serve as a base for discriminating references to individuals, and the solipsist's attempts to win back the necessary independence for it within the mind inevitably fail. They fail, not because the mind just happens to lack the requisite resources, as in Hume's first argument against the theory of the self-impression, but because it necessarily lacks them, as in his second argument.[40] Second, symmetrically, the array is not selected from a more extensive field of objects existing independently.

There is a certain therapeutic value in demonstrating the second deficiency in the solipsist's internalized references to individuals. For it shows why he still has the vestigial feeling that he is pointing to his sensations in spite of the fact that his performance is not selective and does not pick out the material presented to him. Wittgenstein sometimes uses the analogy of a magic lantern to make this point. For example, in the lecture notes taken by G. E. Moore we find this:

> In speaking of these two senses of 'I' he said, as what he called 'a final thing', 'In one sense "I" and "conscious" are equivalent, but not in another', and he compared this difference to the difference between what can be said of the pictures on a film in a magic lantern and of the picture on the screen; saying that the pictures in the lantern are all 'on the same level' but that the picture which is at any given time on the screen is not 'on the same level' with any of them, and that if we were to use 'conscious' to say of one of the pictures in the lantern that it was at that time being thrown on the screen, it would be meaningless to say of the picture on the screen that it was 'conscious'. The pictures on the film, he said, 'have neighbours', whereas that on the screen has none.[41]

This analogy requires some explanation. Consider the contents of my visual field at the moment and suppose that I adopt the convention that I am allowed to 'point' only to them. Then if I say '*They* are seen', 'pointing' to them as I say it, that will not be genuine pointing because it will not be selective. This is because the deictic use of '*They*' has been clamped by logical convention to the contents of my visual field. There are no other things to which I might have pointed instead as I said (falsely) '*They* are seen'.

Now my adoption of this crippling logical convention looks entirely gratuitous at first. However, I do have a reason for it: my visual field has no neighbours,[42] and so if I 'point' inside it, I cannot point outside it in the same way. So it seems to me that my logical convention merely endorses my natural predicament.

Wittgenstein's objection to my procedure starts from his contention that nature never forces anyone to adopt a logical convention.[43] I chose to adopt the rule which stultified my pointing by making it non-selective. True, I had a reason for my choice—the neighbourlessness of the visual field—but it was not a compelling reason and I must be brought to see that the consequence of my choice is that I am no longer really pointing.

In the analogy a certain word 'φ' is introduced to mean 'thrown on the screen at the moment'. Now I can still say of a particular picture that it is φ, but only so long as I am allowed to think of it as the one produced by this slide in the magazine rather than by that one. Each picture has 'neighbours' when it is introduced in that way. But the use of the word 'φ' becomes empty when it is restricted by convention to a range extending no further than the screen and whatever is on it at the moment of utterance. A form of words which would have had sense without the restriction now has no sense.

This is a general thesis about any word 'φ' that is clamped to the world in this particular way. Wittgenstein's example, 'conscious', simply indicates the point of the analogy: I feel forced to adopt the crippling logical convention because my field of consciousness, like my visual field and the picture on the screen, has no neighbours. He applies the thesis to a descriptive word because it is easier to understand this application than the application to pointing. The result is a powerful criticism of the use that the solipsist tries to make of pointing.

It may be objected that the criticism, and, more generally the 'first private language argument' to which it belongs, is unfair, because it assumes mistakenly that solipsism is a theory which has to confine itself to the resources of the present moment. In fact the solipsist can draw on the resources of experience-memory to answer the embarrassing question about the momentary ego: 'How does it achieve the independence that it needs in order to serve as a base for discriminating references to individuals?' For surely the right answer is that it achieves this independence simply by being the ego to which other objects were presented in the past and are now remembered to have been presented.

This move has a certain importance and it will be discussed later

[43] See Vol. I pp. 15–16.

apropos of Strawson's criticism of the 'no-ownership theory'.[44] However, it does not provide the solipsist with a way of escaping the dilemma. For his claim is about all objects presented to his ego. He is saying about all of them, and not just about some of them, that they are the only objects that exist. Therefore, he is not in a position to put some of them outside the scope of his existential thesis so that they may serve to identify his ego independently of the others. If his thesis were restricted to objects paraded before his ego at the moment, he could not rely on objects paraded before it in the past to provide him with an independent identification of it, because he would be implicitly denying their existence. However, his existential thesis does include objects paraded before his ego in the past, but he then needs some way of identifying his ego independently of both sets of objects, present and past.

There are three more comments needed on the suggestion that the solipsist fares better when he is allowed to bring in the temporal dimension and to appeal to his remembered past. First, it looks as if memory is another capacity which cannot be completely internalized. For there has to be a difference between cases where the solipsist actually had the experience that he thinks he remembers having and cases where his memory-impression is mistaken, and this is a distinction which it does not seem possible for him to set up and apply within his mind.[45] If this really is impossible, the solipsist, faced by the threatened loss of his capacity to make discriminating references to individuals, cannot succeed in retaining it by invoking another capacity which would be equally unviable entirely within his mind.

Second, in any case, the resources of experience-memory would not supply the solipsist with a complete answer to Wittgenstein's objections to the internalization of discriminating references to individuals. If those resources really were available to him, and if he really could introduce the inner subject in a way that made it independent of its present objects, that would still not be enough to put it in a position to serve as a base for such references. That function would require the inner subject to be of the same general type, or, at least, in part, of the same general type as the objects presented to it, and how could experience-memory ever make it possible to meet that requirement?

[44] See below, pp. 261–6.
[45] This is the nerve of the second argument against the possibility of a private language. See *PI* I § 243 ff., to be discussed in Chs. 13–15.

Third, it remains an important fact that, when someone has an experience, he does not have to think of himself under any particular physical description. He does not even have to think of himself under a mental description—for example, as the person who yesterday formed a certain intention. If his plane crashes and he survives, at first with none of the memories that would supply him with descriptions of either kind, he can still report his present sensations. Even in such a predicament a person is at home in his mind, and, as his memories return, he can move around in it without making any particular appeal to his body. This is important not only because it is the solipsist's point of departure, but also because it shows how careful Wittgenstein must be not to exaggerate the extent of the mind's dependence on the body.

But what kind of connection between mind and body did Wittgenstein take to be required to sustain the language-game of ascribing sensations to people? This question was close to surfacing at several points in the preceding discussion of his treatment of the solipsist's introduction of the ego, and it must now be answered.

The first step towards answering it is to see that in 1929 he did not think that what was needed was a definitional connection between a particular subject and a particular body. It is easy to miss this important fact because he did argue that the solipsist was wrong to force the ego into a definitional connection with its own objects. That is the point of the criticism in the *Notebooks* and *Tractatus*:[46] the solipsist refused to connect 'his' ego with his body, and, since he never encountered an ego in experience, he could introduce it only as 'the subject to which these objects are presented'. Thus he forced the subject into a definitional clamp which deprived it of its independent mobility. But it does not follow that Wittgenstein's strategy was to substitute another definitional connection, attaching a particular subject to a particular body. On the contrary, he saw two distinct errors in the solipsist's manœuvres. The first error was forcing the subject into a connection with the wrong kind of partner, the array of his sensations instead of his body. The second error was making the connection definitional and, therefore, too rigid. In real life the subject is supported by a web of connections radiating outwards to different points, and though these connections supply criteria of identity, they are not definitional. Their multiplicity is enough to ensure their defeasibility, but they will not be defeated in normal cases, because it is

---

[46] A criticism directed against Russell, among others. See Vol. I p. 161.

only in extreme cases that critical conflicts occur. So it would have been just as mistaken to give the subject a simple definitional connection with his body.

There is a general account of the connection between subject and body in the lectures that Wittgenstein gave in Cambridge in 1932–5:

> . . . Suppose I say 'Although I cannot imagine other people without their bodies, I could nevertheless imagine myself without a body.' It might seem as though there was a sort of knowing expressible by saying 'I know who had the dream and where he is, namely, in this body.' But is it sense to say 'If I did not have a body, I would still know that it was I who had the dream'? What would it be like to *know* I had a dream without having a body? If selves had no bodies, how should we make ourselves understood? Of course, we could imagine that voices came from various places. But what use would the word 'I' have, inasmuch as the same voice might be heard in several places? The fact that it makes sense to suppose that I change my body, but that it does not make sense to suppose that I have a self without a body, shows that the word 'I' cannot be replaced by 'this body'; and at the same time it shows that 'I' only has meaning with reference to a body. A parallel in chess is that although the king is not to be identified with this piece of wood, at the same time one cannot talk of a pure king of chess which has no mark or symbol corresponding to it. The use of the word 'I' depends on an experienced correlation between the mouth and certain other parts of the body. This is clear in the case where the criterion of a person's having pain when *his* hand is pinched is that the words come out of his mouth. It was in order to show that 'I' would have no meaning without such a correlation that I tried to describe a case where there seemed to be a use of the word 'I' [namely, imagining oneself without a body] but where closer investigation indicated there was not. Since 'I' and 'this body', like 'the king of chess' and 'the wooden piece', cannot be interchanged, it is incorrect to say that pointing to this body is an indirect way of pointing to me. Pointing to this body and to me are again different.[47]

The question at issue here is not the one that gave him so much trouble later, 'Are sensation-types necessarily connected through bodies with the external world?' It is still the question whether the owner is necessarily connected with a body. Although Wittgenstein's answer is that it does not make sense to suppose that I have a self without a body, he does not make the connection between me and a particular body definitional. One obvious reason for not making it definitional is that 'it makes sense to suppose that I change my body'. Another equally obvious reason is that, when a particular body is mine,

[47] *CLII* p. 62.

I am neither identical with it nor the inhabitant of it. But there is also a third, less obvious reason: there are two lines connecting the owner, in his mental aspect, through his body to the world around him, one running in from the point of stimulation to his seat of consciousness, and the other running out from that point to speech and other behavioural reactions. In an extreme case, if one could be imagined, these two lines might be attached to different bodies, and so the two connections cannot both be definitional.

But if the connection between owner and body is not definitional, what is it? And why is it needed? What are the sanctions operating against disembodiment? A preliminary, but rather vague answer to the first of these three questions would be that the connection is not definitional but presuppositional—in Wittgenstein's words, 'The use of the word "I" depends on an experienced correlation between the mouth and certain other parts of the body'? The point can be put in the terminology used in Part I: it is a familiar fact that, when a person's right hand is hurt, there is a line running into the seat of his consciousness and out again to his mouth[48] He says 'I am in pain', and though the word 'I', as used by him, does not mean 'this body', it does presuppose the integrity of this personal line. There has to be a connection running back from the mouth that speaks through the seat of the consciousness of the pain to the injured part of the body.

But why is the integrity of this personal line presupposed? If it is only a matter of experience, could we not continue to ascribe sensations to ourselves and others even if our personal lines were disrupted? That is going to depend on the answers to two further questions: 'At what point are we imagining our personal lines disrupted?' and 'Are we imagining universal, or only occasional disruption?'

Wittgenstein describes an extreme case which a neurologist might diagnose as one in which the sensory nerves of one person had been connected up to the cortex of another person:

. . . It is clearly imaginable that I should feel a pain in the hand of a different body from the one called my own. . . .[49]

He does not commit himself to the neurological explanation of the phenomenon and, of course, there might be another explanation, or we

---

[48] See Vol. I pp. 41–3.
[49] *PR* § 60. He carefully distinguishes this achievement, which only has to surmount physical obstacles, from feeling someone else's pain, which is conceptually impossible. Cf. *PR* § 61.

might find the fact, that I reported a pain when his hand was hurt completely inexplicable. Wittgenstein's question is not how it came about that I felt a pain in the hand belonging to a different person's body, but how we would react if it often happened that one person spontaneously reported a pain when another person's hand was hurt. So he does not identify the line which is here called 'personal' with a neural line. It is simply a regular sequence of three types of event, injury, painful sensation, and report of pain, and its actual embodiment is treated by him as irrelevant to the philosophical investigation.[50]

Suppose that the disruption began suddenly and continued for several years. Each of us picked up pains from another person's body and needed empathy to feel pain in his own. We would have to do something about it and our reaction would depend on how chaotic the new situation was. It would be a manageable situation if each of us still had a method of starting from his own felt pain and identifying the injured body, and, more generally, if we found that we could use a similar method on other people, starting from the output body—the mouth that spoke—and tracing the personal line back to a different input body. Of course, there would have to be a fairly simple, regular connection between the body with the mouth that spoke and the body with the injured hand. If there were no regular connection, or if it were too complex to be discovered, we would not be able to sustain a concept of the ownership of sensations like our present one, with three points on the personal line. If the input and output bodies were different, but related in a discoverable, regular way, we would still have a three-point concept, but, of course, not quite the concept that we have now—a knight's move rather than a straight line.

The question asked above was 'Why is the integrity of personal lines presupposed by the language-game of ascribing sensations to people?' So far, the disruption of personal lines has only been considered in one place, between injury and seat of consciousness. The answer proposed was that, if our personal lines were scrambled at this stage, we would no longer have any three-point concept of the ownership of sensations. But would we still have a two-point concept? After giving up the location of sensations in bodies, would we still be able to identify their owners?

At first sight, it looks as if this would depend on what happened on the second section of our personal lines, between seat of consciousness

[50] This is a consequence of the way he draws the line between philosophy and science. See below, pp. 510–13.

and speech or other behaviour. It seems that, if they were not disrupted at this stage, it would still be possible to determine who felt the sensations, even though it would no longer be possible to say where they felt them.[51] So it looks as if the second part of the linkage would still preserve a two-point concept of ownership. However, it is not as simple as that. For it is arguable that complete chaos between input and seat of consciousness would undermine the concept of memory, so that no ascription of pain to a subject could ever be made—not even by the sufferer himself—because there would be no recognized recurrence in his mind to be correlated with the speaking mouth.[52]

The point of all these speculations is to investigate the presuppositions of the language-game of ascribing sensations to people. In it I cannot say that I feel my friend's pain, because the concept of the ownership of sensations simply rules that out as a move that would take me over the edge into nonsense,[53] but I can say that I feel a pain in his hand. This is a good example of the new way of exploring the limits of language: they are no longer revealed by a single, general theory, as they had been in the *Tractatus*, but by careful thought-experiments probing the resistance in order to discover how far we can go without falling into nonsense.[54] In this particular case, though the suggestion that I might feel my friend's pain lacks sense, I can move quite a long way in that direction, because it really would be possible for me to feel a pain in his hand. Naturally, we also want to know why we cannot make the forbidden move, or, to put the question misleadingly, why we cannot feel another person's pain. But here we must be careful, because it is essential not to be fooled by the apparent factuality of these questions about possibilities. We must not expect the answers to be pieces of super-science, because we are never going to be able to identify a candidate for possibility—my feeling his pain—and then go on to explain why the actual achievement of possibility is necessarily out of its reach. Philosophy is not a higher science and the investigation of possibilities must not be modelled on the investigation of facts.[55]

[51] A neurologist would explain disruption on the second stage of the personal line as the effect of scrambling motor-nerves, but Wittgenstein holds his inquiry aloof from all explanations of this kind.

[52] See above, p. 241. It is difficult to work out the effect of chaotic scrambling of the first sections of personal lines without describing the case in more detail. Would these pains be expressed naturally in typical pain-behaviour? And if so, what function in our lives, personal or social, would that have?

[53] See above, p. 252 n. 49.   [54] See above, p. 220.

[55] See above, pp. 215–16.

Then what can philosophy do to satisfy us? It is disappointing to be told that the reason why sensations cannot be shared like umbrellas is that this move would break a rule of the language-game. Is there nothing that philosophy can tell us about the reasons why we follow this rule rather than another more permissive one? Fortunately, there is something more that a philosopher can say in this kind of case. He cannot describe a pre-existing situation and show that it forced us to adopt this particular rule. That would require him to use language in order to get outside language, an impossible feat.[56] But what he can do is to describe the structure of the concept of the ownership of sensations, and, by making certain moves within its structure, he can show us the direction in which this particular piece of nonsense—joint ownership of sensations—lies. As in the *Tractatus*, he can plot the limit of language from the inside, but the difference is that he will now no longer be plotting the whole of it systematically, but only a small section of it experimentally.

This kind of philosophical examination of a concept requires it to have an internal structure. If the concept of the ownership of sensations did not have the three-point structure described above, a philosopher could not manœuvre inside it and orient himself in the direction in which nonsense lies. If it were a simple concept, not based on the central experience connected backwards to the input and forwards to the output, all that he could tell us would be that the word 'ownership' has a meaning and so contributes to the senses of sentences in which it occurs only because it stands for a simple dual relation. But that is not the philosopher's predicament, because the concept is not a simple one. It does have an internal structure, within which Wittgenstein's illuminating moves can be made.

This way of describing his new philosophical method marks one of the main contrasts with the method recommended in the *Tractatus*. In his early work, if he were confronted by a complex concept, he would analyse it into its simple components, standing for simple things, and leave it at that. But he now treats the components in a different way: he imagines situations in which they are arranged quite differently, and he uses these lateral thought-experiments to throw light on their actual arrangement and its effect on our actual language-game.[57] Naturally, these considerations will not justify its rules by showing that they were

---

[56] See above, pp. 214–15 and Vol. I pp. 146–8.
[57] Cf. *LWVC* p. 45, quoted and discussed below, p. 273.

forced on us by a superior metaphysical necessity,[58] but they will show why we impose them on ourselves, how within certain limits we could alter them, and which combinations would take us over the edge into nonsense. What more could be demanded by anyone who wants to understand our remarkable practice of ascribing sensations to ourselves and others?[59]

However, though this description of his new philosophical method marks one of the main contrasts with his earlier method, there is another contrast to which it does less than justice. It is true that his philosophical investigations now involve lateral thought-experiments, but it is also true that the concepts investigated are themselves linked to one another in a network of lateral relations. The two points are distinct but connected, as can be seen from a consideration of our colour-vocabulary. Formerly he had assumed that each colour-word is connected with its own patch of reality and, since they are not logically independent of one another, they must have a structure which the philosopher would analyse down into its simple components. But in 1929 he realized that this was a case in which analysis could go no deeper in spite of the evident logical relations between different words in the vocabulary. So these logical relations were irredeemably lateral and each word could be understood only in its place in the whole network.[60] The connection between this point and the new lateral thought-experiments emerges when he asks if the meaning of a colour-word would have been different if it had belonged to a different colour-vocabulary, either a richer one or a more impoverished one.[61]

The shift from atomism to holism is just as important as the associated shift from depth analysis to description and experimental variation of our language-games. It does not stop us speaking of the structure of a concept like that of the ownership of sensations, but we do have to admit that this is a different notion of structure. There is no longer any implication that a complex concept is one that we must take to pieces and then subdivide the pieces, thus zeroing in on its final atomistic analysis. On the contrary, we mean that the concept has lateral connections radiating outwards in different directions, and it is the exploration of these lateral connections that will yield philosophical understanding.

---

[58] See Vol. I pp. 14–6.

[59] We need to appreciate the strangeness of the ordinary. See Vol. I pp. 17–18.

[60] See Vol. I pp. 83–6.

[61] Cf. L. Wittgenstein: *Remarks on Colour*, ed. G. E. M. Anscombe, tr. L. McAlister and M. Schättle, Blackwell, 1977, § 86.

This point of contrast can be made in another way. It was axiomatic in the *Tractatus* that the sense of a sentence can never depend on the truth of another sentence about one of its components:[62] all such truths must be roped into the sense of the original sentence and none left outside to serve as presuppositions of its sense. Wittgenstein's treatment of the language-game of ascribing sensations to people is based on a repudiation of this axiom. These ascriptions depend on certain conditions, which may fail, but their failure would render the ascriptions senseless rather than false, because it would make the language-game impossible. Of course, these conditions had never even looked as if they were part of the sense of the ascriptions, but, when the earlier axiom had been repudiated, the investigation of sensation-language could be extended to cover them.

So far, more has been said about disruptions of the personal line between point of input and seat of consciousness than about disruptions between seat of consciousness and point of output. But Wittgenstein also has some interesting observations to make on the later section of the personal line. As things are, it connects the seat of consciousness to a mouth which belongs to the same body as the point of input. This connection is, of course, rigidly established for us. Consequently, though the sufferer chooses to speak out, he does not choose the mouth that he uses:

> . . . the man who cries out with pain, or says that he has pain, *doesn't choose the mouth which says it.*[63]

This idea is developed in an interesting, but obscure passage in 'Notes for Lectures on "Private Experience" and "Sense-data" ':

> If I say '*I* see this ↑ ', I am likely to tap my chest to show which person I am. Now suppose I had no head and pointing to my geometrical eye I would point to an empty place above my neck: wouldn't I still feel that I pointed to the person who sees, tapping my chest? Now I might ask 'How do you know in this case who sees this?' But what is *this*? It's no use just pointing ahead of me, and if, instead, I point to a description and tap both my chest and the description and say '*I* see *this*'—it has no sense to ask 'How do you know that it's *you* who sees it?', for I don't *know* that it's this person and not another one which sees before I point. This is what I meant by saying that I don't choose the mouth which says 'I have toothache'.[64]

---

[62] Cf. *TLP* 2.0211 and *Notes Dictated to G. E. Moore in Norway, NB* p. 116, discussed in Vol. I pp. 66 ff.

[63] *BLBK* p. 68.   [64] *NLPESD* p. 310.

This requires comment.

Wittgenstein is describing a situation in which I indicate who is having a certain visual experience by pointing at myself. He does not actually say that I do not choose the hand that points, because he takes it as obvious that I do not have any choice in the matter (except, of course, the unimportant choice between left and right hand). He then mentions two different ways of pointing to myself. The ordinary way would be to tap my chest, but I might also try to indicate the exact place from which I see by pointing to my geometrical eye. That, of course, would be an additional piece of information and it would require me to point at myself in a more discriminating way, aligning my finger with the axis of my field of vision and watching it make its approach. The passage is rather confusing, because, when Wittgenstein describes this way of pointing to myself, he illustrates it with the extraordinary case in which I point to the empty place above my severed neck. Let us eliminate this complication by supposing that I do not try to indicate the exact place from which I see. Evidently, I need not point at any particular part of my body. I can tap my chest, or just hold up my hand like a pupil in class. As a matter of fact, any hand movement would do, because I do not choose which right hand to use. Wittgenstein does not actually say this, because he takes it as obvious. Instead, he moves straight to speech, which is the other way of indicating the person who has the experience—in this case, toothache—and he makes the parallel point, that I do not choose the mouth which says that I am the sufferer.

So far, the line of thought is clear. But why does he go on to say that 'I don't *know* that it's this person and not another one which sees before I point'? This is puzzling, because it looks as if I do know that I am the one who sees—how could I possibly be wrong about that?

However, he is not denying the inconceivability of a mistake, made by me, the owner of this visual experience, about its ownership. He is only making a point about the concept of knowledge: in all cases of knowledge the subject must have made a choice between different possibilities, but no such choice was made in this case. For just as I did not have to choose which right hand would do the pointing, so too, before I pointed, I did not have to make up my mind who was the person who had the visual experience. My personal line only allowed me one answer, 'It is I', without any conceivable alternatives. To put the point neurologically, I did not have to make any selection, because my nervous system had made the selection for me, and so, according to him, this is a case that is too good to be called 'knowledge'.[65]

This point about the concept of knowledge is not so important as the structure which underlies it. Some philosophers disagree with his thesis, that this case, and other similar ones, are too good to count as knowledge. But that issue is less important than the underlying structure of the case, to which he is drawing attention. The deeper point is that there is no intellectual task for me to carry out between the occurrence of the visual experience and my act of pointing. It is exactly the same with the occurrence of the toothache and my act of speaking. The identity of the subject of this experience—i.e. the identity of the mind–body couple, or person—is guaranteed for me by the integrity of my personal line.[66]

If a sceptic hears the mouth that I operate speaking, he may raise the question, 'Do you really know that you are the sufferer?' Now maybe Wittgenstein's critics are right, and I could reply 'Yes, that's something that I really do know'. But the important point is the underlying one: if I know this fact for sure, that is not because I made an infallible choice. I did not choose the mouth that I operated, but simply relied on the integrity of my personal line, and, if that is what the sceptic is questioning, he should reflect that, if my personal line were disrupted between seat of consciousness and mouth, the claim issued by the mouth would not be false but senseless. The sceptic could not say 'You are wrong: it is someone else who is suffering.' For 'you' would mean 'the person to whom the mouth belongs', and the effect of the disruption, in the extreme, chaotic situation, would be that the very idea of 'the person to whom the mouth belongs' would no longer have any application.

Part of the point can be put by distinguishing what is asserted from what is presupposed. Naturally, the integrity of my personal line is only a contingent matter, and it might be impaired either because its first stage started in someone else's tooth or for the different reason implicit in Wittgenstein's remarks—its second stage might terminate in someone else's mouth. These are real possibilities, even if only remote ones, and the question is what would happen if they were realized in the extreme, chaotic way. Now when I make 'my mouth' say 'I am the sufferer', the integrity of my personal line is not part of what I am asserting. It is presupposed by my making any assertion of this kind. If the presupposition failed and there were chaos on both sections of my

---

[65] He, of course, would not put the point neurologically. See above, pp. 252–3.
[66] Cf. the case of the pupil with a headache, Vol. I p. 40.

personal line, the result would not be that the sufferer was not me but someone else. If we multiply out and imagine chaos on both sections of all personal lines, it would no longer be possible for me or anyone else to make any ascriptions of experiences to people. This particular language-game would be one that could no longer be played.

There are two features of Wittgenstein's treatment of the output part of the personal lines that require comment. First, there is the point already made: it is the integrity of this part of the line that explains how the sufferer who complains manages to say something in spite of the fact that he does not pick out the inner subject of his pain.[67] For when he says 'I am in pain', the possibility of expressing his message in a way that uses his mouth instead of the pronoun as a proper part of the propositional sign is a necessary condition of its sense.

The second feature is the use that Wittgenstein makes of the fact that there is no intellectual task for me to carry out between the occurrence of the visual experience and my act of pointing, or between the toothache and my act of speaking. This is because the identity of the owner, conceived in the full three-point way, is guaranteed by the integrity of my personal line. This guarantee is pre-linguistic and it is not restricted to humans, but exploited by other animals not endowed with the capacity to think and speak discursively as we do. The guarantee is a great leveller: we do not need to think at this point and perhaps they could not think, but neither we nor they can go wrong, because thinking is not necessary.

There is a striking parallelism between this feature of the self-ascription of sensations and the feature, mentioned earlier, of the owner's identification of certain sensation-types. When the word for the sensation-type replaces a piece of behaviour which is already linked by nature to the type itself, it insinuates itself into a natural drama which antedates discursive thinking in the life of the individual (and the species).[68] So here too, according to Wittgenstein, there is no intellectual work to be done: if, for example, the sensation is a pain, I do not have to make up my mind whether it belongs to that type or to some other type. Of course, the way in which nature has done the work for me in this case is not exactly the same as in the other case. The naturally established line in this case connects types, whereas in the other case it is a personal line connecting individuals.

---

[67] See above, p. 239
[68] See Vol. I pp. 52–3.

The consequences of this difference are interesting. But before they are drawn out, it is worth quoting the passage in *Philosophical Investigations* in which the point about the natural type-line of pain is made.

How do words *refer* to sensations?—There doesn't seem to be any problem here; don't we talk about sensations every day, and give them names? But how is the connection between the name and the thing set up? This question is the same as: how does a human being learn the meaning of the names of sensations?—of the word 'pain' for example. Here is one possibility: words are connected with the primitive, the natural, expressions of the sensation and used in their place. A child has hurt himself and he cries; and then adults talk to him and teach him exclamations and, later, sentences. They teach the child new pain-behaviour.

'So you are saying that the word "pain" really means crying?'—On the contrary: the verbal expression of pain replaces crying and does not describe it.

For how can I go so far as to try to use language to get between pain and its expression?[69]

This much misunderstood passage does not imply that all sensation-types have natural expressions, or that all words for sensation-types are learned in this way. The point is only that the word for this particular sensation-type, like the words for certain other sensation-types, can be learned in this way, because there is a natural type-line which antedates the very capacity to think and speak discursively. That is why it would be presumptuous of language to attempt to get between the sensation and its natural expression in order to give the sensation an independent classification. There is no intellectual work to be done here just as there was no intellectual work to be done at the corresponding point on the parallel personal line.

Nevertheless, there are differences between the two cases, and one very important difference will be mentioned now but left to be discussed in more detail later: I literally have no alternative to ascribing a sensation that I feel to myself, whereas I do have alternatives to assigning a pain that I feel to that type. So, however unmistakable its type may be, a mistake at this point would not be quite like the other mistake, ascribing it to someone else, which is really inconceivable.[70]

Before this subject is closed, something ought to be said about a well-known criticism of this part of Wittgenstein's later philosophy. Sir Peter Strawson in his book *Individuals*, develops and criticizes a theory

[69] *PI* I §§ 244–5.
[70] See above, p. 239, and Vol. I pp. 57–8.

which he calls the 'no-ownership' or 'no-subject' doctrine of the self and which he attributes to Wittgenstein.[71]

Strawson starts by characterizing the 'no-ownership' move as a rejection of the analogy between the ego and the body: the idea is that the self-ascription of sensations should not be modelled on the ascription of sensations to others through their bodies. To put the point in the terms used earlier, the ego, as an independent entity, is an illusion generated by the assumption that self-ascription requires an internal analogue of the body.[72] This is certainly Wittgenstein's objection to naïve theories of the ego.

Strawson's criticism is that the 'no-ownership' theory, which Wittgenstein then adopts, is incoherent. For the theorist needs to be able to explain how any of us can be in a position to claim that 'All my sensations originate in this body'. Of course, we must suppose that the person who makes this claim either holds up his hand, or else, if his sensory nerves have been linked by surgery to someone else's body, he points to that body. Then what he says will be true, but only contingently true. Now, according to Strawson, the contingency of his claim gives the word 'my' a task that it cannot perform in the 'no-ownership' theory. For 'my' cannot mean 'sensations originating in this body', because that would deprive the claim of its contingency. Nor can it just drop out of the claim, because the speaker evidently does not mean that all experiences whatsoever originate in this body. So, in order to justify the retention of the word 'my' in this claim, the theorist would have to explain it in some non-physical way. But that is something that he refuses to do. Therefore, his theory is incoherent.

This is an interesting criticism of Wittgenstein's treatment of the ego, because it puts pressure on the two parts of it that are most difficult to interpret and defend, the concession that he made to the solipsist in the *Tractatus*, and the account of the phenomenology and semantics of self-ascriptions of sensations that he drew out of that concession in and immediately after 1929. What he conceded to the solipsist was that he had a good point, but he added that his attempt to express it in factual language was mistaken. The field of his consciousness, like his visual field, really was limited, but not by boundaries separating it from neighbours on the same level. This suggested to the solipsist that he might refer to everything in the field of his consciousness without ever relying on anything outside it.

---

[71] See above, p. 238 n. 23.
[72] See Vol. I pp. 159–60.

However, in order to do that he would need a point of origin for his mental system. Now the field of his consciousness also shared another feature with his visual field: it did not contain any representation of its inner focal point. So the solipsist simply took its inner focal point for granted as the point of origin of his system, and went ahead with his claim that the only things that existed were things in the field of his consciousness. Wittgenstein's objection was that he could not possibly take this careless line and rely on a vanishing point of origin, and he offered, as an alternative, his own 1929 account of the ascription of sensations: the subject does not have to say who owns the sensations that he feels, because his personal line leaves him with no choice and, at the same time, shows other people through his body unmistakably (if he is not faking) who the owner is.[73] So though the subject does not have to mention his body or even think about it, that is not because it is not needed: on the contrary, it is essential to, and, therefore, presupposed by, his participation in the language-game of ascribing sensations to people.

The question is, 'What impact does Strawson's criticism make on Wittgenstein's position?' Perhaps the first point that needs to be stressed is that, if Wittgenstein does fail to explain the use of the word 'my' in the perfectly acceptable, contingent claim that 'All my sensations originate in this body', the deficiency can hardly be made good by bringing back the ego. To put the point in another way, the loss of the kind of subject that is eliminated by the 'no-ownership' theory cannot be regarded as a real loss. So the point of the criticism must be not that the ego should be brought back, but that its elimination creates the need for some substitute, something which, unlike the body, really will justify the use of the word 'my' in this contingent claim about the physical origin of 'all my sensations'.

So where should we look for this substitute? There are, as usual, two possibilities: it might be something physical or it might be something mental. Now, at first sight, it may seem that we are forced to look for a physical substitute. For we have to allow for the solipsist who will insist on talking about *everything* in the field of his consciousness, thus, it appears, excluding the possibility of a mental substitute for the eliminated ego. If he is a solipsist of the moment, '*everything*' will mean all the contents of his present field of consciousness, and if he is a diachronic solipsist, it will mean all its contents from birth to death. On

---

[73] See Vol. I pp. 41–3.

the other hand, the search for a physical substitute does look hopeless for the reason given by Strawson: if the substitute is the speaker's body, it looks as if his claim will immediately lose its contingency.

However, perhaps we ought not to give up the physical line of investigation quite so quickly. Maybe we can divide the body notionally and use part of it to identify the sensations and set the other part free to serve as their contingent origin. This, of course, is what is done by someone who claims that his sensations originate in someone else's body. His mouth and the motor nerves connecting his vocal cords with his brain serve to identify the sensations that he means, and when they have been identified in this way, it is a contingent matter whether or not they originated in the body to which the mouth belongs. This way of answering the objection fits very well into Wittgenstein's 1929 treatment of the ascription of sensations to people because it exploits the possibility, implicit in his account, of distinguishing between the two parts of the personal line and treating them differently: the output part serves to identify the sensations, while the input part sustains the contingency of the claim. It is a plausible guess that, if he had been alive to answer the objection, he would have done so in this way.[74]

This answer invites the riposte that it is surely also a contingent fact that all my sensations find their expression unavoidably through this mouth, and how can the 'no-ownership theorist' explain this use of the word 'my'? But there is an answer to this challenge. Our concept of the ownership of sensations would be unusable if simultaneous disruptions on both parts of the personal line produced total chaos. So there is no need for the theorist to explain this use of the word 'my'—on the contrary, the fact that he cannot explain it is some confirmation of his theory, because in these adverse circumstances the concept could not be used. Now it may seem to me that I could still use the word 'my' in my private world even if both parts of my personal line had been disrupted. But, at least, my personal line would have had to maintain its integrity while I was learning to use the word, and after the double disruption it is debatable whether I could rely on the lesson that I had learned in better days and go on using the word. Whatever answer is given to that question, it will not cause the 'no-ownership theorist' any embarrassment.

It was conceded above that the solipsist who insisted on talking about everything in the field of his consciousness left himself with no

---

[74] But, of course, he would not have put the point in neurological terms.

mental basis for his use of the word 'my', if he made the contingent claim that is under examination, and that is why a physical basis was sought for it. It is, of course, obvious that he would not make the claim, but that does not matter, because the question is, what would happen if he did make it. In any case, the solipsist is not the only pebble on the beach, and we should also consider the perfectly ordinary cases in which a person speaks not about all the contents of his mind from birth to death, but about a particular sensation which he ascribes to himself at a particular moment. In such a case there is no need for him to think of himself as the person speaking through 'this mouth'. He can just as well anchor his use of the word 'my' to something mental, provided that it meets the requirement of independence from this particular sensation. He can make this move within his mental system, without denying that it is attached to a particular speaking body, but without making any use of that attachment at the moment. This might be called 'the mind-dividing move' in contrast to 'the body-dividing move', which was made above. The mind, of course, is divided temporally, whereas the body is divided spatially.

Strawson has an objection to the mind-dividing move. He thinks that it succeeds in preserving the contingency of the claim only by paying too high a price for it. Certainly, the 'no-ownership theorist's' Humean move makes the particular sensation sufficiently independent of its mentally identified owner to allow that owner to ascribe it to himself as a matter of contingent fact. But, Strawson argues, it achieves this result only by treating the sensation as a 'logically transferable' item, which it is not. If a domino is added to a particular row, it could have been added to another row instead of this one, but if a sensation is added to the sequence with which I identify myself, there is no sense in the speculation that it might have been added to another sequence instead of this one. A sensation owes its identity as a particular sensation to the identity of the person who owns it.[75]

This objection rests on a questionable assumption. It is true that we start the identity-line of a sensation at the point of its occurrence in the field of consciousness of a particular person, and we veto the possibility that this particular sensation might have been had by a different person. But what need is there for the 'no-ownership theorist' to credit the sensation with the vetoed degree of independence from its actual owner, mentally identified? Maybe Hume did treat impressions

[75] P. F. Strawson: *Individuals*, p. 97.

like stars in space, linked by the laws of the association of ideas just as they are linked by Newton's laws. But there is no need whatsoever for the 'no-ownership theorist' to make this mistake. If Wittgenstein had defended his treatment of self-ascriptions of sensations by dividing the mind, he would merely have had to claim that they get all the contingency that they need from the fact that sensations always add themselves contingently to pre-existing sequences (except in the case of the first one, if it is permissible to talk about 'the first one'), and that they do this without mimicking the criteria of identity of physical objects.

Wittgenstein's treatment of the ego, like so much of his later work, is an example of retrieval. He brings the solipsist back from his free-wheeling fantasy and confronts him with the familiar facts from which he started. It is indeed true that 'any experience is had from a point of view which is not represented in that experience'.[76] However, when the facts about the ascription of sensations are recalled, rehearsed, and thoroughly understood, it becomes clear that nobody needs an ego, or, at least, that nobody needs a pure one. Indeed, I might think it just as well that I do not have one, because, if I did have one, I would have to ask myself whether a sensation in my field of consciousness really did belong to this ego of mine, and how would I answer that question?[77] The whole treatment of the ascription of sensations to people which developed out of the critique of solipsism in the *Tractatus* is a paradigm of Wittgenstein's later method in action.

But what has happened to his original feeling for the mystery of the ego? Where do we now find anything to match this entry in the *Notebooks*?

The I, the I is what is deeply mysterious![78]

Has the old idea, that any language must be understood from a point of view which cannot be represented in that language, completely disappeared?[79] These are questions that have to be asked about the distance that separate the work begun in 1929 from the *Tractatus*.

The first thing that is needed here is a warning against exaggerating this distance. The sense of the mystery of the ego, which had been concentrated at a single point, is now diffused over a wider area. The familiar facts about the self-ascription of sensations are themselves mysterious, but not because they are recondite. On the contrary, the

[76] See Vol. I p. 38. [77] See Vol. I p. 40.
[78] *NB* 5 Aug. 1916. [79] See Vol. I p. 165.

reason why we fail to appreciate them is that they are so much part of our lives, so close up, that it is difficult for us to get them into focus. We have to learn to feel the strangeness of the familiar, and Wittgenstein's treatment of the solipsist's fantasy is imbued with the same spirit as the fantasy itself.[80]

The idea that language cannot represent the point from which it is understood has indeed disappeared, and its place has been taken by an investigation of the solidarity of the community of language-users. This change was a natural one. If the problem of the ascription of sensations and experiences to mind–body couples—in a word, to people—had been successfully solved, it was obviously futile to try to trace the vicissitudes of the detached ego in the rarefied atmosphere of idealism.[81] The point of view from which language is understood is evidently a multiple point of view, and the question is how the community of language-users achieve the necessary integration to communicate with one another. If there were any analogy with the visual field, it would have to be the visual field of an insect with multi-faceted eyes, and the question would be how all these sources of information are co-ordinated.

On the other hand, it must be remembered that the problem which Wittgenstein had successfully solved was only the problem of the subject of experience, and the problem of its objects still lay ahead. It was an achievement to have shown how each subject is tied to his body, but there was still the possibility that the objects of experience might break away from the common world. That is the traditional origin of solipsistic speculations and it still remained to be investigated and neutralized. He had to find a way of extending the successful treatment of the subject of experience to its objects. There ought to be a parallel method for dealing with sensations and their types, but it had yet to be worked out.

If the treatment of sensations and their types, which is the topic of the next five chapters, really does run parallel to the treatment of their owners, it is likely that there will be many points of connection between the two investigations. Some of them have already been mentioned. The solipsist thinks that he can point to his ego and base his fantastic claim on it without giving it any criterion of identity, and, as will appear in the next chapter, he tries to treat his sensation-types in the same

---

[80] See Vol. I pp. 17–18.
[81] See *NB* 15 Oct. 1916, discussed in Vol. I pp. 170–1. It is a mistake to look for this kind of idealism in Wittgenstein's later work. See Vol. I pp. 188–90.

way.[82] Also—to look even further ahead—a mistake of the same general kind is made by anyone who thinks that the constancy of meaning which every descriptive word ought to maintain requires an omni-competent guide in the mind of each of its users.[83] These are the most conspicuous connections between the treatment of solipsism and the two main lines of thought in *Philosophical Investigations*.

There is a risk of misunderstanding here. In the *Notebooks* Wittgenstein argued that, if the ego is detached from the solipsist's body and allowed to float freely, it might just as well be regarded as the universal subject of idealism.[84] So when we find connections between the treatment of solipsism and the two main lines of thought of *Philosophical Investigations*, we may be inclined to think that there is an element of idealism in the later philosophy: the early system is attached to the vanishing 'I' and the later system is attached to the vanishing 'We'.[85] But this is a misunderstanding. The resources for solving the problem of the ownership of sensations were all in the *Tractatus* and it is those resources that were developed in 1929. After that there is no further difficulty about the identification of individual subjects, and there is certainly no suggestion that the community of language-users might have, or ought to have, an elusive collective consciousness. On the contrary, all the emphasis is on their achievement of the necessary solidarity in spite of their separateness. If there is an element of idealism in the later philosophy, it is to be found not in the individuation of the subjects of experience but in the characterization of its objects. To revert to an earlier example, the relevant question is whether Wittgenstein thought that our system for classifying colours is the free invention of our minds, or partly constrained by the colours themselves, or made wholly mandatory by them.[86] But that is an entirely different question.

In any case, the connection between the early treatment of solipsism and the two main lines of thought in *Philosophical Investigations* is more structural than doctrinal. In each of the three cases Wittgenstein argues against a thesis with the same faulty structure. His criticism of the common structure of the three theses has now been fully explained in its application to solipsism, but the explanation of its application to

---

[82] See Vol. I pp. 53–7.   [83] See Vol. I pp. 11–12 and 59–60.
[84] *NB* 15 Oct. 1916.
[85] This interpretation has been proposed by J. Lear. See his article, 'The disappearing "We" ', *Proceedings of the Aristotelian Society*, Supp. Vol. 58, 1984.
[86] See Vol. I pp. 16–17.

the other two theses has only been sketchy. This is a deficiency that will be made good in later chapters. Meanwhile here is an interesting remark from the 'Big Typescript':

I can see—but not at all clearly—a connection between the problem of solipsism or idealism and the problem of the way a sentence signifies. Is it perhaps like this—the I is replaced by the sentence and the relation between the I and reality is replaced by the relation between the sentence and reality?[87]

[87] MS 213, p. 499.

I I

The First Attempt to Extend the Treatment of the Ego to Sensations and their Types: Reactions to Phenomenalism

WITTGENSTEIN'S next task was to give an account of sensations and their types which would steer the same middle course between introspectionism and behaviourism. It was not going to be easy. The elimination of the ego from the position of owner of sensations was the elimination of something unnecessary and its loss no real loss. When we ascribe sensations to others, there is evidently no need to credit them with egos, and even when a person reports his own sensations on the basis of what occurs in the field of his consciousness we do not need to suppose that he has to search it for evidence of ownership by his ego. However, sensations themselves and their types posed a more difficult problem. They were not redundancies to be eliminated, and there was an awkward multiplicity in the range of alternative types to which a sensation might belong.[1]

We feel this awkwardness when we notice the ego's greater amenability to treatment. It may not be true that we use introspection to discriminate sensations of different types, but the suggestion is, at least, not gratuitous, like the idea that the ego ought to be the introspected basis of claims to their ownership. In the case of the ego there is no discriminatory task to perform on oneself, and other people are already distinguished by their bodies, but in the case of sensations the task and its importance are obvious. Sensations really are there— are they not?—waiting for us to describe them, like objects in our environment—well, not exactly like objects, but sufficiently like them to make us try to model inner awareness on outer awareness. There is then a strong tendency for sensations and their types to break away from their ultimate anchorage in the physical world. In certain cases something can be done to check this tendency: we can point out that the type-line of pain shares many of the features of its personal line.

[1] See Vol. I pp. 44–5.

However, even in this kind of example the treatment of type and owner cannot be exactly similar, because, when I feel a pain, the multiplicity of alternative possible types is not matched by any multiplicity of alternative possible owners, out of which I have to pick the right one. There are also other cases, in which the treatment of the type of the sensation is even less like the treatment of the owner than it is in the case of pain. The problem is a difficult one.

The move from the aloof detachment of the *Tractatus* to the new position in which Wittgenstein surfaced in 1929 is not at all easy to understand, because the changes were greater than they immediately appeared to be. The two things that remained constant were so impressive and dominating. First, although the later treatment of the ego included a new reductive argument against the possibility of discriminating reference to individuals, there was no change in the conclusion that it was impossible to detach a private world, based on the ego, from the common world. Second, the theory of language remained for a time substantially unaltered.[2] True, he no longer insisted on the logical independence of elementary sentences, but it was not immediately evident that this was the first open acknowledgement of a general shift towards holism, or that the earlier method of deep analysis was soon to be replaced by the study of lateral implications and the experimental construction of language-games.[3] The process that began in 1929 was the gradual adjustment of a philosophical theory to the predicament of actually being applied. The abstract schema of the *Tractatus* had been developed with an airy neglect of detail and it was suddenly given an ordinary identifiable content. It found this full-bodied realization much more upsetting than was immediately apparent, and it began to undergo a developing series of consequential changes.

At first, the theory of language and the treatment of the ego were the points of minimal change and they fixed the axis around which everything else slowly began to revolve. When the ego had been eliminated, what was left was a person, or rather a number of people, unequivocally placed in the common phenomenal world and somehow communicating with one another about it in a language that was recognizably derived from the *Tractatus*. But given the indirectness of sense-perception, how did they get any idea of that world? And even if they already had some idea of it, how could they know that they all had

[2] See *Wittgenstein's Lectures, Cambridge, 1930–32*, ed. D. Lee, Blackwell, 1980 (henceforth *CLI*), pp. 1–14 and 21–60.   [3] See Vol. I pp. 86–7 and 146–7.

the same idea of it, so that they really were communicating with one another about it? Which ever end of their telescopes they looked down, how could they be sure what was at the other end?

These two problems—the external world and other minds—were hardly new, but Wittgenstein had avoided them in the *Tractatus*, and in 1929, when he began to give his philosophical system a detailed application, they were waiting for him. His first reaction was to assume that, when the subjects of experience had been pinned to the one and only phenomenal world through their bodies, the objects would take care of themselves. But it was not as easy as that. In the *Tractatus* he had simply assumed that the objects of our external senses could be located in the common phenomenal world and left without any further categorization, but when he began to give the system a detailed application, he would, at least, have to work out the connections between bodily sensations and the stimuli and responses that bracketed them before the problem of other minds could be solved.

Near the beginning of *Ludwig Wittgenstein and the Vienna Circle*, there are some remarks of Wittgenstein's which throw a lot of light on the position that he had reached at the end of 1929:

The word 'I' belongs to those words that can be eliminated from language. Now it is very important if there are several languages; in that case it is possible to see what all these languages have in common and that common element is what depicts.

Now it is possible to construct many different languages, each of which has a different man as its centre. Imagine for instance you were a despot in the Orient. All men were compelled to speak the language whose centre you are. If I spoke this language, I should say, 'Wittgenstein has toothache. But Waismann is behaving as Wittgenstein does when he has toothache.' In the language whose centre you are it would be expressed just the other way round. 'Waismann has toothache, Wittgenstein is behaving like Waismann when he has toothache.'

All these languages can be translated into one another. Only what they have in common mirrors anything.

Now it is noteworthy that *one* of these languages has a distinctive status, namely that one in which I can as it were say that I feel *real* pain.

If I am 'A', then I can, to be sure, say 'B is behaving as A does when he feels pain,' but also 'A is behaving as B does when he feels pain.' One of these languages has a distinctive status, namely the language whose centre I am. The distinctiveness of this language lies in its application. It is not expressed.[4]

This is a record of some remarks made by Wittgenstein at a meeting at Schlick's house on 22 December 1929. They occur in a section headed 'Solipsism', which begins like this:

> I used to believe that there was the everyday language that we all usually spoke and a primary language that expressed what we really knew, namely phenomena. I also spoke of a first system and a second system. Now I wish to explain why I do not adhere to that conception any more.[5]

So in December 1929 he had already abandoned the idea that there was 'a primary language that expressed what we really knew, namely phenomena'. It follows that his adoption of that idea has to be assigned to an even earlier date. The editor of *Ludwig Wittgenstein and the Vienna Circle*, Brian McGuinness, points out in a footnote to this passage that in *Philosophical Remarks* 'similar ideas are touched on several times, sometimes as something which has been superseded (e.g. pp. 51 and 84), sometimes with different degrees of assent (pp. 58, 88, 100, 158, 168, and 267). Here Wittgenstein no doubt refers to earlier manuscript volumes in some of which the *PR* may have occurred for the first time.'[6]

There are several problems of interpretation here and they need to be dealt with separately. First, what did Wittgenstein mean by his now abandoned thesis that there was 'a primary language'? Second, when did he adopt it? Third, when did he abandon it? These three questions will have to be answered, and after that it will be possible to explain what he is saying in the longer of the two texts, which discusses the languages with different people as their centres. The answer to the first of the three questions will be that the hypothesis of 'a primary language' never was intended as a contribution to the solution of the problem of our perception of the external world. Its central point was the ontologically neutral thesis that ordinary factual language can be translated into another language which will perfectly mirror the phenomena, whatever their category. If he sometimes suggested that the phenomena were sense-data, there was no implication that sense-data were things standing on the line of perceptual input and curtailing our view of the world.[7] This interpretation will be defended in this chapter and the adoption and abandonment of the hypothesis will be dated. After that, the next chapter will deal with the remarks about languages with different people as their centres. It will be argued that

---

[5] Ibid., p. 45. See Vol. I pp. 92–9.
[6] Ibid., p. 45.   [7] See Vol. I pp. 96–8.

this too is not offered as a solution to the problem of our perception of
the external world: it is an attempt to solve the problem of other minds,
but not a successful one.[8]

There is an important point that can be made immediately about the
relationship between the two texts quoted from *Ludwig Wittgenstein and
the Vienna Circle*. In the longer text, which discusses different
languages centred on different people, he implies that I in my self-
centred language will make direct references to my own sensations, but
indirect references to other people's sensations. So if the 'primary
language', in which, according to the other text, he no longer believes,
had been a sensation-language, the feature of it that led him to give up
his belief in it can hardly have been the subjects' direct references to
their own sensations. For if that had been its objectionable feature, he
could not have gone on to develop, as he does in the longer text, the
theory of interlocking sensation-languages based on the direct
references to sensations that each speaker is supposed to make. It
follows that either we must find some other way of explaining his
abandonment of his earlier hypothesis of the 'primary language'—it
was not a reaction to the difficulty of translating impersonal
descriptions of the phenomenal world into the direct reports that each
person makes of his own sense-data—or else we must find an
alternative interpretation of the theory proposed in the longer text.
There is, of course, also the third possibility, that alternative
interpretations should be adopted for both texts. This third possibility
is, in fact, the one that, according to the argument to be developed in
this chapter, gives the best explanation of Wittgenstein's writings in
this period. However, the immediate point is only that the usual
interpretation, according to which he is concerned with a reduction of
the phenomenal world to our exteroceptive sense-data, cannot be
adopted for both texts.

The longer text reads very naturally as a contribution to the problem
of other minds. It does not raise the question how I can start from my
own sense-data and establish myself as a knowledgeable inhabitant of
the common phenomenal world. The assumption is that I am already
established in that world and am now trying to include other people's
bodily sensations in my picture of it. I am not worried about what I see
when I look out through my own telescope, but only about what I see

---

[8] It is interesting that epistemologists divide quite neatly into those who are more
concerned about our knowledge of the external world and those who are more
concerned about our knowledge of other minds.

when I look back down other people's telescopes. This interpretation is confirmed by the choice of pain as an example, because it is an appropriate choice when the doubt concerns other minds, but less appropriate when it concerns the common phenomenal world. The explanation of the way in which the various self-centred languages are integrated with one another evidently assumes that their speakers can already communicate about things in that world. So, all in all, there is a strong case for taking the longer text to be concerned with the problem of other minds rather than the problem of the external world.

That would make it possible, although no longer very attractive, for us to keep the popular interpretation of his now abandoned hypothesis of 'a primary language': we could still say that it had been adopted as a solution to the problem of our perception of the external world, but that he now thinks that it is not necessary to go to such lengths in order to solve it. However, if he really had been a phenomenalist, it would be strange that his phenomenalism should go so quietly. Why does he no longer think it necessary to go so far for a solution? And what kind of realism has he adopted in its place? The change seems too smooth to be a change from one theory of perception to another.

In any case, the fact is that he never was worried by the thought that each of us might be confined to the world of his own mental sense-data. That was not the possibility suggested by the solipsist in the *Tractatus*. The solipsist's idea there had been that he could cut out of the common phenomenal world a private world centred on his own ego. Wittgenstein's response was to challenge him to identify his ego without placing it in the common phenomenal world. If anyone objected that, until he had solved the problem of perception, he had no right to assume that we are all firmly established in that world, he would have dismissed the objection as rubbish. It would, therefore, be consistent with the whole tenor of his philosophy that his hypothesis of a 'primary language' should not have been a solution to the problem of our perception of the external world. But in that case, what was it?

It is worth pausing at this point to reflect on the reasons why he might have dismissed, or, at least, circumvented the problem of the external world. The point was made in Volume I[9] that he regarded it as the world of phenomena, but not because of any contrasting reality behind the phenomena. That view is endorsed in a passage near the beginning of *Philosophical Remarks*:

[9] Vol. I pp. 96–8.

Time and again the attempt is made to use language to limit the world and set it in relief—but it can't be done. The self-evidence of the world expresses itself in the very fact that language can and does only refer to it.[10]

This refusal 'to use language to limit the world and set it in relief' is a constant feature of his philosophy and it is clearly marked in his early system. Here are two well-known examples from the *Tractatus*:

Thus the aim of the book is to set a limit to thought, or rather—not to thought, but to the expression of thoughts: for in order to be able to set a limit to thought, we should have to find both sides of the limit thinkable (i.e. we should have to be able to think what cannot be thought).[11]

and

Scepticism is *not* irrefutable, but obviously nonsensical, when it tries to raise doubts where no questions can be asked.

For doubt can exist only where a question exists, a question only where an answer exists, and an answer only where something *can be said*.[12]

What has not been so widely recognized is that it is this principle that explains his dismissive attitude to theories of perception both in the *Tractatus* and in 1929. It struck him as incoherent to start by identifying the basic data of perception somewhere within experience—for example, as mental sense-data—and then to draw a line around them and maintain that anything that seemed to lie on the far side of the line must be reduced to things on this side of it. The only way for a philosopher to draw a line around phenomena was to draw it from the inside, and not to pretend to go beyond it in order to draw it, only to confess afterwards that he had not really gone beyond it—that had merely been a kind of geometrical construction for locating the limit.

In the previous chapter the egocentrism into which Wittgenstein forced the solipsist to retreat was called 'sliding-peg egocentrism'.[13] The solipsist tried to use his own ego as a reference-point without first identifying it, and Wittgenstein's response was that in that case it was not a fixed peg, but a sliding peg. The ego was really being allowed to spread to all centres of consciousness instead of being attached exclusively to a single centre, the solipsist's own.[14] Similarly, if

---

[10] *PR* § 47. This is only part of this important text, which is quoted in full in Vol. I p. 95.

[11] *TLP* Preface, p. 3.   [12] *TLP* 6.51.

[13] See above, p. 233 n. 15.

[14] Cf. *NLPESD* p. 281, quoted in Vol. I p. 169 n. 54.

Wittgenstein was a phenomenalist, he was a 'sliding-peg phenomenalist'. For he evidently thought that phenomenalism was right if the line that it drew around phenomena was not drawn within experience, but wrong if it drew the line across the middle of the map of our experience dividing it into two parts. If it drew the line in that way, and then claimed that it was the limit of phenomena, it would be making a mistake exactly like the mistake of first giving one's own ego an identification in the common phenomenal world, and then going on to assert solipsism. So the only correct way of introducing the phenomenal world was to define it as 'whatever is correlated with the unified system of factual language' and then to leave the category of the correlate open. If perception was mentioned in the definition, the perceptual base-line could not possibly be identified empirically. It was by drawing the limit from the inside that he had arrived at the categorically neutral ontology of the *Tractatus*, and he was still in the same position in 1929.

The evidence for attributing sliding-peg phenomenalism to him in the period leading up to the publication of the *Tractatus* was given in Volume I.[15] It was argued that the theory of logic and language put forward in that book was applied to the foundations of empirical knowledge in a way that left many specific questions unanswered, and among them the question of the category of objects. In the *Notebooks* two candidates were canvassed, material points and sense-data, but the decision between them was never made. In the *Tractatus* the question was not even posed, but the plausibility of both candidates was implied both by Wittgenstein's choice of examples and by incidental remarks. The conclusion drawn was that it did not matter for his purposes in the *Tractatus* to what precise category objects belonged, so long as they were phenomenal, and phenomenal in a sense that did not imply a contrast with any reality beyond them.

Given this reason for rejecting phenomenalism with an empirically identified base-line, it would be quite extraordinary to find that in the early part of 1929 he had changed his mind and accepted it. How could such an impressively strong argument go so quietly? But it must be admitted that we do not have a complete picture of the development of his ideas at the beginning of the second period of his philosophy. So how can we be so sure that the text in which he says that he has given up his former hypothesis of 'a primary language' is not simply his

[15] See Vol. I pp. 92–8.

report of a recantation of phenomenalism with an empirically identified base-line? The implication, that at some intermediate date he had abandoned his earlier sliding-peg phenomenalism in favour of the classical version of the theory may be surprising, but how can we resist the testimony of this text? There is also quite a lot of auxiliary evidence for this popular view of the development of his philosophy in his writings in and immediately after 1929, and it will be set out and assessed below.

But first we need an answer to a question that was posed near the beginning of this chapter: 'What was the meaning of his former hypothesis that there was a primary language expressing "what we really knew, namely phenomena"?' It is, of course, very natural to take the distinctive feature of this language to be that it consists of reports of empirically identified sense-data—perhaps mental sense-data, as specified by the early British Empiricists, or perhaps sense-data identified as events in the nervous system of the subject, as they are by Russell.[16] But it would be better to pause and look more closely at what he actually says about the 'primary language':

I think that essentially we have only one language, and that is our everyday language. We need not invent a new language or construct a new symbolism, but our everyday language already is *the* language, provided we rid it of the obscurities that lie hidden in it.

Our language is completely in order, so long as we are clear about what it symbolizes. Languages other than the ordinary ones are also valuable in so far as they show us what they have in common. For certain purposes, e.g. for representing inferential relations, an artificial symbolism is very useful . . .[17]

This contains an endorsement of a remark that he had made long before in the *Tractatus*, but he now adds a very different comment on it. What he had said in the *Tractatus* was this:

In fact, all the propositions of our everyday language, just as they stand, are in perfect logical order. . . .[18]

But then he had continued,

. . . That utterly simple thing, which we have to formulate here, is not a likeness of the truth, but the truth itself in its entirety.[19]

---

[16] Wittgenstein appears not to have noticed that Russell identifies sense-data with physical events, and he takes Russell's popular way of introducing them, as such things as patches of colour in the visual field, to imply that they are mental.

[17] *LWVC* pp. 45–6.

[18] *TLP* 5.5563.

[19] Loc. cit., continuation.

He meant that his task was

> ... to give the most general propositional form: that is to give a description of the propositions of *any* sign-language *whatsoever* in such a way that every possible sense can be expressed by a symbol satisfying the description, and every symbol satisfying the description can express a sense, provided that the meanings of the names are suitably chosen.[20]

He had undertaken to give the unique specification of the essence of all factual languages, and so he had to identify the underlying common structure which the nature of the world imposed on all of them alike, however much they might vary in surface structure. Of course, the truth that he sought was not the truth of individual factual sentences, but the truth about their general form. The question to be answered was, 'What specification of their form would reveal their perfect appropriateness to the possibilities supplied by the world?'

In the conversation at Schlick's house in 1929 he repeats the observation 'that our language is completely in order', but he now makes a very different suggestion about the way to get 'clear about what it symbolizes'. There is no need for philosophers to seek a single way of analysing it which will reveal that its underlying structure is perfectly appropriate to the world. What they must try to do is to understand it as it is, and to penetrate its obscurities without translating it. If they do make any use of 'languages other than the ordinary ones', they will be valuable only in so far as 'they show us what they have in common' (sc. with the ordinary ones). The method recommended is direct examination of ordinary language, without first transforming it by logical analysis, but the examination is to be helped out by the use of invented languages, or invented fragments of language, as aids to understanding. It is interesting that the example of a language invented for comparison that he gives in this passage is an 'artifical symbolism' 'for dealing with inferential relations' or a calculus. The later term 'language-game' was first introduced as a synonym for 'calculus'[21] and it was then developed to mean any operation with language carried out by a group of people in appropriate surroundings.

So the idea that there was a primary or phenomenological language was the leading idea of the *Tractatus*: sentences belonging to the

---

[20] Ibid. 4.5
[21] See *Philosophical Grammar*, ed. R. Rhees, tr. A. Kenny, Blackwell, 1974 (henceforth *PG*), § 31. The point is made by J. and M. Hintikka: *Investigating Wittgenstein*, Blackwell, 1986, pp. 15–16.

primary language would be perfectly appropriate to the phenomena, whatever the category of the phenomena might be. When he abandoned this idea, his whole conception of philosophy changed. He gave up the search for a single analysis of factual language which would be exactly appropriate to the phenomenal world, the perfect mirror hidden deep within all our descriptions of it. Instead, he investigated the obscurities of factual discourse by observing it in action, and, if he constructed new languages, he offered them not as superior analyses or better ways of saying the same things, but, rather, as instructive objects of comparison. We have here the beginning of another way of using language as the key to thought, the comparative method of language-games.[22] What is repudiated is not just the specific idea that the perfect mirror of the world is to be found in the language of exteroceptive sense-data, but the general idea that it is to be found in any single reformulation of the whole of factual discourse.

The message is conveyed rather briefly in these announcements made at Schlick's house. So it is worth comparing them with the parallel passage at the beginning of *Philosophical Remarks*:

I do not now have phenomenological language, or 'primary language' as I used to call it, in mind as my goal. I no longer hold it to be necessary. All that is possible and necessary is to separate what is essential from what is inessential in *our* language.

That is, if we so to speak describe the class of languages which serve their purpose, then in so doing we have shown what is essential to them and given an immediate representation of immediate experience.

Each time I say that, instead of such and such a representation, you could also use this other one, we take a further step towards the goal of grasping the essence of what is represented.

A recognition of what is essential and what inessential in our language if it is to represent, a recognition of which parts of our language are wheels turning idly, amounts to the construction of a phenomenological language.

Physics differs from phenomenology in that it is concerned to establish laws. Phenomenology only establishes the possibilities. Thus, phenomenology would be the grammar of the description of those facts on which physics builds its theories.[23]

It could hardly be made clearer that the phenomenological or 'primary' language that he no longer regards as necessary or possible is the language in which the complete analysis of all factual discourse, as specified in the *Tractatus*, would have been expressed. The quest for a

---

[22] See Vol. I pp. 86–7 and 146–7.   [23] *PR* § 1.

perfect deep analysis is to be given up and it is to be replaced by a direct examination of our use of everyday language helped out by lateral investigations and comparisons designed to separate those features of it that are essential to its function from those that are superfluous and dispensable without loss of function.[24] His point is the general one, that the discovery of a language which would perfectly mirror the common phenomenal world, in whatever terms, is no longer his goal in philosophy.

This puts us in a position to give quick answers to the other two questions posed near the beginning of this chapter, about the date when his search for a primary or phenomenological language began and the date when it ended. It began when he started developing in the *Notebooks* the ideas that he published in the *Tractatus*, and its end in 1929 is recorded in these passages in *Ludwig Wittgenstein and the Vienna Circle* and *Philosophical Remarks*.

However, these answers are not enough in themselves to blow the fog off the mysterious development of his ideas in 1929 and the immediately following years. Maybe his 1929 recantation was entirely general in its scope, the abandonment of the quest for any single language of any kind to express the complete analysis of all factual discourse. But why did he call the object of his quest a 'primary' language, if he did not mean to tie it to the immediate deliverances of the senses? And is the meaning of the other word that he applied to it, 'phenomenological', really exhausted by the explanation that a phenomenological language is one that exactly fits the phenomena, whatever their category? If so, why did he say that phenomenology is concerned not with physical objects but with data?[25] And why did he himself connect his former enterprise with Russell's and say that he 'used to think that . . . one would be able to use visual impressions, etc., to define the concept . . . of a sphere'?[26] Also, how can we discount the fact that in these years he actually subscribed to a common formulation of classical phenomenalism?[27] More generally, it is quite clear that in this period he had a continuing interest in the visual field and its

---

[24] It is worth observing that in *TLP* too he had tried to separate what we use in our everyday language from what we do not use. The difference is that in those days he believed, but now no longer believes, that what we use can be captured in a single, complete analysis. See *TLP* 3.328, discussed in Vol. I pp. 140–1.

[25] See *PR* § 57, quoted below, p. 286.

[26] *PG* p. 211, quoted in full in Vol. I p. 93 n. 18, and below, p. 288.

[27] e.g. in *CLI* p. 81 (quoted below, p. 286) and in other passages cited and discussed below he says that statements about physical objects are hypotheses about sense-data.

contents, and how is that to be explained if he steadfastly refused to categorize phenomena?

There is much that still remains mysterious here, and, before it is investigated in detail, it might be useful to fix the general direction of this inquiry. It will pursue two main lines of interpretation. One will be the suggestion that in 1929 Wittgenstein did start to become interested in the categorization of phenomena, but not because he followed the well-trodden track from scepticism about anything on the far side of mental sense-data to a comforting reduction of all such things to the sense-data themselves. The reason why he became interested in the categorization of phenomena was not that he felt forced by the problem of the external world to adopt a philosophical theory of perception, but simply that people do talk not only about the external world but also about the data of their external senses and, more obviously, about their bodily sensations. The second suggestion will be that, in so far as he was exercised by a problem in this area, it was the problem of other minds.

What has been argued so far is that in 1929 Wittgenstein did not give up classical phenomenalism, because he had never adopted it or any other theory of perception, but that he did give up the quest for any kind of primary language to express the single complete analysis of all factual discourse. However, there is quite a lot of evidence that he was a phenomenalist in this period. Can it really be maintained that all that the evidence shows is that he was developing the sliding-peg phenomenalism of the *Tractatus*? If it shows more than this—if there are passages in which he is clearly concerned with exteroceptive sense-data—we shall have to ask whether he treated them as empirically specifiable things with independent criteria of identity and then went on to make the reductive move of classical phenomenalism. It will also be worth dating the remarks that might be taken to indicate that he was a classical phenomenalist.

Let us start with the question, 'When, exactly, did he show these tendencies to a phenomenalism which is not of the sliding-peg kind?' The answer is surprising: several of the remarks which are taken by some commentators to be the best contemporary evidence for his classical phenomenalism occur in the lectures that he gave in Cambridge in 1931–2.[28] But if this is the correct interpretation of these remarks, it cannot possibly have been classical phenomenalism

---

[28] *CLI* pp. 68–70 (quoted below, p. 290) and pp. 81–2.

that he recanted earlier, in 1929. If there was a crisis in his attitude to classical phenomenalism, it must have been quite distinct from the 1929 crisis in his attitude to the search for a primary language to express the single complete analysis of all factual discourse. On the assumption that there really was a crisis in his attitude to classical phenomenalism, we would have to infer that, first, he dropped the demand for a primary language, and then later, and quite independently, gave up the philosophical theory of perception which determined the category of the objects mentioned in the primary language that would have satisfied his former demand.

This is not an impossible reconstruction of the development of his thought, but there is a point that ought to be made against it immediately. If this is how things went, and if, therefore, it is not possible to treat his 1929 recantation as an abandonment of classical phenomenalism, that robs those who argue that he did at one time adhere to it of one of their main pieces of evidence. There is also the strong objection which has already been brought against this interpretation: the distinctive feature of classical phenomenalism is that it uses an empirically specified perceptual base-line, but if he did at any time adopt this kind of phenomenalism, he must have adopted it in spite of the strong argument against it in the *Tractatus*.[29] Even that is not absolutely impossible, though it would be surprising to find such an impressively strong argument going so quietly. The same point can now be made about his alleged abandonment of phenomenalism with an empirically identified base-line: this second change too must have occurred very quietly, given that it is not what he is reporting that he recanted in 1929. We know that, if it did occur, it must have occurred by 1933–4, because in *The Blue Book* he points out the absurdity of treating exteroceptive sense-data as an empirically identifiable kind of object.[30] But at what earlier point is it supposed to have occurred? And why does he not say in *The Blue Book* that he himself had formerly made the absurd mistake?

These arguments from the dating of the alleged changes in Wittgenstein's supposed theories of perception are not conclusive, but they are enough to raise the suspicion that the interpretation is on the wrong track. This particular drama—scepticism, reductive phenomenalism, and recantation—simply does not seem to be played out in the texts. On the other hand, he does sometimes use the same language as

---

[29] See above, pp. 275–7.
[30] *BLBK* pp. 64 and 70–1; cf. *CLII* pp. 128–9. See below, pp. 292–4.

philosophers who do present the drama. How is this to be explained?

One of the questions posed above was 'Why did he speak of a primary or phenomenological language if he did not mean to tie it to empirically identified sense-data?' Before any attempt is made to answer this question, it is necessary to emphasize the differences between two kinds of sense-data. There are bodily sensations, like pain, and, in the case of our external senses there are impressions which do not always seem to be appropriately classified as sensations. Now we actually have a language for reporting bodily sensations and so we did not need to adopt a philosophical theory of perception in order to introduce it. It is, therefore, not at all surprising to find Wittgenstein announcing his abandonment of his quest for a primary language at Schlick's house and then going on to investigate the way in which we succeed in communicating with one another about pains. Even if the primary language that he abandoned had been the language of phenomenalism with an empirically identified base-line, intercommunication about bodily sensations might still have presented a problem, after its abandonment. Even if we supposed that he tried to solve that problem by suggesting that each of us reports his own pains in a primary language and the pains of others in a secondary language, there would still be no inconsistency. For the primary language that he no longer held to be necessary or possible was not restricted to ordinary reports of bodily sensations—it was a language for expressing the complete analysis of all factual discourse—and it would still leave the analysis of reports of bodily sensations as a residual problem.

So much is obvious. What is more difficult to work out is how much more was implied by the words 'primary' and 'phenomenological'. Granted that they described the universal basic language of completely analysed factual discourse, did he imply anything more specific when he called that language 'primary' or when he called it 'phenomenological'? There are three distinct bids that might be made here in an auction of possible implications. First, he might be taken to imply that reports in a primary or phenomenological language would confine themselves to what was immediately given without adding any interpretation. That implication would be compatible with sliding-peg phenomenalism. Second, he might be taken to imply that these reports of the immediately given would have a different logic from descriptions of physical objects. Third, he might be taken to imply that they would be reports referring to some specific, empirically identified type of object, which stood on the line of perceptual input curtailing our view of the world. That would make him a classical phenomenalist, or, at least, it would put him in that philosophical company.

There is really no doubt that the first of these three bids is correct. In the opening section of *Philosophical Remarks*[31] although his main point is that it is no longer necessary to find a universal basic language, it is also true that he implies that such a language would have confined itself to what is immediately given. For he explains the task of separating 'what is essential from what is inessential in our language' in these terms:

> That is, if we so to speak describe the class of languages which serve their purpose, then in so doing we have shown what is essential to them and given an immediate representation of immediate experience.[32]

There are also several texts in which he marks the contrast between phenomenological and physical descriptions by calling the latter 'hypotheses'. For example:

> The description of phenomena by means of the hypothesis of a material world (*Körper-welt*) is indispensable because of its simplicity, compared with the incomprehensibly complicated phenomenological description. If I see various detached parts of a circle, then an accurate direct description of them is perhaps impossible, but the specification that they are parts of a circle . . . is simple.[33]

However, there is no implication in this passage that what is immediately given belongs to a different category from physical objects. On the contrary, what he says here is compatible with the suggestion that, though reports of the immediately given are very restricted in scope, they are still reports of things perceived in the physical world.

This passage was written in 1929, but, as has already been mentioned, he continued to hold the same view about the relation between the two kinds of description after he had given up his search for a basic language to express the complete analysis of all factual discourse. There is nothing paradoxical about this, provided that we distinguish the main implication of the descriptions 'primary' or 'phenomenological' from any extra implications that they may have had. He had given up the search for a language which would satisfy the main requirement, but there was no reason for him to abandon the

---

[31] *PR* § 1, quoted above, p. 280.   [32] Loc. cit.
[33] MS 106, pp. 102–4, quoted by J. and M. Hintikka in *Investigating Wittgenstein*, p. 164.

subsidiary requirement, that a primary or phenomenological language would have to confine itself to what is immediately given. So in the lectures that he gave in Cambridge in 1931–2 we find him still maintaining that distinction in the same phenomenalistic terms:

> There is a tendency to make the relation between physical objects and sense-data a contingent relation. Hence such phrases as 'caused by', 'beyond', 'outside'. But the world is not composed of sense-data and physical objects. The relation between them is one in language—a necessary relation. If there were a relation of causation, you could ask whether anyone has ever seen a physical object causing sense-data. We can talk about the same object in terms either of sense-data or hypothesis.[34]

He no longer thinks it necessary or possible to find a universal basic language, but he is still interested in one of the features that it would have had, namely its immediacy.

The passages that have been cited are enough to support the first of the three bids set out above: Wittgenstein's 'primary or phenomenological language' really was restricted to the immediately given. But do reports of the immediately given have a different logic from descriptions of material objects? There are several texts that can be adduced in support of an affirmative answer to this question too.

In *Philosophical Remarks* we find this:

> All our forms of speech are taken from ordinary physical language and cannot be used in epistemology or phenomenology without casting a distorting light on their objects.
>
> The very expression 'I can perceive x' is itself taken from the idioms of physics, and x ought to be a physical object—e.g. a body—here. Things have already gone wrong if this expression is used in phenomenology, where x must refer to a datum. For then 'I' and 'perceive' also cannot have their previous senses.[35]

This is not an isolated passage[36] and the differences between the logical grammar of physical space and the logical grammar of visual space continued to interest him between 1929 and 1936, when he formulated his argument against the possibility of a private language.[37] There is nothing surprising about this continuing interest, provided that the main requirement of his concept of a 'primary or phenomenological language' is kept separate from its subsidiary requirements. In our

---

[34] *CLI* p. 81.   [35] *PR* § 57.
[36] Similar points are made in *CLI* pp. 68–71 and in *The Big Typescript* (MS 213).
[37] In *NLPESD*. See p. 297.

everyday language we have locutions like 'It looks . . .' and 'It seems to be . . .', and they do not have to be introduced by a philosophical theory, nor is scepticism about the external world needed to make them interesting to a philosopher. So after Wittgenstein had abandoned the quest for a universal basic language, he continued to investigate the logical grammar of these locutions, just as he continued to investigate the logical grammar of our reports of bodily sensations.[38]

What about the last of the three bids set out above? Did he imply that reports of what is immediately given refer to specific, empirically identifiable types of object standing on the line of perceptual input and curtailing our view of the world? To put it in another way, did he have a theory of perception which forced him to limit the world by pulling it back to an empirically fixed line of sense-data? This is the most important of the three questions about his concept of a 'primary or phenomenological language', because it touches on the problem of identity, which was eventually going to lead to the formulation of his argument against the possibility of a private language. What we want to know is whether in the period that immediately preceded its formulation he himself introduced the data of our external senses as if they were empirically identifiable objects.

There is no doubt at all that in 1929 he treated bodily sensations as if they had independent criteria of identity which would enable them to stand alone and support the language that dealt with them unaided by anything in the physical world. The conversation at Schlick's house in December 1922 makes that very clear,[39] and it is confirmed by a parallel passage in *Philosophical Remarks*.[40] Both texts will be discussed in the next chapter. The point to be made about them now is that bodily sensations are not, in general, exteroceptive, and when Wittgenstein treated them as empirically identifiable things, he was not thereby committing himself to the same treatment of exteroceptive sense-data. In fact, it will be shown in the next chapter that it was the problem of other minds that started his interest in bodily sensations and not the problem of the external world, which would only arise about exteroceptive sense-data.

It is tempting to argue that the sliding-peg phenomenalism of the *Tractatus* could not have survived into the period running from 1929 to 1936. For sliding-peg phenomenalism is not a theory but an evasion, and the investigation of bodily sensations begun in 1929 led to a theory

---

[38] See above, p. 284.   [39] *LWVC* pp. 49–50, quoted above, p. 272.
[40] *PR* § 58, which is quoted below, pp. 297–8.

about them, which, one might suppose, must have been extended to exteroceptive sense-data. The idea is that, if bodily sensations were empirically identifiable things with independent criteria of identity, then so too were exteroceptive sense-data. But that does not follow. His views about sense-data of both kinds were developing and changing, and he started with bodily sensations but did not at first work the other field, external perception, to any great depth. It is true that he was going to recant his account of bodily sensations later, and that, while he still adhered to it, it put his philosophy at risk, because it was so easy to assume that the data of our external senses would have to be treated in the same way. But it is not true that he actually treated them in the same way.

Nevertheless, there is a text, probably written in 1936, in which he seems to admit that he had assumed that exteroceptive sense-data could be treated in the same way as bodily sensations: they too would have independent criteria of identity, so that his account of them too would later become the target of his private language argument.

. . . Formerly, I myself spoke of a 'complete analysis', and I used to believe that philosophy had to give a definitive dissection of propositions so as to set out clearly all their connections and remove all possibilities of misunderstanding. I spoke as if there was a calculus in which such a dissection would be possible. I vaguely had in mind something like the definition that Russell had given for the definite article, and I used to think that in a similar way one would be able to use visual impressions, etc. to define the concept, say, of a sphere . . .[41]

This might appear to settle the question: he was, after all, a classical phenomenalist.[42]

However, the passage is written with later hindsight, and it is quite possible that it rolls up together things that were originally separate, and treats as a formulated theory something that was really never more than a tendency. What this interpretation needs is contemporary evidence for ascribing classical phenomenalism to Wittgenstein. But it is not possible to find anywhere in his work in progress the kind of direct evidence of classical phenomenalism that can be found in the writings of philosophers whose theories of perception belong to the tradition of British Empiricism. He never argues that our supposed view into the outside world is really cut off short at some terminal point

---

[41] *PG* p. 211. See above, p. 281 and Vol. I p. 93 n. 18.

[42] Russell, of course, ended not with phenomenalism but with a different theory of perception. What this interpretation of Wittgenstein's remarks suggests is only that their starting-point was the same.

that can be empirically identified, such as visual sense-data treated as opaque images. He was, of course, aware that other philosophers argued in this way, but he regarded it as their mistake. If he were asked why he condemned their line of argument out of hand he would have replied that it is radically incoherent, because it is impossible to draw any empirical limit around phenomena, and it is no good pretending to have achieved this impossible feat by subsequently reducing everything that seemed to lie on the far side of the limit to things that lie on this side of it.[43] This places his philosophy in a different tradition from Russell's: its line of descent is from Kant rather than from the British Empiricists, and if he was a phenomenalist, he was a sliding-peg phenomenalist.

But can the passages cited from his writings in and immediately after 1929 be plausibly interpreted in this way? Can we really say that the boat was sliding towards the waterfall but not yet over the edge? Is it true that, unlike Russell, he does not place the data of our external senses at any empirically specified point on the causal line of perception and so never curtails our supposed view into the external world by drawing any empirically recognizable phenomenal base-line across that causal line?

It is so in the passages cited so far. When he uses the language of classical phenomenalism and speaks of 'the description of phenomena by means of the hypothesis of a material world', he carefully avoids placing the phenomenological data at any empirically specified point on the causal line of perception. They are identified only by the adoption of a certain style of description—'If I see various detached parts of a circle, then an accurate description of them is perhaps impossible'. The idea is that a phenomenological description is fragmentary or atomistic, but not that it is a description of objects of a special, empirically specifiable kind. To put the point in the terms that he used earlier in the *Tractatus*, a phenomenological description would still be an undoctored description of 'the world as I found it'.[44]

In the passage cited from the *Cambridge Lectures, 1930–1932* he explicitly says that 'the world is not composed of sense-data and physical objects'.[45] Now a classical phenomenalist too might say this, and he, of course, would mean that physical objects must be reduced to sense-

---

[43] See above, pp. 275–7. It is important that the principle invoked in this reply is not only clearly stated in *TLP*, but also repeated in an early section of *PR* § 47, quoted in Vol. I p. 95. See above, p. 276 n. 10.

[44] *TLP* 5.631. See Vol. I p. 154.   [45] *CLI* p. 81, quoted above, p. 286.

data. The difference between them is that a classical phenomenalist
would have begun by giving an empirical specification of sense-data,
but Wittgenstein never begins in that way. On the contrary, when he
ridicules the idea that someone might have 'seen a physical object
causing sense-data', he is attacking a theory which he had never held.
His view is that it is incoherent to treat sense-data as an empirically
recognizable barrier placed across the causal line of perception. This is
confirmed by an earlier passage in the same lecture:

> What really happens is that in visual and physical space the words have
> different grammars, and are *not* describing objects from different points of
> view. If they were, we should at once be involved in a science of some sort, and
> would probably look for a theory which in fact we don't need.[46]

At first sight, this may seem to mean that we are not describing the
same objects from different points of view. However, there are two
reasons why it cannot mean this: first, it would contradict the last
sentence of the later passage, 'We can talk bout the same object in
terms either of sense-data or hypothesis', and, second, if Wittgenstein
believed that we are not describing the same objects from two different
points of view, but two different kinds of objects, it would follow from
his account too that 'we should at once be involved in a science of some
sort'. So the text must mean that we are not describing objects of two
different kinds, each of which is presented to us when we adopt the
appropriate point of view, and the argument for this is that there are
not two distinct kinds of empirically identifiable objects here, one to be
found in physical space and the other in visual space.

It is easy to overlook this difference between Wittgenstein's sliding-
peg phenomenalism and classical phenomenalism, because they are
both expressible in the same formula: statements about physical
objects are hypotheses about sense-data. The crucial difference is that,
when a classical phenomenalist says this, he is reducing the
macrocosm to an empirically specified microcosm,[47] but a sliding-peg
phenomenalist does not start from any empirically specified base-line,
because he believes that a phenomenalism reached from such a
starting-point is incoherent. Of course, sliding-peg phenomenalism is
not a fully determinate philosophical thesis, just as sliding-peg
egocentrism had not been a fully determinate philosophical thesis.

---

[46] *CLI* pp. 69–70.
[47] It is, of course, no accident that classical phenomenalism can be formulated in the
same way as the ego-based solipsism discussed in *TLP*.

They both express undeveloped intuitions about the limit of language, and both would be superseded when the questions that they answered vaguely were given more precise answers. The difference between them in 1929 was that the accurate investigation of the actual way in which we ascribe sensations to their owners had been completed very swiftly, but the parallel investigation of their assignment to types proceeded more slowly.

We may, therefore, conclude that, though Wittgenstein's investigation of the language of exteroceptive sense-data was heading towards the position which he later criticized as untenable, it never quite got there. The idea that he did arrive at the conclusion that they are objects of an empirically specifiable kind is too hard to reconcile with what we know of the development of his ideas. It is, of course, always possible to refuse to draw a smooth curve through a series of points. It is not inconceivable that he quietly took over the assumption that the phenomenal base-line is fixed empirically and then in texts written between 1933 and 1935[48] equally quietly changed his mind. The case against this interpretation is cumulative rather than a knock-out, but it is none the less compelling.

The theme of the *Tractatus* is that the only way to fix the limit of factual language, and, therefore, of its correlate, the phenomenal world, is from the inside. That is the first point that has to be plotted on the graph. It is true that in the *Tractatus* he does not draw the conclusion that a solipsism based on sense-data is either empty or self-refuting—empty, if sense-data are not empirically identified, as they are not in sliding-peg phenomenalism, and self-refuting, if they are empirically identified. But the reason why he does not draw this conclusion in the *Tractatus* is only that he there confines his discussion to ego-based solipsism and does not consider the kind of solipsism that is based on a restrictive categorization of the objects presented to the subject. The suggestion that, if he had considered that version of the theory, he would have let the empirical identification of the phenomenal base-line pass unchallenged, is incredible. How could he have failed to see that a theory which allows the objects to slip their moorings in the physical world is open to the same objections as a theory which allows the subject to slip them? No, the point at which the line of the graph starts is firmly fixed: when he compiled the *Tractatus* the only kind of

---

[48] The relevant texts are cited and discussed below, pp. 292–4. In them he rejects the idea that sense-data are an empirically identifiable type of thing, but he does not say that it was formerly his idea.

phenomenalist that he can possibly be taken to have been is a sliding-peg phenomenalist.

If we now go to the other end of the line, passing over the years 1929–32, for which the evidence has already been given, we may collect the evidence for the later period, 1933–5. What answer do we get from those years to the question whether he was a sliding-peg phenomenalist or a classical phenomenalist? It is important to formulate this question with the terminus placed in 1935. For in 1936 he gave his 'Lectures on "Private Experience" and "Sense-data"', and it is in those lectures that he first developed the argument that any attempt to set up a private sensation language would be crippled by the lack of a viable criterion of identity for sensation-types.[49] After that it was obviously impossible for him to subscribe to phenomenalism with an empirically identified base-line. The question is only whether he subscribed to it before 1936, when he had not yet formulated the argument. If the answer is that he did subscribe to it in 1933–5, the inference will be that it was only the later argument that led him to abandon it; but, if the answer is that he did not subscribe to it in 1933–5, the inference will be that he already had another objection to it, namely the argument given in the Preface to the *Tractatus*. This is obviously an important question of interpretation.

In *The Blue Book* (1933–4) and in *Wittgenstein's Lectures, Cambridge, 1933–1935* there is conclusive evidence that he already had reasons for rejecting any empirical identification of the phenomenal base-line, and, as the chronology of the development of his ideas on this subject would suggest, his reasons do not include his later sharply formulated argument against the possibility of a private-sensation language:

The difficulty which we express by saying 'I can't know what he sees when he (truthfully) says that he sees a blue patch' arises from the idea that 'knowing what he sees' means: 'seeing that which he also sees'; not, however, in the sense in which we do so when we both have the same object before our eyes: but in the sense in which an object seen would be an object, say, in his head, or in *him*. The idea is that the same object may be before his eyes and mine, but that I can't stick my head into his (or my mind into his, which comes to the same) so that the *real* and *immediate* object of his vision becomes the real and immediate object of my vision too. By 'I don't know what he sees' we really mean 'I don't know what he looks at', where 'what he looks at' is hidden and he can't show it to me; it is *before his mind's eye*. Therefore, in order to get rid of this puzzle, examine the grammatical difference between the statements 'I

---

[49] The argument of *PI* I §§ 243 ff. See *NLPESD* p. 297.

don't know what he sees' and 'I don't know what he looks at', as they are actually used in our language.[50]

As usual, the problem here is not the external world but other minds. But what he is attacking is the assumption underlying both problems, that sense-data are empirically identifiable private objects.

A few pages later he criticizes this assumption in terms which show very clearly that his objection to phenomenalism with an empirically identifiable base-line ran exactly parallel to his objection to ego-based solipsism. According to him, both theories exploited illegitimate reification:

> ... The grammar of the word 'geometrical eye' stands in the same relation to the grammar of the word 'physical eye' as the grammar of the the expression 'the visual sense datum of a tree' to the grammar of the expression 'the physical tree'. In either case it confuses everything to say 'the one is a *different kind* of object from the other'; for those who say that a sense datum is a different kind of object from a physical object misunderstand the grammar of the word 'kind', just as those who say that a number is a different kind of object from a numeral. They think they are making such a statement as 'A railway train, a railway station, and a railway car are different kinds of objects', whereas their statement is analogous to 'A railway train, a railway accident, and a railway law are different kinds of objects'.[51]

This passage criticizes the idea that exteroceptive sense-data can be identified empirically just like physical objects and distinguished from physical objects in the same way that one type of physical object can be distinguished from another. But really he is rejecting any reification of exteroceptive sense-data and arguing that it is a false picture projected by grammar:

> Philosophers say it as a philosophical opinion or conviction that there are sense data. But to say that I believe that there are sense data comes to saying that I *believe* that an object may appear to be before our eyes even when it isn't. Now when one uses the word 'sense datum', one should be clear about the peculiarity of its grammar. For the idea in introducing this expression was to model expressions referring to 'appearance' after expressions referring to 'reality'. It was said, e.g., that if two things *seem* to be equal, there *must* be two somethings that *are* equal. Which of course means nothing else but that we have decided to use such an expression as 'the appearances of these two things are equal' synonymously with 'these two things seem to be equal'. Queerly enough, the introduction of this new phraseology has deluded people into

thinking that they had discovered new entities, new elements of the structure of the world, as though to say 'I believe that there are sense data' were similar to saying 'I believe that matter consists of electrons'.[52]

Exteroceptive sense-data are not objects of any kind.

These passages fix the end of the line to be plotted on the graph: in the period 1933–5 Wittgenstein did not subscribe to phenomenalism with an empirically identified base-line. Given that the beginning of the line is fixed on the same co-ordinates on this axis by the *Tractatus*, it is implausible to interpret the texts of 1929–32 as evidence that in those years he did subscribe to phenomenalism with an empirically identified base-line. How could he have changed his mind on this fundamental question and then changed it back again so unobtrusively?

It may be objected that sliding-peg phenomenalism relies on an argument against scepticism about the external world which is too superficial to be attributed to Wittgenstein. But there are three answers to this. First, he does state the argument in the *Tractatus*[53] and there is no evidence that he subsequently abandoned it. Second, in any case, he was never worried by sceptical doubts about the external world: it was the problem of other minds that exercised him in and after 1929.[54] Third, in 1936 he was going to reinforce his implied criticism, that classical phenomenalism was incoherent, by adding the argument that it would not be possible to set up and maintain a sensation-language in complete detachment from the common world, just as it would not be possible to make discriminating references to individuals in such circumstances. How could he have failed to see that the criticism of the reification of exteroceptive sense-data developed in *The Blue Book* is related to the 'second private language argument' in precisely the way in which his earlier criticism of the reification of the ego is related to the 'first private language argument'?

If we only had his own later account of the development of his philosophy between 1929 and 1935, we might well conclude that he subscribed to classical phenomenalism in that period. But given the direct evidence of contemporary texts, it is more plausible to reject this conclusion and to treat his retrospective account as a simplification.

---

[52] *BLBK* p. 70. Cf. *CLII* p. 128: 'There is a fundamental confusion about questions regarding sense data, the confusing of questions of grammar with those of natural science.'

[53] *TLP* 6.51, quoted above, p. 276.

[54] This will be demonstrated in the next chapter.

When he looked back on those years he saw very clearly where he had been heading and so he allowed himself almost to imply that he had actually reached the position that he criticized in 1936. This gives us a more convincing picture of the development of his ideas. He never was a solipsist, and, similarly, he never was a classical phenomenalist. In fact, he extended his successful critique of ego-based solipsism to the classical type of phenomenalism which relies on an empirically specified perceptual base-line. There were, of course, strong forces pushing him into the reification of exteroceptive sense-data which is the decisive step on the road to classical phenomenalism. If bodily sensations could be empirically specified with independent criteria of identity, why could the data of our external senses not be treated in the same way? But he never took this step and he argues against it in the period 1933–5. It is, therefore, a double mistake to claim that he was a classical phenomenalist and that he remained one until he formulated the first private language argument in 1936.

12

The First Attempt to Extend the Treatment of the Ego to Sensations and their Types: Other Minds

THE TWO main interpretative themes of the previous chapter were that Wittgenstein never subscribed to phenomenalism with an empirically identified base-line and that it was not the problem of the external world that exercised him in 1929 but the problem of other minds. Enough has been said on the first of these two themes, but the second one still needs to be worked out in detail and connected with the evidence of the texts. The development of his philosophy in and immediately after 1929 was an intricate and baffling process which has provoked many commentators to over-simplification. So many things were going on, and the record is so private and staccato that there is a strong temptation to simplify the connections between his ideas in these years and their origins in the *Tractatus* and between both and the ideas of his contemporaries. The temptation must be resisted. He was developing the main themes of his early system and this time he was giving them a detailed application to the phenomena. The airy insouciance of the *Tractatus* had gone and the hard work of achieving a real fit now had to be done. It was a slow process, involving many adjustments, and he pushed it forward step by step with an independence that almost amounted to an intellectual form of autism. It is nearly always a mistake to identify his ideas with the ideas that they generated in the minds of his contemporaries.

It was the problem of other minds that started the series of changes in his philosophy which will be examined in this chapter. When he applied his theory of language to the world, he found it increasingly difficult to hold the phenomena together. The problem was not that his own exteroceptive sense-data threatened to detach themselves from the one and only world in which we all live out our lives: it was that other people's bodily sensations seemed to be on a different level from the observed phenomena and in particular from the stimuli and responses that bracketed them. It may seem illogical to be exercised by the second of these two problems without the first one. For the connection between pain and physical injury is related to the connection between the visual sense-data of a circle and a child's hoop. But the fact is that Wittgenstein always felt at home in the world of uncategorized phenomena and the difficulty started for him at the point where he began to reflect on our knowledge of other minds.

His first move was made in the passage quoted from *Ludwig Wittgenstein and the Vienna Circle* near the beginning of the previous chapter.[1] He tried to find a way of splitting the phenomena into two levels which would not be too divisive. The idea was a subtle one and it will be analysed below. He wanted the division to be one that could be accommodated within his system without forcing any radical change on it. He hoped that factual language and the correlated phenomena would remain sufficiently unified, and that his fundamental principle, that their limit must be drawn from the inside, would not be compromised. When he failed in this enterprise, he attributed his failure to the mistaken assumption that each person makes direct context-free references to his own sensations and their types.[2] So his next attempt to extend the treatment of the ego to sensations and their types started from the rejection of the possibility of making such references. He had come to see that, if descriptive language were completely internalized, it would lose the criteria of identity of types on which it depended.[3]

If his problem in 1929 was the problem of other minds, how did he hope to solve it? There are two texts which give his strategy. One is the series of remarks already cited from the discussion of solipsism at Schlick's house on 22 December 1929.[4] The other is the parallel, but rather more explicit passage in *Philosophical Remarks*:

We could adopt the following way of representing matters: if I, L.W., have toothache, then that is expressed by means of the proposition 'There is toothache'. But if that is so, what we now express by the proposition 'A has toothache', is put as follows: 'A is behaving as L.W. does when there is toothache'. Similarly we shall say 'It is thinking' and 'A is behaving as L.W. does when it is thinking'. (You could imagine a despotic oriental state where the language is formed with the despot as its centre and his name instead of L.W.) It's evident that this way of speaking is equivalent to ours when it comes

---

[1] *LWVC* pp. 49–50, quoted above, p. 272.
[3] This is the argument of *PI* I §§ 243 ff.
[2] See Vol. I pp. 51–2.
[4] *LWVC*, loc. cit.

to questions of intelligibility and freedom from ambiguity. But it's equally clear that this language could have anyone at all as its centre.

Now, among all the languages with different people as their centres, each of which I can understand, the one with me as its centre has a privileged status. This language is particularly adequate. How am I to express that? That is, how can I rightly represent its special advantage in words? This can't be done. For, if I do it in the language with me as its centre, then the exceptional status of the description of this language in its own terms is nothing very remarkable, and in the terms of another language my language occupies no privileged status whatever.—The privileged status lies in the application, and if I describe this application, the privileged status again doesn't find expression, since the description depends on the language in which it's couched. And now, which description gives just that which I have in mind depends again on the application.

Only their application really differentiates languages; but if we disregard this, all languages are equivalent. All these languages only describe one single, incomparable thing and *cannot* represent anything else. (Both these approaches must lead to the same result: first, that what is represented is not one thing among others, that it is not capable of being contrasted with anything; second, that I cannot express the advantage of *my* language.)[5]

The first thing that needs to be said about these two passages is that they do make a serious attempt to solve a difficult problem.

This is worth emphasizing, because, if we look back on these texts from the later standpoint of *Philosophical Investigations*, we may easily miss their subtlety, especially if we are completely convinced by his later argument that we cannot make direct, context-free references to our own sensation-types. His rejection of the possibility of a private sensation-language is apt to produce a curious forensic effect: it strikes people as absurd at first, but if they are convinced by it later, the absurdity immediately seems to shift, as it does in certain optical illusions, to their previous hostile reactions to it. It is as if there were no middle ground for their intuitions. So if we look back on Wittgenstein's first attempt to solve this problem from the assumed vantage-point of his second attempt, we shall be likely to be put off by distorting hindsight. The solution sketched in these texts in 1929 may even look naïve, which it certainly is not.

We must appreciate the strategic situation as he saw it in 1929. He had written the *Tractatus* from the point of view of any single person looking out on to the world, avoiding all the complications that are introduced by other people. Instead of adopting a theory of perception,

[5] *PR* § 58.

he made the evasive move which was called 'sliding-peg phenomenalism' in the previous chapter, and he left his ontology incompletely specified. That made it possible for him to represent factual language as a smooth, homogeneous surface without the vortices produced by other minds. Of course, there was always his own mind, but, considered as a configuration of objects, it was just another element in the flat picture presented by factual language, and considered as a subject, it never got into the picture at all. For his ego was merely a presupposed point of view which could not be identified but only vaguely indicated as the focal point of his consciousness. But when he began to work out the application of this abstract schema to real life, he had to give some account not only of himself, but also of all the other users of factual language. Could their different points of view really be treated in the same self-effacing way? That seemed unlikely, because each of them contributed something different to the total picture of the world and there had to be a way of fitting their contributions together.

However, in these two texts he does try to treat them too in the same self-effacing way. His main contention is that it would be possible for each of us to speak a language centred on himself and that, if we did so, we would still succeed in understanding one another. When one of my teeth ached, I would say, for reasons given in Chapter 10, 'There is toothache', but when my friend was the sufferer, I would say, 'He has toothache', perhaps naming him in order to make it quite clear whom I meant. The peculiar form of expression that I reserved for my own case, with no personal pronoun, would indicate that the pain belonged to the centre from which the message originated. A pronoun or a name would be required only when the pain belonged to some other centre. Now it is an accepted fact that we can all understand an ascription of pain to another person just as well as we understand a self-ascription. The indirectness marked by the indispensable pronoun or name is no bar to intelligibility. So much is obvious. But why is it no bar? Wittgenstein's answer is interesting: 'All these languages can be translated into one another. Only what they have in common mirrors anything.'[6] The implication is that anything else that may be conveyed by them—anything idiosyncratic—is not part of factual discourse but something which, in the terminology of the *Tractatus*, can only be shown and not said.

But how are we meant to draw the line dividing the inter-

---

[6] *LWVC* pp. 49–50 quoted above, p. 272.

translatable part of a report in my egocentric language, which is supposed to be all that is actually said, from the idiosyncratic residue, which is supposed to be shown? That is the hard question. However, the difficulties all lie in the details and Wittgenstein's general strategy is tolerably clear. So perhaps it will be best to begin by sketching his overall picture of the interpersonal predicament, leaving the details until later.

His main theme is that the one and only phenomenal world is the correlate of the unified system of factual language. So he says that all these languages, centred on different people, 'only describe one single incomparable thing and *cannot* represent anything else'.[7] The idea is that they all represent the one and only phenomenal world, each from its own point of view, and that it is not possible for any of them to detach itself from its own point of view in order to explain the peculiar adequacy that its speaker would like to claim for it. My self-centred language strikes me as absolutely appropriate, and that is not an illusion, because when I use it, I put myself into it[8] and thereby give it the application to my own point of view that makes it absolutely appropriate to my own case. However, I have no way of identifying my own point of view independently of the way exploited in my self-centred language. I cannot hold the two things apart and slowly demonstrate their perfect fit. The only way in which I could possibly give my point of view an independent identification would be to speak impersonally and locate it in the phenomenal world through my body. But if I do that, I shall be adopting a position for which my self-centred language is no longer appropriate. The special aptness that I would like to claim for it lies only in its application and not in anything that can be said about it.

What its application shows is that communiqués expressed in it come from my centre of consciousness. However, this is not part of what they actually say, but only, as it were, the signature which will guide another person who is trying to fit them into his map of the phenomenal world, which is, of course, primarily based on information collected directly at his centre of consciousness. The point to notice is the way in which my signature is understood by him. He does not understand it through any part of what I actually say, because it is a peculiarity of the self-centred languages described by Wittgenstein that the speaker does not use a name or even a pronoun for himself. So

---

[7] *PR*, loc. cit.
[8] See above, pp. 257–60.

the hearer is reduced to bare essentials and he is forced to take the mouth that issues the communiqué as an indispensable part of its content—that's how it is at his end of the transaction.[9] It is as if the only distinctive feature of my signature were the hand that held the pen.

So far, there is nothing paradoxical about this account of the way in which we all lay each other under contribution when we are constructing our maps of the phenomenal world. When two surveyors, in earshot of one another, are fixing a point by triangulation, they can dispense with their egos, because their centres of consciousness are pinned to the ground through their bodies, and the same is true of any similar but less scientific conversation between two people. Although this is an obvious point, it is worth making, because it is important to appreciate the naturalness of Wittgenstein's explanation of the integration of different perceptual points of view before we look at the difficulties that he encountered when he extended it to intercommunication about sensation-types, especially bodily sensation-types.

The two passages under examination do, of course, concentrate on sensation-types—indeed on one very special type—and it is time to ask what difference that makes. The first distinctive feature of pain that strikes everybody immediately is that pain-sensations are not always caused by physical objects outside our bodies, and even when they are so caused, they do not always give us direct information about the properties of their causes.[10] They were, therefore, bound to modify the flat, homogeneous picture of the world which his sliding-peg phenomenalism had allowed him to maintain so uncritically. He would no longer be able to hold everything together on the same level in such a simple way, and his problem would be to see how to accommodate pain and other bodily sensations without splitting the phenomena into two levels in a way that would make intercommunication between different people impossible.

It is not surprising to find him in this period taking a lot of trouble to fit other people's bodily sensations into his map of the common phenomenal world. They have an obvious importance and when he was applying the abstract schema of the *Tractatus* to real life, he could not just leave them out. Nor would it do justice to their peculiarities to observe that they originate in subjects' bodies, which are just as much parts of the phenomenal world as their environments.[11] There was also a special reason for their appearance on the stage at this turning-point

[9] *PR* § 64, quoted above, pp. 239–40.
[10] Cf. *PI* I § 312, on pain-patches.
[11] See *TLP* 5.631.

in the development of his thought: they force philosophers to think realistically about their attitude to other human beings.

It is worth pausing to see how this comes about. Suppose that we start, as he undoubtedly did, with a predilection for analysing factual language and the deliverances of science.[12] Then we shall be likely to illustrate the problem of intercommunciation between people with examples like the one used above—the two surveyors fixing a point by triangulation. Now it was an understatement to say that they would not be concerned with their egos. The truth is that each of them could regard the other in much the same way that they both regarded their theodolites—as instruments reacting in regular ways to exposure to peripheral stimulation. Anyone who looked at other human beings in this way would not care how their reactions to input were produced so long as they remained regular and reliable. He would treat other people 'despotically'[13] as if they were scientific instruments.

This way of regarding other people finds its exact expression in the theory of language developed by Schlick and Carnap in the early 1930s out of the ideas put forward by Wittgenstein in the two passages that are still under examination.[14] Their theory was that people can communicate with one another only on the physical level. So according to them, A can ascribe a pain to B only by saying that B is behaving as A does when A feels pain, and B's resources, when he ascribes a pain to A, are symmetrical. It follows that, although each of them starts by making direct, context-free references to his own pains, neither of them can make himself understood by the other until he adopts an indirect method of referring to them, as sensations of the type that are bracketed between certain kinds of stimulus and certain kinds of response in his own case. This constraint on intercommunication about sensations is an important element in the theory because it requires each of them to specify the appropriate bracket of stimulus and response. But how will they do that? If one of them specifies it by saying that it is the bracket between which his own directly reported pains occur, the other one, not having access to those pains, will not

---

[12] This may seem to go against the much-quoted letter to Ficker, but what he expresses in that letter is the feeling which had *not* shaped the main body of the *Tractatus*. See Vol. I p. 191 n. 3.

[13] Aristotle's view of slaves.

[14] See M. Schlick: 'Meaning and Verification', in *Readings in Philosophical Analysis*, ed. H. Feigl and W. Sellars, Appleton-Century-Crofts, 1949, pp. 161–70 (reprinted from *Philosophical Review*, 1936). Cf. R. Carnap: *The Unity of Science*, tr. M. Black, Kegan Paul, 1934, pp. 76–92.

know which bracket he means. So Schlick and Carnap specify the bracket in purely physical terms in order to make it immediately recognizable by everybody. They then have to admit that it is a corollary of their theory that the content of experience remains necessarily incommunicable, but, they claim, this does not matter, because if the content of experience does vary from one person to another, the variation will necessarily remain undetectable. It is hardly a fault in a theory of language that it puts the seal of incommunicability on the undetectable.[15]

In *Philosophical Investigations* and *Zettel* Wittgenstein mocks the suggestion that the content of experience is incommunicable.[16] No doubt, he did find it rather absurd when he looked back on it later from the standpoint of his second attempt to extend his treatment of the ego to sensations and their types. But the question is how far he had committed himself in 1929. Now it would be rash to claim to be able to give an exact answer to this question with any confidence. His philosophy was in rapid transition and perhaps it is not too important to establish precisely how far he followed a wrong track which he subsequently abandoned. But what would be interesting, if it could be done, would be to identify the forces already at work in his mind in 1929, and the forces that had yet to make their impact on him.

There are several points that can be made immediately with certainty. First, in the two passages under examination[17] and in many others Wittgenstein had each person making direct context-free references to his own bodily sensations and their types. That is something which he later came to regard as a mistake, because, of course, it implied the possibility of using a private language to report them. But what is not so clear is how far the consequences of this mistake, as he later came to regard it, extended. Did it vitiate his whole treatment of factual language and its correlate the phenomenal world? Or was it only his account of intercommunication about bodily sensations that suffered?

There is a conspicuous gap in both versions of Wittgenstein's account of the way in which two people, *A* and *B*, manage to communicate with one another about their sensations. He seems to

---

[15] An outline of Wittgenstein's ideas on this topic in 1929, and of the way in which Schlick and Carnap developed them was given in Vol. I pp. 45–8.

[16] *PI* I §§ 273–80 and *Zettel*, § 87. Cf. R. Rhees's notes of the lectures given by Wittgenstein in 1936, in *Philosophical Investigations* (the periodical), Vol. 7 No. 1, Jan. 1984, quoted in Vol. I p. 47 n. 19.

[17] *LWVC* pp. 49–50 and *PR* § 58.

have assumed that they are both in a position to talk intelligibly about their environment and their own behaviour in it. The question, whether each of them got into this position by starting from direct reports of his own visual and tactual impressions, and, if so, by what route, is not even raised. It is, therefore, likely that he was simply relying on his sliding-peg phenomenalism at this point, and not treating the claims made by *A* and *B* about the world around them as in any way problematical. The difficulty, as he saw it, was restricted to the claims that they made about each other's bodily sensations.

This interpretation has a lot to be said for it. It is, as has been remarked before, a golden rule to take the problem on which Wittgenstein concentrates in any discussion to be the problem that strikes him as being central.[18] In this case corroboration is provided by the fact that he had never been worried by the possibility that our exteroceptive sense-data might hang like a veil between us and the physical world beyond them. There is also another argument that could be used to support this interpretation: if *A* and *B* were not already in a position to describe the surrounding world and their behaviour in it, they could not possibly hope to achieve intercommunication about their bodily sensations in the way proposed by Wittgenstein in these two passages. So we may take it as proven that the crux here is the problem of other minds rather than the problem posed by the assumption that the physical world is veiled by our mental sense-data, and that the background to the whole discussion is sliding-peg phenomenalism.

There is one more point that can be made with confidence before we raise any of the more speculative questions about the two texts under examination. Wittgenstein's answer to the restricted question, how *A* and *B* manage to communicate with one another about their sufferings, is quite unequivocally that each of them starts by making direct, context-free references to his own pains. But then he is immediately in trouble. For *A* is necessarily deprived of any direct access to *B*'s pains and so he can never tell when *B* is exhibiting behaviour which is from his (*B*'s) point of view pain-behaviour. Of course, this does not prevent *A* from defining 'pain-behaviour' 'despotically' as 'my behaviour when I am in pain'. But then *B* would be in a symmetrical predicament: he could never tell when this description really did apply to *A*'s behaviour, because it would contain

---

[18] See Vol. I pp. 89–90.

an ineliminable reference to something inaccessible to *B*, namely *A*'s pain.[19]

It is important to appreciate exactly why Wittgenstein was in trouble at this point. He was trying to explain how *A* and *B* achieve communication with one another about their bodily sensations, and his leading idea was that 'All these languages can be translated into one another. Only what they have in common mirrors anything.' He was assuming that his sliding-peg phenomenalism made it unproblematical that *A* and *B* were describing the same world around them, and he thought that, if their separate centres of consciousness were pinned to that world through their bodies, their different contributions to the unified system of factual language could be fitted together in much the same way that aerial photographs can be fitted together to make a map. That gave him a platform from which it did not look too difficult to explain how they achieved intercommunication about their bodily sensations too. However, he then made the second assumption that each of them started by making direct context-free references to his own bodily sensations and their types. After that he found their achievement of intercommunication about them inexplicable. Later, when he reviewed his failure, he attributed it to the second of his two assumptions, which he then abandoned. But we must not look back on his predicament in 1929 with narrowly focused hindsight. It is important to appreciate why his mistaken theory seemed plausible to him at the time, and that requires us to look at the available alternatives.

Schlick and Carnap offered a different theory. They shared Wittgenstein's fundamental idea, that factual language must be a single system correlated with a unified field of phenomena, but they differed about the point at which a philosophical reconstruction of language designed to show how this goal is achieved would have to start. Wittgenstein's sliding-peg phenomenalism had given him a conveniently indefinite starting-point for our external senses, while his construal of our references to our own bodily sensations as direct and context-free had given him a definite, but less easily accommodatable starting-point in their case. The obvious objection to this system was that its semi-split levels made it impossible to secure the desired unity for language. Schlick and Carnap inferred that the only way to secure it was to impose a more radical unification on factual language and its correlate,

[19] See Vol. I pp. 45–8.

the phenomenal world, by choosing the same unequivocally specified starting-point for both internal and external perception. They chose physical objects and the physicalistic language, because it seemed to them to be the only way of explaining how people manage to communicate with one another.[20]

However, their explanation was only achieved at a price, the so-called 'incommunicability of the content of experience'. Is it really credible that, when *A* ascribes a pain to *B*, all that he really means is that *B* is behaving as he (*A*) behaves when he is in pain? The suggestion is not much improved if we try to capture the otherwise incommunicable content by saying that what *A* means is that *B* is having a sensation of a type that in his (*B*'s) case is bracketed between the same kind of stimulus and response as *A*'s pain. For that would immediately raise the question whether their similarly bracketed sensations are intrinsically similar, and that is a question which cannot be immediately dismissed like the question about their egos. For though it is not unreasonable to suggest, as Wittgenstein does, that I give up using the first-person pronoun and allow the ownership of my sensations to show itself, this treatment is hardly appropriate to sensation-types. I have to keep the word 'pain' in my report in order to distinguish what I now feel from a sensation of some other type, and the meaning of the word is obviously not exhausted by the bracket in which the sensation is placed. To make the contrast in another way, the sufferer's mouth is literally part of him, but the stimulus and response that bracket a pain are not literally parts of the sensation.[21]

These constraints were mentioned in Volume I, when the problem of other minds was first introduced,[22] but the discussion of them can now be enriched with more detail. First, the problem has now been set against its proper background in Wittgenstein's philosophy, the flat homogeneous surface of factual language and its correlate, the unified field of phenomena. This unity, which these philosophers all wanted to preserve, was obviously threatened by the existence of other minds. How could those difficult vortices be accommodated? What account

[20] See R. Carnap: *The Unity of Science*, tr. and with an introduction by M. Black, Kegan Paul, 1934, § 5, 'The Physical Language as a Universal Language', pp. 67–76, and § 6, 'Protocol Language as a part of Physical Language', pp. 76–93.

[21] See above, pp. 211–14 and Vol. I p. 50, where it was suggested that 'pain is a spreading structure with its roots in the stimulus and its ramifications in the subject's responses.' But the analogy was imperfect, because stimulus and response are not *parts* of the sensation.

[22] See Vol. I p. 43.

could be given of the third dimension which they seemed to require? This problem is not posed by one's own mind. For if, unlike Wittgenstein, one sees one's own exteroceptive sense-data as an impenetrable veil, the problem that this produces is the problem of the external world. One can hardly imagine peering back down one's own telescope and finding the contents of one's own mind problematic. It is other minds that pose the problem, and especially other people's bodily sensations.

There is also another aspect which this problem can now be seen to present. The deficiency of the Schlick–Carnap theory was that, though it was well adapted to the scientific language in which we describe the world around us, it gave a strangely mutilated picture of what it is like to live a human life. Even conversations about the external world make more use of the humanity of the interlocutors than is conceded by this theory. I, of course, am allowed to speak from the depths of my own mind, but I only make use of those properties of other people which they share with scientific instruments. As for their psychology, it is, from my point of view, Hamlet without even the ghost of the Prince of Denmark.

It is quite certain that Wittgenstein never went to those lengths. That is proved by his claim that we all start from direct, context-free references to our own bodily sensations. In fact, it is a plausible conjecture that the origin of his special concern with sensations of this kind was something more than has yet been suggested. Certainly, they presented a threat to the unity of factual language to which he was committed, because they could not possibly be given the same sliding-peg treatment as the objects of our external senses. But he was also staking a claim within the mind, which he was going to modify later, but never abandon, and it is possible that he had already considered and rejected the dehumanizing theory of Schlick and Carnap. Anyway, the fact is that he never did accept it, and the force that prevented him from accepting it was probably already at work in his mind.

When commentators describe Wittgenstein's later liberation from excessive preoccupation with factual language, they usually refer to the well-known passage near the beginning of *Philosophical Investigations*, in which he lists the other things that we can do with words besides stating facts.[23] But perhaps his first and most important step on this road was taken in 1929, when he brought other people into his purview

[23] *PI* I § 23.

and encountered the problem of their minds. For that problem presented him with a dilemma: either his account of factual language would have to be dehumanized—to put the option more accurately, the necessary concessions to humanity would have to be restricted to the first person—or else he would have to admit that factual language did not, after all, present the smooth, homogeneous surface which he had hoped to find. He chose the second alternative, and, if we want to understand why, we must go to later texts for a full development of his reasons.

When two people are talking about their immediate surroundings, they treat each other as equals. Each regards the other as a centre of consciousness and speech rather than as a body reacting to stimulation in an informative way. Those are undeniable facts of life. It is, of course, true, as Wittgenstein points out in the two passages under examination, that *A* can insist on speaking the language centred on himself, in which he makes direct, context-free references to his own sensations and their types. But however difficult it may be to see how he can communicate with *B* about their types, he really cannot avoid treating *B* as another centre of consciousness and speech. If he tries to monopolize the ego, he cannot succeed and he will be left where he started, one person among others in the physical world, each with a body and each with his own personal line.[24] Wittgenstein's treatment of the ego had neutralized any attempt to cut out of the common world a private world based on the superficially asymmetrical concept of the ownership of sensations. As owners, and as speakers who could refer to what they owned, *A* and *B* were already established as equals, treating each other as human centres of consciousness and speech rather than as soft scientific instruments. That step forward had been taken before the special case of pain was considered in 1929.

The peculiar importance of the example of pain must lie in some feature of its type. It is a plausible suggestion that pain was chosen because it blocked any attempt to solve the problem of intercommunication about sensation-types by eliding experiential content in the way that Schlick and Carnap elided it. Their theory does not even succeed in giving a completely successful account of a conversation between two people about their immediate surroundings, but it is, at least, persuasive in that kind of case. The reason for this limited persuasiveness is that we would be less inclined to worry about the

[24] See above, p. 233.

types of other people's exteroceptive sense-data. Isn't it obvious that any variations of this kind within a community speaking the same language would not matter so long as all their responses to stimuli were the same, so that they could agree in their descriptions of the world?

But though the Schlick–Carnap theory is persuasive in this kind of case, it really will not do. When intercommunication about the world around us is presented in this way, people become like Geiger counters, whose souls show up only when they speak in the first person, and then irrelevantly. Pain was an especially effective counter-example to this kind of physicalism, and that is almost certainly why it is so prominent in Wittgenstein's writings in this period. It was not that he accepted the Schlick–Carnap analysis of statements about the physical world and only demurred when it was extended to reports of bodily sensations. It was just that the inadequacy of a theory which elides the 'painful content' of toothache is particularly obvious.

The point can be put in the terms introduced in Chapter 10. When *A* and *B* converse with one another, their personal lines make it easy for them to treat each other as equal owners, each of his own sensations, and so as equal centres of consciousness and speech. But it is more problematic how their type-lines can put them in a position to communicate with one another about all the different kinds of sensation that they experience in their lives. The simplest solution to the problem is the semi-behaviourist theory proposed by Schlick and Carnap: the placing of different sensation-types between their appropriate stimuli and responses is all that can, and need, be caught in the net of language, and their intrinsic properties slip through the mesh inevitably but unregrettably. But pain, because of what it is like for the person who expresses it, is an especially convincing counter-example to that theory.

It is also an example with an especially well-marked type-line. Consequently, Wittgenstein could use the argument sketched in Chapter 10 to show that there was a firm pre-linguistic foundation for the introduction of the word 'pain'.[25] There is, then, a certain incoherence in scepticism about other people's pains: it treats the matter purely intellectually, when the intellectual framework for posing it is itself based on something more primitive. This important line of thought was taken one stage further in his later writings. Instead of stopping at the end of the type-line with the natural expression of pain,

[25] See above, pp. 260–1. Cf. Vol. I pp. 56–7.

he added other people's reactions to the sufferer's plight and included them too in the primitive pattern on which language was superimposed:

> It is a help here to remember that it is a primitive reaction to tend, to treat, the part that hurts when someone else is in pain; and not merely when oneself is—and so to pay attention to other people's pain-behaviour, as one does *not* pay attention to one's own pain-behaviour.
>
> But what is the word 'primitive' meant to say here? Presumably that this sort of behaviour is *pre-linguistic*: that a language-game is based *on it*, that it is the prototype of a way of thinking and not the result of thought.
>
> 'Putting the cart before the horse' may be said of an explanation like the following: we tend someone else because by analogy with our own case we believe that he is experiencing pain too.—Instead of saying: Get to know a new aspect from this special chapter of human behaviour—from this use of language.
>
> My relation to the appearances here is part of my concept.[26]

This is a late development. The ascription of pain to another person is supported even more extensively than in 1929 by the web of human reactions and feelings which antedates the intellectual problem of other minds. The passage was written after Wittgenstein's second attempt to adapt the treatment of the ego to sensations and their types, at a time when he believed pains and their expression to be very unlike physical objects and their description. The situation was different in, and immediately after, 1929, when he was still treating the assignment of sensations, one's own and other people's, to types as if it were really quite like the description of physical objects. Of course, he already saw the peculiarities of sensation-language—so close-up in the first person and so remote in the second and third persons—but it still seemed to him that the need to incorporate it in the unified system of factual discourse could be met without treating sensations altogether differently from objects. That was the point on which he was to change his mind.

The question that he faced in 1929 was how one person's pain could be sufficiently closely connected with anything accessible to another person. He had succeeded in relating their two points of view, but he still had to connect what was actually felt from one point of view with what seemed to be merely gathered inferentially from the other. This proved to be a difficult task so long as it was treated as an ordinary investigation of a connection between objects established scientifically by observation and inference. On the one hand, *A*'s conviction that *B* is

[26] *Zettel*, §§ 540–3.

in pain seemed to be beyond anything that would be warranted by a scientific inference verified in only one sequence of cases, *A*'s own pains. On the other hand, *B*'s pain, as accepted by *A*, could hardly be reduced to its setting of stimulus and response. For *A* had to admit that *B*'s pain amounted to more than the physical phenomena that bracketed it, and the behaviourist's denial of that platitude should not even be considered as a possible solution to the problem, but, rather, as a sign that it must have been posed in the wrong way. There has to be a better way of posing it, a new *mise-en-scène*, which will concede that what is given to *B* is distinct from what is given to *A*, but without making it impossible to explain how *A*'s conviction, that *B* really is suffering, manages to leap this logical gap.

In 1929 Wittgenstein was still working within the general framework of the *Tractatus*. He was trying to accommodate the eddies and vortices created in the otherwise smooth surface of phenomena by the existence of other minds, but he had not yet measured the depth of the problem. Because he retained the assumption that factual language is flat and homogeneous, his first attempt to solve it reads very much like a *reductio ad absurdum* of the terms in which he was posing it. Naturally, that was not what he intended. His intention was to solve it, but to do so without realigning the structure of his philosophy. He had not yet seen that only a radical change would make a solution possible.

In all his discussions of this problem the fixed point around which everything else revolves is the correctness of ordinary ascriptions of pains to other people. He never questions the general legitimacy of claims like *A*'s that *B* is suffering. Of course, it has to be a normal case, but there is never any suggestion that it would be necessary to go beyond the ordinary standards of evidence in order to answer scepticism. Here, as elsewhere, the assumption is that the sceptic must be wrong, because his doubt would make sense only against the background of a further world with further resources unavailable not only to his adversary but also to himself.[27] However, in 1929, when he set this fixed point of certainty in the framework of a unified factual language, he found himself pushed towards the extreme paradox of behaviourism:

The two hypotheses, that other people have toothache, and that they behave just as I do but don't have toothache, possibly have identical senses. That is, if

---

[27] See *TLP* 6.51, quoted above, p. 85. Cf. *PR* § 47, quoted above, pp. 84–5, and more fully in Vol. I p. 95.

I had, for example learned the second form of expression, I would talk in a pitying voice about people who don't have toothache, but are behaving as I do, when I have it.

That is a passage that comes fairly early in *Philosophical Remarks*.[28] On the next page we find this:

The two hypotheses, that others have pain, and that they don't, and merely behave as I do when I have it, must have identical senses if every *possible* experience confirming the one confirms the other as well. In other words, if a decision between them on the basis of experience is inconceivable.[29]

If these remarks had implied behaviourism, he would have treated the argument as a *reductio*, retraced his steps and rejected the premiss that this was an ordinary investigation of a connection between objects, established by observation and inference in the usual manner of science. However, it was several years before he moved in that direction, and in the mean time he must have believed that he could keep all his premisses without being forced into behaviourism. But how was that possible?

There are some hints in the notes take by G. E. Moore of the lectures given by Wittgenstein in Cambridge in 1930–3:

. . . the fact that it is nonsense to talk of verifying the fact that I have it [sc. toothache], puts, he said, 'I have it' on 'a different level' in grammar from 'he has it'. And he also expressed his view that the two expressions are on a different grammatical level by saying that they are not both values of a single propositional function '*x* has tooth-ache'; and in favour of this view he gave two definite reasons for saying that they are not, namely (1) that 'I don't know whether I have tooth-ache' is always absurd or nonsense, whereas 'I don't know whether he has tooth-ache' is not nonsense, and (2) that 'It seems to me that I have tooth-ache' is nonsense, whereas 'It seems to me that he has' is not.

He said, that when he said this, people supposed him to be saying that other people never really have what he has, but that, if he did say so, he would be talking nonsense; and he seemed quite definitely to reject the behaviourist view that 'he has tooth-ache' means only that 'he' is behaving in a particular manner; for he said that 'tooth-ache' doesn't in fact only mean a particular kind of behaviour, and implied that when we pity a man for having toothache, we are not pitying him for putting his hand to his cheek; and, later on, he said that we *conclude* that another person has toothache from his behaviour, and that it is legitimate to conclude this on the analogy of the resemblance of his behaviour to the way in which we behave when we have toothache.[30]

---

[28] *PR* § 64.   [29] Ibid., § 65.

[30] G. E. Moore: 'Wittgenstein's Lectures in 1930–33', *Mind*, Vol. 64, No. 253,

Now if it was possible for him to avoid behaviourism in this way, the two hypotheses that he had seemed to identify with one another in *Philosophical Remarks* could not be identical after all. But had he really meant to commit himself to their identity? In the first of the two passages he had only said that they 'possibly have identical senses', and in the second one he had only said that they 'must have identical senses, if every *possible* experience confirming the one confirms the other as well'. However, though this phrasing indicates his reluctance to commit himself to the identity of the two hypotheses, there is no hint of any good way of avoiding the identification, given the framework within which he was operating. His predicament stands out very clearly in the next part of the lectures recorded by Moore. He paces round and round behind the bars of his assumptions, uncomfortable in any position that he adopts, but not yet quite ready to break out.

It is easy to understand his predicament with hindsight. He had set up the problem of other minds as if it merely required an appreciation of the way in which a kind of primitive science had already taken care of it in our infancy, almost without our connivance. However, there was a gap between pain felt and pain observed—between the experience of the sufferer and the so-called 'inference' of the spectator—which he could neither eliminate nor accommodate. He could not eliminate it, because he was unable to accept behaviourism, but he could not accommodate it within his unified system of factual language, because it seemed to rely on an inference of a type that was verifiable only in a single sequence of cases, one's own, and was, therefore, quite unscientific.

So was there, perhaps, a way of treating the inference as something presupposed by discourse about other minds, but not actually included in it? But given the framework within which he was operating, how could that possibly be so? The ego could drop out of this discourse, because the fact, that A's sensations were A's, really was something that was shown directly to A and indirectly, through A's body, to B. Thus the inference to A's ego was dispensable. But sensation-types could not possibly drop out in the same way. For A's sensation-types constituted a range directly accessible to A, and, if the multiplicity of the phenomena that bracketed them really did put B in a position to infer them, his inferences could not be treated like the dispensable

Jan. 1955, p. 12. When Wittgenstein allows the argument from another person's behaviour to his toothache, he need not be committing himself to the view that the concept of other people's suffering is *set up* by analogy.

inference to *A*'s ego. To put the point in another way, *A*'s ego was something that was shown but not mentioned in *A*'s report that he was in pain, and so it did not figure in any way in *B*'s agreement that he (*A*) was in pain. But *A*'s sensation-types were mentioned both in *A*'s report and in *B*'s agreement with it, and, if *B* really did infer them, his inferences ought to conform to the ordinary canons of a unified factual or scientific language. However, they did not conform to those canons, and yet the legitimacy of *B*'s conviction in a normal case, that *A* was suffering, quite evidently remained unimpaired. The mysterious survival of this common conviction proved that its real foundations were more secure than the ones proposed for it by this theory.

However, even in the passages which show Wittgenstein most clearly at an impasse, the clue that would eventually indicate his line of escape can already be discerned. He was trapped by the assumption that the problem of other minds could be solved by a sufficiently subtle analysis of the way in which this very special connection between objects was established by ordinary scientific observation and inference. But even in this period he often points out that *A*'s relation to his own pain is not an exceptionally close example of a relation between subject and object. It is not just that *A* does not know by introspection that he is in pain: the very question how he knows it lacks sense.[31] This turned out later to be the clue to his line of escape from the impasse.

Meanwhile he adhered to the theory that in a case like pain, *A* and *B* would each speak about their own sensations in a basic language founded on direct, context-free references to the sensations themselves. The consequences of starting from these isolated points of view have already been described. Not only could their certainties about each other's pains never be justified, but—worse—they could not even establish communication with one another about them. For *A* could describe *B*'s pains only in phrases derived from his own basic language; they would be 'sensations bracketed between the same kinds of stimulus and response as my pains'. But *B* would not be able to understand this phrase, because the direct references to *A*'s pains, on which it relies for its meaning, would be something in which he could never participate. Naturally, *A*'s reply to *B*'s complaint would be that

---

[31] See G. E. Moore: 'Wittgenstein's Lectures in Cambridge, 1930–33', p. 12: '. . . there is no such thing as a verification for "I have [sc. toothache]", since the question "How do you know that you have toothache?" is nonsensical'.

he was equally disqualified from understanding *B*'s attempts to communicate about pain in his self-centred basic language.

If this theory made intercommunication about pains inexplicable, how far did the crisis extend? What other cases are sufficiently like the case of pain to produce the same apparently insoluble problem? The first step towards answering this question is to specify again what the problem that may have extended to other sensory fields was. It was not the problem of the external world, but the problem of other people's minds. The mere fact that Wittgenstein's central example was pain, a non-exteroceptive sensation, or, at best, an incompletely and unsystematically exteroceptive one, is enough to prove that. He was not looking out on to the world and trying to show that his sensation-language was not so detached from descriptions of physical objects that he really could not make any claim to knowledge of anything outside the circle of his own sensations. He was looking back into the minds of other people and trying to show that his sensation-language and theirs were connected with one another through descriptions of stimuli and responses in a way that made genuine intercommunication about sensations possible.

That identifies the problem that may have extended to other sensory fields. Did it? At this point it is necessary to distinguish three different questions. Does the problem of the inscrutability of other people's sensations in fact extend to further cases besides pain? If so, was Wittgenstein aware that it does? And in 1929 did he generalize his account of intercommunication about pain to other sensory fields, thus producing the same impasse in every other case too?

The answer to the first of these three questions is obviously 'Yes'. It is just as easy for a philosopher to box himself into a position in which he finds other people's visual impressions inscrutable, and the same is true of all the other sensory fields. It is equally obvious that Wittgenstein was aware of this. How could he fail to be? It is true that philosophers like Russell, writing in the British Empiricist tradition, were far more concerned about the problem of the external world than about the problem of other minds, because what struck them most forcibly was the risk that the detachment of sensations from any connection with physical objects might make the external world inscrutable rather than the risk that it might make other minds inscrutable.[32] That put the main emphasis on exteroceptive sensations

---

[32] However, there is a discussion of the problem of the inscrutability of other people's sense-data in Russell's *Philosophy of Logical Atomism*. See *Essays in Logic and Knowledge*,

in their writings. Wittgenstein's concern with the problem of other minds shifted the emphasis to interoceptive sensations, for reasons that have already been explained. But naturally he was aware that the problem of the inscrutability of other people's sensory experiences spread across the whole board. If evidence is needed, we have his reactions to the general theory of incommunicability of content which Schlick and Carnap developed out of his ideas in this period.[33]

It is not quite so obvious what the answer to the third question is. On the one hand, when he was illustrating his 1929 explanation of intercommunication about sensations, he nearly always chose pain as his example. This must be because pain is so obviously not amenable to the treatment proposed by Carnap and Schlick. It may be possible to treat other people like scientific instruments aiding one's own investigation of the phenomenal world and to elide their visual impressions, but it is evidently not possible to elide another person's suffering and merely comment that he has run into a patch of painful stimuli.[34] On the other hand, there is nothing in Wittgenstein's writings to suggest that he confined his 1929 treatment of sensations to pain, or even to interoceptive data. His 'phenomenological language' had been mainly concerned with the 'immediate data' of our exteroceptive senses, and he began to concentrate on bodily sensations only after he had ceased to look for a single, uniform analysis of all factual discourse. However, even after that change of goal and method

ed. R. C. Marsh, Allen and Unwin, 1956, pp. 195–6, where Russell foreshadows the solution later adopted by Schlick and Carnap.

[33] See above, p. 303 n. 16. Cf. Wittgenstein's letter to Schlick quoted by J. and M. Hintikka in *Investigating Wittgenstein*, pp. 145–6, in which he complains that Carnap's recent article (probably 'Die physikalische Sprache als Universalsprache der Wissenschaft', *Erkenntnis*, Vol. 2 Nos. 5–6, 1932, pp. 432–65) would make his own work look like 'a rehash or plagiarism of Carnap'. They infer that Wittgenstein saw himself as the originator of the theory of a physicalistic language. But the letter does not force us to draw such a strong conclusion. It may only mean that Wittgenstein's treatment of sensation-language puts a heavy load on physical criteria. If it meant more than this, it would be incompatible with the development of his philosophy of mind from the examination of solipsism in the *Tractatus* to his 1929 investigation of the ownership of sensations and his attempt to extend the same treatment to the sensations themselves and their types. (See above, Chs. 10 and 11, and the first part of this chapter.) It is a constant feature of all this work that mental phenomena are neither independent of, nor reduced to, physical phenomena. That explains why in a slightly later letter to Schlick Wittgenstein claimed that he himself had dealt with the problem of 'physicalism' in the *Tractatus*. This is hard to reconcile with the view taken by J. and M. Hintikka. However, it must be admitted that Wittgenstein's 1929 explanation of intercommunication about bodily sensations is an asymptotic approach to Carnap's theory. He will not go all the way to that destination, but it is impossible to see where he can justifiably stop.

[34] Cf. *PI* I § 312.

it would be quite natural for him to extend to all kinds of 'immediate data' the question that he tried to answer about bodily sensations—'How do we manage to communicate with one another about them?'

Of course, it must have struck him as much easier to answer it for the data of our external senses. For the connection between 'It looks blue' and 'It is blue' is comparatively unproblematic, provided that the visual datum is not treated as an independent thing.[35] So though he was prepared to generalize the problem, posing it for visual impressions in several passages,[36] all the hard work that he did on it in these years is concentrated on the more difficult field of bodily sensations. If he had reified exteroceptive sense-data in the way in which he reified bodily sensations when he allowed that we start from direct, context-free references to them, the difficulty would have been equalized across the whole field of perception. But as was shown in the previous chapter, the tendency of the problem to spread was overtaken by the general critique of the reification of sense-data in 1933.

The theme of this chapter and the previous one has been Wittgenstein's first attempt to extend the treatment of the ego to sensations and their types. This way of presenting his work in and immediately after 1929 is not the usual way and its appropriateness to the texts may be questioned. Does it not, perhaps, impose a structure on his philosophy rather than describe what is actually to be found in what he wrote? To put the question in Kantian terms, is it not a regulative device which may help us to understand the direction in which his thoughts were moving without actually being constitutive of them?

A complete defence of this way of looking at his work in these years would involve moving forward to the next stage and looking back on this one from that vantage-point. However, the dangers of using that method have been mentioned more than once. There would be a risk of treating a line of development which could only be traced with hindsight as something which was actually constitutive of the earlier stage of his thought. The defence of this interpretation really has to start at the beginning of the period.

So consider once again Wittgenstein's remarks at Schlick's house on

---

[35] The problematic reification of sense-data only surfaced gradually. See above, pp. 289–95, and below, Ch. 13.

[36] It is significant that many of these passages occur in *NLPESD*, which contains the first formulation of the argument against the possibility of a sensation-language completely detached from physical criteria.

22 December 1929.[37] They occur in a section headed 'Solipsism', in which there are no retractations of his earlier views on that topic. In the setting of conversations which do contain criticisms of parts of the *Tractatus* the absence of self-criticism at this point must indicate that he is not abandoning his earlier ideas about solipsism, but building on them. This is confirmed by the exact match between many of these later remarks and what he had said in the *Tractatus*. In that book the solipsist claimed to have a true theory, but the claim had to be withdrawn, because the ego vanished just when it was needed to serve as the point of origin of the map of the new private world. That disappearance is matched in these later remarks by the elimination of the word 'I' from first-person reports of experiences. In both texts alike the message is that the ownership of an experience is shown directly to the owner himself, and indirectly, through his body, to others. The illusion of the solipsist begins when he assumes that he can take the direct presentation of his own ownership, throw away its physical basis, and still use it to formulate a significant restrictive thesis.

But if in these later reflections Wittgenstein was building on his earlier treatment of solipsism, what exactly was new in them? What had not yet been done and still remained to be done in 1929? The answer proposed here has been that, when he abandoned the point of view of any single person, 'I', looking out on the phenomenal world through the conceptual grid described in the *Tractatus*, he was faced with the problem of integrating the points of view of different people using ordinary factual language in everyday life to communicate with one another. So his first task was to tie each person's point of view into the one and only phenomenal world and to show how their evident intercommunication was possible. That is his primary concern in this section of *Ludwig Wittgenstein and the Vienna Circle* and in the parallel passage in *Philosophical Remarks*.[38] In both texts he concedes that the would-be solipsist can speak the language centred on his own point of view without the personal pronoun 'I', but in both he argues that he cannot detach his self-centred language from the unified system of factual discourse about the one and only phenomenal world. His language, like anyone else's, is unavoidably egocentric, but that does not provide any support for his theory that he is really speaking a private factual language about a private world.

[37] *LWVC* pp. 49–50, quoted above, p. 272.
[38] *LWVC*, loc. cit., and *PR* § 58, quoted above, pp. 297–8.

The point emphasized in this chapter and in the previous two is that this part of the development of Wittgenstein's earlier treatment of solipsism was only concerned with the location of our different points of view in the common phenomenal world. It is quite distinct from his second task, which was to explain how we communicate with one another about our sensations and their types. Now it may look as if his first task had already been completed in the *Tractatus*, but even that is not really so. He had offered the solipsist the simple dilemma that his theory is either incoherent or empty, but he had not explained how we make discriminating references to individuals in real life, and so he had not been in a position to follow up his dilemma with the necessary supplementary argument against the solipsist's next move, which was to deny that there was any need to identify his ego by description when he restricts all such references to his private mental world.

It was pointed out in Chapter 10 that this supplementary argument might well be called 'the first private language argument'. For it is related to the argument of the *Tractatus*, that if ego-based solipsism is not empty it is incoherent, in exactly the way in which the later private language argument of *Philosophical Investigations* is related to the argument that classical phenomenalism with an empirically identified base-line is incoherent. In both cases incoherence is the first charge against the theory to be rejected. In both cases the theorist tries to meet this charge by claiming that when he retreats into his private world, he can take with him the linguistic equipment required for reproducing in that world the performances of speakers in the public world. Wittgenstein argues that both claims are mistaken because in each case the theorist exaggerates the resources that he is able to retain. The first private language argument shows that he would lose discriminating references to individuals, and the second private language argument shows that he would lose discriminating references to sensation-types. So these two reductive arguments are exact counterparts on two parallel lines of investigation.

But this anticipates later developments. If we focus more narrowly on to Wittgenstein's 1929 criticism of solipsism, we find a certain difference in the perspicuousness of the moves that he makes on the two lines of investigation. The critique of the solipsist's treatment of the subject of experience is not too difficult to follow, because it is concerned exclusively with the subject's location in the common phenomenal world among other subjects. But the development of his ideas does become more baffling when he takes on his second task, the explanation of intercommunication between different subjects about their sensation-types. The trouble is that at this point his investigation has split into two levels and the original discussion of the location of different subjects in the world is overlaid by a second stratum on which he is concerned with the objects presented to those subjects, or, at least, with the most 'private' objects presented to them, bodily sensations. This is a confusing complication and an exegetic strategy was required to meet it. The strategy was to start the interpretation of his remarks by uncovering the lower stratum first, and reporting what was found there before dealing with the upper stratum. The finding was that the solipsist's attempt to set up a private language about a private world centred on his detached ego was defective.

In the two parallel passages cited from *Ludwig Wittgenstein and the Vienna Circle* and *Philosophical Remarks*, this criticism of solipsism is taken as made, and attention is switched to the other line of investigation. There is a certain range of objects presented to different subjects, namely, bodily sensations, about which he asks questions closely related to those that he has already asked and answered about the subjects themselves. How are these objects tied into the common world? And how do different subjects manage to establish communication with one another about their types? At this point, we have to pause and remind ourselves that these questions were posed long after the original questions about the subjects of experience, and that Wittgenstein at first underestimated the difficulty of answering them. The discussion of them begins almost as a footnote to the long discussion of the subjects to whom all objects are presented. It goes without saying that it is essential to avoid reading these further questions about bodily sensations and their types back into the original treatment of solipsism.

It is worth emphasizing another point that has been made in this chapter. When Wittgenstein did raise these questions about sensations, he did not ask them indiscriminately about the immediate deliverances of all our senses, but concentrated on a subclass which was especially difficult to include in the unified system of phenomena, bodily sensations and their most dramatic representative, pain. He remained unworried by the usual philosophical doubts about our perception of the external world, relying on his sliding-peg phenomenalism to keep them silenced. His problem was other minds, and it was posed more starkly by pain than by the data of our external senses.

His first proposed solution to it failed, and an explanation of its failure has been offered in this chapter. It started from the obvious impossibility of eliminating sensations and their types in the way in which he had succeeded in eliminating the ego. Behaviourism, or the semi-behaviourism of Schlick and Carnap, were convincing only when they did not involve any real loss within the mind. There was no quick way of disposing of the problem of our intercommunication about bodily sensations and their types, and he set out on the long quest for a solution to it without modifying the general framework of a unified factual language which he had set up in the *Tractatus*. So he began by holding on to the assumption that our conversations about our pains must be supported by primitive scientific observations of objects and by inferences based on them. But this explanation did not work.

It is at this point that doubts are most likely to be felt about the structure attributed to his thought in this chapter and in the previous two. It may be conceded that up to this point the clue that he had been following was the parallelism between the treatment of the subject and the treatment of its objects. But after he had found that he could not accept any behaviouristic or semi-behaviouristic elimination of bodily sensations and their types, what further guidance could he hope to get from the supposed parallelism?

There is an answer to this challenge and it will serve as an introduction to the next chapter. When he failed to explain how our intercommunication about bodily sensations could be supported by primitive science, he asked himself whether sensation-types really do have the intrinsic criteria of identity that would be needed for any attempt to pin them down for scientific observation and inference, like types of physical object. This is a profound question and one that is easily overlooked by philosophers who hold that we make direct, independent references to our experiences in the basic language that each of us employs in his own case. Once asked, it led him into an investigation of the criteria of identity of the objects of experience which exhibits a striking parallelism with the subjects' criteria of identity. This opened up a new field in which his thought manifests the same structure, and, not surprisingly, the identity of structure was obvious to him.

The further parallelism shows up very clearly in the texts. There is a good indication of it in a passage in *The Blue Book*, where he is discussing the application of solipsism to sight and says:

Now let us ask ourselves what sort of identity of personality it is we are referring to when we say 'when anything is seen, it is always I who see'. What is it I want all these cases of seeing to have in common? As an answer I have to confess to myself that it is not my bodily appearance. I don't always see part of my body when I see. And it isn't essential that my body, if seen amongst the things I see, should always look the same. In fact I don't mind how much it changes. And I feel the same way about all the properties of my body, the characteristics of my behaviour, and even about my memories.—When I think about it a little longer I see that what I wished to say was: 'Always when anything is seen, something is seen.' I.e., that of which I said it continued during all the experiences of seeing was not any particular entity 'I', but the experience of seeing itself. This may become clearer if we imagine the man who makes our solipsistic statement to point to his eyes while he says 'I'. (Perhaps because he wishes to be exact and wants to say expressly which eyes belong to the mouth which says 'I' and to the hands pointing to his own body.) But what is he pointing to? These particular eyes with the identity of physical objects? (To understand this sentence, you must remember that the grammar of words of which we say that they stand for physical objects is characterized by the way in which we use the phrase 'the *same* so-and-so', or 'the identical so-and-so', where 'so-and-so' designates the physical object.) We said before that he did not wish to point to a particular physical object at all. The idea that he had made a significant statement arose from a confusion corresponding to the confusion between what we shall call 'the geometrical eye' and 'the physical eye'.[39]

He then explains the difference between 'the geometrical eye' and 'the physical eye'. It is the difference between the focal point behind the visual field conceived in an abstract way, without any independent criterion of identity, and the point of collection of the visual field conceived physically, and so with an independent criterion of identity.[40] After that he goes on to develop the parallelism between solipsism founded on the ego and solipsism founded on its objects in a passage that was quoted above.

. . . The grammar of the word 'geometrical eye' stands in the same relation to the grammar of the word 'physical eye' as the grammar of the expression 'the visual sense datum of a tree' to the grammar of the expression 'the physical tree'. In either case it confuses everything to say 'the one is a *different kind* of object from the other'; for those who say that a sense datum is a different kind of object from a physical object misunderstand the grammar of the word 'kind', just as those who say that a number is a different kind of object from a numeral. They think they are making such a statement as 'A railway train, a railway station, and a railway car are different kinds of objects', whereas their

[39] *BLBK* p. 63, the first part of which was quoted and discussed above, pp. 242–3. This was written in 1933–4.
[40] His explanation of the difference between the two concepts was analysed above, pp. 242–6.

statement is analogous to 'A railway train, a railway accident, and a railway law are different kinds of objects'.[41]

There really cannot be any doubt that the parallelism between the treatment of the solipsist's ideas about the ego and the treatment of his ideas about the objects presented to the ego was constitutive of Wittgenstein's thought at the time, or that he himself saw it in this way. For in the discussion that follows he first deals with the solipsist's mistaken ideas about the subject of experience[42] and then goes on to deal with his similarly mistaken ideas about its objects.[43]

Incidentally, it is instructive to study the way in which he presents the connection between the 'I' that lacks an independent criterion of identity and the visual objects that suffer from the same lack. These objects are, of course, visual sense-data, but nothing is said about their ontological status and nothing depends on it. The crucial fault in the solipsist's treatment of them is that he does not single them out from a more extensive array of objects that could have been seen, but were not seen. The principle on which they are selected is merely that they are the whole contemporary visual show.[44] This is a logical fault in the solipsist's concept of internalized pointing—unlike pointing in real life, it does not really pick anything out—and the diagnosis of this fault does not presuppose that the targets of this internalized pointing are mental sense-data. It is, of course, natural for the solipsist to go on and give his sense-data a specific ontological status, but his mistake begins earlier than that. His mistake is pointing without picking out, and it is a development of the logical mistake that was imputed to him in the *Tractatus*. The criticism is made very clearly in the continuation of the discussion of the targets of the solipsist's pointing in *The Blue Book*:

Now we can make use of such an expression as 'pointing to the *appearance* of a body' or 'pointing to a visual sense datum'. Roughly speaking, this sort of pointing comes to the same as sighting, say, along the barrel of a gun. Thus we may point and say: 'This is the direction in which I see my image in the mirror'. One can also use such an expression as 'the appearance, or sense datum, of my finger points to the sense datum of the tree' and similar ones. . . .

Now when in the solipsistic way I say '*This* is what's really seen', I point before me and it is essential that I point *visually*. If I pointed sideways or behind me—as it were, to things which I don't see—the pointing would in this case be meaningless to me; it would not be pointing in the sense in which I wish to point. But this means that when I point before me saying 'this is what's

---

[41] *BLBK* p. 64, quoted above, p. 293.
[43] Ibid., pp. 70–1.
[42] Ibid., pp. 64–70.
[44] See above, pp. 244–7.

really seen', although I make the gesture of pointing, I don't point to one thing as opposed to another. This is as when travelling in a car and feeling in a hurry, I instinctively press against something in front of me as though I could push the car from inside.

When it makes sense to say 'I see this', or 'this is seen', pointing to what I see, it also makes *sense* to say 'I see this', or 'this is seen', pointing to something I *don't* see. When I made my solipsist statement, I pointed, but I robbed the pointing of its sense by inseparably connecting that which points and that to which it points. I constructed a clock with all its wheels, etc., and in the end fastened the dial to the pointer and made it go round with it. And in this way the solipsist's 'Only this is really seen' reminds us of a tautology.[45]

It has already been explained that this argument is a reinforcement of the first private language argument, against the possibility of discriminating reference to individuals in the solipsist's private world.[46] According to that argument, it is an essential feature of such references that they should be made from an independent base of the same general type as their targets, but this requirement cannot be met within the mind because nothing mental could possibly serve as such a base.[47] In the external world the subject's body is mobile and it serves as a sight-seeing vehicle, but it is not possible for anything in the mind to match that role. The reinforcing argument that has just been sketched indicates the consequence of the lack of resources within the solipsist's mind: given the poverty of his mental resources, the only way for him to make discriminating references to individuals is to fall back on the external world: genuine selectivity requires him to go beyond what he sees at the moment and, therefore, beyond the limits of his mind.[48]

Although these remarks in the *The Blue Book* are concerned with the selection of the objects seen by the solipsist, they do not yet touch on the selection of their types. The whole passage is still focused on to the way in which he picks out objects, and the discrimination of different types of sensation is not mentioned. This is probably because Wittgenstein assumed that his account of our self-centred basic language would take care of their types, and it had not yet occurred to him that there might be a real difficulty about reidentifying them. He was still some way from his later claim that the solipsist's excerpt from the total system of factual discourse was not viable, because it

---

[45] *BLBK* p. 71. Cf. *BRBK* pp. 174–5, quoted above, pp. 231–2.

[46] See above, pp. 235–7.   [47] See above, pp. 244–5.

[48] See G. E. Moore's notes of Wittgenstein's lectures in 1933, quoted above, p. 247.

depended on, but at the same time deprived itself of, the criteria on which the differentiation of sensation-types is ultimately based.

If we want to see the beginning of the next stage in the parallelism between his treatment of the ego and his treatment of its objects, we must go to his 'Notes for Lectures on "Private Experience" and "Sense-data"'.[49] There is a revealing passage in which Wittgenstein argues with an interlocutor who complains, in effect, that his account of our conversations about our bodily sensations is indistinguishable from the account given by Schlick and Carnap:

'But doesn't what you say come to this: that it doesn't matter what the persons feel as long as only they behave in a particular way?'

'Do you mean that you can define pain in terms of behaviour?'

'But aren't you neglecting something—the experience or whatever you might call it—? Almost *the world* behind the mere words?'[50]

These three questions express a misunderstanding of Wittgenstein's position which is the inevitable first reaction to it. He is giving pain a criterion of identity which we naturally, but, in the end, disastrously, regard as 'extrinsic', and he is trying to do this without denying what we all in the same way regard as its 'intrinsic' character. This is an enterprise which is always misunderstood at first, because the immediate reaction is always to assume that the 'extrinsic' criterion will necessarily fail to capture the 'intrinsic' character. So in the continuation of this text he asks his interlocutor to reflect on the way in which he himself originally got into a position to identify the 'intrinsic' character of pain. Was it not by using precisely the 'extrinsic' criteria which strike him as inadequate when Wittgenstein reminds him of them in a philosophical context? His treatment of his interlocutor's discontent indicates where he differs from Schlick and Carnap and at the same time reveals the parallelism between the two lines of his own investigation:

But here solipsism teaches us a lesson: It is that thought which is *on the way* to destroy this error. For if the *world* is idea it isn't any person's idea. (Solipsism stops short of saying this and says that it is my idea.) But then how could I say what the world is if the realm of ideas has no neighbour? What I do comes to defining the word 'world'.

'I neglect that which goes without saying.'

'What is seen *I* see' (pointing to my body). I point at my geometrical eye,

---

[49] These lectures were given in 1936.

[50] *NLPESD* p. 296.

saying this. Or I point with closed eyes and touch my breast and feel it. In no case do I make a connection between what is seen and a person.

Back to 'neglecting'! It seems that I neglect life. But not life physiologically understood but life as consciousness. And consciousness not physiologically understood, or understood from the outside, but consciousness as the very essence of experience, the appearance of the world, the world.

Couldn't I say: If I had to add the world to my language it would have to be one sign for the whole of language, which sign could therefore be left out.

How am I to describe the way the child learns the word 'toothache'—like this?: The child sometimes has toothache, it moans and holds its cheek, the grown-ups say '. . .' etc. Or: The child sometimes moans and holds its cheek, the grown-ups . . .? Does the first description say something superfluous or false, or does the second leave out something essential? Both descriptions are correct.

'But it seems as if you were neglecting something.' But what more can I do than *distinguish* the case of saying 'I have toothache' when I really have toothache, and the case of saying the words without having toothache. I am also (further) ready to talk of any *x* behind my words so long as it keeps its identity.

Isn't what you reproach me of as though you said: 'In your language you're only *speaking*!'[51]

The crucial point is made in the penultimate paragraph: 'I am also (further) ready to talk of any *x* behind my words so long as it keeps its identity.' The concession is ironical, because he has already pre-empted all the available criteria of identity, and the remarks that lead up to it are a brilliant coda recapitulating the themes that had led him, one by one, from his first ideas about solipsism to this apparently remote point.

The lesson that solipsism teaches us is that in everyday life the solipsist satisfies the criteria of personal identity, like anyone else, and if he detaches the ego or consciousness from those criteria, he cannot claim them as his own or even treat the words for them as count-nouns. Consciousness becomes a mass-noun designating 'the world as we find it' or, to put the emphasis on the human end of the transaction, it designates sentient life as it constitutes the world.[52] Now the human constituent of the phenomenal world is not something that slips through the net of ordinary language and can only be captured by a

---

[51] *NLPESD* p. 297. Wittgenstein does not mention Schlick or Carnap, but he was aware of their theory and must have realized how easy it was to confuse his treatment of this problem with theirs.

[52] See Vol. I pp. 174–6.

special philosophical description. All that the philosopher needs to do, and all that he can do, is to remind us how words for ordinary types of bodily sensation, like toothache, are introduced by so-called 'extrinsic' criteria in everyday life. There are no other criteria for him to use, and if his critic complains that the words introduced in this way get no grip on the actual things, he can retort that a reality that eludes everything that anyone can possibly say in the language that was specially invented for it is an illusion of exactly the same kind as the pure ego.

I3

The Private Language Argument of Philosophical Investigations

IT would be simplistic to suppose that it is possible to take a late text of Wittgenstein's, cut along the dotted lines, and find that it falls into neatly separated arguments. The structure of his thought is too holistic for that kind of treatment. However, though this is generally true of his later work, his private language argument is something of an exception. It is brief, looks self-contained, and, after it has been cut out of the text of *Philosophical Investigations*, it proves to be memorable and eminently debatable:

. . . But in the present case I have no criterion of correctness. One would like to say: whatever is going to seem right to me is right. And that only means that here we can't talk about 'right'.[1]

The topic is the reidentification of sensation-types, and the argument is that a case can be described in which there would be no distinction between applying a word to a sensation-type correctly and applying it incorrectly. The case that he has in mind has been introduced like this:

. . . But could we also imagine a language in which a person could write down or give vocal expression to his inner experiences—his feelings, moods, and the rest—for his private use?—Well, can't we do so in our ordinary language?—But that is not what I mean. The individual words of this language are to refer to what can only be known to the person speaking; to his immediate private sensations. So another person cannot understand the language.[2]

The case is specified as one in which the vocabulary of the private language is completely detached from everything in the physical world, so that the most that could be expected is that the originator of the language should understand what he was doing with it although nobody else could. The question is, 'Could even he understand what he was doing with it?', and that immediately introduces further, more

---

[1] *PI* I § 258.
[2] Ibid., § 243.

radical questions, 'Would he really be doing anything with it? Would it be a language at all?'

Wittgenstein argues that even the originator would be at a loss. But languages are made, not found. So if he could not understand what he was doing, he would not be succeeding in doing anything that he intended to do, and the sense in which he was doing something would not be the sense in which speaking a language is doing something. Coleridge desribes the case of an uneducated German servant who began to 'speak' in Hebrew,[3] but Wittgenstein's point is that such a case would not really count as speaking a language. Of course, in the case that he describes, nobody else can understand what the speaker is doing, but even if they could, and even if they explained it to the speaker, what he originally did would still not count as speaking a language. The disqualification is a radical one: if the speaker did not know what he was doing because he did not understand it, and if he did not understand it because he started without any viable criteria of doing it correctly, his performance would be linguistic only in the sense that he would be using his tongue.

This is a striking argument and one that looks easy to excerpt from the text of *Philosophical Investigations* in which it is developed. Indeed, the argument must have a certain independence, because it is a *reductio ad absurdum*, and it is essential to such arguments that the thesis under attack should be clearly formulated, and that all the premisses should be unequivocally identified. If these conditions were not met, an argument of this kind would be frustrated, because the impact of the absurdity would be uncertain. It would be possible that all that it showed was that the original thesis was not stated precisely enough, or perhaps what would have been proved to be absurd would be an extra premiss which had not been formulated in spite of the fact that the argument needed it. A *reductio* has to avoid these uncertainties. So there can be no doubt that Wittgenstein's private language argument was offered as a self-contained unit, and the question is, 'What would a complete list of its premisses look like?'

It is worth recalling the position of the argument in his later philosophy. In the preceding chapters it was called 'the second private language argument', because it was modelled on an earlier private language argument against the construction of a microcosm based on the ego. Both arguments were introduced as supplements to a general

---

[3] See S. T. Coleridge: *Biographia Literaria*, Vol. I Ch. 6 (Vol. 7 pp. 112–13 in *The Collected Works of Samuel Taylor Coleridge*, Princeton, 1983).

thesis first formulated in the Preface to the *Tractatus*: the limit of factual language and of its correlate, the world, can be drawn only from the inside. From this it follows that it would be incoherent first to identify the ego in the common world, and then to go on to cut out of that world a microcosm based on the ego; and similarly, it follows that it would be incoherent first to identify a phenomenal base-line within experience, and then to go on to shrink the world into the area bounded by that base-line. Each of the two private language arguments then adds a further consideration: if, contrary to the arguments just given, a private microcosm could be set up in either of those two ways, the solipsist would still lose something essential to language when he retreated into his private world—in the first case, he would lose discriminating references to individuals, and in the second case, discriminating references to types.[4]

It is immediately evident that the private language argument of *Philosophical Investigations* cannot possibly rely on the second of the two conclusions drawn from the general thesis about the limit of language,—classical phenomenalism, with an empirically specified base-line, is incoherent. The argument against the possibility of private reidentification of sensation-types has to make a further, independent point. It must start by allowing, for the sake of argument, that the stage really can be set in the way proposed by the classical phenomenalist: the subject reviews his sensation-types in complete detachment from the external world, and yet the sensations themselves are specified empirically in precisely the way that someone at home in the external world would specify them—'my bodily sensations', 'my visual impressions', etc. Maybe this is incoherent, but that is not an objection that can be exploited by the private language argument of *Philosophical Investigations*, because it has to show that after the stage has been set in this way nothing that is done on it can possibly count as speaking a language.

The point must not be exaggerated. It is still possible that some of the considerations that figured in the case against classical phenomenalism can be counted in as premises of the private language argument, and this possibility will have to be explored later. What is not possible is that the argument should rely on the incoherence of classical phenomenalism deduced from the general thesis about the limit of language.

---

[4] See above, pp. 233–5, 276–8, and 289–95.

Here then is one question of interpretation which will have to be answered: 'Granted that the private language argument is an independent *reductio*, what exactly are its premisses?' Now the boundary between it and the general argument for the incoherence of classical phenomenalism is not the only line that has to be drawn in this area. There is also some uncertainty about the relation between the private language argument and the description of the pre-linguistic structure into which sensation-language was originally introduced. It must be significant that this structure is mentioned and illustrated by the case of pain immediately after the question about a private language has been posed:

> . . . Here is one possibility: words are connected with the primitive, the natural, expressions of the sensation and used in their place. A child has hurt himself and he cries; and then adults talk to him and teach him exclamations and, later, sentences. They teach the child new pain-behaviour. . . .[5]

But what exactly is the connection between the structure that makes it possible to teach a child to use the word 'pain' by this method and the private language argument? The obvious answer is that if this method of teaching is used, the language will not be private. But Wittgenstein immediately goes on to make a further, deeper point about the underlying structure:

> For how can I go so far as to try to use language to get between pain and its expression?[6]

The implication is clear: in the pre-linguistic structure pain is already distinguished by its natural expression in behaviour, and he must have felt it important to indicate right at the beginning of the discussion of the possibility of a private language that classical phenomenalism over-intellectualizes our linguistic reactions to perceptual input.[7]

If this is the right interpretation, it opens up a whole new vista. It is true that pain is a special case, because the output end of its type-line is very simple and very clearly marked.[8] However, there are other cases which do not fall far short of it in simplicity and clarity, and which, unlike pain, carry information about the external world in their pre-linguistic structure. When someone crosses a stream on stepping-stones, there is an almost equally straight-forward correlation between what he sees ahead of him and what he has to do with his feet. Now

---

[5] *PI* I § 244, quoted above, p. 261.   [6] Ibid., § 245.
[7] See above, pp. 309–10 and Vol. I pp. 56–7.   [8] See above, p. 261.

classical phenomenalists try to internalize the spatial properties of what he sees ahead of him, claiming that the words for them can be applied directly and independently to his visual sense-data. What they forget is that when these words are pulled back into the microcosm, they carry with them 'hypotheses' about the external world.[9] This is not the case with colours, because there are no natural reactions to the colours themselves and it is only the colour-edges which give us spatial information about our surroundings. But that only shows that the spatial 'hypotheses' carried by colour-words are attached to patterns of colours rather than to single colours, and that the key to the information that they provide is not atomistic, as Locke supposed, but holistic.

Perhaps Wittgenstein's point about pain can be put like this: the concept has a pre-linguistic structure and when we plant the word 'pain' in it, it takes. It takes, because the output end of the type-line is ready for it with a well-established reaction, and this reaction matches an equally well-established connection at the input end, namely the connection between pain and injury. The 'hypothesis', if there is one in this case, is that the cause of the pain felt by the subject is damage to his body. But it comes more naturally to us to speak of 'hypotheses' picked up by words in more complicated cases, like visual impressions of spatial properties. In such cases when the vocabulary is introduced, and our reactions are intellectualized, a whole range of 'hypotheses' is packed into the words. But there is nothing wrong with extending the same account to pain, with the qualification that the 'hypothesis' in that case is not about the external world, but about the world beneath the subject's skin. We can even point to a range of 'hypotheses' in this primitive case, because pains have many different locations.

This avenue will need to be explored carefully. There is a real possibility, overlooked in many commentaries on Wittgenstein's private language argument, that the error that he was trying to eradicate seemed to him to start with the characteristic philosophical over-intellectualization of our reactions to perceptual input.

There are two other questions of interpretation, which will not need much introduction, because they have received such a lot of attention

---

[9] A point well made by G. Evans in his brilliant article, 'Things without the Mind: A Comment on Ch. 2 of Strawson's *Individuals*', in G. Evans: *Collected Papers*, Oxford 1985 (reprinted from *Philosophical Subjects: Essays presented to P. F. Strawson*, ed. Z. van Straaten, Oxford, 1980). Cf. M. Merleau-Ponty: *Phénomenologie de la perception*, Gallimard, 1945.

in the literature. Why does Wittgenstein claim that there must be a distinct step from seeming right to being right, if the performance is going to count as speaking a language? And if sensation-language is completely detached from the external world, what exactly is the crucial loss that it suffers? Is it the loss of any chance to check one's own impressions by asking other people for theirs? Or is it the loss of any chance to check them on standard material objects which might be assumed to provide the same stimulation on every occasion of perception?

All these questions will need discussion, and perhaps it will be useful to start by putting the last two in perspective. Speaking a language, unlike writhing in pain, is an artificial accomplishment with standards of correctness which have to be learned and maintained. Neither of these achievements would be possible if the material on which people practised did not give them any indication of success or failure. Imagine, for example, trying to become a good marksman on a rifle-range where you were the only person who ever saw your target, and even you only glimpsed it down the sights of your rifle before you fired and never again. In such circumstances there would be no point in pulling the trigger, and similarly, according to Wittgenstein, if your sensations were completely detached from the external world, there would be no point in opening your mouth to speak about them.

In general, someone who can never discover what he is in fact doing will not be in a position to maintain any proficiency at doing it, and will never have been in a position to learn to do it, or even to try to do it. An acquired skill, like speaking a language, is not like an automatic performance. Blinking in a bright light is something that you might never know that you did, because, not being an intentional action, it stands in no need of a test of success. You might even be born without the capacity to do it and be given it by neural surgery, but the 'gift of tongues', without any test of success available to the speaker, would not count as the gift of language. The point is not that you could not acquire or maintain the skill because it would be too difficult to acquire or maintain in such circumstances, but that whatever you did in such circumstances would not count as the exercise of a skill.[10]

The crucial loss inflicted on the would-be speaker of a private language is not too easy to identify in the text of *Philosophical Investigations*. On the frustrating rifle-range there would evidently be

[10] See above, p. 329.

two deprivations: nobody could ever tell you the pattern of your shots, and you yourself could only glimpse the target down the sights of your rifle before you fired. In this case there is no need to choose one of the two deprivations as the crucial one rather than the other. For each of them could be made good without the other, and it would not matter which one was made good, because either one would be enough by itself to allow you to learn to shoot accurately.

The case of the detached sensation-language is not so clear. This is because there are several important differences between the predicament of a would-be speaker of a private language and the predicament of the marksman on the frustrating rifle-range, and the effect of these differences is hard to assess. It may be that Wittgenstein believed that they would make it conceptually impossible for an intelligent wolf-child to set up a private language to record his life in the forest, and that is why this kind of case is not mentioned in *Philosophical Investigations*. Or perhaps he considered the case too exceptional and marginal to be worth discussing. His attitude to it in the book is enigmatic.

The differences between the two cases are not hard to locate. Because the two resources available on an ordinary rifle-range are independent of one another, it is not unusual for a marksman to shoot alone and to verify the pattern of his own shots. But could the intelligent wolf-child set up his language alone, and check the regularity of his use of words on standard physical objects? In *Philosophical Investigations* Wittgenstein certainly never says that he could do this.[11] However, that may only be because he had come to think that this kind of case is too exceptional and too marginal to be worth discussing.[12] He may have thought it advisable to ignore cases in which the would-be speaker is alone and so is reduced to calibrating his skill on standard objects, and better to concentrate on ordinary cases in which we are in a position to appeal through physical objects to other people. That, after all, is our normal practice both when we are acquiring a vocabulary and later when we want to test the accuracy of our use of it. In both these situations we calibrate our reactions on objects, but instead of being reduced to making the wolf-child's

---

[11] This would be treated as an understatement by those who take Wittgenstein to be denying the possibility of such an achievement in *PI* I §§ 240–2. Their view will be discussed in the next chapter.

[12] He did discuss similar cases in texts earlier than the final draft of *PI*, and did allow that they were cases of speaking a language. See below, pp. 372–9.

assumption, that they are standard objects, we make the easier and less risky assumption that our mentors' reactions to them are reliable.

The alternative explanation of his not saying in *Philosophical Investigations* that the wolf-child could manage his language on his own is, of course, that he thought that the task would be beyond him. If that was his view, he adopted it not because he believed that no wolf-child would be clever enough to achieve anything so difficult, but because he believed that nothing that it was logically possible for him to do would count as devising and using a language.[13]

The conflict between these divergent interpretations will be resolved in the next chapter. Meanwhile, there is a further point worth making about the two resources normally available to the speaker of a natural language. It has already been remarked that the two resources available to a marksman on an ordinary rifle-range are independent of one another. The reason for this is plain: if the target happens to be too far away for the marksman to make out the bullet-holes, he can get the information by telephone from someone at the other end, and, if there is nobody at the other end, he can walk down the range and inspect the target himself. But when someone sets out to learn a descriptive language, the two resources that might help him are not independent of one another. One important link between them shows up when we reflect that he could not profit from the instruction offered by other people unless there were something that he could do without them. For suppose it were granted that anything that he did on his own would not count as acquiring a language, not because he would not be communicating with anyone else, but for the more fundamental reasons that he would not have a firm criterion for the regularity of his reactions to things. Even so, what he could do on his own would contribute to his learning a language later, when he met other people. For it would be impossible for him to learn from them unless he understood that they were reacting correctly to the things to which he would certainly take himself to be trying to react correctly. This raises an important question which we do not need to ask about the two resources normally available on a rifle-range: 'Just how much is added by the information provided by the reactions of a language-learner's mentors and how much was already in place?'

Finally, to complete this introductory sketch, something should be said about the difference that the private language argument made to

---

[13] See above, p. 329.

his philosophy. Some commentators suppose that he subscribed to classical phenomenalism until he devised this argument against it. It is worth repeating that this is doubly mistaken. He never was a classical phenomenalist, and, before he formulated this argument, he relied on his argument from the limit of language to show that it was an incoherent theory.[14] True, the steps in that argument are not clearly marked in his writings between 1929 and 1932, but that is only because he was preoccupied at first with his investigation of the subject of experience. In *The Blue Book*, when he turned to the parallel investigation of the objects presented to the subject, he did criticize classical phenomenalism for starting from a perceptual base-line that was specified empirically. So his private language argument must be a second shot aimed at the same target. It must be aimed at any theory that treats sense-data as empirically specified things with independent criteria of identity. What the new argument adds to his philosophy is another criticism of classical phenomenalism—this time a criticism from the inside: even if the stage could be set in that way, still nothing that could be done on it would count as speaking a language.

It is not too hard to get a general picture of Wittgenstein's private language argument and its place in the development of his philosophy. The difficult thing is to establish the details from the text of *Philosophical Investigations*. The trouble is not the usual one with original thinkers, that they forge ahead with their own ideas hoping to carry objectors along with them without pausing to hear out their misgivings. On the contrary, he nearly always argues dialectically, but though each instalment of his reasoning is sharply focused on to its own issue, it is often unclear which objections have already been answered and which lie ahead. That is why aphoristic writing often produces convictions far beyond the believer's ability to defend them.

The way to interpret a reductive argument is, or course, first to identify the hypothesis under attack, and then to identify the premises on which the attack relies. It may be seen as a parade of propositions, which together produce an absurdity, and the question is 'Which one is responsible for it?' In a good argument of this kind the answer will be clear, because all the other propositions will point the finger of blame at the hypothesis under attack. If this is going to work, the guilty hypothesis must be clearly identified, a complete list of the premises must be available and they must all be seen to be true.

---

[14] See above, Ch. 11.

Wittgenstein formulates the hypothesis under attack very carefully:

> A human being can encourage himself, give himself orders, obey, blame and punish himself; he can ask himself a question and answer it. We could even imagine human beings who spoke only in monologue; who accompanied their activities by talking to themselves.—An explorer who watched them and listened to their talk might succeed in translating their language into ours. (This would enable him to predict these people's actions correctly, for he also hears them making resolutions and decisions.)
>
> But could we also imagine a language in which a person could write down or give vocal expression to his inner experiences—his feelings, moods, and the rest—for his private use?—Well, can't we do so in our ordinary language? But that is not what I mean. The individual words of this language are to refer to what can only be known to the person speaking; to his immediate private sensations. So another person cannot understand the language.[15]

A line is being drawn here between something which we can imagine—people 'who spoke only in monologue'—and something else which, he is going to argue, we cannot imagine—a person 'speaking a language' strictly unintelligible to anyone else. He is, as usual, prepared to concede that we think that we can imagine the second achievement, but according to him, that is only because we are operating with a picture which is protected from criticism by its own vagueness. We avoid giving our hypothesis of a private language any precise application to human life, and we make no attempt to work out its testable consequences. These are things that we would do if we were treating it as a serious scientific possibility, but we keep it in the philosophical limbo, from which he has to force it to the surface, draw out the details, and demonstrate that it is not just false but absurd.[16]

It is a good idea to start by looking at the phenomenon which he places on the near side of the line, people speaking only in monologue. That, of course, is not the case that interested him, and he mentions it only to mark it off from the 'possibility' which is going to be the object of his investigation. But if we look at the phenomenon lying just on this side of the line where absurdity begins, we may be able to identify the resource which these soliloquists possess, but which the speaker of a private language would lack. The difference between the two cases is, up to a point, very clear. The soliloquists are applying their language to the physical world, and their own activities in it, but the speaker of a private sensation-language would be doing no such thing. So we can

---

[15] *PI* I § 243.
[16] See above, pp. 206–7.

see immediately that the soliloquists do, at least, have the resource available to the intelligent wolf-child: one of them can tell himself to get an oyster, remember his intention, check his successful execution of it, and congratulate himself before consuming it. We can also see, or, at least, Wittgenstein intends us to see that the speaker of a private sensation-language would not have anything like this resource.[17] However, there is something else, which is not so clear. Do these soliloquists have, and do they need to have, the opportunity to overhear each other?

The emphasis on the connection between their language and behaviour is understandable in a discussion which opens with a criticism of the common philosophical tendency to over-intellectualize the beginnings of language. A little earlier in *Philosophical Investigations* something had been said about the conclusions that would be drawn by 'explorers', if they discovered people whose actions were intelligible and appeared to be accompanied by language but without any regular connection between what they did and what they said:

> Let us imagine that the people in that country carried on the usual human activities and in the course of them employed, apparently, an articulate language. If we watch their behaviour we find it intelligible, it seems 'logical'. But when we try to learn their language, we find it impossible to do so. For there is no regular connection between what they say, the sounds they make, and their actions; but still these sounds are not superfluous, for if we gag one of the people, it has the same consequences as with us; without the sounds their actions fall into confusion—as I feel like putting it.
>
> Are we to say that these people have a language: orders, reports, and the rest?
>
> There is not enough regularity for us to call it 'language'.[18]

The reason why this is not a language is that the requisite regular connections between vocalizations and actions are lacking. Such regular connections were a feature of the soliloquies described in § 243, and that was at least part of the reason why they counted as examples of speaking a language in spite of the absence of intercommunication.

This suggests that in § 243 Wittgenstein may implicitly be allowing that the resource available to the intelligent wolf-child would be enough by itself to support a language. For if those people 'spoke only

---

[17] Of course, a classical phenomenalist would dispute this. See below, Ch. 15, for a discussion of his objection.

[18] *PI* I § 207.

in monologue', they would never appeal to one another for confirmation of the correctness of what they said. However, the text does not really commit him to that thesis. For he does not stipulate that the soliloquists of § 243 do not overhear or imitate one another, and his phrase 'their language' certainly allows for the possibility that they all speak the same language and achieve conformity by eavesdropping instead of openly appealing to 'human agreement'.[19]

On the far side of the dividing line drawn in § 243 there are several questions that need to be asked about the would-be private sensation-language. The one that should be taken first is, 'How complete is its detachment from everything outside my mind supposed to be?' The answer to this question can be gathered from a passage that occurs some way into the discussion. His first move had been to stipulate that the private sensation-language can be understood only by me (if indeed even I can understand it). While that remains in force, he reminds us that my sensation-vocabulary is not 'tied up with my natural expressions of sensation', because 'in that case my language is not a "private" one'.[20] Later, he relaxes the stipulation, but the relaxation is on the input half of the type-line rather than on its output half: he gives my sensation-type, 'S', a regular connection with something outside my mind:

Let us now imagine a use for the entry of the sign 'S' in my diary. I discover that whenever I have a particular sensation, a manometer shows that my blood-pressure rises. So I shall be able to say that my blood-pressure is rising without using any apparatus. This is a useful result. And now it seems quite indifferent whether I have recognized the sensation *right* or not. Let us suppose I regularly identify it wrong, it does not matter in the least. And that alone shows that the hypothesis that I make a mistake is mere show. (We, as it were, turned a knob which looked as if it could be used to turn on some part of the machine; but it was a mere ornament, not connected with the mechanism at all.)

And what is our reason for calling 'S' the name of a sensation here? Perhaps the kind of way this sign is employed in this language-game.—And why a 'particular sensation', that is, the same one every time? Well, aren't we supposing that we write 'S' every time?[21]

This is an unusually telegraphic text even for Wittgenstein, and though

[19] However, Wittgenstein does not actually mention this possibility, and a comparison of this text with its earlier versions shows that he is writing even more cautiously than usual in this passage. The reason for his caution will be discussed in Ch. 14, when the question about the necessity and sufficiency of the two resources—calibration on standard objects and appeal to other people—is taken up.

[20] *PI* I § 256.

[21] Ibid., § 270.

the individual points in it are not hard to understand, the choice of example allows him to link them together, so that you scarcely have time to take in the first one before the second one is upon you. It is a case of persuasion by saturation.

His first point is a simple one: 'S' would cease to be a word in a would-be private sensation-vocabulary if I noticed and began to exploit a regularity on the input half of its type-line. He has already made the parallel point about the output half of its type-line, and his strategy so far is perspicuous. However, it is not so clear what the new status of the word 'S' would be. There are, in fact, two possibilities. First, I might be able to monitor my own blood-pressure without having any definite sensations to guide me. In that case I might still say 'I feel as though my blood-pressure is going up', but I would only mean 'It seems to me that it is going up'. The word 'feel' would merely signify that this was not a case of exteroceptive perception: that is to say, I was not in a predicament like that of a short-sighted person who could not quite read the figures on the manometer. The second possibility is that I might have definite sensations to go on—for example, sensations of pressure in my temples, slight dizziness, etc. The final paragraph warns us against assuming that, because we started with the idea that 'S' belongs to a private sensation-vocabulary, it will still be a sensation-word after it has gone public: it may merely indicate interoceptive seeming.

Wittgenstein's second point is that, when the new regular connection on the input half of its type-line threatens 'S' with the loss of its private status, it cannot possibly retain that status in the way that is criticized in 'Notes for Lectures on "Private Experience" and "Sense-data" '.[22] In that dialogue the interlocutor protested that all sensations have 'intrinsic' properties which cannot possibly be captured by any 'extrinsic' criteria derived from the circumstances that bracket them. But that did not work, because all the available criteria had been pre-empted, and so, if these 'intrinsic' properties really did remain uncaptured, they would only be wheels that could be spun independently of the rest of the mechanism. So in the case of 'S', 'wrong identifications' of this extra element would not even be detectable, provided that my use of the word remained firmly correlated with a rise in my blood-pressure.[23]

---

[22] *NLPESD* pp. 316–18, quotes and discussed pp. 353–8, and p. 400. Cf. the child who asks his mother how she knows that her visual impressions of red are not like his of blue (see above, p. 218).

[23] See below, pp. 351–2 for the details of this argument. The question, whether in

This point is not one that could be established in a brief Wittgensteinian paragraph. It would take a great weight of argument to drive it home, and in this text we only get quick thrusts. So we feel that it all goes by so quickly that we don't quite know whether to agree or disagree. Where might the interlocutor have been best advised to dig in and resist? That is not at all clear—all the less so, because the example is intermediate between two different cases. It is easy enough to show that, if 'S' is tied to something's seeming so, it cannot be entirely independent of the physical criteria for its actually being so.[24] But the parallel demonstration for 'I have an S sensation' is not so simple, and the full development of it is not undertaken in this brief text.

In other philosophers' books the question about the possibility of a completely detached sensation-language is usually discussed in the extreme case in which there is nothing whatsoever outside the circle of sensations to which 'S' or any other sensation-word could be attached. That is our original position as it is presented by classical phenomenalists. If it is not a possibility in that case, then in the ordinary course of everyday life it ought not to be possible to pick out an 'intrinsic' property of a sensation which is bracketed between stimulus and response, but which cannot be captured by anyone using any part of the bracket itself as a criterion. Here, as elsewhere, Wittgenstein's strategy is to bring the discussion down to earth. He does this not by asking how we would react to the original position described by the phenomenalist but how we would react to a particular case that might occur in our daily lives. Naturally, the case that he chooses is not the case of a philosopher who claims that all our sensations have 'intrinsic' properties bracketed between their stimuli and responses, but uncapturable by any criteria taken from the brackets themselves. He brings the discussion down to earth by asking how we would react if someone who was not a philosopher claimed to have a new type of sensation unconnected with anything in the physical world.

This strategy has been criticized because, it is said, the plausibility of Wittgenstein's argument depends on the scope of the private language that he is considering. If it is the whole of the speaker's language, the agument may carry conviction. But if it is only part of it, the speaker will be able to establish his general competence with words

fact my reports of my sensation-types are immune from error, is discussed below, pp. 359–60.

[24] Cf. *Zettel*, §§ 409–25.

in areas where he can use tests based on the external world, and then he can extend his operations back into the private sector, where they cannot be checked but can still serve to support a genuine language.[25] But how much mileage can the critic get out of this suggestion? Suppose that some range of ordinary bodily sensations suddenly became completely detached from everything in the physical world. Would we really allow that the next generation of speakers could acquire complex but uncheckable skills in this private sector by extrapolating their general competence established in the public sector?

The suggestion, that in such a case we would credit vocalizers with uncheckable skills in the private sector, may well strike us as incredible. But here, as usual, we have to be careful. If Wittgenstein is right, what is incredible is not what these people are supposed to do, but the way in which we are supposed to describe their performance. This is not armchair science, but philosophy, and his point is that we could not bring anything that they did under the concept of *an acquired skill*. Now it may not look as easy to make this point perspicuously in this kind of case as it is to make it against classical phenomenalists, who develop a scenario of total privacy. But the trouble with that scenario is that it is difficult to see how it is connected with our normal lives, and, therefore, difficult for us to project ourselves into it. Whatever the outcome of this controversy, Wittgenstein was surely right to bring it down to earth in the way that he does.

The next step in the interpretation of his private language argument must be to look more closely into a question that has already been introduced: 'Granted that it is a self-contained *reductio*, what exactly are its premises?' Several commentators take the view that its most important premiss is the verification principle.[26] Why else would Wittgenstein argue that a speaker of a private sensation-language would lack the distinction between 'It seems S' and 'It is S'? Now classical phenomenalists would retort that it just is not true that the speaker of a private sensation-language would lack this distinction: according to them, he would have a perfectly good basis for it within his private world.[27] But that is not the objection made by those who claim that his

---

[25] See A. Donagan: 'Wittgenstein on Sensation', in *Wittgenstein: The Philosophical Investigations*, ed. G. Pitcher, Doubleday, 1966, p. 340.

[26] e.g. J. J. Thomson: 'Private Languages', in *American Philosophical Quarterly*, Vol. 1 No. 1, Jan. 1964, pp. 20–31.

[27] See below, Ch. 15, for a discussion of this very natural objection.

argument depends on the verification principle. They are trying to undercut the argument between Wittgenstein and classical pheno-menalists by questioning the need for any criterion for distinguishing 'seems' from 'is'. Their objection is that he sees a need for such a criterion only because he makes the dubious assumption that, without it, the speaker of the language would not be able to understand the suggestion that he might feel that he was applying the word 'S' to the sensation correctly when, in fact, he was applying it incorrectly, because he would have no way of verifying it. They ask why he would need a method of verifying this suggestion. Wouldn't his pronounce-ments be incorrigible after he had set up the language? So earlier, while he was engaged in setting it up, wouldn't he just edge his way forwards into the position of arbiter in his own case?

But it is not possible to neutralize Wittgenstein's argument so easily. His response would be that he was not arguing that the speaker would need the criterion in order to understand the possibility that he might be applying 'S' incorrectly when he thought that he was applying it correctly, but, rather, that he would need it in order to check his applications of the word for correctness, especially when he was first learning how to use it. It is, of course, true that people can claim incorrigibility for their applications of the word 'pain' to their own sensations. But there are two different stages in a speaker's career at which his self-ascriptions of pain might be assessed for incorrigibility. After he has attained proficiency in the use of the word, it is, perhaps, impossible for him to make a mistake,[28] but it is obviously possible for him to make one while he is still learning to use it. If he had not been in a position to claim independently verified successes while he was learning to use it, what would his later reports—his postgraduate performances—be about? The objector cannot possibly backdate the incorrigibility to the pupil's first tentative efforts. Even if the method of teaching were merely to get a child to substitute the word 'pain' for his natural reactions,[29] it would still be possible for him to make mistakes

---

[28] See *PI* I § 288: '. . . I can't be in error here'. This is true of pain, which is the example used in this passage, but its extension to all other types of bodily sensation is questionable. See Vol. I p. 58, and see below, pp. 359–60. However, although Wittgenstein may sometimes go too far in this matter, that does not weaken his reply to the objection. His reply is, in effect, that, even if the speaker does finally achieve incorrigibility, his early efforts are certainly not incorrigible, and when he is learning how to use the word 'pain', he must have some way of correcting any early mistakes that he may make.

[29] See above, p. 261, and Vol. I pp. 57–8.

when he first started to practise these substitutions. If it seems impossible to us, that is only because we suppose that, if he did make a mistake at that stage, it would be just as surprising as a mistake made by people like ourselves, already proficient in the use of the word. But that is a confusion of two different stages in the speaker's career.

What has to be explained is how the learner ever manages to start to make any progress. The critic of Wittgenstein's argument suggests that in the early stages he 'just edges his way forward into the position of arbiter in his own case'. But how is he supposed to do that, if he has no way of telling whether he is really progressing or only seeming to do so? There must be a discoverable difference at this stage between his merely feeling that he has got it right this time and his actually getting it right. Learning is possible only if there is a standard of success which the pupil can apply to what he does in order to improve his performance. In real life a learner progresses by recognizing his mistakes and avoiding them next time. If he lacked any criteria of objective error, any progress that he made would not be attributable to learning but to a miracle.

Wittgenstein's idea is that the language for reporting bodily sensations does not make its own origins immediately clear. After it has been mastered, it operates with an independence from the external world that appears to be complete, and it strikes us as the paradigm of an internalized sector of language. That is not a mistaken impression, but the trouble is that it so easily leads to the illusion of the solipsist or the classical phenomenalist, that even in its early stages the language had the same independence from the external world. The truth is that this impressively independent linguistic competence can be achieved only by someone who starts by exploiting the connections between sensations and the external world. It is a language with an internal field of application but though it is not learned at the interface between body and external world, it does owe its development to something that happens there.

When Wittgenstein's position is set out like this, it can be seen to survive the objection that it relies on the questionable assumption that meaning extends no further than actual verifiability. He is not relying on the verificationist theory of meaning at this point and, as far as the needs of this argument are concerned, he could allow that our understanding of factual sentences is not restricted to what we can verify. That would still permit him to make his point that inaccessible facts are no good to anyone trying to acquire a skill. This is obvious in the case of marksmanship, but it needs to be emphasized in the case of language, because we tend to see our earlier learning from the point of view of our later proficiency as speakers and so to discount the indispensable physical setting of the original lesson. The remedy is to remind ourselves that we cannot even try to acquire a skill without a usable criterion of successful performance.

It is important to appreciate the role of incorrigibility in this argument of Wittgenstein's. There are two distinct points at which it comes in. First, there are certain cases in which proficiency in the use of a sensation-word makes it impossible for a person to apply it mistakenly to one of his own sensations.[30] This is one of the many peculiarities of pain, and cases of this kind tend to produce an effect which has already been described: they give the solipsist or classical phenomenalist the illusion that, because reports of such sensations on the lips of a good pupil finally achieve incorrigibility, they must, therefore, always have been independent of anything physical which might show an observer that the pupil had not yet learned the correct use of the word. This illusion is one of Wittgenstein's main targets and, as usual, his treatment of it is designed to make us feel its persuasiveness before he eradicates it.

It is instructive to look at the similarities and differences between the introduction of the word 'I' on the personal line and the introduction of a word like 'pain' on its type-line. The use of the word 'I' has to be learned, but if there is any difficulty in the lesson, it will not be the difficulty of remembering to whom it should be applied— still less, of recognizing that person—but, if anything, some hesitation about the production of the right word. Consequently, at a very early stage a mistaken insertion of the word 'I' in the sentential function '*x* is in pain' is extremely unlikely. It could only occur as a momentary mistake, perhaps in a crisis, and it would never lead to the judgement that the sufferer did not know who the sufferer was. But if the effect of introducing the word 'pain' on its type-line in the way described by Wittgenstein really is incorrigibility, it will still not be quite the same as the effect of introducing the word 'I' on the personal line. For it is not generally true that proficiency in the use of words for sensation-types rapidly, or even in the end always, produces incorrigibility. In this matter, as in several others, pain is a special case.[31]

Anyway, the first role of incorrigibility in this argument of

---

[30] But of course he could lie. See *NLPESD* pp. 293–6.
[31] See Vol. I p. 58.

Wittgenstein's is its contribution to his diagnosis of his adversaries' errors. Impressed by the independence of a report of pain on the lips of someone who has achieved proficiency in the use of the word, they forget the way in which the lesson had to be learned. They then generalize across the board and claim that a complete sensation-vocabulary could be set up without any recourse to the external world.

The second role of incorrigibility is its contribution to the development of Wittgenstein's own ideas rather than to his diagnosis of his adversaries' errors. It is not easy to gauge this positive contribution and it is best to start with the question, whether first-person reports of all sensation-types achieve incorrigibility, and, if not, how we are to explain the line dividing cases in which incorrigibility is achieved from cases in which it is not achieved. This inquiry need not be restricted to sensation-types, because it would also be possible to ask how widely the phenomenon of incorrigibility extends into other areas.

Full answers to these questions are beyond the scope of this book. They would require it to range across the whole of Wittgenstein's philosophy of mind and to pay particular attention to cases which do not even look like examples of infallible description. When someone announces a decision, he does not first have to focus on to an isolated object which has just made its appearance in his mind and try to get its description right. The announcement is itself part of what introspectionists treated as the performance that had to be accurately described, and this makes it impossible, but at the same time unnecessary, for the announcement to play any descriptive role. In fact, in quick, unreflective cases, it is often the only isolatable element and so it can actually be identified with the deciding, provided that its immediate context in the mental history of the subject is appropriate.[32] Wittgenstein's ideas are close to J. L. Austin's at this point. For Austin too saw the importance of cases where something which looks like a description is really a performance describable by other people, but neither containing, nor itself requiring, any description from the performer himself, and in such cases he too saw the need for the right background and context.[33]

[32] In *PI* I § 304 Wittgenstein attacks the 'idea that language always functions in one way, always serves the same purpose: to convey thoughts—which may be about houses, pains, good and evil or anything else you please'. The passage is quoted in full below, p. 351.

[33] See J. L. Austin: *Philosophical Papers*, Oxford, 1961, Ch. 10.

But to what extent did Wittgenstein take this new model to be applicable to sentences about sensations? If it could be extended into that field without any modification, the result would be fairly spectacular. The incorrigibility of 'It hurts' would no longer be attributable to the extreme simplicity of the descriptive task carried out by the speaker. His utterance would appear as part of the spontaneous line of behaviour that partly constitutes being in pain.

However, this is not a result to be generalized unguardedly. The application of the model to sensations is most appropriate in cases like pain, where there is a clearly marked line of spontaneous behaviour. In such cases the speaker sends his words down a parallel line and gives expression to what he feels rather than describing it.[34] But those cases shade off into others where the classification of sensation-types is more elaborate and artificial. When a patient gives his doctor a precise description of an internal pain, the appropriateness of the model is obviously less complete. When we move across the spectrum, leaving behind cases of automatic expression and taking examples which require the subject to make more of an intellectual effort to get his words right,[35] there is no longer the same reason to credit his utterances with incorrigibility. So it seems that there are two distinct factors that tend to produce incorrigibility in this area. One is the simplicity of the descriptive task, and the other, which is arguably more

[34] Wittgenstein sometimes seems to rest too much weight on the concept of expression, but, as usual, it is the fact underlying the difference between expressing and describing that is important. The fact is that in cases where a word replaces the natural expression of a sensation, the use of the word is not a purely intellectual reaction to the sensation. The sensation, considered as a natural phenomenon, has already made the first move towards its own publication in words. It is hardly necessary to add that an external phenomenon could never achieve this result, because it would not lie on any neural circuit in the speaker's system. So if a journalist had to describe the eruption of a volcano, that would be a purely intellectual task. What interests Wittgenstein in the cases where the phenomenon is one's own sensation is the natural blurring of the line between speech and what is spoken about. It is at this point that the differences between his ideas and Austin's become apparent. When someone uses a performative expression, like 'I promise', Austin's point is that he does not speak about anything, but in this case the effect is achieved not by nature but by artifice. The overlap between the two philosophers' ideas is apparent in the intermediate case of a person announcing a decision.

[35] Many of Wittgenstein's examples of inner states that can be described instead of being expressed are emotions rather than sensations. See *PI* II pp. 188–9 and *Remarks on the Philosophy of Psychology*, Vol. II, ed. G. H. von Wright and Heikki Nyman, tr. C. G. Luckhardt and M. A. E. Aue, Blackwell, 1980 (henceforth *RPPII*), §§ 722–35. However, in *Zettel*, § 482 he does allow that pain can be described spatially and temporally.

important, is amenability to the new treatment derived from an entirely different model.

If we find this new treatment difficult to accept at first, that is probably because we are so inveterately attached to the simple idea that there are two worlds, the linguistic and the non-linguistic, set over against one another, and that our task as truth-seekers is the purely intellectual one of making the former match the latter. But when people succeed in understanding the new treatment, they often switch like solenoids to accepting it as the complete truth about all sensation-statements.[36] They then find it mysterious that Wittgenstein should allow that inner states can ever be described. Is he not betraying his own cause? But there never was any reason to suppose that he was promoting a universal account, applicable to all sentences about inner states.

Even at the near end of the spectrum, among cases of automatic expression, to which the new model is most appropriate, it is important not to forget its limitations. After all, the spontaneous cry 'It hurts', is a reaction to sensory input, and this simple fact is enough to show that being in pain cannot be entirely reduced to a line of expressive behaviour. Really, this is not something that needs to be shown, because it is so obvious that an account of pain and its language must avoid any accidental implication of anaesthesia.[37] It is here that Wittgenstein's proviso, that the immediate context must be right, makes an essential contribution to his account. He is not trying to eliminate what lies in the middle of the type-line, but to make us realize that it is not another section of the line, but a point which spectators can approach asymptotically from either end of it. We should think of the sufferer's feeling as another line cutting it at right angles and we should think of his pain as the point of intersection with no magnitude. There would then be no section of the type-line that was inaccessible to us, and we would be able to see that, as we approached the central point, we could pick sections of it which, given that everything else was in order, would be sure signs of pain. What we cannot do is to get on to the suffer's personal line, but we must not think that this involves an exclusion from yet another section of the type-line of pain, like all the other sections except in this one baffling respect—it is inaccessible to us.

---

[36] See above, p. 298, for another case of this pattern of resistance to Wittgenstein's philosophy followed by over-enthusiastic acceptance.

[37] This is how the interlocutor interprets Wittgenstein's remarks in *PI* I § 304.

Naturally, the proviso, that everything else is in order, neither includes, nor is tantamount to the stipulation, that the person really is in pain. It would obviously trivialize the analysis to include it, and it is equally necessary to avoid implying that our observations actually add up the the central fact about him.[38] What the proviso excludes is exceptional circumstances on sections of the type-line which happen to be unexplored by us, but which might have shown us that he was not in pain after all. If it is objected that even if all such matters are in order, he still may not be in pain, because no possible observations on our part will ever add up to pain on his part, Wittgenstein would remind us of a crucial distinction: instead of saying that, in spite of everything, he may not be in pain, we ought to be prepared to say something quite different, because this may be a limiting case in which the conditions required for playing this particular language-game are no longer satisifed. If, as we suppose, the type-line of pain really is disrupted in this apparent sufferer, his case will not be one of a person possibly not being in pain, but one in which it is possible that the question cannot be asked because the presuppositions of the language-game may have failed.[39] If it is difficult to witness one's own funeral, it is equally difficult for a language-game to tell the story of its own demise, but that does not mean that the story could not be told in other words.[40]

People who study this part of Wittgenstein's philosophy often find it hard to extract a better understanding of sensation-language from his ideas without being led into enthusiastic absurdities. It is sometimes necessary to pinch oneself and reflect on the obvious difference between a case of input, like feeling a sensation, and a case of output, like making a decision or acting. Whatever the limitations of the old model—the isolated object of introspection and description—its appropriateness to sensations must be greater than its appropriateness to decisions. The difference shows up clearly when we ask whether the problematical thing—the felt sensation or the decision as it is made— can actually be identified with something accessible to others. In the

[38] That would be behaviourism.

[39] The breakdown of this part of the language-game is parallel to the breakdown of the other part—ascription of sensations to owners—which would be produced by disruption of the personal line. See above, pp. 252–61. Naturally, we must not jump to the conclusion that there has been a breakdown, but if we do draw a conclusion, that is what it should be. See *Zettel*, §§ 543 and 555.

[40] See above, pp. 254–7, for a discussion of this point and its connection with the early doctrine of showing.

output case there is often something with which the decision can be identified, and Wittgenstein's proviso gives the conditions under which the identity holds, but the actual sensation, as it is felt in the input case, cannot be dragged out into the open in the same way.

These issues are relevant to the interpretation of the private language argument. For we need to see not only how Wittgenstein sets up the thesis that he charges with absurdity, but also which philosophical theories about sensation-language commit their supporters to that thesis. It is one thing to give an abstract account of an intellectual malady, and quite another thing to give instructions which will put people in a position to diagnose it in the field. So any interpretation of the private language argument will remain incomplete until it has told us exactly what indicates commitment to the unacceptable theory. The abstract reductive argument needs to be connected with actual examples of philosophical theorizing.

There are three main questions in this area. First, how can we tell when sensations or their properties really have been given a philosophical treatment which makes them idle cogs to be spun capriciously without producing any detectable change in anything else? Second, does any philosopher who rejects the thesis, that all first-person sensation-reports are incorrigible, thereby commit himself to a reification of sensations and their properties which would make them, if Wittgenstein is right, free-wheeling extras. Third, is the scope of his incorrigibility thesis really restricted in the way that was suggested above, or does the incorrigibility of all first-person reports of sensations simply follow from the conclusion of the private language argument?

At first sight, it looks easy enough to give Wittgenstein's method of testing a philosophical theory about sensations and their properties for the free-wheeling detachment that he is out to diagnose. The test gives a positive result for any theory that treats them as 'private'. But what does that word mean here? His adversaries take it to mean 'something which only I can feel', like pain, and they protest that it must be a mistake to try to get rid of such things. But that does not exhaust what he means by the word 'private'. He uses it with the extra implication that what I feel has intrinsic properties which cannot be captured by any physical criteria. All that he is trying to get rid of is pain construed as something completely detached from all physical criteria. If the private language argument is valid, we could not possibly speak about any such thing, and 'what we cannot speak about we must pass over in silence'.[41] How could it possibly be what is discussed in casualty-clearing stations and hospitals?

It is only too easy for his adversaries to misunderstand his strategy at this point and take him to be a behaviourist trying to eliminate pain as it is felt:

> 'But you will surely admit that there is a difference between pain-behaviour accompanied by pain and pain-behaviour without any pain?'—Admit it? What greater difference could there be?—'And yet you again and again reach the conclusion that the sensation itself is a *nothing*'.—Not at all. It is not a *something*, but not a *nothing* either! The conclusion was only that a nothing would serve just as well as a something about which nothing could be said. We have only rejected the grammar which tries to force itself on us here.
>
> The paradox disappears only if we make a radical break with the idea that language always functions in one way, always serves the same purpose: to convey thoughts—which may be about houses, pains, good and evil, or anything else you please.[42]

The placing of this remark indicates that it is part of the private language argument. What it offers is a careful restatement of the argument's conclusion. It 'was only that a nothing would do just as well as a something about which nothing could be said'. He diagnoses the same absence of any contribution and the same free-wheeling detachment in the inner objects that are sometimes invoked to explain seeing aspects:

> (The temptation to say 'I see it like *this*', pointing to the same thing for 'it' and 'this'.)[43] Always get rid of the private object in this way: assume that it constantly changes, but that you do not notice the change, because your memory constantly deceives you.[44]

The idea is not that the familiar 'intrinsic' character of a sensation-type like pain cannot be captured by language. It has already been captured in a subtle way which Wittgenstein is trying to describe sympathetically, at length, and in all its complexity. Indeed, it may well be that the effect of his description ought to be the abandonment of the distinction between 'intrinsic' and 'extrinsic'. However, his adversaries' reaction is more straightforward: they ignore what has actually been caught by

---

[41] *TLP* 7. [42] *PI* I § 304.

[43] This is the way in which the point was put in *BRBK* pp. 174–5. See above, pp. 231–2. This way of putting it highlights a feature of the structure of the private language argument which was mentioned in Vol. I pp. 58–60, and which will be discussed in Ch. 15.

[44] *PI* II p. 207.

language in this complex way, because they think that it must be 'extrinsic', and they then demand something more, which, they insist, really will be 'intrinsic' and so can only be captured by language in an extremely simple way, like the beetle in the box. But then this further element remains forever disengaged.

His argument in this passage may seem to be too swiftly dismissive, but it has an interesting structure which is often exemplified in his later writings: his adversaries propose something which he sees as absurd, but not obviously so—a sensation-language completely detached from the physical world. It takes the whole private language argument to show up the absurdity, and so, as a quick alternative, he suggests that they move further out on the same line and try thinking of a sensation-language which is not even connected by uncheckable memory with the intrinsic characters of the sensations reported in it. As he says elsewhere, the method is to get people to see the absurdity of a piece of unobvious nonsense by pushing the same idea over the edge into patent nonsense.[45]

It was pointed out in Volume I that, when he is describing the subtle way in which sensation-types are captured by language in real life, he is walking a narrow path between two impossible theories, behaviourism and the theory of the detached inner object of introspection.[46] He must not only walk this path but also be seen to walk it, and that too is difficult, because his debate with his adversaries is bedevilled by a misunderstanding. It is as if they do not even see the narrow ridge, but only the abysses on each side of it. So when he carefully avoids one of the two absurd theories, it seems to them that he must be adopting the other one. They draw this conclusion, because there is no discernible third theory. What they overlook is that he is not professing to offer a third theory, but only a long and careful description of the way in which we set up and maintain sensation-language in real life.[47] They succeed in understanding what he is denying only by misunderstanding what he is asserting.

Their bafflement is produced in a way that is easy to grasp but not so easy to hold on to. They start from an assumption which he rejects, but which we, who follow this controversy, find it only too easy to mistake for common ground. They assume that there must be a third theory of sensation-language which draws the line between the inner and the outer in a way that succeeds in avoiding the objections to the two

---

[45] See *PI* I § 464.
[46] See Vol. I pp. 44–5.   [47] See Ch. 9.

opposed theories. But his view here, as elsewhere, is that this kind of
theorizing can never lead to philosophical understanding. The reason
why I cannot feel other people's pains is not that there is a section of
their type-lines from which I am excluded.[48] So he flatly refuses to
accept his adversaries' picture as the right framework for the
discussion. It is, according to him, not true that if we separated inner
from outer more carefully and more faithfully to the phenomena, we
would get rid of our doubts about successful intercommunication in
sensation-language. In any case, a quasi-scientific description of two
different kinds of object is not what is needed. What is needed is a full
description of the actual working of the language which will allow us to
see beyond the distinction between the inner and the outer:

. . . 'But do you assume that it [sc. the child who has told a lie] has only the
facial expression of shame, e.g. without the feeling of shame? Mustn't you
describe the inside situation as well as the outside one?'—But what if I said that
by 'facial expression of shame' I meant what you mean by 'the facial
expression + the feeling', unless I explicitly distinguish between genuine and
simulated facial expressions? It is, I think, misleading to describe the genuine
expression as a *sum* of the expression and something else, though it is just as
misleading—we get the function of our expressions wrong—if we say that the
genuine expression is a particular behaviour and nothing besides.

But couldn't one say that if I speak of a man's angry voice, meaning that he
was angry, and again of his angry voice, not meaning that he was angry, in the
first case the meaning of the description of his voice was much further-
reaching than in the second case? I will admit that our description in the first
case doesn't *omit* anything and is as complete as though we had said that he
was really angry—but somehow the meaning of the expression reaches below
the surface.

But how does it do that? The answer to this would be an explanation of the
two uses of the expression. But how could this explanation reach *under the
surface*? It is an explanation about symbols and it states in which cases these
symbols are used. But how does it characterize these cases? Can it in the end
do more than distinguish two expressions? i.e. describe a game with two
expressions?

'Then is there nothing under the surface?!' But I said that I was going to
distinguish two expressions, one for the 'surface' and one for 'what is below
the surface'—only remember that these expressions themselves correspond
just to a *picture*, not to its usage. It is just as misleading to say that there is just
the surface and nothing underneath it, as that there is something below the
surface and that there isn't just the surface. Because once we make use of the

[48] See above, p. 348.

picture of the 'surface', it is most natural to express with it the distinction as on and below the surface. But we misapply the picture if we ask whether both cases are or aren't on the surface.[49]

It is natural to think of a person's behaviour and speech as lifeless products, lying on the surface and waiting to be given a special philosophical description with the power to reach deep into his soul. We forget that the ordinary description of his behaviour and speech already does just that. Impressed by the idea that we ought to do better, we produce the picture which seems to us to succeed in meeting our imagined need. But there is something very wrong with this fugue of ideas. If the picture really did do better, it would remain forever unattached, because all the available attachments have already been pre-empted by the ordinary description. That description has not only done its best: it has done the best that anything could possibly do with the available material. No picture can succeed in doing any better than the language-game which it is supposed to illustrate, because, if the language-game is not already understood by us, we shall not get any help from a picture which derives all its real content from the same familiar sources as the language-game. Finally, it will only make things worse if, when we discover that we are not making any progress, we start tinkering with the details of the picture and attempt to draw a more accurate line between the inner and the outer. We must try to understand our philosophical predicament: the picture cannot add a new dimension to a language-game which already deals with all the material in its own unimprovable way.

It is this misunderstanding that generates the idea of the 'private object' in Wittgenstein's pejorative sense of the phrase. Such objects would be completely detached from the physical world, so that only I could speak about mine, if, contrary to the private language argument, anyone could speak about them. On the other side, his adversaries are likely to protest that they cannot see anything wrong with private objects. Certainly, there is nothing wrong with the claim that sensations are unsharable. That is just their logic. He, of course, would agree with that,[50] but he would ask them whether they think that on the private stage of the mind our references to sensations and their properties are just like our references to physical objects and their properties in the external world. The point of the question is that physical objects stand out from their background and endure, and that is why we are able to set up a descriptive language by isolating them

[49] *NLPESD* pp. 302–4.   [50] See *PR* §§ 60–1, discussed above, pp. 252–3.

and sorting them into types. Do they or don't they think that this is how it is with sensations?

It is obvious that solipsists and classical phenomenalists do think that this is how it is with sensations. But many people will want to compromise at this point. After all, it does not seem to be a necessary part of the meaning of the word 'private' that sensations should be quite so like physical objects. Why be so literal-minded? Why not treat it as a metaphor which gives an apt, if rather vague picture of each person's relation to his own sensations. So the controversy slides back and forth over the shifting use of its central phrase.

Fortunately, this is easily fixed. One remedy is to look again at a text in which he makes his point most concisely:

> 'But it seems as if you were neglecting something.' But what more can I do than *distinguish* the case of saying 'I have toothache' when I really have toothache, and the case of saying the words without having toothache? I am also (further) ready to talk of any *x* behind my words so long as it keeps its identity.
>
> Isn't what you reproach me of as though you said: 'In your language you are only *speaking*!'?[51]

Language cannot very well ingest its subject-matter, but that is a message that is really too telegraphic. What is needed is an investigation of the philosophical development of the word 'private' which will show how far its application to perceptual input is legitimate, at what points it begins to be illegitimate, and why the limit of its legitimate application runs through those points.

It has already been explained that there is nothing wrong with calling sensations 'private' provided that it only means that they are unsharable. It is a plain necessary truth that only I can feel mine. There are, however, two distinct, but connected, ways of developing the philosophical use of the word 'private' beyond this uncontroversial point. One line of thought would be that I can make discriminating references to the individual sensations that I have without relying in any way on my body at any time—not even when I was learning this language-game. The argument which in Chapter 11 was called 'the first private language argument' shows that, if this is the implication of the word 'private', it is illegitimate to apply it to sensations. The other line of thought is that I can make discriminating references to the different sensation-types that I experience without relying in any way on my body or its physical environment. The private language

[51] *NLPESD* p. 297.

argument of *Philosophical Investigations* shows that it is illegitimate to apply the word 'private' to sensations, if this is its implication.

Not surprisingly, some of Wittgenstein's criticisms of these two transgressions make an impact on both of them. For example, it is not even quite right to call the unsharability of sensations 'privacy', because that dramatizes the owner's exclusive privilege in a way that is already inappropriate. If I have a pain, I am not in the position of a collector who has a picture locked in a strong-room where only he can see it. That would be a kind of necessary privacy, but the necessity is too weak for it to serve as a model for my relations with my own sensations.[52]

So much is obvious, but it needs to be emphasized that it is not just bad luck that frustrates the search for a physical analogy which will be perfectly appropriate to my logically exclusive privilege. The word 'private' suggests that there ought to be some such analogy, if only we could think of it, but in fact there could not possibly be any such thing. One way of appreciating the necessary failure of the search for it is to go back to a thesis put forward in the *Tractatus*: when something is only physically impossible, you can identify the unsuccessful candidate for physical possibility, but when something is logically impossible the unsuccessful candidate cannot be identified.[53] It follows that the search for a physical analogue for my logically exclusive privilege is bound to fail. So here is one suggestion implicit in the thesis that sensations are 'private' which must be eradicated. It was argued above that nothing is achieved by shifting the line dividing the inner from the outer, but it now appears that we do not even start with a field of what may properly be called 'objects' waiting to be divided into two sets.

There is another way of appreciating why physical analogies necessarily make a poor showing when they are used to illustrate the exclusiveness of my relation to my own sensations. Physical objects endure and their identity-lines do not start when they are first owned, if indeed they are owned, so I can speculate that my car might have belonged to someone else. But the criteria of identity of sensations do not allow me to speculate that one had by me might have been had by someone else instead. For the identity-line of a sensation begins when it is had by a particular person and the speculation would make sense only if it began before it was had.[54]

---

[52] See *PI* I § 293 on the beetle in the box. Cf. the discussion of the filling of the sandwich in Vol. I pp. 45–7.

[53] See above, pp. 215–16, and Vol. I p. 172.　　　　　[54] See above, pp. 265–6.

These deficiencies in the analogy between the private ownership of sensations and the private ownership of physical objects put heavy constraints on both the developments of the philosophical use of the word 'private'. The last deficiency is particularly interesting, because it suggests a question about the criteria of identity of sensation-types: 'Is it possible that the "intrinsic" property of the sensations which I, relying on their effects, have learned to call "sensations of giddiness", might have been different from what it actually is in my case?'[55] If this is not possible, at least the reason for its impossibility cannot be quite the same as the reason why a particular sensation of mine could not have been had by someone else instead. For sensation-types are not unsharable and their identity-lines do not begin when a particular person experiences them. Which person would it be?

There is also another question about sensation-types that might be asked at this point. Suppose that the speculation about giddiness that has just been put forward is empty—would it be equally empty to speculate that the 'intrinsic' property of the sensations which I have learned to call 'sensations of giddiness' might change in my case over the course of time? It is obvious and important that, if this second speculation about the 'intrinsic' property of giddiness is empty, its emptiness cannot be explained in the same way as the emptiness of the first one.[56]

The next step out along this line would be to maintain that properties of sensations, like giddiness, are 'intrinsic' in the stronger sense that they are completely detached from anything in the physical world. This is the main target of the private language argument of *Philosophical Investigations*, which denies that a person who tried to set up a vocabulary for describing his sensations in complete detachment from the external world, would find that he was related to their properties in anything like the way in which he was related to the properties of physical objects. The idea is that his mind can get a purchase on physical properties independently of their background, but it cannot get any purchase on the properties of sensations when they are completely detached from the external world. To put the point in another way, physical objects supply us with constancies against which we can push when we are acquiring proficiency with a

---

[55] The question will be discussed in Ch. 15.
[56] This question too will be discussed in Ch. 15.

vocabulary for describing them, but detached sensations do no such thing.[57]

The point has already been made, that it is a mistake to look for a positive theory of sensation-language in *Philosophical Investigations*. Wittgenstein's reductive argument clears the ground not for another theory, but for an accurate description of the phenomena. True, he does offer a new model, but he does not intend it to have a universal application. This is not a field for the kind of pitched battle that has been fought over the private language argument. However, in spite of its lack of universality, the new model does have conspicuous merits. It does succeed in connecting our sensation-language, which is by now quite a sophisticated affair, with its original pre-linguistic foundations. It thereby opens up a new way of dealing with scepticism about other minds. It also has another advantage, more general and more important—it allows us to see the whole phenomenon of language in a new way.

We no longer have to see it as a neat, artificial system set over against an indefinitely complicated world, all of which is at first equally opaque. On the contrary, it is itself part of the natural order which it has to sort out and record. This produces two connected consequences, one positive and the other negative. On the positive side, it allows us to construe certain questions about the world as questions, at least in part, about ourselves, and this gives us a head start in our attempts to answer them. *Philosophical Investigations* is a sustained exploitation of this advantage, and so too, in a different way, was Hume's *Treatise of Human Nature*.[58] The other consequence, on the negative side, is that certain restrictions are imposed on the range of possible alterations to the world which would still leave us in a position to play our various language-games. This is an important point, and one that is often made in the course of Wittgenstein's long critique of solipsism and its heirs. The linguistic rules that we follow no longer have the sanctity that realism tried to give them. Logic, according to the old conception of it, dictated to the world from its own independent rostrum, but now that it has been naturalized, its necessities are all conditional and its writ more precarious.[59] However there may be a compensating

---

[57] A classical phenomenalist would not agree with this. His objection will be examined in Ch. 15.

[58] See my 'Hume's Empiricism and Modern Empiricism' in *David Hume*, Macmillan, 1963, and S. A. Kripke: *Wittgenstein on Rules and Private Language*, Basil Blackwell, 1982. Kripke's version of the relationship beween Wittgenstein's naturalism and Hume's will be discussed in Ch. 18.   [59] See Vol. I pp. 27–33.

advantage: perhaps we can now really see some reason for obedience.

The third question raised above can be dealt with more briefly. Did he deduce the incorrigibility of all first-person reports of sensations from the conclusion of the private language argument? This question should be approached without too much expectation of an affirmative answer. Wittgenstein is not a philosopher given to sweeping generalizations, and he usually thinks in curves, leaving it to his commentators to fly off on the tangents. In this particular case, there is a plausible alternative to crediting him with the simple thesis that all first-person reports of sensations are incorrigible: he may have believed that many of them are, and that these examples of incorrigibility have an importance that is more than statistical—they demonstrate the appropriateness of his new model, but without any idea of a total take-over.

The textual evidence for attributing the simple, universal thesis to him is not decisive, because it is not clear how far he intended to generalize his remarks.[60] It is, of couse, always risky to offer universal propositions in philosophy, and he was especially aware of the risk and always on guard against it. However, it is, perhaps, more important to show that at least it is not true that the private language argument rules out corrigible first-person sensation-reports.

This is easily demonstrated. Let Q be a property of sensations and assume that the word for it is learned in a perfectly ordinary way which exploits the physical setting of its occurrence. Suppose now that the word presents a certain difficulty to learners: even after much practice some people still hesitate about its applicability and occasionally change their minds about it. On such occasions there is often circumstantial evidence which makes onlookers judge them right to change their minds, and sometimes the evidence leads the onlookers to conclude that the subjects' reports were mistaken in spite of the fact that they did not subsequently change their minds.[61]

None of this is incompatible with the conclusion of the private language argument. It would be incompatible with it only if the degree of stability that a Q-type sensation required for the subject's self-corrections would necessarily have been sufficient to provide him with

---

[60] See above, p. 343 n. 28.

[61] Even if no type of statement is, as such, incorrigible, it may still be true that for every type of statement there are circumstances in which it is incorrigible. In *On Certainty* Wittgenstein argues that certain statements about the physical world have to be taken as fixed paradigms of truth. The matter will not be pursued here.

a firm basis for his original learning of the meaning of the word without any appeal to physical circumstances. But why should anyone believe that? It is much more likely that Wittgenstein took the new model, which eliminated corrigibility, to be appropriate to no more than a majority of cases, and, what is perhaps more important than its exact scope, that he took those cases to be 'good medicine'. The further question, whether any of the cases that do not fall within its scope exhibit corrigibility, was then left open to investigation.

14
The Disabling Defect of a Private Language

THE private language argument is the centre-piece of *Philosophical Investigations* and there are several aspects of it that still need further scrutiny. Something has been said about its connection with the thesis that sensation-language is grafted on to a pre-linguistic structure of considerable complexity, but that is a topic which deserves to be taken further. Also more needs to be said about its connection with the proof of the incoherence of classical phenomenalism derived from the early thesis about the limit of language. It is notorious that classical phenomenalists reject the private language argument and the question, whether their rejection of it is justifiable, can be answered only after a more thorough examination of the links between Wittgenstein's two arguments. Both these lines of inquiry touch on a difficult issue raised in the previous chapter: granted that the private language argument is a self-contained *reductio*, what exactly are its premises? There is also another, more general point of view from which the structure of the argument can be surveyed. It is evidently a criticism of a theory which collapses together two things which are, and must be, independent of one another, seeming right and being right. But the precise structure of the criticism still remains to be explored, and it merits closer examination, because it is a structure which manifests itself at other points in his philosophy.[1]

However, these rather abstract questions may be deferred to the next chapter, because there is another, more concrete question to be settled first. If sensation-language is completely detached from the physical world, what exactly is the crucial loss which leaves us without a distinction between seeming right and being right? The question was introduced in a general way at the beginning of the previous chapter, but Wittgenstein's answer to it has yet to be identified.

There are two rival views about his answer. According to one, the crucial deficiency is the impossibility of checking one's own judgements

---

[1] See Vol. I pp. 58–60, where this aspect of the private language argument was first introduced.

by asking other people for theirs,[2] while the other claims that it is the impossibility of checking them on standard physical objects which could be assumed to provide the same stimulation on different occasions of perception, and could be used whether or not there were other people around.[3] It was pointed out in the previous chapter that the second deficiency would make the first one inevitable, because the only way to get into a position to seek confirmation from other people is to establish communication with them through the physical world.[4] But the first deficiency would not make the second one inevitable, because it is possible to imagine an intelligent wolf-child exploiting physical objects to set up a language for his own use without the help provided by a typical human family—or rather, to beg no questions, it is possible to think that one can imagine such an achievement.[5]

It is a good idea to begin by placing this question of interpretation on a larger map of Wittgenstein's philosophy. The general drift of his thought is against solipsism, or, to put it in a way that makes his adversary look less *outré*, against solipsism developed as classical phenomenalism or as some other restrictive theory of perception. His strategy is to argue on two fronts, first about the subject, and then about the objects of experience. On each front he uses two distinct arguments, one to show that solipsism is incoherent, and the other to show that, even if it could be set up coherently, there are two essential linguistic devices available in the macrocosm, which the solipsist cannot take with him when he retreats into his microcosm—discriminating references to individuals and to types. So the second argument is developed in two stages: the impossibility of discriminating references to individuals is demonstrated by the first private language argument, while the second private language argument in *Philosophical Investigations* establishes the same conclusion for types. At least, these are Wittgenstein's claims.

There is also another, parallel development in Wittgenstein's later philosophy, which was introduced in Volume I and will be examined in

---

[2] This view is taken by S. A. Kripke, *Wittgenstein on Rules and Private Language*, pp. 3, 79, and 89, and by N. Malcolm, *Nothing is Hidden*, Ch. 9.

[3] This view is taken by P. M. S. Hacker and G. Baker, *Scepticism, Rules and Meaning*, Blackwell, 1984, pp. 1–112, and by C. McGinn, *Wittgenstein on Meaning*, Blackwell, 1984, pp. 1–92.

[4] See above, pp. 334–5.

[5] McGinn seems to succeed in describing such a case, op. cit., pp. 196–7, but Malcolm will not allow that he has succeeded, op. cit., pp. 176–8. The issue is discussed below, pp. 372–86.

the final chapters of this volume. He argued that the meanings of our words are not guaranteed by any independent pattern already existing in the world and waiting for language to be attached to it.[6] On the contrary, the pattern that we see depends on what we do with our words, albeit not entirely arbitrarily, in the world. Either way—whether a fixed pattern is imposed on any language by the world, or we ourselves contribute to forming a more fluid pattern—the attachments of words to things will evidently be indispensable. But can they really be retained in the solipsist's microcosm?

When Wittgenstein argued in the way already described, that discriminating references to individuals and types cannot be successfully transplanted into the microcosm, his conclusion was more far-reaching and destructive than at first sight it appeared to be. The two private language arguments were offered as a demonstration that classical phenomenalists give an unacceptable account of the language in which we report our sensations and identify their owners. But is any language possible in the solipsistic world from which they start? If Wittgenstein is right in his contention, that discriminating references to individuals and types cannot be retained in that world, it seems that no language whatsoever could be spoken in it. For what would guarantee the correctness of any attachments of words to things?

One response to this challenge—and it is an influential one—is Platonism, which postulates fixed rails of correct use, already laid out in advance and somehow serving as a guide for the speakers of a language. Wittgenstein's objection to this theory is that it removes the basis of the distinction between obeying and disobeying a linguistic rule. Speaking a language is a practice and it is an essential feature of any practice that its followers cannot slavishly conform to any fixed paradigm, even a metaphysical one. What they actually do necessarily makes some contribution to determining what counts as what they ought to do.

Nobody would deny that speaking a language is a practice, but the importance of the thesis can be appreciated if we look at the theory of language that is produced by those who ignore it. Platonists, who believe that the meanings of our words are guaranteed by the pre-existing structure of reality, are bound to underestimate the dependence of their meanings on what we do with them. What we do with them will seem to be a consequence of their meanings which will look as if they

[6] See Vol. I pp. 10–12.

are already secured by independent lines to reality.[7] It will then be completely mysterious how the one-off attachment of a word to a thing puts it in a position to pick up all and only the possibilities inherent in the thing.[8] Wittgenstein's later view was that it is really the other way round: meaning is a consequence of our practices, and so the question, whether the solipsist can completely internalize our practices without any loss is one that ought, at least, to be taken seriously.

If this is the right way to look at Wittgenstein's later philosophy, one would not necessarily expect him to choose a precise point on the line of escalating deprivations resulting from the solipsist's retreat into his microcosm, and to claim that it is just here that language becomes impossible. The more dramatic of the two losses is, of course, other people, and it deprives the solipsist of something more widespread and less obtrusive than explicit appeals to them for confirmation. For when we talk to one another, we seldom doubt that we are using our words with the same constant meanings, and the mere fact that we contrive to communicate with one another gives us a reserve of reassurance to settle any doubts that we might feel.[9] We know that the backing is there without having to ask for it because each time two people agree on a simple matter of fact they make a small contribution to it.[10] Explicit appeals for confirmation are, therefore, not common except among learners and teachers, and especially in the early life of a child in a family. It is the tacit reassurance derived by speakers of a language from successful communication with one another that is important. However, even if this much more widespread resource were lost, Wittgenstein might well treat the deprivation as a serious handicap without making it the single decisive turning-point at which language becomes impossible. A crippling handicap is no less real than an immobilizing one.

There are several considerations which might reinforce the suspicion that he did not mean to commit himself to the theory of a single decisive loss. One, which was mentioned in the previous

---

[7] See Vol. I pp. 59–60.

[8] This is what the picture theory of sentences had to explain. See Vol. I Ch. 6.

[9] See *Zettel*: §§ 428–32. Cf. L. Wittgenstein: *Remarks on the Foundations of Mathematics*, eds. G. H. von Wright, R. Rhees, and G. E. M. Anscombe, tr. G. E. M. Anscombe, Blackwell, 3rd edn., 1978 (henceforth *RFM*), VI § 39. Constancy of meaning in the later works is not judged by a criterion independent of language, because what counts as constancy is partly dependent on the practice which maintains it. See Ch. 17.

[10] What they are saying on a given occasion is shown by their practice, which is partly determined by this particular linguistic episode.

chapter, is that the possibility, that an intelligent wolf-child might set up a minimal language for his own use, may have seemed to him to be too marginal to deserve separate investigation. Now there is a common misunderstanding to be avoided here. If he did think that the possibility was too marginal to merit separate treatment, that would not be because he doubted whether such a creature could manage to produce the appropriate performance without any instruction. There is no reason why he should suppose that a wolf-child would be able to produce the appropriate performance in the wild only if he had already acquired the rudiments of language from his parents before he was adopted by wolves. This is an opinion which is hardly likely to be held by a philosopher who puts so much weight on the pre-linguistic foundations of language.[11] There is also something much more important that is wrong with the attribution of this line of thought to him. Even if he had held that opinion, it would only be a speculative thesis in developmental psychology, and he was surely the last person to draw a philosophical conclusion from a premiss which would be, at best, only contingently true.

His procedure in this kind of inquiry is always quite different. He sets up a case like this as a contrast to the usual situation and asks us what we would say about it. What would we say if we found regular connections between the wolf-child's apparent symbols and his predicaments and actions?[12] Would we call this 'a language' in spite of the fact that it was not being used for intercommunication? Or in spite of the fact that the performer had not learned even its rudiments from any one else? It would be quite extraordinary to find him arguing that it

[11] Malcolm holds this opinion and argues for it in the following way: the wolf-child would need to adopt the plan of setting up signs now to guide himself in the future, and a plan of that complexity could only be formed by a creature already endowed with language (*Nothing is Hidden*, p. 176). But why so? An animal that always used the same track on the journey out would be setting up signs which would guide it on the return journey, without any such plan, and perhaps without even the capacity to make plans. It might even enhance its track through the forest by breaking twigs—still without any plan—in a way that was no help on the way out, but very useful on the way back. Is there anything to stop the development of a system of self-addressed signs out of this kind of pattern of behaviour, given the intelligence of a human child? But this inquiry throws no light on Wittgenstein's argument, because he was only concerned with the classification of logically possible performances. Would we, or would we not, count them as speaking a language? See above, p. 329.

[12] There is a good example of this procedure in *PI* I § 207, where he discusses the question whether a tribe, rather than a solitary human being, would be said to be speaking a language in a problematical case which he has described, and *not* the question whether the situation, as described, is a possible one.

would be psychologically impossible for the wolf-child to achieve a level of performance that would meet our criteria for speaking a language, and then using this scientific conclusion as one of the premisses of his philosophical criticism of solipsism. How could a philosopher who was so careful to preserve the purity of his method make such a compromising mistake?[13]

The sense in which the case of the wolf-child is marginal is different. It is not that it is a case in which it is doubtful whether the performance could be achieved, but, rather, that it is a borderline case for anyone who asks himself whether it satisfies the criteria for 'speaking a language'. The trouble is that it is not clear whether the way in which the child acquired the capacity to perform as we suppose ourselves to have observed him perform in the field ought to affect our answer to the question whether we would call his performance 'speaking a language'. This is a new problem and an entirely different source of doubt: the wolf-child's performance is appropriate and he relies on one of the two tests of its correctness—calibration on standard objects—but is that enough to make us call what he is doing 'speaking a language'? Is it not, perhaps, also necessary that the whole 'game' should not have been spontaneously generated in solitude?

In the middle 1930s we find Wittgenstein conceding that someone might be born with the capacity to speak a language,[14] and even if he later came to doubt whether the capacity should be described in that way, the capacity itself—to perform in the appropriate way—is obviously a logically possible element in a person's endowment at birth. So this gift could surely be vouchsafed to the child in the wolf-pack on his seventh birthday. Of course, both these cases would be miraculous and the second one would be the more spectacular of the two, but that is not the point. Such 'gifts of tongues' are certainly logically possible, and the question that is being asked is whether we would describe them as cases of 'speaking a language' if we encountered them. When a philosopher thinks up such cases in his study, he is only asking himself whether they would satisfy the criteria for 'speaking a language', and not how they could have come about.

[13] So, as one might expect, his argument in this case is quite different. It is that speaking a language is an acquired skill and an acquired skill requires a usable test of correct performance; therefore an appropriate performance with no such test available is something which we would not call 'speaking a language'.

[14] See *BLBK* pp. 12–14, and *MS* 165, paraphrased by G. P. Baker and P. M. S. Hacker in *Scepticism, Rules and Language*, p. 20 n. 29. The concession will be discussed below, pp. 375–7.

The question, whether the wolf-child could manage to produce the correct performance if he had not already made some progress with language in his human family before being adopted by the wolves, is irrelevant to this kind of inquiry. We simply suppose that he has not had that advantage and yet his performance is correct, and then we ask whether it would count as speaking a language.[15]

However, there is also the other source of doubt introduced above. Is it really so clear that the origin of a capacity which is normally acquired from others is irrelevant to its later classification?[16] It may well be that he had begun to feel less confident about this by the time that he compiled *Philosophical Investigations*. If so, that might explain why the final version says little about ordinary, solitary language-users, and nothing about their original acquisition of the capacity.[17] On the other hand, it does not contain anything that implies that we would actually be wrong to apply the description 'speaking a language' to a performance by an intelligent wolf-child with no previous linguistic training in his own family, and the absence of this implication must be deliberate. If Wittgenstein had come to think that it would definitely be a mistake to describe the imagined case as 'the solitary, unaided invention and use of a language', he would surely have said so. Therefore, his silence on this point gives us a strong reason for not taking his later view to be that, in default of other people, and, therefore, without any opportunity to exploit agreement in judgements, whatever was done could never be described as 'speaking a language'.

When he leaves a question open, it is usually because it lies off the main track of his thinking.[18] In this particular case there is another consideration which helps to explain why he may have taken that view

[15] Or, to put the question in another way, we ask whether anything that went on in his mind would count as thinking in unspoken words.

[16] There are several possible objections to constructing bizzare cases in philosophical thought-experiments. This particular objection is simply that the origin of the case described may be overlooked in spite of its relevance to its classification. H. Putnam makes this point about the classification of diseases by their causes (see 'The Meaning of Meaning' in *Collected Papers*, Vol. 2, Cambridge, 1981). Its relevance to logical atomism was mentioned in Vol. I p. 69. This objection needs to be distinguished from another one which sounds confusingly like it: 'In a sufficiently altered world the concept of *speaking a language* would no longer have any application.' See above, pp. 255–7. There is also a third entirely general objection, which in this area is easily confused with the first two, namely the objection that it is a mistake to draw a firm line between physical and logical possibility.

[17] The only reference to this topic is an oblique one in *PI* I § 243, discussed above, p. 337. See also below, pp. 374–5.

[18] See Vol. I pp. 89 and 120 for other examples of this procedure.

of the matter. It was pointed out above that, when there are other people around, the links between sensation-language and the physical world immediately make both stabilizing resources available—standard objects and reassuring interlocutors.[19] This is our usual, indeed, our almost universal, situation. So why should he think it necessary to investigate the exceptional case of a speaker who has the first of these two resources without the second one? Maybe if he had investigated it, he would have given us a better understanding of the exact effect of each deprivation. However, it was a solipsistic renunciation of the physical world that he was criticizing, and a solipsist is not someone who just happens to find himself on his own. So Wittgenstein may not have seen any real need to tell his story in two chapters, like a German fairy story, in which the hero's predicament gets worse and worse until help arrives.

There is also something else which gives further support to the view that he may not have actually rejected the possibility that certain logically possible case-histories of children brought up in isolation from their species might elicit the verdict that they really would be speaking a language. The point has just been made that the second reassurance—by other people—would not be available without the first one—by physical objects—and that this helps to explain why Wittgenstein did not separate the two deprivations in *Philosophical Investigations* or pronounce on the rare case of the wolf-child. But this line of thought can be taken one stage further: it is not just that both stabilizing resources are available to members of a linguistic community—they actually exploit them simultaneously. For when I check my use of a word by asking another person how he uses it, I am, of course, assuming that his use of it has remained constant, so that I can treat it as a touchstone. But what is the test of the constancy of his use of the word?

The answer to this question must bring in the other resource. The popular answer, which does not mention it, must be treated with great circumspection: 'His use of the word agrees with the use that other members of the linguistic community make of it.' That is certainly correct as far as it goes, but it does not go far enough. For suppose that everybody's use of 'left' and 'right' were switched overnight and they then had to find their way around in their cities with the help of written instructions. All the predictions made before the switch would come

[19] In Wittgenstein's later philosophy a resource which 'stabilizes language' contributes to what counts as the stability that it maintains. See above, p. 364 n. 9 and below, Ch. 17.

out false. For example, it would no longer be true, with the new uses of 'left' and 'right', that turning left here would get you to Trafalgar Square. This is one of those points that loom so large and so close that they are overlooked.[20] The appeal to the community is not final, because factual language, whether spoken by a solitary person or by millions, has to preserve the constancy required if yesterday's predictions are to come true today. The individual gets confirmation of the constancy of his own usage from the community only on the assumption that the community's usage has itself remained constant.

One way of making this point is to show that there are purely aesthetic features of our use of language which might dominate our choice of words nowadays, but not in fifty years' time after a change of taste. For example, Humpback Whales always sing the same song in any given year when they congregate around Hawaii, but each year the song is different. Dictionary-writers are aware that something not entirely unlike this happens to the meanings of descriptive words over the centuries. But there is a crucial difference between factual language and artistic improvisation. Factual language is answerable to the world, and a statement about the way things go in the world, if it was made two centuries ago in English words with different meanings, must be translated before it can be understood and tested for truth today. There is a requirement of constancy in this case which is independent of the vagaries of taste.

It follows that, when an individual checks his own use of a word against the community's use of it, he is really exploiting both the stabilizing resources simultaneously. On the surface, he is appealing to 'agreement in judgements',[21] but underneath he is assuming the constancy of the community's use. True, the assumption is a latent one, because it is so very unlikely that there would be a communal, but coincidental overnight shift in the use of a word like the kind of shift that actually does occur co-operatively, and, therefore, explicably, over the centuries, and, anyway, most of the information on which we rely for guidance is expressed in contemporary language. This is, no doubt, the origin of the popular illusion that the verdict given by the community today is final. We see the importance of the stabilizing effect of the continuing success of our communications with one another, but we overlook the fact that both the uniform language of our contemporaries and our changing language stretched out over time are

[20] See Vol. I p. 18.
[21] Wittgenstein's phrase. See *PI* I § 242, quoted and discussed below, pp. 382–5.

subject to the same constraint as the idiosyncratic language of the wolf-child—they must yield true predictions.

There is another way of making this important point. It is true that a communal overnight shift in the use of descriptive words is enormously improbable. But it is also true that even in my own case, taken in isolation, an overnight shift in my use of descriptive words is very unlikely. Consequently, it would not occur to me that the constancy of my use of them in a locked diary needed any authentication. However, if this question of constancy were forced on me in philosophical discussion, part of my answer to it would be that the constancy of my usage would be authenticated by the verification of my unpublished predictions. Although no single language-user invented language, there is, as it were, a wolf-child inside each of us trying to get out and appeal to the community, but not entirely bereft of resources if it can not do so.

The community of my contemporaries is in an analogous position, but without any possibility of further appeal to people because it already contains all the living speakers of the language. It is, therefore, forced to rely on the sole resource available to the wolf-child—the verification of untranslated predictions. We must not treat the contemporary community as infallible simply because of the enormous improbability of coincidentally identical overnight slippages in its uses of descriptive words. It really is logically possible that a community of language-users should be caught out in the same way as a wolf-child whose shifting use of his symbols for colours tricked him into eating poisonous fruit. Agreement in factual judgements is not like whistling the same tune. An improvised tune is responsible to nothing outside itself, but factual judgements have to be true of the world.

There is another way of dramatizing this difference: we can imagine that agreement in factual judgements might have been achieved by pure coincidence—one person makes what is, for us, a factual judgement, and all the others just happen to vocalize in the same way. In that case the world would not come into it, and the judgements would not really be factual. It would not even be an ordinary case of shared taste, because these people would not influence one another. But what Wittgenstein meant was that people agree because they react to objects independently, but in the same way, and that this, in its turn, is because each of them remembers what he has previously learned and because all their lessons are part of the same tradition. The stability of the tradition itself cannot be assessed by its agreement with anything else, but only by its persistently high score of true predictions. We discover the regularities in nature's behaviour only by first establishing regularities in our own behaviour.

If this is right, it lends further support to the suggestion that in *Philosophical Investigations* Wittgenstein did not think that he needed to tackle the question whether anything that it was logically possible for a wolf-child to do in isolation from his species would count as speaking a language. Certainly, it is logically necessary that a skill should be maintained in circumstances that yield a viable test of success and, if it is acquired, the same is true of its acquisition. But in the case of speaking a language, the two resources that yield such a test are almost inextricably bound up together in our daily lives. Moreover, the target of Wittgenstein's criticism was solipsism, which would deprive us of both resources simultaneously. So it is quite plausible to infer that he did not think that he needed to analyse the effect of each of the two deprivations separately. There is also the other factor mentioned above, which may have contributed to the rather impacted structure of this part of *Philosophical Investigations*: he may have come to think that the effect of separating the two resources was not so easy to assess, because the case of the wolf-child lay on a difficult borderline. Was it necessary that language should be learned? If so, is a self-taught person a learner?[22] These are not easy questions to answer.

Before the textual evidence is reviewed, a word of warning is needed about these introductory remarks. They have cut two corners for the sake of brevity. First, they anticipate the topic of rule-following, which will be examined in detail in Chapters 16–18, and what has been said here about the establishment and maintenance of the regular use of a word is only a small excerpt from Wittgenstein's wide-ranging discussion. Much more is needed on the point of insisting that speaking a language is a practice, about the indispensability of the self-imposed regularity of such a practice as a means to discovering regularities in nature, and about the impossibility of establishing and maintaining any self-imposed regularity without a viable test of success. Second, these introductory remarks have taken the peculiar position of sensation-language rather for granted. If Wittgenstein is right, nobody could learn it without at least being sufficiently at home in the physical world to be able to learn the language for describing the objects in his environment. Normally, both languages are learned

---

[22] See below, pp. 375–7 and 380–1.

together, *pari passu*, but if there is a deviation from the normal course of events, it cannot be that sensation-language is learned first. Some details of this unequal partnership have been given in previous chapters, but more needs to be said about it if the precise impact of the private language argument is going to be determined.

The texts show a certain development in Wittgenstein's views between 'Notes for Lectures on "Private Experience" and "Sense-data"' and *Philosophical Investigations*. When he first formulated the private language argument in the notes for his lectures, he mentioned the two resources available to us—standard physical objects and other people—and he described the effect of the loss of both of them, but made no attempt to assess their relative importance by examining the predicament of someone who had lost other people but still had physical objects:

> We learn the word 'red' under particular circumstances. Certain objects are usually red, and keep their colours; most people agree with us in our colour judgements. Suppose all this changes: I see blood unaccountably sometimes one, sometimes another colour, and the people around me make different statements. But couldn't I in all this chaos retain my meaning of 'red', 'blue', etc., although I couldn't now make myself understood to anyone? Samples, e.g., would all constantly change their colour—'or does it only seem so to me?' 'Now am I mad or did I really call this "red" yesterday?'[23]

Nothing is said in this passage about the predicament of someone who can get reassurance from standard physical objects, but not from other people because there are none around. The significance of such cases would be obvious—they would throw light on the relative importance of the two resources—but that is a matter that he did not touch on in this passage.

The notes do, however, contain another passage in which he does seem to imply that the second resource, the appeal to other people, is indispensable:

> In fact, if he is to play a language-game, the possibility of this will depend on his own and other people's reactions; i.e. they must *call* the same things 'red'.
> 'But if he speaks to himself, surely this is different. For then he needn't consult other people's reactions and he just gives the name "red" now to *the same colour* to which he gave it on a previous occasion.' But how does he know that it is *the same colour*? Does he also recognize the sameness of colour as what he used to call sameness of colour, and so on ad infinitum?[24]

[23] *NLPESD* p. 306.   [24] Ibid., pp. 287–8.

This certainly seems to imply that the would-be speaker of a language would be lost without other people. However, he ends not with a statement to that effect, but with questions, and he does not actually exclude the possibility that, if he had the other resource, standard objects, he would not be reduced to 'just giving the name "red" to the same colour', and would not be launched on an infinite regress like the one that made Russell conclude that there must be universals.[25] There is a long footnote on the same page explaining the importance of the constancy of the weights of objects for our practice of weighing them.[26] Why not also for someone's solitary practice of weighing them? Has he just temporarily forgotten this resource?[27]

The predicament of someone who can get reassurance from standard objects, but not from other people, because there are none around, is discussed in several manuscripts written between *The Blue Book* and the final draft of *Philosophical Investigations*.[28] In one of them he says that a solitary caveman could devise a picture-language or even develop a spoken language entirely for his own use.[29] This is not offered as a contribution to developmental psychology, because he explains that what he means is that the painter's pictures or the speaker's words might be connected with his behaviour in regular ways which would have justified the verdict that he was speaking a language, if an observer had been there to give it.[30] There is also another manuscript in which he discusses cases of this kind and finds no difficulty in imagining people who talk only to themselves.[31] He even

[25] See Russell: *The Problems of Philosophy*, Oxford, 1911, Ch. IX.

[26] *NLPESD* p. 287 n. 11.

[27] The footnote was taken by the editor, R. Rhees, from a later context in the notes and placed by him at the foot of p. 287.

[28] *BLBK* pp. 12–14. See above, p. 000 n. 14.

[29] MS 165. This MS, like several others that throw light on the development of the private language argument of *Philosophical Investigations*, has not been published, but the relevant passage is paraphrased by G. P. Baker and P. M. S. Hacker in *Scepticism, Rules and Language*, pp. 20–1 n. 29.

[30] The same point is made in MS 129, p. 89. The need for this kind of regularity is explained in *PI* I §§ 206–7. It is, of course, the observer's only clue to what is going on, but he does not merely use it as the premiss of a scientific inference. For he also faces the criterial question, 'What would count as speaking a language?' According to Wittgenstein, a single spectacular performance would not count. See *PI* I § 199. But if an individual performance has to belong to a regular sequence, does the regularity itself need to have been set up by the kind of teaching that passes down language from parents to children? That was an inevitable question, but not an easy one to answer. See above, p. 371, and below, pp. 376–9.

[31] MS 124, pp. 213 and 221. See Baker and Hacker, *Scepticism, Rules and Language*, p. 41 n. 57.

allows that each of them might have his own separate language, and he says that the way in which it was acquired would not affect its present status as a language.

These texts demonstrate conclusively that when he first separated the effect of solitude from the effect of restriction to the resources of sense-data, he held that it would definitely be possible for a person to speak a language even if there were nobody else around.[32] The fact that, if someone else had arrived on the scene, he could have shared the language, does nothing to show that the original stabilizer, standard physical objects, was not previously sufficient by itself.[33] It follows that, if Wittgenstein did change his mind about this in *Philosophical Investigations*, it would be reasonable to expect an unequivocal statement of his new view and some indication of his reasons for adopting it.

Is this what we find in *Philosophical Investigations*? Before this question is answered, there are two points that ought to be made. First, he might have distanced himself from his earlier position without actually occupying the opposite position. He could simply have left it open whether anyone could set up and use a language without having other people around. The difference between the line that he took with fairly high consistency from *The Blue Book* to the drafts of *Philosophical Investigations* and the line that he took in *Philosophical Investigations* itself need not have been the difference between a non-social and a social theory about the threshold marked by the judgement 'x is speaking a language'. Second, his thinking about this matter evidently underwent a certain change, and if it is not explained as the change from a non-social to a social theory, another explanation will have to be found.

Now consider what he says in *Philosophical Investigations* about speaking a language without the co-operation of other people:

A human being can encourage himself, give himself orders, obey, blame and punish himself; he can ask himself a question and answer it. We could even imagine human beings who spoke only in monologue; who accompanied their activities by talking to themselves.—An explorer who watched them and

[32] This is confirmed by what he says about Robinson Crusoe in MS 116. See Baker and Hacker, loc. cit.

[33] A point made by Baker and Hacker (ibid., p. 38) against Kripke: *Wittgenstein on Rules and Private Language*, pp. 79 and 89. The original stabilizer makes it possible for explorers who arrive later to interpret the language (see *PI* I § 205), but, when the speaker was on his own he was, of course, helped not by this possibility but, rather, by the original stabilizer, which made it a possibility.

listened to their talk might succeed in translating their language into ours. (This would enable him to predict those people's actions correctly, for he also hears them making resolutions and decisions.)[34]

This is the first paragraph of the remark in which he goes on to introduce the other kind of private performance, which, he will argue, would not count as speaking a language. His point is that the kind of private performance about which he is going to prove his negative conclusion is not the kind described in this paragraph. He is still zeroing in on the main topic of this part of the book. Of course, there may be an important doctrine put across in this specification of the case that he is not going to talk about. But is there? It is surely significant that, whereas in the earlier version of this passage he gave a negative answer to the question whether it matters how these soliloquists acquired the capacity to behave as described, in this version he does not even raise the question. Nor does he mention the possibility, which he had allowed in the earlier version, that each of them might be talking to himself in a different language. What he says here is compatible with the possibility that they all speak the same language, having learned it by eavesdropping on their elders' soliloquies. Naturally, nobody would claim that this is what he *meant*, but it must be significant that he left himself open to this interpretation. If this is not the way to reaffirm the sufficiency of standard physical objects without other people's co-operation, it is, equally, not the way to deny the sufficiency of that resource.[35]

If he is doing neither of these two things, we can only guess the scruple that made him show more caution in his discussion of this topic in *Philosophical Investigations* than in his earlier manuscripts. The point has already been made that there are several texts in which he says that, when we ask whether a regularity in a person's vocalizations and actions would make us say that he was speaking a language, we do not have to find out how he acquired the capacity to carry on as he does, because that is irrelevant. It is interesting that at least one of these texts antedates the first formulation of the private language argument.[36] The explanation of his later caution may be the one suggested above: he had come to doubt the legitimacy of separating

----

[34] *PI* I § 243.

[35] It does almost look as if he is reaffirming the sufficiency of physical objects without other people, but in fact the text is non-committal. See above, p. 371.

[36] The passage in *The Blue Book*, quoted immediately below. See above, p. 366 n. 14.

speaking a language quite so sharply from having learned to speak it.[37]
If so, this would be yet another example of the increasing holism of his
later philosophy. The verdict 'He is speaking a language' has the load
of its meaning spread from the particular performance to the exercise
of the general capacity, and thence, but tentatively, to the normal way of
acquiring the capacity—from other people.

But who could claim to know the truth of this matter? Here, for what
it is worth, is the main passage in which he dismisses as irrelevant the
way in which a person learned the behaviour that is a candidate for the
title 'speaking a language':

> In so far as the teaching brings about the association, feeling of recognition, etc.
> etc., it is the *cause* of the phenomenon of understanding, obeying, etc.; and it is a
> hypothesis that the process of teaching should be needed in order to bring about
> these effects. It is conceivable, in this sense, that *all* the processes of under-
> standing, obeying, etc., should have happened without the person ever having
> been taught the language. (This, just now, seems extremely paradoxical.)[38]

If it is paradoxical to suggest that everything that constitutes my
understanding English today might have started suddenly on my last
birthday, instead of going back to its actual origin in my gradual
acquisition of the language as a child, that is only because it would
have been a miracle. So Wittgenstein explains that in this passage he is
thinking of teaching as the cause of understanding. But it is also
possible to focus on to the lesson that has been learned and to think of
teaching 'as supplying a *reason* for what one did; as supplying the road
one walks'.[39] A typical example of this way of thinking about teaching
would be a case in which I see it as having supplied me with a rule
which I actually apply today:

> Teaching as the hypothetical history of our subsequent actions (understanding,
> obeying, estimating a length, etc.) drops out of our considerations. The rule
> which has been taught and is subsequently applied interests us only so far as it
> is involved in the application. A rule, so far as it interests us, does not act at a
> distance.[40]

He then tries to explain why it might be wrongly taken to be
inconceivable that a person should speak a language without previous

---

[37] See above, p. 367.   [38] *BLBK* p. 12.
[39] Ibid., p. 14.
[40] Loc. cit. There is something slightly wrong with the first sentence. The intended
meaning must have been 'Teaching as the hypothetical historical cause of our
subsequent actions'.

teaching, when really it would only be miraculous. His explanation is that people see the contingent causal connection between my performance today and my earlier teaching, but confuse it with the logical connection between my performance today and the rule which, as a result of the lesson, I am now applying. His idea is that they fall into this confusion because the rule was in fact imparted by the teaching.

It would certainly be a mistake to suppose that it is inconceivable that my understanding of the English language today might have been produced by teaching in any way different from the teaching that in fact produced it, and it may also be a mistake to suppose that it is inconceivable that it might not have been produced by any teaching at all. But though Wittgenstein's explanation looks as if it works just as well for the second mistake, if it is one, as it does for the first mistake, it is possible that he began to doubt whether the second supposition really is mistaken. Is it really so obvious that the essence of speaking a language is purely functional and in no way genetic? But we can only conjecture at this point, because we do not know what scruple led him to take a more cautious line in *Philosophical Investigations* about the possibility of speaking a language without having other people around.

At this point those who credit Wittgenstein with a social theory of the threshold marked by the verdict '*x* is speaking a language' will certainly protest. They will deny that he takes a more cautious line about this matter in *Philosophical Investigations*—he takes the same line, they will say, and it is only misguided concentration on a single remark, § 243, which has produced the illusion of greater caution.

It is time to look at the rest of the evidence. In *Philosophical Investigations* he actually poses the question whether the description 'obeying a rule' might be applied to something that a person might do on his own. However, instead of answering it, he immediately compounds it with the further question, whether it might be applied to something that he did once in his life:

Is what we call 'obeying a rule' something that it would be possible for only *one* man to do, and to do only *once* in his life?—This is, of course, a note on the grammar of the expression 'to obey a rule'.[41]

If he had really changed his mind and decided that contact with other

---

[41] *PI* I § 199, first paragraph. As usual, he warns us that this is not a question about what a person could manage to do, but about the way in which we ought to describe what we are supposing that he does only once in his life.

people was necessary after all, it is very unlikely that he would have rolled these two questions up together. He would have asked whether someone could establish a rule and obey it repeatedly without having other people around, and he would have returned a negative answer. In fact, he substitutes the double-barrelled question, and he answers it very guardedly:

> It is not possible that there should have been only one occasion on which someone obeyed a rule. It is not possible that there should have been only one occasion on which a report was made, an order given or understood; and so on.—To obey a rule, to make a report, to give an order, to play a game of chess, are *customs* (uses, institutions).
>
> To understand a sentence means to understand a language. To understand a language means to be master of a technique.[42]

This is a very carefully composed answer. The first sentence requires a person to do whatever is going to be described as 'obeying a rule' more than once. But none of the examples used to illustrate this requirement are like talking to oneself: each of them involves at least one other person right from the start because of the very nature of the performance—making a report, giving an order (at least, in the normal use of these phrases), or playing a game of chess. How baffling that he should choose illustrations like these, when what we needed was a case that does not involve a partner almost by definition, so that at least we could ask whether someone could produce the performance on his own! But no, the question that we want to hear him answer is jostled off the stage, and the final paragraph merely repeats the requirement of the first sentence and explains it: repetition is needed because understanding a language is mastering a technique.

The point that Wittgenstein is making is not that repetition is needed because it is difficult to master a technique. That may be true, but what he is saying does not exclude miracles, but only affects how we would describe them. Nor is he saying that repetition is needed to convince other people that the technique has been mastered, although that too is true. His point is that repetition is of the essence of understanding language:[43]

---

[42] *PI* I § 199, second and third paragraphs.

[43] This is brought out very clearly by C. McGinn in *Wittgenstein on Meaning*, Blackwell, 1984, p. 39. But what about the learning which produces mastery of the technique? Is that too part of the essence of understanding and speaking a language? And can the learning be a solitary achievement? See above, p. 367.

In order to describe the phenomenon of language, one must describe a practice, not something that happens once, *no matter of what kind*.[44]

This is a subtle point and it is worth looking at the way he formulates it when he applies it to the rather different case of mathematical calculation:

'But how often must a rule have actually been applied in order for one to have the right to speak of a rule?' How often must a human being have added, multiplied, divided, before we can say that he has mastered the technique of these kinds of calculation? And by that I don't mean: how often must he have calculated right in order to convince *others* that he can calculate? No, I mean: in order to prove it to himself.[45]

If he fails to prove it to himself, that can only be because what he does lacks something essential to calculation, namely sufficient repetition. For he will know what he is doing on each particular occasion up to a point, the point at which he asks himself the same question that his examiners ask about him, 'Does it count as calculating?' That question will force him to check the general pattern of his performances, because a single correct performance, even if it were accompanied by an impressive flash of understanding, would not count as calculating.[46]

It is not easy to appreciate Wittgenstein's point. Even when people grasp it, they find that it turns in their hands into one of the two things that he did not mean—that it takes repetition to master a technique or to prove to others that one has mastered it. So here is another, longer and more subtle explanation of his point, this time applied to reading:

Consider the following case. Human beings or creatures of some other kind are used by us as reading-machines. They are trained for this purpose. The trainer says of some that they can already read, of others that they cannot yet do so. Take the case of a pupil who has so far not taken part in the training: if he is shown a written word he will sometimes produce some sort of sound, and here and there it happens 'accidentally' to be roughly right. A third person hears this pupil on such an occasion and says: 'He is reading.' But the teacher says: 'No, he isn't reading; that was just an accident.'—But let us suppose that this pupil continues to react correctly to further words that are put before him. After a while the teacher says: 'Now he can read!'—But what of that first word?

---

[44] *RFM* VI § 34.   [45] Ibid., VI § 32.
[46] Cf. *PI* II. xi, p. 217: 'If God had looked into our minds, he would not have been able to see there whom we were speaking of.' Wittgenstein's reason for insisting on what a person actually does was that he did not think it possible to reduce computing a result or speaking about a particular person to anything that occurs momentarily in his mind. See Ch. 17.

Is the teacher to say: 'I was wrong, and he *did* read it'—or: 'He only began to read later on'?—When did he begin to read? Which was the first word that he *read*? This question makes no sense here. Unless, indeed, we give a definition: 'The first word that a person "reads" is the the first word of the first series of 50 words that he reads correctly' (or something of the sort).

If on the other hand we use 'reading' to stand for a certain experience of transition from marks to spoken sounds, then it certainly makes sense to speak of the *first* word that he really read. He can then say, e.g., 'At this word for the first time I had the feeling "Now I am reading".'

Or again, in the different case of a reading-machine which translated marks into sounds, perhaps as a pianola does, it would be possible to say: 'The machine *read* only after such-and-such had happened to it—after such-and-such parts had been connected by wires; the first word that it read was . . .

But in the case of the living reading-machine 'reading' meant reacting to written signs in such-and-such ways. The concept was therefore quite independent of that of a mental or other mechanism.—Nor can the teacher here say of the pupil: 'Perhaps he was already reading when he said that word.' For there is no doubt about what he did.—The change when the pupil began to read was a change in his *behaviour*; and it makes no sense here to speak of 'a first word in his new state'.[47]

In the final paragraph of this passage Wittgenstein rejects the kind of solution that a materialist would propose for this problem about the moment when a capacity is acquired. Even if he is wrong to set his face against injecting neural information into the concept of reading, it remains true that, when we apply the concept in everyday life, there is no precise moment at which we can say that a person began to read. This is because the only change accessible to us is a change in his behaviour and not in any states that may be postulated to back up his behaviour.[48] Even his first impression that he is reading will not serve to identify the precise moment when he begins to read, because there is no such moment. It is not like the change in a traffic-light from red to green.

This may be connected with the doubt that Wittgenstein seems to feel in *Philosophical Investigations* about his earlier view that speaking a language has no logical connection with having learned to speak it. For

---

[47] *PI* I § 157. The possibility that 'reading' might be used to stand for a certain experience of transition would have appealed to Hume. See Ch. 18.

[48] Cf. *Zettel*, §§ 608–10. His rejection of materialism is criticized by C. McGinn in *Wittgenstein on Meaning*, pp. 112–17, and defended by N. Malcolm in *Nothing is Hidden*, Ch. 10. His refusal to allow that a full account of such concepts as *reading* and *speaking a language* would mention neural states is, of course, more difficult to defend than his refusal to allow that it would mention separate mental states.

if the acquisition of the capacity cannot be assigned to a definite moment in time, anyone who holds that learning is necessary can always claim that it occurs when a person is producing, albeit tentatively, his first correct performances. But though this is the first step towards allowing us to say that the wolf-child learned to apply his symbols, it remains an obstacle that he was not taught them, unless we can count being self-taught. Perhaps it was a doubt about this last point that made Wittgenstein hesitate about such cases. If so, he would certainly have felt doubts about the other kind of case, in which someone suddenly and miraculously finds himself completely proficient.

Whatever the explanation, it is certainly no accident that in *Philosophical Investigations* he smothers the question that we all want to hear him answer, 'Is what is called "obeying a rule" something that it would be possible for only *one* man to do?[49] For he makes exactly the same evasive move in two parallel passages in *Remarks on the Foundations of Mathematics*:

> The prophecy does *not* run, that a man will get *this* result when he follows this rule in making a transformation—but that he will get this result, when we *say* that he is following the rule.
>
> . . . we should not call something 'calculating' if we could not make such a prophecy with certainty. This really means: calculating is a technique. And what we have said pertains to the essence of the technique.
>
> This consensus belongs to the essence of *calculation*, so much is certain. I.e.: this consensus is part of the phenomenon of our calculating.
>
> In a technique of *calculating* prophecies must be possible.
>
> And that makes the technique of calculating similar to the technique of a *game*, like chess.
>
> But what about this consensus—doesn't it mean that *one* human being by himself could not calculate? Well, *one* human being could at any rate not calculate just *once* in his life.[50]

This can only mean that whatever looks as if it is lost by a would-be calculator working in complete isolation is certainly lost by one who only performs once. But what can that possibly be if it is not the opportunity to acquire a skill by exploiting a viable criterion of correct performance? So the passage makes for mathematics the same point that is made about the use of language in *Philosophical Investigations*, § 199.[51] It is also equally evasive about the need for other people.

[49] *PI* I § 199, quoted above, p. 377.
[50] *RFM* III § 66 and § 67, first four paragraphs.
[51] This should throw some light on Wittgenstein's treatment of applied mathematics, but the topic is not within the scope of this book.

The second passage in *Remarks on the Foundations of Mathematics* confines itself to posing several questions:

> Could there be arithmetic without agreement on the part of calculators?
>
> Could there be only one human being that calculated? Could there be only one that followed a rule?
>
> Are these questions somewhat similar to this one: 'Can one man alone engage in commerce?'[52]

Malcolm's comment on this is, 'The point is that just as carrying on a trade presupposes a community, so too does arithmetic and following a rule.'[53] But Wittgenstein does not say this. He only asks a question, and the question that he asks is only whether the question about solitary arithmetic is somewhat similar to the question about solitary trading. Naturally, he was aware that a performance like trading, unlike doing arithmetic, involves at least one other person by definition, so that the question, whether a solitary person could do it, is just not worth discussing.[54] So he could hardly have agreed with Malcolm that '*just as* carrying on a trade presupposes a community, *so too* does arithmetic and following a rule' (my italics). Even the question that he does ask, about the more remote similarity of the two performances, is left unanswered by him. There must be a reason for his tentative handling of this topic, and it is a plausible guess that he saw the consequence of pushing a rewarding line of thought too far. But it must be admitted that he gathers too much momentum on his approach to the point where he is going to halt, like a horse that gallops at a fence only to stop suddenly so that the rider flies on. Anyway, in this passage he is certainly not propounding a social theory of following a rule. He is inviting us to think about it.

But what are we supposed to think about it? It is worth examining some of the other texts which are commonly taken to show that he was inviting us to adopt a social theory of rule-following:

> Disputes do not break out (among mathematicians, say) over the question whether a rule has been obeyed or not. People don't come to blows over it, for example. That is part of the framework on which the working of our language is based (for example, in giving descriptions).
>
> 'So you are saying that human agreement decides what is true and what is false?'—It is what human beings *say* that is true and false; and they agree in the *language* they use. That is not agreement in opinions but in form of life.

---

[52] *RFM* VI § 45.
[53] N. Malcolm: *Nothing is Hidden*, p. 175.   [54] See above, p. 378.

If language is to be a means of communication, there must be agreement not only in definitions but also (queer as this may sound) in judgements. This seems to abolish logic, but does not do so.—It is one thing to describe methods of measurement, and another to obtain and state results of measurement. But what we call 'measuring' is partly determined by a certain constancy in results of measurement.[55]

There is a parallel passage in *Remarks on the Foundations of Mathematics*:

We say that, in order to communicate, people must agree with one another about the meanings of words. But the criterion for this agreement is not just agreement with reference to definitions, e.g., ostensive definitions—but *also* an agreement in judgements. It is essential for communication that we agree in a large number of judgements.[56]

It is surely significant that in each of these passages the requirement of agreement in judgements is subject to a condition—in the first one, 'If language is to be a means of communication', and in the second one, 'In order to communicate'.[57] Wittgenstein would not have needed to mention this condition, if he had held it impossible for anyone to set up a language for his own use without any contact with other people. He would simply have insisted on agreement in judgements whether or not language was to be a means of communication. The case of the wolf-child, as described above, would then not count as a case of speaking a language, because his vocalizations did not at any stage exploit the resource that only a community could supply.

There is another way of making this point. A philosopher who asks what it takes to establish communication will naturally start with the vocalizations of two or more people. A case in which the conditions that he believes to be necessary are not met will be one in which these people apply the same words in different ways. It will not be a case in which a speaker does not even have a companion whose uses of words he can examine to see if they agree with his own. With whom would he be unable to communicate in such a case?

Communication requires agreement in judgements because mere agreement in definitions is not enough, and the reason why it is not enough is that two people might make the same definitional substitutions in a given sentence and then go on to apply the

---

[55] *PI* I §§ 240–2.   [56] *RFM* VI § 39.
[57] C. McGinn rightly stresses the importance of this condition. See *Wittgenstein on Meaning*, pp. 53 and 89.

substituted words to different things. That would show that, in spite of their agreement about the verbal translation of the original sentence, they had not really understood it in the same way. Similarly, if a group of people all agreed about the relative lengths of two rulers except for one of them who applied a ruler twice to any object to be measured, while the others followed our practice and applied it only once, that would show that an instruction like 'Get some ten-inch logs' would be understood in a different way by the one with the eccentric practice.[58] Incidentally, it would be quite implausible to argue that it would be impossible for someone who had no contact with other people to take a stick of standard length with him when he went foraging for firewood, so that he could bring back logs that would fit his fireplace.[59]

It is not obvious why he says that it is logic that looks as if it would be abolished by reliance on agreement in judgements. For logic does not seem to depend on the application of words to things. On the contrary, it appears to rely entirely on regulated moves within language from one sentence to another, and these are moves made on safe, surveyable territory. So it might look as if logic would not be affected if our moves between sentences and facts were completely unregulated.

However, the results obtained by logic have to be applied, at least when it is being used in everyday life, and any logical connection between two descriptions will put a restriction on their applications. For example, if one description implies another, it will not be possible to apply the first one to something, and then go on to refuse to apply the second one. But that is just what might be done by someone whose applications of words to things were completely unregulated. For if such a person were not thinking of the logical connection between the two descriptions when he was asking himself whether or not to apply them to the thing, he might well feel impelled to apply the first one but to withhold the second one.[60] Of course, we ourselves sometimes make mistakes of this kind in the application of pairs of logically connected descriptions, but the reason why we make them is not that we are applying descriptions in a completely unregulated way, and so we would never go astray with a perspicuously connected pair like 'coloured' and 'red'.

---

[58] We would have to suppose that they judged the equality in length of two rulers by what was marked on them rather than by juxtaposition. So perhaps coiled tapes would provide a more credible example.

[59] See above, p. 373 n. 27.

[60] See the discussion of this point in Vol. I pp. 31–3.

Now if the results obtained by logic are applied to the world, and if completely unregulated descriptions of things would conflict with logic, we would not even have logic if our descriptions of things were not governed by rules. So logic relies on the application-rules of our descriptive words in spite of the fact that they reach out beyond the safe, surveyable territory on which we make moves from sentence to sentence within a language. It follows that if these risky moves made on the unmappable territory between words and things were completely unregulated, logic really would be abolished, just as a system of measurement would be abolished if people always used their tape-measures capriciously. So logic depends on rule-governed behaviour beyond what is usually taken to be its frontier. If this dependence seems to abolish it, that is only because we have made excessive claims for it.

The old conception of logic was that it dictates to the world as we describe it from some higher vantage-point. Wittgenstein's idea is that its writ is neither so unconditional nor so far-reaching, because it depends on what we do on the extreme edge of its territory. If Platonists object that this abolishes logic, his reply is that, on the contrary, it makes its claims more convincing by limiting them. The whole argument should be read as an answer to a question posed in the *Tractatus*: 'If there would be a logic, even if there were no world, how could there be a logic given that there is a world?'[61]

At this point those who credit Wittgenstein with a social theory of the threshold marked by '*x* is speaking a language' may claim that, when all has been said, it cannot be denied that in the passage quoted from *Philosophical Investigations* Wittgenstein does imply that logic,

---

[61] *TLP* 5.5521. Naturally, his later answer to this question is quite different from the answer that he gave in the *Tractatus*. See Vol. I pp. 23–5, 117–18, and 124–5. What he said there was that logic depends on the world, but only on its unalterable essence and not on its contingent layout. His idea was that logic develops out of elementary sentences, which are true or false with no third alternative, because their senses never depend on further contingent facts. So all necessity came out as logical necessity and there were no necessary connections embedded in the natures of things. His later view of the relation between logic and the world differs from this in two ways. First, he no longer sees logic as a system threatened by its dependence on contingencies. A language-game like that of ascribing sensations to their owners does depend on contingent presuppositions, but if that means that its sentences would lack sense if the presuppositions failed, that is only because it implies that they could no longer be used. In any case, he has now abandoned his idea that logic depends on sentences without presuppositions. Second, if logic is still under a threat, it is one that comes from a different direction. It is no longer subject to constraints imposed by the world and it will not be easy to establish that its internal stabilizers are an adequate substitute.

and, therefore, language depends on agreement in judgements. True, but the implication is restricted to cases in which 'language is a means of communication'. There is nothing in the passage to rule out the possibility that there might be a language used in solitude which depended on its rule-governed applications without the easy test of regularity that is available when there are other people around.

There is another puzzling fature of the two parallel texts that have been quoted. Wittgenstein seems to be drawing a distinction between opinions and judgements and to be saying that the agreement that he has in mind is not agreement in opinions but agreement in judgements. This might make us look for a definite difference between the meanings of the two words 'opinion' and 'judgement'.[62] But it may only be that he is writing informally and making the point that, when someone makes a factual claim, there are two different ways of looking at it: we may take it as an opinion, to be assessed for truth, or we may take it as something done by him, an act of judgement, which contributes to the meaning of the sentence that he uses. We can, of course, regard the same claim in both ways, because the second way does not amount to treating the sentence used by him as an ostensive definition. The point is only that people can neither agree nor disagree about a particular matter of fact unless they have already achieved general agreement in their applications of the disputed word.

The full weight of this thesis will be assessed below.[63] It has been introduced here for a limited purpose, to explain Wittgenstein's answer to the question 'What does it take to set up and maintain a language?' The question arose about a special case, sensation-language. That was because he was concerned with the persistent attempts of solipsists and classical phenomenalists to retreat into their private worlds taking with them, if they can, all the intellectual devices that are set up and maintained in our common world. One such device is the reidentification of types, and the private language argument was designed to show that, though, of course, this device does work on sensations, the condition of its success in that field is that it should have started, and should continue to be used, in the public world. The argument was that my impression, that this is the same sensation-type again, needs an independent standard of correctness. The question then arose whether Wittgenstein believed that such a standard would

---

[62] So McGinn suggests that an opinion is a reasoned belief, and a judgement, a reaction that needs no justification. See *Wittgenstein on Meaning*, pp. 56–7.

[63] See below, Chs. 16–18, on Wittgenstein's investigation of rule-following.

necessarily involve other people, or only the possibility of communicating with other people, if there happened to be any around.

The interpretation of his answer to that question went through three stages. First, it was necessary to establish his view of the way in which sensation-language is learned: children pick it up together with the language for describing objects in their immediate environment, and it would not be possible for them to acquire a vocabulary for sensations without, at least, being in a position to acquire one for physical objects. Second, his reason for believing that sensation-language cannot be learned separately had to be explained: it was that the requirement of an independent standard of correctness could not be met by a sensation-language completely detached from everything in the physical world. That introduced the third stage, an inquiry into his account of rule-following, which has been taken only so far as is necessary in order to explain his views about the reidentification of types. This is a performance with a standard of correctness which is imparted to us by other people in the ordinary course of life. However, that does not mean that a community of language-speakers, taken collectively, is not answerable to anything outside the circle of its own agreed practices. If everyone else started to improvise wildly, but, by shere coincidence, in perfect unison, I would not necessarily be wrong if I rejected the tyranny of the majority. On the contrary, if in these circumstances, I accepted it, and we all continued to speak with one voice, it would not be the voice of science, but, at best, of art.

That is the real point of the speculation about the wolf-child. A philosopher who holds that a human being in such circumstances would have nothing to keep his vocalizations on the rails ought to ask himself what keeps the vocalizations of the whole linguistic community on the rails. For whatever it is, it is going to be the same stabilizing resource in both cases.[64] 'Not at all', the defender of the social theory of rule-following will reply, 'No doubt, the community would be kept on the rails by the same thing, if anything kept it on the rails. But in fact the suggestion that something is needed to keep it on the rails is mistaken. For it was an understatement to say that the community

---

[64] It is important to keep in mind the peculiarity of the sense of the phrase 'stabilizing resource' when it is applied to 'what keeps language on the rails'. See above, pp. 333–5 and pp 361–3. Although such a resource does have a certain independence of language, its independence is not complete and so it contributes to what counts as stability in addition to producing it. This difficult point will be explained in Ch. 16.

imparts the standard of correctness to the hesitating individual—it sets it.'[65]

The really difficult thing is to see through all the superficialities to what underlies this controversy. It is not a question of the inventiveness of the wolf-child.[66] Nor is it a question whether his 'invention' of such a language would not really have to involve thinking out a plan of such complexity that he could have adopted it only if he already had a language—as if we knew how to judge that! What makes the wolf-child's case important is that it isolates a resource which certainly underpins the practice of the community, but not in a way that allows us to point to particular uses of it. The isolated resource is the discovery of regularities in nature through self-imposed regularities. But naturally, we cannot point to particular occasions when the community exploits this resource. We could hardly expect a learned academy to review progress annually and check whether the self-discipline of our linguistic practices was paying off by unlocking enough of the secrets of nature, or whether it needed tightening up.

It is easy to react in too simple a way to the evident absurdity of such a suggestion. We find it so natural to regard the standards of the community as autonomous. How could a philosopher step outside factual language and find any independent support for it? Isn't that precisely the kind of theory of meaning that is rejected in the long investigation of rule-following which develops out of the critique of the *Tractatus* in *Philosophical Investigations* and leads into the private language argument?

But we must not forget that we really do have something that gives us a purchase on these difficult matters. We can point to other uses of language which, unlike its scientific use, are not designed to unlock the secrets of nature. What supporters of the social theory of rule-following tacitly assume is that the community still speaks with the original purpose of the wolf-child. This assumption is brought out into the open when I imagine that the other members of the community might all start to improvise wildly but in coincidental unison, leaving me in a position very like that of the wolf-child, the only scientist on earth. But that is only the first step in this investigation of meaning and truth, which will be continued in the chapters on rule-following.[67]

[65] See Kripke: *Wittgenstein on Rules and Private Language*, pp. 88–9.
[66] See *PI* I § 257: 'Well, let's assume that the child is a genius and invents a name for the sensation.' As usual, the discussion that follows is a discussion of what we ought to say about such a case.   [67] See Chs. 16–18.

15

The Structure of the Private Language Argument

THERE are several aspects of the private language argument that have not yet been fully investigated. Perhaps the most important unanswered question, or, at least, the one to which an answer is most overdue, is how Wittgenstein would deal with classical phenomenalists, who simply retort that there is really nothing to stop an isolated subject setting up the necessary distinction between seeming so and being so in his private world without any support from the public world. That is a very straight response to his strategy and many have found it convincing. When he argues that nobody could learn the language of appearances before the language of reality, classical phenomenalists merely reply that there is no question of priority here because reality is only a matter of multiple appearances. There is a similar confrontation over bodily sensations. He claims that people could never learn the vocabulary for reporting them unless they had already learned to describe the physical setting of their occurrence, but they reject that too, arguing that the physical setting is only a configuration of exteroceptive sense-data.

It is by no means obvious how this controversy should be settled. Classical phenomenalists take over Wittgenstein's theme, that a criterion is needed to distinguish seeming so from being so, but they play it back to him in a different key, and it is not at all easy to adjudicate the contest.[1] Perhaps the first thing that is required at this point is a reminder of the structure of the private language argument and of its place in Wittgenstein's philosophy.

The *Tractatus* had provided him with a very simple argument against classical phenomenalism: the limit of language had to be drawn from the inside, and so if factual language really were restricted to sense-data, it would be impossible to specify them empirically by giving their position on a larger map. But that is precisely what classical

[1] See Vol. I pp. 53–7.

phenomenalists try to do. They identify the phenomenal base-line of the private world by indicating where it runs in the public world. Of course, their excuse is that the public world is, in the end, reducible to the private world. His objection is that the reduction comes later, if it comes at all, and at the earlier stage when they are drawing the limit within 'the world as they find it', it can only be understood as a line running between two fields each containing its own kind of identifiable things. Therefore, according to him, classical phenomenalism is incoherent.

The claim made in defence of the theory is that a subject can identify objects in his private world without placing them in the public world. All that he needs to do is to specify them as objects presented to him, the subject, and then, instead of relating the subject to the public world, he can let its identity speak for itself [2] Wittgenstein's first private language argument was directed against this way of identifying private objects. But, of course, his adversaries also claimed to be able to go on and describe them without relating their descriptions to anything in the public world, and it was against this claim that he developed the second private language argument in *Philosophical Investigations*. Given their position in his philosophy, both private language arguments had to be independent of the argument developed in the *Tractatus* against drawing the limit of language on the larger map of the world as we find it. So the second private language argument, like the first one, was offered as a self-contained *reductio* deriving no support from the conclusion of the earlier argument about the placing of the limit of language. In effect, Wittgenstein was saying that even if the stage could be set in the way in which the classical phenomenalist wants to set it, there are certain essential linguistic devices that he would not be able to use on that stage and the reidentification of types is one of them.

This obviously makes it impossible to count the conclusion of the argument about the limit of language among the premises of the private language argument of *Philosophical Investigations*. However, it might well be that some of the considerations that figured in the earlier argument could be used again in this private language argument.[3] But were they? That is an important question about the structure of the argument and one that will affect the outcome of the confrontation between Wittgenstein and the classical phenomenalist.

One consideration that played a role in the earlier argument was the

---

[2] See above, pp. 40–2.
[3] See above, pp. 244–8.

opacity of the sense-data presented to the subject in the original position as described by classical phenomenalists. They are all that he has to go on and he has to set up a vocabulary for reporting them without any inkling of anything existing beyond them. Now it is easy to forget that this is supposed to be his predicament, because the natural way of thinking about visual impressions is quite different: they may be interposed between the subject and the physical world, but they are not pictured as an opaque screen. So we have to remind ourselves that the way in which classical phenomenalists think of sense-data when they are trying to identify them empirically is not the natural way. According to them, the subject in the original position confronts his sense-data with no hint of anything existing beyond them, and he has to take it from there. He must set up his basic language at the interface between his ego and his sense-data in much the same way that the wolf-child was supposed to set up a language for physical objects at the interface between his body and the outside world.[4]

This conception of the original position of the subject produces a familiar effect: he is unable to make any use of the outside world, and the smooth surface presented to him by his own sense-data with nothing behind the mask is something that he has to take at face value, like the wolf-child's environment. There are really two points here, one of them obvious, and the other more in need of argument to support it. The obvious point is that he cannot rely on physical checks as such. But can he appeal to them surreptitiously as sequences of sense-data, which is the way in which they finally figure in the reductive chapter of the story told by classical phenomenalists? Wittgenstein's second point, which is more controversial, is that he cannot do this either. For in the first chapter of the story he is supposed to stand with both feet in the original position, and the resources provided by physical objects, as reduced in the final chapter, are not yet available to them. They will become available to him only after he has made considerable progress in setting up his basic language. But how will he be able to start on that task *before* these resources have been made available to him?

Evidently, classical phenomenalists believe that the subject can not only start on the task in the original position but also go on to complete it. For if physical objects are configurations of sense-data, the necessary resources are already available to the subject in the original

---

[4] See above, Ch. 14.

position. Whichever side is right, it is important to remember the actual disposition of their forces on the field of their controversy. We must receive the story told by classical phenomenalists strictly as they tell it. It is, unfortunately, very natural to fail to do this, and to take a break from their narrative without realizing that one is doing so. Because they are describing the way in which people start to use language in real life, we tend to embellish their austere story with details taken from the process that we know them to be describing. This eases the way for the concession that it is all right to allow the subject in the original position to exploit physical objects, provided that they only figure as patterns of sense-data. But this concession must not simply be donated to Wittgenstein's adversaries. They must fight for it, because the subject in the original position described by them really does have a handicap that needs to be assessed. He has to take the first steps towards setting up his basic language without being able to check his performance for success against physical objects as such, and it is questionable whether he can appeal to them as configurations of sense-data. For it is far from clear whether he can pick out any patterns among his sense-data before he has made considerable progress with reidentifying their types in the original position. Of course, Wittgenstein is not basing his argument on the sheer difficulty of the beginner's task. His point is that, like the marksman on the frustrating rifle-range,[5] he cannot be exercising a skill, because his behaviour is, at best, a miraculously accurate mixture of automatism and guesswork.

But is this a valid argument? The best approach to answering this question is through a general conspectus of the strategic situation. We need to see exactly how this way of answering the classical phenomenalist's objection to the private language argument of *Philosophical Investigations* is related to the argument from the limit of language presented in the *Tractatus*. Now the defence of the private language argument cannot rely on the conclusion of the argument from the limit of language, because that would be an inappropriate reinforcement for a piece of reasoning which sets out to explore the consequences of allowing that the classical phenomenalist can do what the earlier argument had shown it to be incoherent to imagine him doing. However, it is quite legitimate for the defence to exploit the same principle as the earlier argument, and it will not take long to

[5] See above, p. 333.

demonstrate that that is what the defence sketched above actually does.

The point made in support of the private language argument of *Philosophical Investigations* was that the classical phenomenalist tells a story with several distinct chapters but fails to appreciate the relationship between them. According to the argument from the limit of language, if he starts by identifying the phenomenal base-line empirically, he cannot go on to adopt a theory which would rob the identification of its original character. An alternative way of exploiting the principle of this argument would be to insist that, if in the original position the subject is simply confronted by a sequence of sense-data, he will not have the advantage of a person who has already picked out patterns in their occurrences. The general principle is this: whether the subject is at home in the public world or confined to his private world, he stands wherever he does stand with both feet in the same world. So the defence of the private language argument against the classical phenomenalist's objection does rely on the same principle as the argument from the limit of language. If they make the subject start in an original position which does not include physical checks, they cannot sneak them in from a later stage in which, according to their story, they become available to the subject only because he has completed a task which he could not even have begun without them. If restrictions are imposed on the subject in the original position, their effects are imposed on him too.[6] The effect of the restriction imposed by classical phenomenalists is, according to Wittgenstein, a devastating disability, and, to repeat a point that bears repetition, he does not mean that, if the subject was cut off from all the resources that might have allowed him to check the success of his efforts to set up a language, he would not be clever enough to bring it off, but, rather, that we could not even call them 'efforts' or say that he was acquiring and exercising a skill.

But is it true that the subject in the original position described by classical phenomenalists is deprived of so much that nothing that he did could possibly count as setting up a language? It is, of course, obvious that he cannot learn the meaning of 'It looks red' before the meaning of 'It is red'.[7] No doubt this is why philosophers who end with classical phenomenalism, or with some other theory of perception in

---

[6] This is one of those cases in which Wittgenstein would say that his adversaries, unlike scientists, do not take their own theories seriously, do not work out their detailed application to the phenomena, and leave them in limbo. See above, pp. 206-7.

[7] See above, p. 341 n. 24.

the same family, often start from bodily sensations, which really do have something of the character of objects, and then edge their way forwards to exteroceptive sense-data. But if the private language argument is convincing, physical checks are just as necessary in the early stages of setting up a language for reporting bodily sensations. Anyway, the defence of the private language argument against the objection has to be conducted in parallel for both cases, bodily sensations and exteroceptive sense-data. If there is nothing wrong with conceding the need for physical checks but construing them as patterns of sense-data, Wittgenstein's claim fails in both cases alike.

Does it in fact fail? If not, he must have convincing arguments to support the proposed defence of the private language argument against the objection. This is all the more necessary because the objection is an obvious one, and anyone who believes in classical phenomenalism will immediately see, or think that he sees, the possibility of construing the required checks as patterns of sense-data or sensations.

The objector will, of course, admit that the subject can test his competence in the use of one word only if he is already competent in the use of other words describing sensations in the surrounding pattern. But, he will ask, why must the subject adopt a stepwise procedure in the original position, never trying to attain proficiency in the use of his second word before he has consolidated his competence with his first one? A scientist who is trying to explain some phenomenon may well propose a theory with several independent variables, for which he is not immediately able to determine the values separately. So surely, in the same way, the subject in the original position described by the classical phenomenalist can acquire proficiencies with several words simultaneously, adopting the most economic hypotheses about his successes and failures.

However, though this blanket method may work when a phenomenon is being explained by an appeal to a pattern of interactions already established in nature, it does not follow that it will work for the acquisition of a set of independent skills. For we have to establish, improve, and maintain each skill in the set, and when we are working on one of them, we cannot assume that the pattern of our exercise of the others today will be held constant so long as we do not deliberately change it tomorrow or the next day. That pattern is not something that is given to us by nature, already firmly established and waiting for us to discover it by ingeniously interlocking experiments. It is a pattern established by our own efforts and so we need to be able to master the skills that maintain it one by one.

Suppose that a marksman had to learn to shoot on a rifle-range even more bizarre than the one already described.[8] On this new range there are several different kinds of target, each requiring a different skill, or, equally good, the various skills are needed for different kinds of gun. But the trouble on this range is that the marksman's indication of the point where his shot strikes a target of the first kind is always given in the form of a conditional report: 'If you scored a bull's-eye on a target of the second kind, then the point when you hit the first target was . . .'. It is evident that he would never be able to adjust his performance on the first kind of target unless information about the grouping of those shots were given to him outright. If this information were conditional on success on the second kind of target, and so on indefinitely, he could never get started. The acquisition of different skills necessarily proceeds stepwise. As usual, we can imagine anything we like happening on the range, but in the circumstances described the most accurate performance that we can think up, without separate feedback, would only be a miracle of automatism and not the establishment and maintenance of a skill.

To this the classical phenomenalist may reply that it can hardly be put forward as an objection to his theory. For any account of the origin of language, even one that starts squarely in the physical world, will have to face the same problem of explaining how the whole system ever gets going, and it is no harder for him to deal with this problem than it is for anyone else.

But at this point Wittgenstein has another card to play. He can point out that his adversary is over-intellectualizing the acquisition of language. When a child learns the word 'pain', the sensation-type will already have been exemplified for him on many occasions and he will have reacted to it in discriminating ways established not by artifice but by nature.[9] Painfulness is not like an unobvious property of a painting, the sort of thing that he could see many times without ever noticing it until it was pointed out to him by a critic. Pain is not something that first becomes an important part of his life when his attention is drawn to it by his parents who give him the word for it. True, the acquisition of the word does have a certain importance, and in certain cases where

---

[8] See above, p. 333.
[9] See *PI* I § 244, quoted and discussed above, pp. 261 and 331, and in Vol. I pp. 52–3.

the system of classification is complex and subtle, words may even put people in a position to make discriminations that they would not have been able to make before. However, that kind of thing does not justify the extent to which the classical phenomenalist intellectualizes the learning of language.

His account of the original position treats the lesson as if it were learned in a void. The teacher is supposed to see that the circumstances are right and then to tell the pupil that pain is what he now has. This lesson makes its impact on the pupil as a sequence of sense-data, out of which he has the purely intellectual task of selecting the one that is to receive the word as its name. It is as if he had to react to points of coloured light against a background of total darkness in some psychological experiment. All the pre-existing physical connections of pain are ignored by this theory, and the result is a radically false intellectualization that would make human learning impossible. Or so Wittgenstein thinks.

When we reflect on teaching, we often underestimate the foundations in the pupil's mind on which the discipline builds. The history of developmental psychology is full of examples of this kind of misjudgement, which must have powerful causes. It is obviously difficult to describe what antedates language in the pupil's mind, and, once language has been acquired, it appropriates what was there before and takes the credit for it. Parents are especially prone to exaggerate their own contribution to their children's mental achievements, and, if Freud is right, the exaggeration is reinforced by the dogma of previous innocence. But this misconception is nowhere more conspicuous than in philosophical accounts of the learning of language, perhaps because it comes so naturally to philosophers to assume that their own mental lives began with the advent of words.

But how is all this connected with the structure of the private language argument? In Chapter 13 there was some discussion of the self-contained independence of the argument, and one of the questions posed was whether Wittgenstein's thesis, that language rests heavily on the pre-linguistic network on which it supervened, should be counted among its premises.[10] This question can now be sharpened and put in a more precise form: 'Did he think that it would be impossible for us to learn a language for reporting sensations if we did not already react to different sensation-types with pre-linguistic

---

[10] See above, pp. 331–2.

discriminations?' Put like this, the question has an obvious importance in the interpretation of the private language argument. For since it is a reductive argument, we ought to be able to identify all its premisses, reduce the set to absurdity, and point to the culprit. If he held that it would not be possible for anyone in the classical phenomenalist's original position to establish a group of discriminating reactions to several different sensation-types by interpreting his successes and failures holistically' it may make all the difference to the argument if that thesis is included in it as a premiss, or, perhaps, as a lemma deduced from some anterior premiss.

Now, as already explained, classical phenomenalists object to a cardinal point in Wittgenstein's reasoning: they allow that the distinction between 'seems' and 'is' must be based on two different things, but they claim that it can perfectly well be drawn within the circle of the subject's sense-data. He evidently cannot answer this objection by appealing to the incoherence of classical phenomenalism deduced from his early account of the limit of language. So did he think that he could show that language could not possibly be learned in the original void presupposed by his adversary? Did the pupil's task, as set in the first chapter of the classical phenomenalist's story, seem to him to be as impossible as the task of the marksman on the second frustrating rifle-range?[11]

That is a surprisingly difficult question to answer. A reductive argument must, of course, be complete and the impact of the deduced absurdity must be clear. However, Wittgenstein's mode of presenting his philosophy does tend to blur the structure of his thought. If it is at all possible, he will pack an argument into a single paragraph, and what gives his reasoning its strength is seldom its reliance on conclusions established by him elsewhere. He was not a thinker like Kant, who bolted together an elaborate framework on which to hang his solutions to different problems. Wittgenstein preferred his arguments to be relatively independent, concise, and concerned with some familiar aspect of our lives, so that they would get the response, 'Of course, that's how it is.' This is not to say that his philosophy lacks structure, but only that it is not like the extruded structure of certain contemporary buildings. It is more elusive, both because it lies deeper, and because its relation to the details is less simple, but it is something

---

[11] As usual, the question means, 'Whatever the pupil did, would it be impossible to describe it as "learning a lesson"?'

that can always be felt behind his descriptions of our ordinary modes of thought and speech.

As a matter of fact, he does not develop his disagreement with the classical phenomenalist in the order in which it has been presented here—first, the private language argument, then the objection that the demand for an independent test of correctness can be met within the circle of sense-data, and finally the rejoinder that in an original position which exploits none of the advantages of the pre-linguistic basis of language the subject could never succeed in getting his system of signs off the ground. However, the order in which these thoughts are developed in *Philosophical Investigations* is not too important. The important thing is the way in which they are connected with one another, and the placing of the description of the clearest example of the pre-linguistic basis of language that is given in the book must be intended to indicate a connection. It comes immediately after the first formulation of the question about the possibility of a private language,[12] and the implication must be that this is a resource which a philosopher who holds that it is a possibility needs, but cannot have.

However, it remains surprising that he does not make the importance of this claim very clear in his presentation of the private language argument. If nature has already linked pain with the behaviour that expresses it, there will be two complementary ways of criticizing the classical phenomenalist's view of our acquisition of the word for it. One way would be to argue that it gives a false account of pain as observed by the sympathizer, and the other would be to argue that it gives a false account of pain as felt by the sufferer. However, when Wittgenstein is presenting the private language argument, he uses the resource provided by the natural link to develop the first of these two criticisms much more extensively than he uses it to develop the second one. You know that your infant is happy because she smiles and could not fake a smile.[13] He approached the subject through the problem of other minds and so he was inclined to play down the phenomenology of feeling pain. It may also have struck him as too obvious to be worth saying that, if the intrinsic character of pain is captured by a word substituted for its natural expression in behaviour, that will be because feeling pain necessarily involves a felt tendency to exhibit that behaviour. But the point is important; for the behaviour, avoidance of the cause of pain, has a natural appropriateness to the

---

[12] *PI* I § 244. See above, p. 395 n. 9.
[13] Cf. *NLPESD* pp. 293–5.

sufferer's predicament, and so when the word 'pain' is introduced in this way, it incorporates 'hypotheses' about the cause of pain in its sense.

Anyway, it is not obvious and it needed to be established by argument that if this kind of natural expression in behaviour were not available at any point, no language could be learned, or, to put it more accurately, nothing that could conceivably be done would count as learning a language. If this is a valid point, it is not self-evidently valid, and it is one that is well worth developing, especially when it is extended to exteroceptive perception. For it is when the function of the pre-linguistic structure is brought in to explain the perception of spatial properties that the full power of this line of argument can be felt.

Pain is an exceptional case in several ways.[14] First, from the sympathizer's point of view, the evident simplicity of its natural links not only with behaviour but also with the circumstances that cause it makes it easier to argue that its outward criteria really do capture its intrinsic character. Second, from the sufferer's point of view, the spontaneous tendency to take avoiding action is perspicuously appropriate to the fact that the usual cause is physical damage. The whole drama is so simple that in an extreme case the sympathizer does not infer the sufferer's pain—he sees it; and similarly, the sufferer does not infer the damage and decide to take avoiding action—it hits him and he reacts in the way that nature, relieving him of the need for thought, has made spontaneous.

These two features of the special case, pain, can also be found in the wider field of exteroceptive perception. In fact, the pre-linguistic structure, on to which language is grafted, is most elaborate in the perception of space, and it is quite impossible to treat visual impressions of spatial properties in the pointillist way that is favoured by the classical phenomenalist. The man who sees the stepping-stones ahead of him does not first pick out the corresponding impressions in his visual field, one by one, and then set up the hypothesis that their visual layout corresponds to the actual layout of the physical objects ahead of him. On the contrary, the so-called 'hypothesis' was imprinted on his nervous system before he found names for his impressions, and so the names, when they were introduced, immediately picked up connections which already existed, not, of course, as inferences, but as actual links in his nervous system. Cartesian philosophy ignores these

---

[14] See above, pp. 308–10 and 331.

connections in their early pre-linguistic form, and tries to introduce them at the later intellectual stage. But it is then too late, and the desperate philosophical remedies that are proposed have much the same character as the theories that are brought in to explain paranormal psychological achievements.[15]

The relation between this case and Wittgenstein's preferred case, pain, is not entirely straightforward. So before visual impressions of spatial properties are investigated any further, it will be useful to review his account of pain. Something has already been said about his rejection of the idea that its intrinsic character cannot be captured by any outward criteria,[16] and there is a résumé of his treatment of this topic in 'Notes for Lectures on "Private Experience" and "Sense-data" ':

'But surely I distinguish between having toothache and expressing it, and merely expressing it; and I distinguish between these two in myself.' 'Surely this is not merely a matter of using different expressions, but there are two distinct experiences!' 'You talk as though the case of having pain and that of not having pain were only distinguished by the way in which I expressed myself!'

But do we always distinguish between 'mere behaviour' and 'experience + behaviour'? If we see someone falling into flames and crying out, do we say to ourselves: 'there are, of course, two cases: . . .? Or if I see you here before me do I distinguish? Do you? You can't! That we do in certain cases, doesn't show that we do in all cases. That to some of you must sound silly and superficial; but it isn't. When you see me, do you see one thing and conjecture another? (Don't talk of conjecturing subconsciously!) But supposing you expressed yourself in the form of such a supposition, wouldn't this come to adopting a 'façon de parler'?[17]

In extreme cases, at least, the sympathizer sees the sufferer's pain. If this puts too much weight on the use of the verb 'to see', there is also the negative argument, that anything extra and completely detached from outward criteria could not possibly be what people talk about in casualty-clearing stations and hospitals.[18]

Wittgenstein might have reinforced this account of pain as observed by the sympathizer with a complementary account of pain as felt by the sufferer, which would, as it were, meet the sympathizer half way. He

---

[15] Some of the clearest examples of theories in the philosophers' limbo are to be found among classical treatments of perception. See above, pp. 206–7 and 337.

[16] See above, pp. 000–0.

[17] *NLPESD* p. 318.   [18] See above, pp. 351–5.

could have included in what the sufferer feels his intimation of what has happened to his body and his spontaneous tendency to react in the appropriate way. His treatment of experiences is generally holistic, and he mentions many examples where an experience which seems to be self-contained really gets most of its content from its surroundings. Experiences which are tied to a felt tendency to specific behaviour are a special case of this sort of thing, and pain illustrates it most dramatically.[19] However, he says very little about the phenomenology of pain, perhaps because he took it to be obvious, or maybe the course of his inquiry was set by its starting-point, the problem of other minds.[20]

There is no mystery about the connection between the fact that pain is typically caused by injury and the sufferer's tendency to take avoiding action. The fact itself is so simple and so much part of our lives that, when we learn the word 'pain', it scarcely strikes us as a word that derives from the sensation-type an imprinted 'hypothesis' about its cause. But if the tendency to shrink or run is essential to pain, so too is the intimation of its cause. It is unfortunate that in our philosophical tradition so much emphasis has been put on the fact that sensations of pain are not correlated in any simple way with the world outside our skins, and so little on its regular correlation with damage or malfunction inside our skins.

If we want to see the full development of this pattern, we need to look at exteroceptive impressions. They exhibit an interesting variety of cases, ranging from visual impressions of colours at the least theory-laden end of the scale to visual impressions of spatial properties at the most theory-laden end of it. The range of cases is worth analysing, because it helps to show what is wrong with the classical phenomenalist's account of language. It may be that words at the theoretical end could not be learned in the way that they propose because their account of learning is pointillist and these words carry 'hypotheses' about the physical world.[21] Certainly, when we learn such words in real life, we are greatly helped by the fact that the links which we now try to set out as hypotheses were imprinted on our nervous systems before the advent of language. Incidentally, there is another lesson to be learned

---

[19] His most discussed example is the flash of understanding and its follow-up (see *PI* I §§ 138–40). He sometimes seems to assume that pain is the only type of sensation that lays a train for specific behaviour (see *Zettel*, § 483). But itching leads to scratching, and there are also more subtle cases, like the sensation that people get before yawning.

[20] See above, p. 398.

[21] Cf. G. Evans: 'Things without the Mind', pp. 270–1.

from this range of exteroceptive impressions: it is at the non-theoretical end of the scale that we tend to suppose that we can understand the suggestion that there might be undetectable variations between the impressions of different people. No doubt that is why this speculation is usually developed for visual impressions of colours and not for visual impressions of spatial properties.

But is it possible to get any support for the private language argument of *Philosophical Investigations* from an examination of exteroceptive sense-data at the theory-laden end of the scale? If so, they would reinforce the lesson that he extracts from his favourite example, pain. Now the lesson, as he formulates it, is that the word 'pain' is introduced into a pre-linguistic pattern of connections. This lesson would be reinforced if it could be shown that many words for types of exteroceptive sense-data are introduced into similar patterns. For that would show that this mode of introduction is widespread rather than the exception. However, what the private language argument needs in order to protect it from the classical phenomenalist's criticism is a demonstration that, if pre-linguistic patterns of this kind were not available at many points in the mass of material which confronts a child trying to acquire language, the achievement would be impossible. But can this be shown?

We may start from the less ambitious of the two lessons to be extracted from these theory-laden cases. There can really be no doubt about their importance. It has just been remarked that it is easier to imagine that one can understand the speculation that there might be undetectable variations between the intrinsic properties of different people's impressions of red and blue than it is to imagine that one can understand the same speculation in the case of words like 'above' or 'on the left', and the suggestion was that this difference is explained by the fact that these spatial words, unlike colour words, carry a load of theory. This point does not involve agreement that the speculation really is intelligible for colours. It is merely that the spatial properties of visual impressions, unlike their colours, are linked to our actual location and possible movements in physical space in a way that so obviously captures their intrinsic character.

This is immediately apparent to anyone who tries to speculate that his visual impressions of spatial properties may be different from other people's. The idea does not even give the illusion of being easy to handle, as it does in the case of colours. Suppose that he tries imagining that *left* in the visual field represents *right* in the cone of physical space ahead of him, and *right* represents *left*, whereas in the visual fields of other people like is correlated with like. But what would 'the left half of his visual field' mean, if it did not mean 'the half that is correlated with the left half of the cone of physical space'? True, people might put on spectacles that transposed left and right, but, if they did that, they would soon revert to seeing left as left.[22] Visual impressions of spatial properties evidently get their intrinsic character from their regular connections with something else, but this does not seem to be true of visual impressions of colours.

There is another way of showing that visual impressions of spatial properties get their intrinsic character from their regular connections with something else. If colours really do lack regular connections with other things and are, in that sense, free variables, there will be no decisive test not involving language which will indicate that someone is seeing red as conclusively as seeing him struggling in flames will indicate that he is in pain. But if what has been said so far is correct, we would expect there to be a decisive test for his seeing something on the left, and there is: if he flinches to the right when a blow is aimed at him from the left, he saw it on the left.[23]

It is paradoxical to say that visual impressions of spatial properties get their intrinsic characters from something else. How then can their characters be intrinsic to them? It would be more accurate to say that the words that we apply to them directly really carry hypotheses about physical objects and our own movements among them. That is how Gareth Evans puts it,[24] and it carries the corollary that someone who did not understand the hypotheses would not understand the words. Whichever way we put it, the point is that seen spatial properties are very unlike seen colours. For seen colours guide our behaviour only when we happen to have other beliefs, like the belief that scarlet berries are poisonous. This, of course, is not true of patterns of colours, because colour-edges do indicate the boundaries of objects in physical space, but it is true of individual colours.[25] So people get the illusion that the colours of visual impressions are genuinely intrinsic, unlike their spatial properties, which are properties borrowed from elsewhere. But how could colour-edges in the visual field possibly be

[22] This type of 'seeing as' is not among those examined in *PI* II. xi, where Wittgenstein's discussion of this polymorphous concept concentrates on cases involving a recognizable internal relation between what is seen and something else.

[23] See *RPPII* § 506.

[24] Cf. G. Evans: 'Things without the Mind', p. 269.

[25] See above, p. 332.

less intrinsic than the colours themselves? We should content ourselves with describing the facts without bringing in the distinction between intrinsic and extrinsic properties of exteroceptive impressions.

The important point is that such impressions can be arranged on a scale starting with the least theoretical and ending with the most theoretical. For since the theories are essentially about the physical world, the idea behind the private language argument can be developed in an area in which Wittgenstein deployed it less fully than he deployed it for bodily sensations. The idea is that many of the words that the classical phenomenalist persuades us to see as pure descriptions of sense-data really carry 'hypotheses' which cannot conceivably be passed off as 'hypotheses' about further sense-data. The argument for this is simple: when these theoretical words are learned, they find their place in a pre-existing framework of type-lines, because in each case the link brought out by the theory has already been imprinted on our nervous systems. Since so much of language is acquired in this way, the classical phenomenalist's intellectualization of the process cannot be right. His error shows up at two places in the development of this idea. First, and most important, these theoretical words will be undetachably rooted in the physical world because the original imprinting was done at the interface between the human body and its environment. Second, we are able to learn their meanings only because their type-lines were firmly established before the advent of language. If that were not so, our predicament as learners would be as hopeless as that of the marksman on the second frustrating rifle-range.

Wittgenstein did not develop this idea in any detail for exteroceptive impressions.[26] He developed it very fully for bodily sensations and especially for pain, where it leads to an account of the meaning of the word which puts a lot of weight on the social importance of pain-behaviour and on the responses of sympathizers.[27] Pain is a special case and in some ways a very illuminating one, but it is uncharacteristic of Wittgenstein to be drawn so exclusively to the bright light of a single example.[28] It is also regrettable, because it diverted his attention from the errors in the classical phenomenalist's account of the origin of scientific language. It is all very well to mock the positivists Schlick and

[26] He did, of course, apply it to exteroceptive impressions (see above, p. 403 n. 23), but not in the fully worked out detail of its application to pain, and even in the case of pain not enough is said about its perceptual relation to its cause.

[27] See above, pp. 309–10 and 331–3.

[28] Cf. *PI* I § 593: 'A main cause of philosophical disease—a one-sided diet: one nourishes one's thinking with only one kind of example.'

Carnap for leaving out the humanity of human observers, and for treating them like mechanical recorders of cold facts.[29] But that really is one side of human life, and Wittgenstein's later philosophy would have been more balanced if he had not allowed so many of the fundamental problems of this kind of factual language to fade into the background. Pain is an important example, beause it leads philosophy away from its preoccupation with science[30] into our social lives and emotional reactions. But it would have been better to develop the new idea in full detail not only for pain but also for exteroceptive impressions. It is a source of weakness in his philosophy that he was not sufficiently worried by his relations with the physical world.[31]

If he had worked out the implications of the new idea for exteroceptive impressions in as much detail as he put into its application to pain, the private language argument would have been more perspicuous.[32] It is not just that the premisses of the *reductio* are hard to identify, or that it is not entirely clear what further considerations, if any, would have been used by him to defend it against the obvious criticism made by ordinary phenomenalists. The trouble is that the decisive role of the pre-linguistic network of type-lines is not fully presented. It is explained in some detail for bodily sensations, but not for exteroceptive impressions, and it occupies the position of a reserve force never fully committed on the field of battle.

If this line of thought had been developed further, it would have supported a more ambitious conclusion than the one sketched above. That conclusion was that many types of exteroceptive impression are essentially connected with their physical causes, so that, when words are coined for them, they immediately pick up 'hypotheses' about those causes. But if the reasoning had been taken further, it would have proved possible to argue that, if this had not been so, we would not have been able to include in our language any words for the other types of sense-data which strike us, albeit misleadingly, as having independent intrinsic properties. So we would never have been able to start on the task of setting up a language, because we would have found ourselves

---

[29] See above, pp. 300–3. Understandably, this has proved to be one of the most popular aspects of Wittgenstein's later philosophy, but really it corrects one excessive emphasis only by substituting another one.

[30] See above, pp. 309–10. [31] See above, pp. 274–7, and Vol. I p. 194.

[32] G. Evans's development of the idea in this area is independent of Wittgenstein's private language argument, but if the line taken above is right, it can be connected with it. It can also be connected with the work of Merleau-Ponty, and, earlier, with the ideas of the American Pragmatists.

in a position like that of the marksman on the second frustrating rifle-range.

But isn't this precisely what Wittgenstein does argue? It is certainly the conclusion of his private language argument and it is equally certainly the line of thought that leads him to it. What is lacking, or, at least, not fully developed, is the detailed application of the reasoning to exteroceptive impressions. It is as if the private language argument, instead of including these thoughts as premises, was developed in the atmosphere that they created. This gives people the illusion that the classical phenomenalist's objection to his argument had not occurred to him and that, perhaps, he had no answer to it. No doubt, this is why there has been such extensive disagreement about the interpretation and assessment of the private language argument. Some treat it as a superficial sophism easily refuted, while others see it as a profound piece of reasoning which has changed the face of philosophy.

The structure of the private language argument of *Philosophical Investigations* is not the only aspect of it which received too little attention in the previous two chapters. There is also another aspect which still remains to be investigated. In the course of the discussion of its structure that has just been concluded, it was remarked that it seems easier to imagine that there might be undetectable differences between the 'intrinsic' characters of two people's visual impressions of red or blue than it is to imagine a similar difference between the 'intrinsic' characters of their visual impressions of left and right. An explanation of this apparent difference was suggested and the subject was dropped. It must now be pursued further, because it raises more questions than those brief remarks implied, and the answers to them will affect the interpretation of the whole argument. Is it, perhaps, possible that the 'intrinsic' characters of my impressions of red and blue might be switched overnight? If so, is it also possible that they might have been switched from the very beginning, when I was first acquiring my colour-vocabulary? And if that is possible, comparisons between the 'intrinsic' characters of the impressions of two different people must be intelligible, must they not?

These questions are evidently relevant to the interpretation and assessment of the private language argument. So far, attention has been focused on the situation in which language is learned. The point selected for development from Wittgenstein's discussion has been the need for a viable criterion of identity of each sensation-type. That was, of course, his central point, but since the use of a criterion of identity is spread out over time, his examination of the conditions that make it possible for a person to learn a vocabulary leads without any sharp transition into an examination of the conditions that make it possible for him to maintain it, like a currency, with the meanings of its words unchanged. Now there are various crises that might threaten words in our vocabulary for reporting our bodily sensations or our exteroceptive impressions, and perhaps the most dramatic one that you can imagine would be the sudden transposition of the 'intrinsic' characters of your visual impressions of red and blue. But can you really imagine that? And if you can, does that not prove that, contrary to what Wittgenstein has been represented as saying so far, exteroceptive impressions really do have intrinsic characters that cannot be captured by any external criteria?

These questions need to be handled with care, because it is not clear what imaginability is supposed to indicate here, or even whether it is an effective test of anything. In the other situation, in which language was being learned, the question was not whether we can imagine a child, who had been adopted by wolves before he had acquired even the rudiments of language in his human family, then going on to set up a language entirely for his own use. The question was whether anything that we can imagine a child doing in such a predicament would count as setting up a language. Similarly, in this situation, the question is not whether you can imagine yourself, after going through the crisis of transposition, still continuing to use the words 'red' and 'blue' with their original meanings preserved, but whether anything that you can imagine yourself doing after such a crisis would count as maintaining them in use with their original meanings. It is particularly important not to fall into the trap of saying 'Yes, of course, it would be easy and I am sure that I would bring it off.' For that would be like saying that the wolf-child would have no difficulty in setting up a language, given his human intelligence. Perhaps it is better to change the story and make it someone else who goes through the crisis:

Consider this case: someone says 'I can't understand it, I see everything red blue today and vice versa.' We answer, 'It must look queer!' He says it does and, e.g., goes on to say how cold the glowing coal looks and how warm the clear (blue) sky. I think we should under these or similar circumstances be inclined to say that he saw red what we saw blue. And again we should say that we know that he means by the words 'blue' and 'red' what we do, as he has always used them as we do.[33]

[33] *NLPESD* p. 284.

This is not a case involving a comparison between the 'intrinsic' characters of this man's impressions of red and blue and anyone else's. Nor does it even involve a contrast with an alternative possible world, in which his impressions of the two colours are imagined to have 'intrinsic' characters different from those that they actually have. 'Intrinsic' characters are not even mentioned by Wittgenstein, who simply observes that in a case like this 'we should say that we know that he means by the words "blue" and "red" what we do, as he has always used them as we do'. To put his verdict in the terms used above, what we are imagining that this man does would count as maintaining the two words in use with their original meanings.

It is tempting to go on and ask a further question, which Wittgenstein does not ask about this case: 'How long would this man's behaviour go on counting as maintaining the two words in use with their original meanings?' Suppose that ten years later he still says that the sky looks red, and that, though it no longer looks 'queer' to him, it does look the colour that geraniums used to look in the time before the crisis. Would this too count as maintaining the two words in use with their original meanings?

Before this question is tackled, it is a good idea to remind ourselves that it is not asking how long the sky would go on looking queer to him, or how long he would continue to remember seeing geraniums with the colour that the sky looks to him now. Those two questions are empirical, and they can be settled, if at all, by experiment.

Incidentally, the second empirical question, about his memory, would be especially difficult to answer. For it is not asking whether he would remember that geraniums once looked the colour that the sky looks to him now. That would be an uninteresting question about the range and reliability of his factual memory. The second empirical question is asking something much more interesting—how long would he actually remember seeing geraniums with that colour? This introduces philosophical considerations about the criteria of different kinds of memory into the designing of any experiment intended to give us the answer to the question. For the experimenter would have to distinguish factual memory from experience-memory, and he would have to make sure that it was the latter that he was testing. The investigation would be interesting because, if it could be carried out, it would show how much the man's reports of his experience-memories were influenced by the new connections that the words 'red' and 'blue' had acquired for him in the physical world.

Anyway, the original question—the one that Wittgenstein does not ask—was 'How long would this man's behaviour go on counting as maintaining the two words in use with their original meanings?' In order to answer it, we merely have to imagine that the experiment gets a positive result: ten years later he does still remember seeing geraniums with the colour that the sky looks to him now. Would that count as maintaining the two words in use with their original meanings?

It may be that the reason why Wittgenstein does not ask this further question is that it is peripheral. On the day after the crisis, the man really would be maintaining the use of the two words with their original meanings. Wittgenstein is categorical about that and he is surely right. Ten years later, given no further upsets, the new connections with the physical world acquired by the two words will give the man all the resources that he needs in order to maintain their meanings unaltered throughout the period after the crisis, and the question about the geraniums of his distant past will be completely detached from his present practice. That makes it a peripheral question in the investigation of the ways in which constancy of meaning is preserved. Our assessment of the resources that are available and actually used is not affected by our conclusions about the phenomenology of the man's memories of the way things looked ten years ago.

There is, however, something more to be learned from this case. It is possible to discuss it in perfectly ordinary language without any use of the phrase 'intrinsic character', which hints at something which might elude all 'extrinsic' criteria. The reason why it can be discussed in a way that does not lead into such runaway speculations is plain: in the first chapter of the story about the crisis the characters of the victim's visual impressions are tied to their ordinary physical criteria while in the second chapter these attachments are suddenly broken and replaced by a new set of attachments of the same kind. There is no point in the story at which we feel that, in order to understand what is going on, we have to introduce a distinction between the 'intrinsic' characters of his impressions and characters captured by 'extrinsic' criteria. Yet his impressions do have characters which are not *reduced* to their links with stimuli and responses in the way envisaged by behaviourists. That is the point of the story of the crisis produced by the startling transposition.

Wittgenstein's treatment of the case of the sudden transposition may be summarized briefly. He presents it in perfectly ordinary language, avoiding any use of the distinction between 'intrinsic' and 'extrinsic'. He merely observes that, on the day of the crisis, 'we should say that this man means by the words "blue" and "red" what we do, as he has always used them as we do'. The question whether he would still be doing so ten years on is not raised.

The best way to appreciate his treatment of this case is to contrast it with what he says about the other two cases, in each of which something is lacking. This is what he says about the first deficient case:

> On the other hand: Someone tells us today that yesterday he always saw everything red blue, and so on. We say: But you called the glowing coal red, you know, and the sky blue. He answers: That was because I had also changed the names. We say: But didn't it feel very queer? and he says: No, it seemed all perfectly natural. Would we in this case too say: . . .?[34]

What is lacking in this case is a phenomenological feature which played an important role in the other case: this man does not find the appearance of the sky at all queer, and he says that he immediately made the linguistic adjustment required to bring his reports of colours into line with other people's, like someone who is accustomed to the wobbly steering of his car and adjusts it without thinking.

If this is not a case of maintaining the use of the two words through a crisis of transposition with unaltered meanings, the reason why it is not such a case is not that their use is not maintained, but, rather, that it is not clear that the case, as described, really is an example of the crisis. An essential feature is lacking in this man's experience, and so it is not a clear case of transposition. This brings out an important point about the imaginability of these bizarre cases. If you want to present such a case, it is no good just saying 'Imagine a switch in the characters of a person's impressions of blue and red'. You have to tell the story in a way that will make the case count as an example of such a switch, and this story fails to pass the test, although, of course, it does seem to count as a case of maintaining the use of the two words with unaltered meanings.

The case deserves closer scrutiny, because it makes a subtle point. It is a case of a person who takes the first step towards detaching the 'intrinsic' characters of his impressions of the two colours not only from their previous physical criteria, but also from his own apprehension of them. He tells us that yesterday, during the crisis, he 'saw everything red blue, and so on', but he denies what ought to follow from this, that

[34] *NLPESD* p. 284.

it felt queer. The next step along this road is to try to imagine a case in which the 'intrinsic characters' of the two impressions are also detached from the subject's apprehension of them:

> . . . Always get rid of the private object in this way: assume that it constantly changes, but that you do not notice the change because your memory constantly deceives you.[35]

In this case the 'intrinsic' character of the 'internal' object is supposed to be detached from everything that ties a sensation-type into our lives as we live them—even from the subject's own apprehension of it. Wittgenstein is inviting us to take a further step along the road of imagined detachments. Naturally, he does not ask us to imagine a case in which the subject has no awareness of the 'private object', because that would be going too far—there would then be no reason left to suppose that there was an object at all. So what he suggests is that we try to imagine a case in which the line connecting the sensation-type to the subject's memory is completely disrupted, so that there is no way of gathering the actual type from what his memory tells him about it.[36] This is an example of a technique often used by Wittgenstein in his dialectical treatment of philosophical problems: when his adversary puts forward a thesis which is really senseless, but not obviously so, he suggests a further move in the same direction—away from our normal practice—thus producing a piece of patent nonsense which will show up the fault that is latent in his adversary's less extreme position.[37]

There is a feature of these presentations of imagined cases which is worth noting. We really would describe the central case as 'the crisis of transposition'. But though we would not be so sure about applying the same description to these cases which lack something that played an important role in the central case, there is no implication that it would be meaningless to describe them in the same way. Wittgenstein is not using the verification principle to cut his adversaries' speculation down to the ground, as it were with a single hatchet blow. He is not saying to them, 'Look, your suggestion about the "intrinsic" characters of sensation-types is unverifiable and so, since the meaning of a sentence is the method of its verification, it lacks meaning.' It is not necessarily meaningless to suggest that the 'intrinsic' characters of certain

---

[35] *PI* II. xi, p. 207.

[36] This disruption is the limiting case of the disruptions of type-lines introduced above, pp. 406–7.

[37] See above, p. 352. Cf. *PI* I §§ 464 and 524.

impressions of colour might undergo a shift which could not be captured by the 'extrinsic' criteria that we use at present. He is making the more subtle point, that his adversaries must give it a meaning by tying it into our lives. They must not assume that it already has a meaning in its own right, a meaning so independent that it will survive the stepwise detachment of this 'intrinsic' character from all the 'extrinsic' criteria on which it now relies. That is the point of his parody. In effect, he is saying 'All right. Sever the external connections if you like, but, if this character really is "intrinsic", you can sever its internal connection too. Then you really will be able to understand your mistake.'

Incidentally, when a suggestion does not yet have a meaning in our language, as the suggestion in Wittgenstein's parody does not, he would say that we have not even identified a candidate for possibility. So we must not allow ourselves to be deluded by a vague picture into supposing that there is a definite piece of non-sense out there in the cold waiting for language to make contact with it.[38] The only thing that we can do here is to give the suggestion a sense by changing our language. In some cases this is easily done, but in a case like this one, there is no more material left for us to use. However, that does not mean that we have to choose between the two extreme alternatives, either condemning the suggestion as meaningless or else relying on a vague picture which has not been given a definite application. In such cases the work of inventing modified language-games is most needed precisely because it is most difficult.

So much for the first deficient case, lying on one side of the straightforward case of the crisis of transposition, in which the subject is amazed to wake up finding the sky looking steadily red and burning coals looking steadily blue. The deficiency is something in the phenomenology of the experience: the subject does not find it at all queer. There is also a second deficient case, lying on the other side of the straightforward crisis, in which what is lacking is a steady connection between the old impressions and their new physical settings. Here is Wittgenstein's description of this kind of case:

We learn the word 'red' under particular circumstances. Certain objects are usually red, and keep their colour; most people agree with us in our colour judgements. Suppose all this changes: I see blood, unaccountably sometimes one, sometimes another colour, and the people around me make different

[38] See above, pp. 215–16.

statements. But couldn't I in all this chaos retain my meaning of 'red', 'blue', etc. Although I couldn't now make myself understood to anyone? Samples, e.g., would all constantly change their colour—'or does it only seem so to me?' 'Now am I mad or did I really call this "red" yesterday?'[39]

This text's equal emphasis on our two resources, calibration on standard objects and appeal to other people's judgements, has already been discussed.[40] The point that needs to be made about it now is that he carefully refrains from giving any verdict and leaves it an open question whether I would still be able to maintain the use of the two colour-words with unaltered meanings. The reason why he does not commit himself in this case is that nothing stable takes over the role of the old physical criteria. True, my use of the two colour-words does start off in the normal way, and that creates a presumption that it is not immediately derailed by the crisis. But how long would it remain on the old rails without any discoverable new physical criteria to take over from the old ones?

As usual, this question needs to be split in two. First, there is the empirical question, how long my practice would in fact continue to exhibit any confident regularity. As Wittgenstein presents the story, I am immediately thrown into complete confusion. There is, therefore, no occasion for the philosophical question how long my practice would count as maintaining the use of the two colour-words with their meanings unaltered. So he returns an open verdict. Presumably, he felt it unnecessary to consider the other logically possible outcome, in which I record the continually changing colours of the sky, burning coals, and everything else with amazement but nevertheless with complete confidence. If that were what happened, the philosophical question would be how long my practice would count as maintaining the original use of the two colour-words. Perhaps he thought that there was no need to go into that question. Complete chaos in the new physical settings of the impressions would make us say, sooner or later, that it would not count, and it would be foolish to ask for the exact point at which it would cease to count.[41]

This chapter opened with a question about the structure of the private language argument of *Philosophical Investigations*. Has it any unobvious premisses? The answer proposed was that it does have a premiss that is easily overlooked: language must be superimposed on a

---

[39] *NLPESD* p. 306.   [40] See above, p. 372.
[41] Cf. his discussion of the question 'Which was the first word that this person read?' (*PI* I § 157, quoted and discussed above, pp. 379–80).

pre-existing network of connections running from physical stimuli into the seat of consciousness and out again to behaviour,[42] because there is no way in which it could get started without those connections. Indeed, it is only this premiss that provides Wittgenstein with an answer to the obvious objection of the classical phenomenalist.[43]

That part of the examination of the private language argument was concerned with the learning of language. But there is also the question how language is maintained after it has been learned. Although this is not an entirely separate question, it does focus attention on a different aspect of language, namely the continuity of an established tradition. Wittgenstein investigates the presuppositions of this continuity by presenting a case of a crisis of transposition and asking whether a speaker's practice after the crisis would count as maintaining his former vocabulary in use with the meanings of its words unaltered. That is his central case, and it is flanked by two related cases, one showing a deficiency in the phenomenology of the speaker's experience, and the other showing a deficiency in the connections between the original impressions and their new physical settings.

It is time to ask what the investigation of these cases contributes to the line of thought started by the private language argument. A simple answer to this question would be that it demonstrates the difference between Wittgenstein's position and behaviourism. If the subject's impression-types before the crisis were reduced without residue to their physical criteria, then it would follow that, given the different physical criteria after the crisis, his impression-types would be different too. But that is not Wittgenstein's position. His verdict is that in the central case of the straightforward crisis, the subject's later reports would count as reports of the same impression-types. True, as time went on, the preservation of the established tradition through the crisis would become less and less important for the contemporary use of the language. Nevertheless, his verdict on the immediate sequel to the crisis sharply distinguishes his position from behaviourism.

If that were all that could be learned from these cases, it might leave us with the impression that each impression-type has a definite

---

[42] Evidently these connections run through our nervous systems. But the lines presupposed by language are only lines connecting the immediate environment with our awareness of it and then with appropriate behaviour. These are the three things that are regularly and repeatedly connected in the essential pre-linguistic patterns. the embodiment of the connecting lines in our nervous systems is something that is not essential to the philosophy of mind as practised by Wittgenstein. See above, pp. 252–3.

[43] See above, pp. 405–6.

'intrinsic' character, which gives any word that is attached to it its meaning, and that the 'extrinsic' physical criteria are merely devices which are necessary for the identification of this character in other people's impressions, but which are completely unnecessary in our own cases. But that is not Wittgenstein's view. The further, and equally important lesson that he derives from these cases is that the criteria of identity of these 'intrinsic' characters are strictly limited in their scope. They allow us to ask and answer certain questions about sameness of impression-types in our daily lives, and they provide answers to such questions across the gap produced by the straightforward crisis of transposition that he describes. But their scope is limited, because they fail to provide us with answers in the two deficient cases which flank the straightforward case.

It is important to appreciate the nature of this failure. In the two deficient cases the criteria of identity of impression-types fail to give us any answer to the question whether the type is still the same. So though Wittgenstein's view of these two cases is that the subject's reports would not count as reports of the same impression-types, he is not implying that they would count as reports of different impression-types. His idea is that we have reached a point where the criteria do not supply us with any answer to the question about identity of type. The presuppositions of the language-game are not fulfilled and so questions of identity cannot be answered either positively or negatively.

It is from this point of view that we can appreciate his reluctance to discuss the problem of the identity of phenomenal types in the terms used by his adversaries. They speak of 'intrinsic characters' and 'extrinsic criteria', but, as already observed, he confines himself to perfectly ordinary language when he is presenting the cases which lead to his solution. This is not because he thinks that it is an unreal problem, created by his adversaries' terminology. That would be the behaviourist's view of the matter. His view is that their determination to rely on the words 'intrinsic' and 'extrinsic', as if they marked a distinction when no distinction has been drawn, makes the problem insoluble for them.[44]

He would concede that it is not actually wrong to sum up the straightforward case of the crisis of transposition by saying that the 'intrinsic' characters of the subject's impressions of red and blue were detached from their usual 'extrinsic' physical setting and attached to a

---

[44] Cf. *PI* I § 308, and *NLPESD* pp. 304–5.

new 'extrinsic' physical setting, provided that we realize that we have no criterion of identity for a character, completely detached from all physical settings. However, that is precisely what those who use this terminology do not realize. They talk themselves into the delusion that the identity of phenomenal types will endure through all vicissitudes—even those described in the two deficient cases—because it is genuinely 'intrinsic' identity. Naturally, they concede that there are cases in which we will be unable to tell whether the type is, or is not, the same, and that perhaps this is how the two deficient cases should be classified. But they cling with unalterable determination to their idea that in any case that can be described, however far out from human life, there must be an answer to the question of identity—yes or no—if only we could discover it.

The analogy with physical objects is plainly influential at this point. This wineglass is an object which I could describe in full detail if it were a valuable antique and it vanished. If ten years later Interpol sent me a matching description of a glass seen in a private collection in Japan, I would know that it either was, or was not, the same glass. More interestingly, if it had a rare sheen of iridescent amber, I would know that this either was, or was not, the colour of certain Roman goblets described by an author in Antiquity. These are our paradigms of 'intrinsic' identity. These things do not 'borrow' their identities from their circumstances, and so in this kind of case, when we hear of a candidate for identity but find that the circumstances are baffling, we do not conclude that there is no answer to the question of identity, positive or negative. Wittgenstein's point is that his adversaries have no right to extend this treatment to phenomenal types in all imaginable circumstances. They are merely following the suggestion of their arbitrarily chosen phrase 'completely intrinsic character'.

The maintenance of a word in use, like the original acquisition of the ability to use it, must not be allowed to rest on the exaggerated analogy between phenomenal things and physical things. The point made in Chapter 14 about learning how to use a word was that it is possible only when there is an independent criterion for 'the same again'. This independent criterion is available for physical objects and their properties, and also for anything which has an identity connected with the identities of physical objects and their properties. But it is no longer possible to reidentify phenomenal types when all their connections with the physical world have been severed, and so it is no longer possible to learn to use words for them. However, this disability

is overlooked by Wittgenstein's adversaries because they assume that
they can start all over again within the mind, treating sensations and
their types as if they had the necessary independent criteria of identity,
which they do not have, but physical objects do have. When they go on
to consider the maintenance of a word in use across the gap made by a
crisis of transposition, they make the same mistaken assumption. So at
both stages of the investigation they are trying to exploit points of
analogy between phenomenal types and physical types beyond the
point where they have ceased to exist.

Two of the questions raised above[45] still remain to be answered. Is it
possible that the 'intrinsic characters' of my impressions of red and
blue might have been switched from the very begining, when I was first
acquiring my colour-vocabulary? And if that is possible, does it follow
that comparisons between the 'intrinsic characters' of the impressions
of two different people are intelligible? Perhaps it would be prudent to
start following Wittgenstein's example now and to give up using the
misleading phrase 'intrinsic character' because the so-called 'intrinsic
characters' of our sensations, as they are reported in our actual
language-game, have 'extrinsic criteria'. So we had better switch to
plain English and simply ask whether my impressions of red and blue
might have been switched from the very beginning.

It may now look as if there is a way of giving this question an
affirmative answer. If it is possible that the switch might occur in the
form of the later crisis described by Wittgenstein in the straightforward
case, then it is also possible that it might have occurred at some earlier
date. However, if a person who went through it in later life said that he
wished that it had happened to him at birth, so that he could have
avoided all this disorientation and rehabilitation, there would be
something wrong with his wish. It is really an understatement to say
that it would have been easier for him if it had happened at birth. For
in that case there would have been no point of view from which it was a
switch. His first impressions of red and blue simply set him the
standard for those two types.

He may object that, of course, he understands the possibility that he
has formulated perfectly well, and it is just a verificationist prejudice
which generates the objection that, if it had been realized in his case, it
would have been exactly the same for him as if it had not been realized,
and, therefore, the formula lacks sense. Maybe, but the language

which deals with these matters is intended for use, and it should at least give us pause when we notice that we are moving out of the zone of possibilities that would be recognizable if they were realized. Wittgenstein is not intolerant in his treatment of the outer circle into which this speculation takes us. He observes that the proposed formula has not been given a use, but he does not argue dogmatically that it could not be given one. What he opposes is the procedure of his adversaries who go on as if they had given it a use, when they have not done so. He also often hints that, if it were given a use, it would not be what they wanted, because their aspiration is to decant all the meaning of the phrase 'impression of blue' into its 'intrinsic character' and then to argue that, *as things are*, it is entirely possible that this 'intrinsic character' varies in complete independence of its physical setting.[46]

At this point Wittgenstein's adversaries are likely to say that they were manœuvred into an impasse only because they were making no use of the 'intrinsic characters' of other people's impressions. You should start from a case in which, when someone else looks up at the clear sky, his impression of blue differs from yours, and you speculate that it might have been the same.

This suggestion does not look so good when it is put in plain English. We already have criteria for determining when two people have impressions of the same type, and we do not find it necessary to qualify such criteria as 'extrinsic'. If this word means 'belonging to the common world', it does not need to be added, while if it means 'failing to capture the "intrinsic" character of the impressions', it had better not be added, because our criteria just are the criteria of sameness of impression-type.[47] What others could we have in mind?

But the opposition will not collapse so easily. It is precisely in the case of other minds that people's doubts are strongest. In one's own case, one can remember how the sky looked before the straightforward crisis described by Wittgenstein. Consequently, the idea of an elusive 'intrinsic character' gets no grip on their imaginations in the first-person case. But we lack any such line into other people's minds, and so, according to them, it is only practical convenience and not a concern for truth that leads us to treat the ordinary criteria of sameness of impression-type as decisive in the third-person case.

Against this, Wittgenstein would make all the moves that have

---

[46] It is against this argument that Wittgenstein develops his parody. See above, p. 411.
[47] See above, pp. 351–5 and 400–1.

already been described. Why should even your memory be trusted in the crisis of transposition? If you discount the so-called 'extrinsic' criteria, you might as well suppose that your memory deceives you about the character of the impressions that you used to get from the clear sky. Or suppose you try moving in the other direction, establishing new links which provide new criteria of identity, instead of severing the old links. Suppose, for example, that the speech-centre in your cortex were connected to the visual centre in the other person's cortex. Even that could be rejected as not giving you what you really wanted, and that would show that nothing would satisfy you—your complaints about the inadequacy of 'extrinsic' criteria are creeping complaints.

But his most effective attack on this position is developed in the passage in *Philosophical Investigations* in which he inveighs against the illusion that behind the ordinary criteria of sameness of impression-type there is another deeper criterion which is so obvious that it need not be formulated:

But if I suppose that someone has a pain, then I am simply supposing that he has just the same as I have so often had.—That gets us no further. It is as if I were to say: 'You surely know what "It is 5 o'clock here" means; so you also know what "It's 5 o'clock on the sun" means. It means simply that it is just the same time there as it is here when it is 5 o'clock.'—The explanation by means of *identity* does not work here. For I know well enough that one can call 5 o'clock here and 5 o'clock there 'the same time', but what I do not know is in what cases one is to speak of its being the same time here and there.

In exactly the same way it is no explanation to say: the supposition that he has a pain is simply the supposition that he has the same as I. For *that* part of the grammar is quite clear to me: that is, that one will say that the stove has the same experience as I, *if* one says: it is in pain and I am in pain.

Yet we go on wanting to say: 'Pain is pain—whether *he* has it, or *I* have it; and however I come to know whether he has a pain or not.'—I might agree.—And when you ask me 'Don't you know, then, what I mean when I say that the stove is in pain?'—I can reply: These words may lead me to have all sorts of images; but their usefulness goes no further. And I can also imagine something in connection with the words: 'It was just 5 o'clock in the afternoon on the sun'— such as a grandfather clock which points to 5.—But a still better example would be that of the application of 'above' and 'below' to the earth. Here we all have a quite clear idea of what 'above' and 'below' mean. I see well enough that I am on top; the earth is surely beneath me! (And don't smile at this example. We are indeed all taught at school that it is stupid to talk like that. But it is much easier to bury a problem than to solve it.) And it is only reflection that shows us that in this case 'above' and 'below' cannot be used in the ordinary way. (That we might, for instance, say that the people at the antipodes are 'below' our part of the earth, but it must also be recognized as right for them to use the same expression about us.)

Here it happens that our thinking plays us a queer trick. We want, that is, to quote the law of excluded middle and to say: 'Either such an image is in his mind, or it is not; there is no third possibility!'—We encounter this queer argument also in other regions of philosophy. 'In the decimal expansion of π either the group "7777" occurs, or it does not—there is no third possibility.' That is to say: 'God sees—but we don't know.' But what does that mean?—We use a picture; the picture of a visible series which one person sees the whole of and another not. The law of excluded middle says here: It must either look like this, or like that. So it really—and this is a truism—says nothing at all, but gives us a picture. And the problem ought now to be: does reality accord with the picture or not? And this picture *seems* to determine what we have to do, what to look for, and how—but it does not do so, just because we do not know how it is to be applied. Here saying 'There is no third possibility' or 'But there can't be a third possibility!'—expresses our inability to turn our eyes away from this picture: a picture which looks as if it must already contain both the problem and its solution, while all the time we *feel* that it is not so.

Similarly when it is said 'Either he has this experience, or not'—what primarily occurs to us is a picture which by itself seems to make the sense of the expressions *unmistakable*: 'Now you know what is in question'—we should like to say. And that is precisely what it does not tell him.[48]

What could be more forceful?

There is, finally, another more distant vantage-point from which the structure of the private language argument can be viewed. We may ask a very general question about Wittgenstein's later philosophy of language: 'Why so much emphasis on activity, practice, and use?' A quick answer would be that this way of looking at language seemed to him to put if firmly in its place in the world. It is interesting that in the earlier theory of language, developed in the *Tractatus*, he had tried to secure the same advantage by treating sentences as facts. They were facts of a very special kind—pictorial facts—but still facts belonging, like other facts, to the one and only world.[49] So why is this egalitarianism[50] presented in a new way in the later theory? Speaking a language is obviously something that we do, but why is that so important?

---

[48] *PI* I §§ 350–2.　　　　　　[49] *TLP* 2.141. See Vol. I pp. 140–1.

[50] The egalitarianism is important. It is only too easy to assume that language and thought are set apart from the rest of the world, enjoying privileges which we need not question.

Again, a quick answer is available: 'This way of looking at language is the best corrective for a bad habit of thought which is endemic in Western philosophy—the inveterate tendency to narrow down the mind's access to reality, constricting it to point-to-point contact.' The treatment of names in the *Tractatus* was a clear example of this habit of thought. For though the name-relation was supposed to draw in the combinatorial possibilities of named objects,[51] there was no explanation of how this was done, and the subject's grasp of the objects was simply called 'acquaintance'[52] and left at that.

Wittgenstein was trained as an engineer and he often used mechanical analogies to illustrate his preferred way of looking at language. Here is one that throws light on the structure of the private language argument:

> The example of the motor roller with the motor in the cylinder[53] is actually far better and deeper than I have explained. For when someone showed me the construction I saw at once that it could not function, since one could roll the cylinder from outside even when the 'motor' was not running; but *this* I did not see, that it was a rigid construction and not a machine at all. And here there is a close analogy with the private ostensive definition. For here too there is, so to speak, a direct and an indirect way of gaining insight into the impossibility.[54]

This may not be very illuminating for those who are on less familiar terms with machines. The unsuccessful motor-roller is described elsewhere:[55] the piston and cylinder are not mounted on a chassis, and so they cannot turn a wheel from which the drive could be transmitted to the drum of the roller (*Walze*, here mistranslated 'cylinder', which makes the construction unintelligible); instead, they are mounted inside the drum of the roller, replacing one of its spokes, which are, of course, held rigidly in place. The point that he makes about this contraption is that there are two ways of appreciating its uselessness. One way is to see that, whatever the piston and cylinder are doing inside the drum of the roller, it produces no effect at the point where the drum is in contact with the ground—there is not tractive effort. This must be the indirect way of discovering that this motor-roller is a bad buy. The other way—the direct way—is to look inside the drum and see that, in fact, the piston and cylinder are not doing anything,

---

[51] See *NB* 4–5 Nov. 1914, quoted in Vol. I pp. 118–19.   [52] *TLP* 2.0123.
[53] i.e. the drum of the roller.
[54] *Remarks on the Philosophy of Psychology*, Vol. I, ed. G. E. M. Anscombe and G. H. von Wright, tr. G. E. M. Anscome, Blackwell, 1980 (henceforth *RPPI*), § 397.
[55] *PG* § 141 and *Zettel*, § 248.

because they are held rigidly in place like machine-parts in a Picasso sculpture.

The application of this mechanical analogy to the private language argument is interesting. The indirect way of appreciating what is wrong with the private use of a word is to see that the user is not getting any purchase on the surface presented to him by the external world. Whatever he is doing with the word, it produces no effect at the interface between his body and his environment. There is no physical test of the correctness of what he is doing and the world slides by without his would-be practice engaging with it.

The direct way is to look inside his mind and see that he is not really doing anything. He may seem to have set up a practice, because he does produce the word in the presence of a sensation, but point-to-point contact is not enough. A practice can be established only when there is an acknowledged connection between a sequence of attempts and a sequence of independently checkable achievements. No skill can be acquired and maintained without a viable criterion of success independent of the fact that the attempt has been made—if there were no such criterion, what would have been attempted?

The structure of the private language argument is indicated very clearly by Wittgenstein's mechanical analogy. Two things, which ought to keep a certain independence of one another—what is done as it is for the doer, and what is done as the successful achievement—are collapsed together, and the result is that, in the sense of 'doing' in which doing is a practice, nothing is done. The same structure is exemplified in a somewhat different way in the argument developed in *Philosophical Investigations* against Platonizing accounts of rule-following, which will be the topic of the next three chapters.[56]

[56] See Vol. I pp. 58–60.

16

Rule-following: Meaning and Doing

THE philosophical problems traversed in the last six chapters were all given a similar treatment. They presented themselves as questions that ought to be answerable in something like the way in which questions of fact can be answered, and the treatment was to remove this mask and reveal their true nature. However much they looked like scientific questions, they were really something else. Naturally, they had never quite pretended to be scientific questions and their answers were never really expected to be the sort of thing that would simply be incorporated in the main text of human knowledge. The inquiry into the ownership of experiences could not quite masquerade as a straightforward empirical inquiry which might result in something like a psychological theory of the ego, and the investigation of sensation-types could not really try to pass itself off as an extension of the ordinary study of colour-blindness. Nevertheless, the assumption was that the method used by philosophers on their problems would not be so very different from scientific method and that, though their results would not belong to the main text, they would be important marginalia, the deep afterthoughts of metaphysics. The treatment was designed to demonstrate that their problems were much more different from scientific problems than at first sight they seemed to be.

The method was to examine the problems one by one, and to show that the forces that power them really do take thinkers over the edge, but not into a rarefied factual inquiry—only into an investigation of their own thought and its pre-conditions. I ascribe experiences to people, myself and others, but this is a task which is very unlike describing the physical world in impersonal language. I assign sensations, my own and others', to definite types, but there is a great difference between doing this and sorting out things in the physical world, a difference which cannot be explained by any theory about private objects, additional to physical objects and modelled on them. The treatment was a sober, realistic description of these performances which made it clear how they are achieved.

In the last six chapters the direct line of inquiry followed by philosophers who took science as the example to which their thought should conform was abandoned. If we could not think our way into a quasi-scientific orbit beyond the limits of science, it was better not to try to do so, but to ask, instead, what drives us so relentlessly in that impossible direction. But if philosophy is not like science, why have so many thinkers found the assimilation of the two disciplines irresistible? The way to get an answer to this question is to inspect the wreckage of their systems in order to discover why they tried to take scientific thought beyond its limit and why they failed. If we could understand what went wrong, our thinking might achieve the kind of self-criticism that is needed to protect it from these disasters.

That proved to be a difficult task because thought has no external vantage-point from which to criticize itself. Its predicament is uncannily like the egocentric predicament of the solipsist,[1] and there were two possible reactions to it. Given that the limit of thought and language had to be fixed from the inside, one possibility was to draw it as a single firm line, in the style of the *Tractatus*. However, that turned out to be a curiously disappointing way of dealing with the predicament. One could feel that the *Tractatus* was right in principle, and yet get very little understanding from it, because it was written from a single, abstract point of view. The alternative reaction, developed in the later writings, was to manœuvre between ordinary points of view all of which are definite and unambiguously occupiable. Instead of taking up a notional position at the centre of all factual language, philosophers could move from one carefully specified language-game to another. They did not even have to confine themselves to actual language-games, because they could invent variations which had never been put into practice, provided that their inventions were always perspicuously related to the linguistic procedures that are already established in our lives. The advantage of this method was that it offered the comparisons necessary for understanding without at any point transgressing the limit of language.

This method treated language as an empirical phenomenon instead of treating it as something sublime and quintessential:

'A proposition is a queer thing!' Here we have in germ the subliming of our whole account of logic. The tendency to assume a pure intermediary between the propositional *signs* and the facts. Or even to try to purify, to sublime, the

---

[1] See above, p. 422, and Vol. I p. 153.

signs themselves.—For our forms of expression prevent us in all sorts of ways from seeing that nothing out of the ordinary is involved, by sending us in pursuit of chimeras.[2]

The remedy was to examine the actual working of language. If a philosopher wanted to understand the ownership of experiences, he had to start by finding out how we manage to think and speak about the phenomenon in everyday life. It was no good assuming that there must be an ego related to the contents of a person's mind in the same way that he, mind and body, was related to the objects around him. That would be a piece which simply did not belong to our jigsaw, and the attempt to force it into a place would produce multiple distortions in what ought to be a smooth surface.

One of the great successes of this treatment was achieved by its distinction between the contingent facts asserted within a language-game and the facts presupposed by the very possibility of playing it. This distinction had no place in the *Tractatus*, where the truth-conditions of a factual sentence had to include everything that was to be found in its total demand on the world; or, to put the point in another way, the more problematical part of its total demand, its sense-conditions, could never be presented as facts, because the objects on which its sentences depended for their senses were simple and their existence could not be asserted but only shown.[3] But when language was studied as an empirical phenomenon rather than as something sublime, it immediately became clear that the sense-conditions of moves made within language-games included contingent facts. There were conspicuous examples of this kind of presupposition in the analysis of the ownership of sensations. Certain disruptions of our personal lines would make it impossible for us to engage in the language-game of ascribing sensations to one person rather than to another. If the sceptic was thinking about this kind of contingency when he suggested that a particular sensation might not after all belong to the person to whom the usual criteria indicated that it did belong, then he was expressing his thought in the wrong way. For these disruptions would make the denial just as senseless[4] as the assertion.

The same criticism was made of the sceptic's speculation that the

---

[2] *PI* I § 94.

[3] See Vol. I pp. 71–2 and 145 for an explanation of this view.

[4] It would be more accurate to say that their senses did not allow for this kind of contingency. They could, of course, be extended to allow for it, but then they would be different senses.

colour-impression that you received from a geranium might differ from his colour-impression. When he raised this doubt he was assuming that the language-game of reporting impression-types would continue unaffected by anything that happened to their type-lines. But that is not so. There are disruptions of type-lines which would immediately put a stop to this language-game. If all the connections between an impression-type and the physical world were severed, as they were in the second deficient case described by Wittgenstein,[5] it would be just as impossible to reject the assignment of an impression to the type as it would be to accept it.

There are several things that made it hard to accept this way of dismissing the sceptic's development of these two speculations. One obstacle that stood in the way of its acceptance was the evident fact that there are also disruptions both of personal line and type-line which would not be serious enough to stop the language-game. So we start with these milder cases and acquire a momentum which carries our imagination along in the extreme cases. I can imagine a situation in which a pain would be correctly assigned to myself in spite of the fact that it was a pain in your tooth.[6] Similarly, I can imagine a situation in which my colour-impression of the clear sky would be correctly assigned to the type to which I formerly assigned my colour-impressions of burning coals.[7] These mild cases, in some of which the criterial links are still preserved, create the illusion that we would still have a concept of type-identity in extreme cases where all the criterial links had been severed. This is one of the routes by which we arrive at the mistaken idea that the sceptic is right to force the choice between two answers, Yes or No, in all contingencies.

The route to this erroneous conclusion is related to the theory of meaning of the *Tractatus* in an interesting way. We feel driven to draw the conclusion because we find it unacceptable that a line of identity should peter out in certain contingencies. Surely there must still be a definite answer to the question whether the sensation would be mine or not mine, and, equally, to the question whether it would or would not belong to the same type! We are, of course, merely whistling in the dark to encourage ourselves, but the force that drives us to

[5] The case described in *NLPESD* p. 306, quoted and discussed in the previous chapter, p. 407.

[6] The case was discussed in Ch 10. See pp. 252–4.

[7] Wittgenstein's straightforward example of the crisis of transposition, discussed in the previous chapter. See pp. 407–10.

postulate the continuing possibility of identifying owner or type is powerful. The connection with the theory of meaning of the *Tractatus* is very close. For according to that theory it would be intolerable if the sense of a sentence depended on any contingencies. But that is precisely what drives us to the erroneous conclusion that, whatever happened, we could still go on playing the language-game of ascribing sensations to owners and types. For that would be possible only if the sentences which described the embarrassing contingencies were treated as implications of sentences, positive or negative, belonging to the original language-game in the way recommended in the *Tractatus*. So in both cases alike the driving force is the exigence of the dogma of far-reaching sense.[8]

Naturally, this dogma does not produce an atomistic theory when it is brought to bear on ascriptions of sensations to owners or types. What it produces is the idea that we can take the total demand made on the world by an ascription of either of these two kinds, analyse it into its components, and then, for all their possible combinations, assign a definite truth-value to the original ascription. However, that does raise a question which can be posed from the logical point of view of the *Tractatus*: 'Are we then to conclude that a word like "pain" designates a complex entity consisting of the three elements on the type-line, namely stimulus, experience, and response?'

The answer is, of course, negative. The word 'pain' neither designates this triple, nor does it designate a type of experience which is completely detachable from its physical setting. It was at this point that the earlier discussion led to a diagnosis of the error that lies at the heart of the sceptic's misrepresentation of these matters.[9] He presents the three sections of the personal line and the three sections of the type-line as if each of them were independently identifiable and amenable to an ordinary scientific investigation of a kind that would have appealed to Hume. But though input and output really are independently identifiable, the central section of each line cannot be identified independently of the other two. So there is a profound mistake behind the sceptic's treatment of the speculation: what we have at the midpoint of each of the two lines is not the independent object that he offers us, but something much more elusive—'It is not a *something*, but not a *nothing* either!'[10] We have to avoid behaviourism

---

[8] His early view on this matter was discussed in Ch. 4. See Vol. I pp. 70–2. Cf. *NB* p. 64.

[9] See above, pp. 313–15 and 320–1.   [10] *PI* I § 304, quoted in full above, p. 351.

without falling into the opposite error of treating 'pain' as the name of a type of experience which is completely detachable from its physical setting,[11] and, of course, without adopting the really desperate expedient of treating it as the designator of a complex consisting of all three parts of the type-line. The three parts of the line are not a triple posing an ordinary scientific problem, and the word 'pain' is not a wanderer looking for the kind of place in the world that was offered to names in the *Tractatus*.

Then what sort of word is it? Wittgenstein believed that the only way to answer this question is to describe its place in our lives. There are certain constraints imposed on our learning of sensation-language and the main thrust of his private language argument was against philosophical theories which ignore these constraints and represent it in a way that would make it unlearnable. He also investigated the closely related question of the conditions under which a language can be maintained in use. It was in that part of his inquiry that he developed his ideas about the limited scope of the criteria of identity for sensation-types. It is only our inveterate tendency to assimilate them to physical types that makes us push their identities beyond their natural limits. If we find that their criteria of identity break down under this treatment, that is no slur on them and it certainly lends no support to scepticism.

Various illusions come in at this point to reinforce the misleading assimilation of mental 'objects' and their properties to physical objects and their properties. People feel that there is a firm line drawn between the 'intrinsic' character of a sensation-type and its character judged by 'extrinsic' criteria when they have not really drawn it. This gives them the idea that every experience has an essential core too obvious to need demarcation and completely detachable from any physical setting. The idea is encouraged by the evident fact that in the straightforward crisis of transposition described by Wittgenstein something really is detached from, and then reattached to, the physical world. So that must be 'what it is like' to get an impression of blue! But he would object that, if this phrase is applied to his other cases where the ordinary criteria of identity peter out, it merely gestures in the direction of a new criterion of identity without actually supplying one: 'I am also (further) ready to talk of any *x* behind my words so long as it

---

[11] There is no simple way of making this point. If we talk about lines, it is better to treat their centres as cuts rather than sections. See above, p. 348.

keeps its identity.'[12] It would be a useful exercise to try to develop a parallel account of the essential core of ownership. Could there be 'something that it is like to be the owner of a sensation', extractable from ordinary cases of ownership and extrapolatable to the extreme cases in which he would say that the language-game of ascribing sensations to owners is no longer possible?

There is another source of confusion which was hinted at, but not fully described in the last six chapters. A philosopher like Wittgenstein tries to achieve an understanding of the place of sensations in our lives by manœuvring within the limits of language. When people read the record of his linguistic investigations, they sometimes protest that he has left out the essence of the matter, the actual quality of sensory experience. He would reply, 'Isn't what you reproach me of as though you said: "In your language you're only *speaking*!" '[13] But they might point out that in the *Tractatus* he did at least speak about the intrinsic nature of the objects which language tries to capture when it arrives on the scene. Why does he no longer make any attempt to get beyond the language that we use in everyday life? Why does he not even try to achieve the independent viewpoint that is expected of philosophers? Surely it is obvious that philosophy needs its own language-game in which to comment from the sidelines on all the others.[14]

This criticism comes from a misunderstanding. When Wittgenstein manœuvres between different language-games, he is, of course, only adopting their various standpoints in imagination. He does not have to look at the clear sky and the glowing coals in order to write about the crisis of transposition. So if what he writes fails to capture the essence of the matter, that will not be because he is a poor phenomenologist, but because there are criteria of identity for impression-types better or more profound than the ones that we use in everyday life. If that is so, his fault will be that he does not even try to find anything better but is content to let his dramatic sketches show us how our language manages in this difficult area without opening the way to improvements.

So much is obvious, but if the critic is suggesting that Wittgenstein ought to have looked for improvements, he faces a difficult question. How could a special philosophical language, if there were such a thing,

---

[12] *NLPESD* p. 297, quoted and discussed above, pp. 325–6 and 355.
[13] *NLPESD* p. 292.
[14] J. Lear argues that in *Philosophical Investigations* Wittgenstein needs, but cannot find, an independent basis for the language of philosophy. See his article, 'The Disappearing "We" ', *Proceedings of the Aristotelian Society*, Supp. Vol. 58, 1984.

go one better than ordinary language? The criteria of identity for impression-types make full use of all the available material, leaving nothing to be picked up by a better, philosophical language, and, if they are more limited in their scope than the criteria of identity for physical objects, that is something which we must accept and try to understand.

Or is the point the more general one, that beyond all our ordinary language-games there must be an ultimate truth of the matter, to be revealed in the manner of the *Tractatus*? But the trouble with that kind of metaphysic is that it is expressed in a language which transcends the conditions of ordinary language without setting up any new conditions of its own. The wheels turn idly without engaging with anything in our lives.

This does not mean that philosophy has nothing special to say. When we look out on the world, or on part of it, from the point of view of a particular language-game, there will be features of our experience which strike us as having a depth which can only be appreciated if we shift to another point of view. That is why a comparison with another language-game, perhaps an invented one, is often illuminating, and it has the advantage that it does not draw on any dubiously available resources. There is always a purpose behind Wittgenstein's dramatic sketches of different language-games. His comments on them, which are also made in ordinary, non-technical language, give the key to his strategy. He is trying to determine the scope of the criteria of identity of sensation-types, or he is explaining the conditions of the viability of our concept of the ownership of sensations. These investigations certainly require a special kind of insight, but they do not have to be carried out from a special vantage-point, like our ordinary standpoints but better, because it would give us a more penetrating view of reality. If a philosopher could walk on a Möbius ring, he might realize that beneath the surface on which he was moving there was only a further stretch of the same surface.

This review of the treatment given to the philosophical problems traversed in the last six chapters will not convince everybody that subjectivity is not a runaway vehicle, but it does, at least, indicate the importance of treating language as an empirical phenomenon. If we think of it as something sublime, spoken from nowhere, the demands that it makes on the world will be too exorbitant to be satisfied and the outcome will be scepticism. If, on the other hand, we place different language-games against their proper background in our lives as we live them, we shall be able to see an alternative to drawing simple sceptical conclusions from the sceptic's speculations.[15] For there will be the better possibility of dividing his doubts into two categories, doubts about truth-conditions and doubts about sense-conditions. This will have two advantages. First, when we restrict the scope of claims made in a language-game, it will be less difficult to show how they can be established, and, second, legitimate speculations that take us beyond the limit of one language-game can often be presented in another one.

If these philosophical problems are given a linguistic treatment, what about the philosophical problems posed by language itself? If language-games are the custodians of thinking, *quis custodiet ipsos custodes*? When language is studied as an empirical phenomenon rather than as something entirely *au-dessus de la mêlée*, it too must generate problems that require philosophical treatment. What are they? And how should they be treated? The remaining chapters will be concerned with these questions.

The best place to start is the early theory of meaning, which must be taken up again at the point where it was left in Volume I. Nothing explicit had been said in the *Tractatus* about the reidentification of things, and it was not even clear at what points, if at any, the problem would arise in the early system. Would it arise only for particulars or also for types?[16] Rules were mentioned in the book,[17] but only rules for connecting words with words and never rules for connecting words with things. Connections of the latter kind were called 'correlations' and they were not examined in any detail.[18] However, they did begin to receive attention in the lectures in which Wittgenstein explained the leading ideas of the *Tractatus* to a Cambridge audience between 1930 and 1932. In fact, it was in those lectures that he first developed a point which was implicit in the *Tractatus* and which was to prove important later: when the meaning of a word is specified, the specification will contain further words with meanings which can in their turn be specified, but sooner or later the leap from language to the world will have to be made without more words.[19]

---

[15] See L. Wittgenstein: *On Certainty*, ed G. E. M. Anscombe and G. H. von Wright, tr. D. Paul and G. E. M. Anscombe, Blackwell, 1969, *passim*.

[16] See Vol. I p. 120.   [17] See e.g. *TLP* 3.334 and 3.343–4.

[18] Ibid., 2.1514. See Vol. I pp. 9 and 115.

[19] In the *Tractatus* a sentence, or its analysis, showed its sense, but neither it nor any other sentence could say fully and finally what its sense was. No sentence could get to the end of saying that, because the end could not be put into words. Cf. *TLP* 4022 and 4.1212. See Vol. I pp. 142–6.

This is the point of origin of the topic in the philosophy of language that receives most attention in *Philosophical Investigations*, rule-following. The philosophical problems that it raises are not easy to locate. In everyday life we might say that the difficult cases are those where we have to do something but do not have a rule telling us what to do and so we must improvise. The score leaves the violinist free to add his own cadenza or the recipe leaves the chef free to adjust the flavour of the dish. This sort of thing can be worrying, but, at least, we know where we are—on our own. However, Wittgenstein seems to write as if we ought to feel the same anxiety even when we do have a rule. But how can it possibly be right to let the anxiety produced by the lack of a rule spread into the safe area where there are rules to guide us in what we do?

The simplest way of explaining his extension of what looks as if it ought to be a limited anxiety is not quite accurate, but it is, perhaps, best to start with it: if a sentence cannot give us a complete specification of what it is telling us to believe, then equally a rule cannot give us a complete specification of what it is telling us to do. The point is not just that there is often a need to interpret rules by defining their terms, but also that this process of defining a term and then defining the terms in the definition cannot possibly close all gaps, because sooner or later there will have to be a leap, not guaranteed by any verbal definition, from language to the world. Case-law provides an ordinary example of the need for interpretations, but Wittgenstein's point is that, though the quest for meaning usually starts along the road of verbal substitutions, the final stage of the journey must be quite different from any of its preceding stages, because it will bring in things as well as words.

It is important and worth emphasizing that he was not specially interested in the kind of doubt that rule-followers often feel about borderline cases. Is this ink blue or green? Ought we to take counsel's opinion before signing this contract? These are ordinary cases in which a ruling might be needed to close a gap and, until it was given, a real doubt might be felt. But he was not concerned with that kind of case. What interested him was the possibility of always capping a doubt that had been settled up to a point with a further doubt which still remained to be settled beyond that point.

However, even this does not locate his problem sufficiently accurately. It is the right approach to the area in which he was working in *Philosophical Investigations*, but it does not pin-point his problem, because it makes it look as if he was worried by the endlessness of the quest for a really self-explanatory definition, because it left him without an answer to radical scepticism about rule-following. But his interest in the interminable sequence of definitions had a different source.[20] He wanted to know *what counts as* knowing how to follow a rule for the use of a word, and the conclusion that he drew from the necessarily endless sequence of verbal interpretations was that the answer could not possibly be 'The ability to give a verbal interpretation of the word'.

The question 'What counts as knowing how to follow a rule?', like others of the same form in his later writings, was a request for the criteria that we use in everyday life. He asked it without assuming that, in order to satisfy those criteria, we would have to get to the end of a sequence of verbal interpretations which he had shown to be endless. That was the assumption that led to scepticism, but he did not share it. He took the reasonable view that, since we do manage to follow rules in our daily lives, the criteria for following them must be readily accessible and often seen to be satisfied much nearer home. He also believed that the sceptic's assumption can be shown to be absurd.[21]

These two philosophical enterprises, giving the criteria for knowing how to follow a rule and refuting scepticism about following a rule, are easily confused, because they overlap one another. The distinctive feature of the scepticism is the assumption from which it starts, that there ought to be a completely decisive verbal criterion for the application of a word. Wittgenstein did not share this assumption and so he was free to look for a viable criterion in a less restricted area in which there was, at least, some chance of finding one. The relation between the sceptic's necessarily unsuccessful quest for a viable criterion and Wittgenstein's more promising method of search is the key to many ordinary disagreements in everyday life. Suppose, for example, that three employees are discussing the character of their boss. One of them admits that she has not known him long enough to fathom his character. Another says that, however long and carefully she observes him, she will never be able to complete her assessment satisfactorily, because every piece of behaviour is always open to reinterpretation in the light of some further piece of behaviour. The

---

[20] S. A. Kripke in *Wittgenstein on Rules and Private Language* argues that the threat of this kind of recursive scepticism about rule-following really was Wittgenstein's concern. The evidence for his interpretation will be reviewed and discounted in the next chapter.

[21] The *reductio ad absurdum* that he used against it will be examined in the next chapter.

third one takes the reasonable view that enough is enough. The second speaker is on the verge of philosophical scepticism, while the view taken by the third speaker is closest to Wittgenstein's.[22]

The question 'What counts as knowing how to follow a rule?' is closely connected with the question discussed in Chapter 14, 'What counts as following a rule?' Wittgenstein's guarded answer to that question was that, though it might not be necessary to have other people around, in the case of linguistic rules we did in fact have the benefit of their company, and the easiest way for me to check the correctness of my practice was to compare it with theirs. So the main criterion of following a linguistic rule correctly was agreement in judgements. However, it was evident that purely coincidental agreement would not indicate that a group of people were following a rule, and that agreement by direct imitation, without independent consideration of the objects described would not do so either. Therefore, even if agreement in judgements was the main resource, it could not be the only one, and in fact there was also the possibility of calibration on standard objects, which is something that could be done without other people. This second resource was shown to be fundamental even in a community of language-users, but not because they make frequent appeals to it. They do not have to appeal to it explicitly, but they would soon notice if it ceased to be supportive. If man is the measure of the world, and if he discovers its regularities by imposing regularities on his own thought and language, his investment of self-discipline has got to pay off.[23]

In Chapter 14 the two resources were described as 'stabilizing'. However, it was explained that that did not mean quite what it might be taken to mean at first sight. A gyroscope is stabilizing because it keeps a vehicle level in an independently specified plane, but Wittgenstein was interested not only in how a speaker maintains the correctness of his usage, but also in what counts as correct usage. Consequently, the resources mentioned in Chapter 14 were stabilizing in two different senses at once: they maintained stability, but they also helped to set the standard of the stability that they maintained, unlike a

[22] The similarity is not exact, because the sceptical employee does not refuse to exploit an indispensable type of evidence, whereas the sceptic about rule-following does refuse to consider how the person using the word actually applies it to things, and that is an essential supplement to whatever verbal instructions he may be following.

[23] This is a rough formulation of the reciprocal connection between the two regularities. It would be more accurate to say that the investment will necessarily pay off given the conditions governing the setting up of the language. See below, pp. 456–7.

gyroscope, which merely maintains a stability with a standard set by something else.

So in his treatment of the possibility of a private language the question at issue was not whether a child adopted by wolves would be clever enough to invent and maintain a language for his own use. It was whether anything that we could imagine the child doing in such circumstances *would count as* speaking a language. Wittgenstein did not choose an independently fixed standard of stability of meaning and then inquire whether the child would be able to attain it. His investigation was conceptual and he started from the fact that the concept of speaking a language is the concept of an acquired skill. Then the method that he used in his search for an answer to his question was to inquire whether the necessary conditions for the acquisition and maintenance of a skill were satisfied in this case.

If the concept of speaking a language is the concept of an acquired skill and if it is conceptually necessary that an acquired skill should have some stabilizing resource, the investigation of private language is in both its stages a conceptual investigation—both when it draws out the implication that speaking a language is doing something that has to be learned, and when it assesses the resources available for the stabilization of the practice. That is why it is not concerned with the question whether the wolf-child would be sufficiently clever to achieve anything that we would call 'speaking a language', or with the question whether there is any independently specified standard of stability which we language-speakers have attained, but which he could not attain. Those would be questions of contingent fact and, though they lie in the background of the conceptual investigation, they are not part of it. It is concerned only with the concept of language as it is, and not with the psychological constitution that produced it, nor with the benefits that it secures for its users. It is, of course, true that language is impossible for creatures below a certain level of intellectual endowment, and that it would secure no advantages for its users if it fell below a certain standard of stability, but, however important those two theses may be, they are not part of the conceptual inquiry.

We may well begin to feel doubts at this point, if not before, about the purity of Wittgenstein's method. Is it really possible to draw such a firm line between conceptual and contingent matters? No doubt the two fields can be separated for most of their length and their separation has an undeniable importance, because philosophy really is not another science.[24] However, when language itself is seen as a natural phenomenon, that looks like the end of the line and it is no longer so clear that the two fields can still be neatly separated.

There are two main points in Wittgenstein's later philosophy where this difficulty surfaces. One is his treatment of logic and mathematics, which is beyond the scope of this book, and the other is his general treatment of language, which is now under examination. How exactly does the difficulty present itself in the case of language? The exclusion of questions about variations in mental endowment does not seem to be problematical. It is on the operational side of language, among its aims and effects, that the difficulty lies. Factual assertions aim at truth, which cannot consist merely in agreement in judgements, regardless of the way in which it has been achieved. The connections between learning, meaning, assertion, and truth form a linked circuit, so that, though agreement in judgements is a serviceable, it is not a final, criterion of truth. However, the conviction, that truth involves something more, is not very impressive unless we can say what more it is.

One of Wittgenstein's favourite ideas is that language is an instrument of measurement. In its simplest form the suggestion is that a sentence containing a descriptive word is laid against a thing in order to see if the thing measures up to it.[25] However, we have to sophisticate the metaphor, because it is not just the word that gives us the measure of the thing, but the word with the meaning conferred on it by its previous use. So there are really two tasks that a speaker performs in a case like this: in general, he contributes to maintaining the meaning of the word by his use of it, but when he adds this particular episode to his practice, he does not intend it to modify the meaning of the word, but rather, given the meaning conferred on it by previous episodes, to be, here and now, a shot at the truth.

The fact that a speaker does two things with a word but only one thing with a yardstick marks an important difference between the standards of measurement used in the two cases. A yardstick is a physical object made of a material chosen for its rigidity and low coefficient of expansion, but in the case of language the standard is set by a regularity in speakers' practice over a period of time. This makes a particular speaker's shot at the truth a more precarious performance. If there is any kind of spatial measurement that it is like, it would be

---

[24] See Ch. 9.
[25] It is said to be laid against reality in *TLP* 2.15121, which is criticized in *PR* p. 317, quoted in Vol. I pp. 85–6.

pacing out the distance between two points far out of sight of one another.

If the use of language is the application of a measure to the world, the study of language seems to belong to anthropology at least as much as to conceptual analysis. Or, perhaps we should say that it becomes hard to see how the two disciplines can be kept separate at this point. Whichever way we put it, the difficulty is to see what happens to meaning and truth when language is studied as an empirical phenomenon. The sublime treatment that they received in the *Tractatus* kept the question silenced, but the naturalization of semantics in the later writings made it unavoidable.

The question that Wittgenstein asks about measurement by words is one of those fundamental questions that have an almost childlike simplicity:[26] 'What, if anything, forces me to apply this word to this thing when I make a shot at the truth?' His answer is that nothing *forces* me to do it: I do it as an exemplification of the acquired regularity of my own reactions.[27] This is not intended as a sceptical observation, and he is certainly not suggesting that I do not really know that, for example, this harebell is blue. The apparently shocking remark, that nothing forces me to say, as my shot at the truth, that it is blue, is only intended as a contribution to an account of what is involved in using language to measure the world: the measurement relies on the regularity of the speaker's reactions and so he is himself functioning as the instrument of measurement.

It is, of course, possible to place this answer at the end of a line which begins with real doubts about the way to apply a rule in practice. But if we do that, we must not allow the superficial continuity of the series of answers to blind us to the fact that, when we have reached the end of the line, we are beyond the doubts raised and settled within a language-game like describing colours, and into the presuppositions of this and every other use of descriptive language.

[26] In *PG*, pp. 381-2, he himself describes the question that he raises about mathematics in this way: 'A mathematician is bound to be horrified by my mathematical comments, since he has always been trained to avoid indulging in thoughts and doubts of the kind I develop. He has learned to regard them as something contemptible and, to use an analogy from psycho-analysis (this paragraph is reminiscent of Freud), he has acquired a revulsion from them as infantile. This is to say, I trot out all the problems that a child learning arithmetic, etc., finds difficult, the problems that education represses without solving. I say to those repressed doubts: you are quite right, go on asking, demand clarification.'

[27] See Ch. 18 for a discussion of the connection between this answer and Hume's account of causal necessity.

There are two areas in which the fact, that nothing forces me to
continue a series in this way rather than that, makes itself felt. One is a
person's development of a mathematical series, and the other is the
unrolling sequence of his applications of a descriptive word. They are
brought together in a discussion in *Remarks on the Foundations of
Mathematics*:

> *How do I know* that in working out the series + 2 I must write
>   '2004, 2006'
> and not
>   '2004, 2008'?
> —(The question: 'How do I know that this colour is "red"?' is similar.)
>
> 'But you surely know for example that you must always write the *same*
> sequence of numbers in the units: 2,4,6,8,0,2,4, etc.'—Quite true: the problem
> must already appear in this sequence, and even in *this* one: 2,2,2,2, etc.—For
> how do I know that I am to write '2' after the five hundredth '2'? I.e. that 'the
> same figure' in that place is '2'? And if I know it *in advance*, what use is this
> knowledge to me later on? I mean: how do I know what to do with this earlier
> knowledge when the step actually has to be taken?
>
> (If intuition is needed to continue the series + 1, then it is also needed to
> continue the series + 0 .)
>
> 'But do you mean to say that the expression " + 2 " leaves you in doubt what
> to do e.g. after 2004?'—No; I answer '2006' without hesitation. But just for that
> reason it is superfluous to suppose that this was determined earlier on. My
> having no doubt in face of the question does *not* mean that it has been
> answered in advance.
>
> 'But I surely also know that whatever number I am given I shall be able,
> straight off and with certainty, to give the next one.—Certainly my dying first is
> excluded, and a lot of other things too. But my being so certain of being able to
> go on is naturally very important.'[28]

The idea that I might doubt whether 2006 follows 2004 in the series
governed by the rule 'Add 2' is explicitly rejected, and so too, by
implication, is the idea that I might doubt whether this geranium is
red. Those are not things that might be doubted because their
foundations go deeper than knowledge. They are founded on what I
do, and not on anything complicated that I do, but on utterly simple,
basic routines that a child could master. When I am taught one of these
routines, provided that I have the necessary intellectual endowment—
and, in the other case, colour vision too—there is only one way in which
I find it natural and unavoidable to continue. That does not mean that

---

[28] *RFM* I § 3. Cf. *PI* 187, quoted below, p. 444.

I could never raise either of the two doubts, but only that I could not raise either of them within its language-game after mastering the relevant techniques. To raise it at that stage would be to move out of the language-games, but we must not forget to add, not into an area in which there is nothing more to be said, because a philosopher can describe the two language-games in a way that indicates their foundations—as, indeed, Wittgenstein does in this passage.[29]

What he says here about knowledge is rather compressed and it is worth unpacking some of his points, because they will serve to introduce the argument that will be analysed in the next chapter. After I had written out part of a mathematical series I might reflect that there were two different ways in which knowledge had helped me. First, I knew in advance that I had to write '2006' after '2004', and, second, when I reached that point, I knew at that moment that I had to write '2006'. But Wittgenstein would object that the word 'know' is not appropriate to my situation immediately before I write '2006'. This is one of those cases mentioned before[30] that are just too good for knowledge:

> I turn to stone and my pain goes on.—Suppose I were in error and it was no longer *pain*?—But I can't be in error here; it means nothing to doubt whether I am in pain!—That means: if anyone said: 'I do not know if what I have got is a pain or something else', we should think something like, he does not know what the English word 'pain' means; and we should explain it to him.—How? Perhaps by means of gestures, or by pricking him with a pin and saying: 'See that's what pain is!' This explanation, like any other, he might understand right, wrong, or not at all. And he will show which he does by his use of the word in this as in other cases.
>
> If he now said, for example: 'Oh, I know what "pain" means; what I don't know is whether *this*, that I now have, is pain'—we should merely shake our heads and be forced to regard his words as a queer reaction which we have no idea what to do with. (It would be rather as if we heard someone say seriously: 'I distinctly remember that some time before I was born I believed . . .'.)
>
> That expression of doubt has no place in the language-game; but if we cut out human behaviour, which is the expression of sensation, it looks as if I might *legitimately* begin to doubt afresh. My temptation to say that one might take a sensation for something other than what it is arises from this: if I assume the abrogation of the normal language-game with the expression of a sensation, I need a criterion of identity for the sensation; and then the possibility of error also exists.
>
> 'When I say "I am in pain" I am at any rate justified *before myself*.'—What

[29] See above, p. 429.   [30] See above, pp. 257–60.

does that mean? Does it mean: 'If someone else could know what I am calling "pain", he would admit that I was using the word correctly'?

To use a word without a justification does not mean to use it without right.[31]

Similarly, I have a right to put '2006' after '2004' because I have internalized the rule, not just in the sense that I can repeat it on demand, but in the deeper sense that I can apply it correctly. This acquired skill is an exceedingly simple matter in a case like this, but that is why Wittgenstein chose the example. His point is that, when I have mastered this technique, the step from '2004' to '2006' is so basic that I cannot see it as a matter for possible doubt, and, anyway, even if I had been able to feel doubt at this point, there would be no justification available. I am alone and without textbooks and so I simply take the step, and taking it is something that I do without even a smidgeon of hesitation, because my training has set me up in this business. Someone less thoroughly trained might have written '2008' and defended it by saying that for any number over 2003 the instruction 'Do the same again' meant 'Add 4'. But I have mastered the technique and so, when I write '2006', it is not a case of my knowing, but of something too basic for knowledge, my rule-governed doing. My self-imposed regularity simply manifests itself in one more episode. This primitive form of regular behaviour is something that underlies all language and so language cannot covenant for it. It might be called 'maintaining the linguistic instrument of measurement'.

When Wittgenstein reveals the true nature of our predicament, as he sees it, people tend to feel anxiety or, at least, surprise: 'Is it possible that so much should be contributed by me?' They then begin to experience the intellectual vertigo for which they convince themselves that Platonism is the only effective antidote.[32] But his view of their case is quite different: the cure is unworkable, but, fortunately, the malady is an illusion, because he is only telling them something which they really knew already, but which they would rather not hear. Except for a few eccentrics, they all responded to their original training by taking the same lines through the infinite field of alternatives that lay before them. When they are being subjected to the steadying force of social conditioning, they do not feel that too much depends on them. It is when they sit back and theorize about their practices that they begin to think that there ought to be real barriers already lining the routes which they agree in taking. So they reject what he tells them and

---

[31] *PI* I §§ 288–9.   [32] See Vol. I pp. 12–16 and 59–60.

protest that any gap left by their instructions needs to be, and always can be, closed. But his point was the more basic one, that the process of closing gaps in their instructions by adding verbal riders to them is necessarily endless. They must actually do something, because they themselves by what they do will contribute something indispensable to making an instruction a guide pointing one way rather than another. When they refuse to accept this, they are like people who have been hypnotized and told that they are not standing on firm ground but on a narrow foot-bridge across a gorge, and then the only way to get them to walk is to tell them that there are high parapets on each side of them.

There is another passage in *Philosophical Investigations* which shows very clearly how he was trying to transform our view of the foundations of meaning:

'All the steps are really already taken' means: I no longer have any choice. The rule, once stamped with a particular meaning, traces the lines along which it is to be followed through the whole of space.—But if something of this sort really were the case, how would it help?

No; my description only made sense if it was to be understood symbolically.—I should have said: *This is how it strikes me.*

When I obey a rule, I do not choose.

I obey the rule *blindly*.[33]

My obedience is 'blind' not because I shut out considerations that might have influenced me, like the officers who led the Charge of the Light Brigade, but because, when I have worked my way down to the foundations, where the only question left is 'What in this case would count as the same again?', there are no more considerations, doubts, or jutifications. I do not even have to listen to the rule, because it speaks through my application of it.

This is not offered as an answer to the sceptical question, 'How can I possibly know that I really am maintaining language as an accurate instrument of measurement?' Wittgenstein's question is the deeper one, 'What counts as maintaining it?' He is not taking it for granted that we all know what counts as maintaining it and merely asking whether our resources are sufficient to allow us to achieve that standard. True, he does attach great importance to the two resources that evidently act as stabilizers, calibration on physical objects and other people's reactions, but he does not think that they maintain an independently identified standard of stability, like gyroscopes. On the contrary, they help to constitute the stability that they maintain.

Kripke treats this as 'a sceptical solution to a sceptical problem'. The problem, according to him, is that language would have the stability required for an accurate system of measurement only if the meanings of words were anchored in some firm ground which was completely independent of the unrolling sequences of our applications of them. However, there is no such anchorage available, and so we must rest content with a second-best, internal stabilizer.[34]

That was not Wittgenstein's view of the matter. In *Philosophical Investigations* he places all questions about knowledge, doubt, and justification within our various language-games, each of which comes with instructions for answering them. If after full training and all the recommended checks I still 'doubt' whether I am using a word correctly, my 'doubt' goes beyond the particular language-game and is automatically transformed into a request for an answer to the conceptual question 'What counts as following a rule?' I cannot possibly take my doubts outside all language-game without producing this metamorphosis in them. The outer void, in which they would retain their sceptical character but lose all hope of finding non-sceptical answers, is treated by Wittgenstein as a fantasy.

If he heard philosophers complaining that they never really knew that they were following a rule correctly, because even full training was not enough to ensure that they really were doing the same again, he would ask them what they thought counted as 'doing the same again'. If they refused to accept as criteria the two stabilizers, agreement in judgements and calibration on standard objects, and treated them as mere indications that some other, external standard was being attained, he would challenge them to specify that external standard. If they could not specify it, he would not tell them that their sceptical problem could only be solved sceptically. On the contrary, he would argue that they had not really got a problem, but thought that they had one only because they had misunderstood their predicament.

When the study of language is naturalized, the investigation of the conditions of raising, and the methods of settling, doubts becomes wholly empirical. There is no external vantage-point from which

---

[34] The internal stabilizer, according to him, is agreement in judgements: *Wittgenstein on Rules and Private Language*, pp. 89–90. If he had added the other resource, calibration on standard objects, his central point would still have remained unaltered: language cannot get the independent support that it needs in order to be a reliable system of measurement and Wittgenstein's theory of meaning is, in the Humean sense, 'sceptical'.

philosophers can pose sceptical questions about rule-following without the resources for answering them. That does not mean that such questions are empty. They do not have any sceptical content but, if we go along with them and move outside the orbit of a particular language-game, we will see them change into something quite different—requests for a general answer to the question 'What counts as following a rule?' Not surprisingly, the answer to this question too will be put together entirely from internal resources.[35]

Nevertheless, Kripke's interpretation of *Philosophical Investigations* is not the complete misunderstanding that some of his critics have taken it to be. He asks the same questions as Wittgenstein about the maintenance of language as a system of measurement and, like Wittgenstein, he argues that it can only be maintained by internal resources. The main difference lies in the assessment of this conclusion. Kripke's verdict is that the best available resources are not really adequate. That is not the verdict of Wittgenstein, who argued that the quest for external resources is the result of a misunderstanding. Now it might have been possible to take Kripke to be challenging this way of blocking recursive scepticism about rule-following.[36] But unfortunately, his account of what Wittgenstein says is inaccurate[37] and he misinterprets his argument for the self-sufficiency of language.[38]

The discussion of the development of a mathematical series in *Philosophical Investigations* touches on the other point at which knowledge might help me when I am writing one out:[39] I might have thought out what I was going to do before I started. In the discussion in *Remarks on the Foundations of Mathematics*[40] he does not deny that this would give me knowledge in advance, but he does point out that it is only another manifestation of the same internalized regularity that will,

---

[35] Cf. *TLP* 6.51: 'Scepticism is *not* irrefutable, but obviously nonsensical, when it tries to raise doubts where no questions can be asked. For doubt can exist only where a question exists, a question only where an answer exists, and an answer only where something *can be said*.' This gives us a small-scale map of the ground on which the more sophisticated later moves are made.

[36] See below, p. 447 n. 44.

[37] He makes no claim to complete accuracy and says that the message that he gets from the text of *Philosophical Investigations* may not be what Wittgenstein intended (*Wittgenstein on Rules and Private Language* p. 5), but he does not try to locate the point of possible divergence.

[38] These criticisms of Kripke's interpretation will be developed in the next chapter.

[39] *PI* I § 187, quoted below, p. 444.

[40] *RFM* I § 3, quoted above, p. 438.

I hope, produce the right figure when I reach that point. He also observes that I shall then have to apply my advance knowledge, and my application of it will raise the same question that would have been raised by my unpremeditated application of the rule—'What counts as "doing the same again"?'

These points are made very clearly in *Philosophical Investigations*:

'But I already knew, at the time when I gave the order, that he ought to write 1002 after 1000'.—Certainly; and you can also say you *meant* it then; only you should not let yourself be misled by the grammar of the words 'know' and 'mean'. For you don't want to say that you thought of the step from 1000 to 1002 at that time—and even if you did think of this step, still you did not think of other ones. When you said 'I already knew at the time . . .' that meant something like: 'If I had been asked what number should be written after 1000, I should have replied "1002".' And that I don't doubt. This assumption is rather of the same kind as: 'If he had fallen into the water then, I should have jumped in after him.'—Now what was wrong with your idea?[41]

The critic who suggests that there is no mystery about 'doing the same again' because we have advance knowledge of what we are going to do is simply floundering on the surface of the problem.

In all these details of meaning and doing it is easy to lose sight of the concept of truth. It is an important fact that, when I call this harebell 'blue', I am not just avoiding a disagreement with other people, like a chorister trying to hit the same note as his companions. I am making a shot at the truth. The strange thing is that this important fact seems to be left out by Wittgenstein or, at least, to be pushed into the margin of his text. Why is this? Consider, for example, this passage in the other set of lectures on the foundations of mathematics:

This is a difficulty which arises again and again in philosophy: we use 'meaning' in different ways. On the one hand, we take as the criterion for meaning, something which passes in our mind when we say it, or something to which we point to explain it. On the other hand, we take as the criterion the use we make of the word or sentence as time goes on.

First of all, to put the matter badly and in a way which must be corrected later, it is clear that we judge what a person means in these two ways. One can say that we judge what a person means by a word from the way he uses it. And the way he uses it is something which goes on in time. On the other hand, we also say that the meaning of a word is defined by the thing it stands for; it is something in our minds or at which we can point.

The connection between these two criteria is that the picture in our minds is connected, in an overwhelming number of cases—for the overwhelming majority of human beings—with a particular use. For instance you say to someone 'This is red' (pointing); then you tell him 'Fetch me a red book'—and he will behave in a particular way. This is an immensely important fact about us human beings. And it goes together with all sorts of other facts of equal importance, like the fact that in all the languages we know, the meanings of words don't change with the days of the week.

Another such fact is that pointing is used and understood in a particular way—that people react to it in a particular way.

If you have learned a technique of language, and I point to this coat and say to you, 'The tailors now call this colour "Boo" ' then you will buy me a coat of this colour, fetch one, etc. The point is that one only has to point to something and say, 'This is so-and-so', and everyone who has been through a certain preliminary training will react in the same way. We could imagine this not to happen. If I just say, 'This is called "Boo" ' you might not know what I mean; but in fact you would all of you automatically follow certain rules.

Ought we to say that you would follow the *right* rules?—that you would know *the* meaning of 'boo'? No, clearly not. For which meaning? Are there not 10,000 meanings which 'boo' might now have?—It sounds as if your learning how to use it were different from your knowing its meaning. *But the point is that we all make the SAME use of it.* To know its meaning is to use it *in the same way* as other people do. 'In the right way' means nothing.

You might say, 'Isn't there something else, too? Something besides the agreement? Isn't there a *more natural* and a *less natural* way of behaving? Or even a right and a wrong meaning?'—Suppose the word 'colour' used as it is now in English. 'Boo' is a new word. But then we are told, 'This colour is called "boo" ', and then everyone uses it for a shape. Could I then say, 'That's not the straight way of using it'? I should certainly say they behaved unnaturally.

This hangs together with the question of how to continue the series of cardinal numbers. Is there a criterion for the continuation—for a right and a wrong way—except that we do in fact continue them in that way, apart from a few cranks who can be neglected?

We do indeed give a general rule for continuing the series; but this general rule might be reinterpreted by a second rule, and this second rule by a third rule, and so on.

One might say, 'But are you saying, Wittgenstein, that all this is arbitrary?'— I don't know. Certainly as children we are punished if we don't do it in the right way.

Suppose someone said, 'Surely the use I make of the rule for continuing the series depends on the interpretation I make of the rule or the meaning I give it.' But is one's criterion for meaning a certain thing by the rule the using of the rule in a certain way, or is it a picture or another rule or something of the sort?

In that case, it is still a symbol—which can be reinterpreted in any way whatsoever.

This has often been said before. And it has often been put in the form of an assertion that the truths of logic are determined by a consensus of opinions. Is this what I am saying? No. There is no *opinion* at all; it is not a question of *opinion*. They are determined by a consensus of *action*: a consensus of doing the same thing, reacting in the same way. There is a consensus but it is not a consensus of opinion. We all act the same way, walk[42] the same way, count the same way.

In counting we do not express opinions at all. There is no opinion that 25 follows 24—nor intuition. We express opinions by means of counting.[43]

This passage raises the question that we all want to ask, when we are told that 'right' and 'wrong' can be applied to what we do when we are following a particular rule, but not when we are choosing which rule to follow. If language is a device for attaining truth, won't its success depend on the rules that are chosen to govern it, just as certain eccentric systems of measurement would have to be avoided by a builder laying tiles on a floor? It would, for example, be no good using a plant that was still growing as an instrument of measurement, and, similarly, it would be no good gearing the use of seven colour-words to the days of the week in such a way that what was called 'blue' on Sunday would be called 'red' on Monday, and so on. So won't some rules be right, when they are judged by their effectiveness as devices for attaining the truth, and others simply wrong?

The answer given in this passage is 'No'. All we can say is that the adoption of certain rules is natural and the adoption of others unnatural, and 'right' and 'wrong' apply only to behaviour governed by a rule already adopted. This is apt to strike people as paradoxical. Surely truth is too fastidious to yield itself to an eccentric system of rules? Surely the correctness of claims made in a really 'cranky' system will not be equatable with truth?

This is a mind-spinning question and, when we are answering it, we must be careful to separate two different possibilities. First, there is the possibility that my use of a particular word might be eccentric in a way which was latent at the moment but which was going to emerge very soon when it was compared with other people's use of it in a testing situation. This seems to open the door to a familiar kind of scepticism, because at any point in the sequence of my applications of the word, however many eccentricities had been ironed out, there might be

---

[42] Or did he really say 'talk'?　　　[43] *LFM* pp. 182–4.

others that still remained undiscovered.[44] The second possibility is that, even if my application of it was always going to agree with everyone else's, we might all be deviating from the ideal truth-seeking system.

The first possibility does not present Wittgenstein with an unmanageable sceptical problem. A particular eccentricity of mine will be eliminated when it is discovered, and even if it remains undiscovered, it will not distort my record of the world as I found it, though it could well cause confusion if my record were added without correction or comment to the common stock of knowledge. Now it is a familiar sceptical move to generalize such ordinary doubts and to place their settlement beyond any contemporary horizon of investigation. However, this does not pose too formidable a problem for a philosopher who treats language as the measure of the world. Each of these ordinary doubts can be settled within the language-game, and, though their settlement is an open-ended process, so that I never really *know* that my use of a word is not still in some way eccentric, that does not prevent the common language from being an effective system of measurement. It is a continually self-refining system, like any metric system, and none the worse for that.

The principle behind these ways of dealing with the first possibility is a simple one: a doubt is real only if there is a method of answering it, and in all such cases there is a method laid down in the language-game. But if we push these doubts beyond the limit of the language-game, they will immediately be transformed into a request for an answer to the general question 'What counts as following a rule?', to which the response will be a description of the ways in which we maintain the system of language in our daily lives. It is a self-correcting system, because it is used for communication and that automatically tends to produce agreements in judgements and the ironing out of anomalies.[45]

It is the second possibility that raises the problem that we all want to hear discussed. However perfect our agreement, may it not be the case that the whole system deviates from the ideal truth-seeking system?

[44] It is important that there will always be such points (see Kripke: *Wittgenstein on Rules and Private Language*, pp. 8–9 and 17), but it is a further question whether Wittgenstein saw them as openings for scepticism about rule-following, and reasons for rejecting Kripke's answer, that he did see them in that way, will be given in the next chapter.
[45] See above, p. 442.

Or, to put it more concisely, how do we know that our system is the right system?

Wittgenstein's objection to this question is given in the passage quoted from *Lectures on the Foundations of Mathematics*. It is that, whatever the questioner is trying to get at, he is going about it in the wrong way. If ordinary rules could be right or wrong, there would have to be super-rules governing their formulation. This objection goes back to the original structure of the system of the *Tractatus*. The idea there was that there are real possibilities, which may or may not be realized as facts, but that there are no identifiable candidates for real possibility which may or may not achieve that status.[46] When rules are introduced, they put us in a position to identify real possibilities and to discover which of them are realized as facts, but there are no super-rules identifying candidates for real possibilitiy, some of which will succeed in achieving it. Rules define possibilities and enable us to recognize when they become actual, but we have to resist our inveterate tendency to see this relationship reproduced on the next level between candidates for possibility and real possibilities. The idea that there is an outer zone into which we could move in order to answer the question 'Which are the right rules?' is pure fantasy.

However, fantasies do not spring into existence gratuitously and the source of this one is interesting. Everyone would agree that it is silly to ask whether it is better to think in English or French. But those are established languages and, except for finer nuances, intertranslatable. Consequently, the choice between them does not raise any deep question about truth and it could not possibly be represented as a choice between a right alternative and a wrong one. At the very most, the issue is pragmatic. But many of the alternative language-games envisaged by Wittgenstein have never been tried out and we might well wonder whether they are suitable instruments for the discovery of truth. If this question rests on an illusion, it is a deep illusion, not to be dismissed out of hand. Maybe it is correct to insist that truth can only be relative to a particular language-game and that we cannot judge language-games by their effectiveness in attaining an independently determined truth. Maybe all that we can say about the more bizarre alternatives envisaged by Wittgenstein is that they are unnatural. But the adequacy of this response does need to be established, because there is a real force behind the question that provoked it.

[46] See above, pp. 215–16 and Vol. I p. 146.

At this point there is an obstacle familiar to students of his later philosophy. It has just been mentioned that natural languages, like French and English, are, not surprisingly, intertranslatable. But when we are looking for a really bizarre alternative to these natural languages, or to some part of them, we face a dilemma. If the bizarre language-game cannot be translated into ours, we shall not be able to understand it, but if it can be translated into ours, it will not raise the deep question that we wanted it to raise about its suitability for discovering an independently determined truth. For its bizarre character will merely be a feature of the way in which it expresses the things that we say in our language—perhaps it lumps together what our language distinguishes or vice versa—and that will not raise any questions about truth that we could not use our own language to raise.

Before this inquiry is taken any further, it must be pointed out that this obstacle to understanding speculations about alternative language-games must not be cited, without further reflection, as an objection to Wittgenstein's procedure. We complain about the thinness of his specifications of bizarre alternative language-games,[47] but perhaps he could actually exploit it to support his own view, that we cannot survey candidates for possibility in some outer zone, but can only make lateral movements within the inner zone of real possibilities, introducing new language-games by progressively modifying our existing ones.[48] If this is our situation, it really does severely limit the intelligibility of bizarre alternatives.

His attempts to construct fantastic alternative practices need to be scrutinized more closely. Suppose that we pick seven colour-words, put them in order in a table, and gear their application to the days of the week in such a way that it agrees with ours only on Sundays. Then if red followed blue in the table, it would be correct in this language-game to call a harebell 'red' on Mondays. This language-game obviously cannot be used to raise problems about the suitability of different linguistic systems for the discovery of absolute truth. *Ex hypothesi* we understand what anybody playing this language-game would be doing, but that is only because it introduces no new

[47] See Vol. I, p. 32.
[48] Cf. *PG* § 68, 'The thing that's so difficult to understand can be expressed like this. *As long as* we remain within the province of the true–false games a change in the grammar can only lead us from *one* such game to another, and never from something true to something false. On the other hand, if we go outside the province of these games, we don't any longer call it "language" and "grammar", and once again we don't come into contradiction with reality.'

possibilities, but merely expresses familiar ones in a new and very clumsy way. Imagine saying in this language 'Red berries may be poisonous, but blue ones never are'!

Colour-vocabularies which do not discriminate where our own colour-vocabulary does discriminate, or vice versa, are rather more interesting, because we can give them an intelligible origin—elaborate discriminations of shades of green would be made by inhabitants of a rain forest, and of blues and greys by sailors. But they too fail to advance the inquiry and, in any case, Wittgenstein firmly repudiated the idea that such pragmatic explanations are any part of philosophy. He always held that philosophy does not include the investigation of the adaptation of language to the needs of its users:

> Darwin's theory has no more to do with philosophy than any other hypothesis in natural science.[49]

The thought is elaborated in *Philosophical Investigations*:

> If the formation of concepts can be explained by facts of nature, should we not be interested not in grammar, but rather in that in nature which is the basis of our grammar?—Our interest certainly includes the correspondence between concepts and very general facts of nature. (Such facts as mostly do not strike us because of their generality.) But our interest does not fall back upon these possible causes of the formation of concepts; we are not doing natural science; nor yet natural history—since we can also invent fictitious natural history for our purposes.
>
> I am not saying: if such-and-such facts of nature were different, people would have different concepts (in the sense of a hypothesis). But: if anyone believes that certain concepts are absolutely the correct ones, and that having different ones would mean not realizing something that we realize—then let him imagine certain very general facts of nature to be different from what we are used to, and the formation of concepts different from the usual ones will become intelligible to him.
>
> Compare a concept with a style of painting. For is even our style of painting arbitrary? Can we choose one at pleasure? (The Egyptian, for instance.) Is it a mere question of pleasing and ugly?[50]

In this important passage he is not denying that the viability of our language-games often depends on contingent facts.[51] He is replying to the objection that, if he cites general facts of nature or imagines them altered, he must be offering scientific hypotheses about the adaptation

---

[49] *TLP* 4.1122.   [50] *PI* II § xii. Cf. *RPP* I § 46.
[51] The point emphasized in Ch. 10.

of language to circumstances. On the contrary, he is only trying to undermine the complacent assumption that our concepts are the only possible ones by giving our imaginations a jolt.

Nevertheless, the passage does raise a difficult question of interpretation. How can his appeal to the naturalness of certain practices stop short of an investigation of what makes them natural? Maybe his 'interest does not fall back upon these possible causes of the formation of our concepts', but if language has grown out of a pre-linguistic pattern of discriminations which is locked into our environment in complex ways, how can the philosophical study of language avoid including this part of its natural history? But before these questions are tackled, more needs to be said about the obstacle that stands in the way of the attempt to make bizarre alternative language-games intelligible. A dilemma was presented: either the alternative practices do not differ in any profound way from our own, or else we shall not be able to understand them. The second horn is worth inspection.

It can be discerned very clearly in the sequel to the passage quoted from *Remarks on the Foundations of Mathematics* earlier in this chapter:[52]

'But then what does the peculiar inexorability of mathematics consist in?'—Would not the inexorability with which two follows one and three two be a good example?—But presumably this means: follows in the *series of cardinal numbers*; for in a different series something different follows. And isn't *this* series just *defined* by this sequence?—'Is that supposed to mean that it is equally correct whichever way a person counts, and that anyone can count as he pleases?'—We should presumably not call it 'counting' if everyone said the numbers one after the other *anyhow*; but of course it is not simply a question of a name. For what we call 'counting' is an important part of our life's activities. Counting and calculating are not—e.g.—simply a pastime. Counting (and that means: counting like *this*) is a technique that is employed daily in the most various operations of our lives. And that is why we learn to count as we do: with endless practice, with merciless exactitude; that is why it is inexorably insisted that we shall all say 'two' after 'one', 'three' after 'two', and so on.—But is this counting only a *use*, then; isn't there also some truth corresponding to this sequence? The *truth* is that counting has proved to pay.—'Then do you want to say that "being true" means: being usable (or useful)?'—No, not that; but that it can't be said of the series of natural numbers—any more than of our language—that it is true, but: that it is usable, and, above all, *it is used*.

'But doesn't it follow with logical necessity that you get two when you add one to one, and three when you add one to two? and isn't this inexorability the same as that of logical inference?'—Yes! it is the same.—'But isn't there a truth

[52] *RFM* I § 3, quoted above, p. 438.

corresponding to logical inference? Isn't it *true* that this follows from that?'—The proposition: 'It is true that this follows from that' means simply: this follows from that. And how do we use this proposition?—What would happen if we made a different inference—*how* should we get into conflict with truth?

How should we get into conflict with truth, if our footrules were made of very soft rubber instead of wood and steel?—'Well, we shouldn't get to know the correct measurement of the table.'—You mean: we should not get, or could not be sure of getting, *that* measurement which we get with our rigid rulers. So if you had measured the table with the elastic rulers and said it measured five feet by our usual way of measuring, you would be wrong; but if you say that it measured five feet by your way of measuring, that is correct.—'But surely that isn't measuring at all!'—It is similar to our measuring and capable, in certain circumstances, of fulfilling 'practical purposes'. (A shopkeeper might use it to treat different customers differently.)

If a ruler expanded to an extraordinary extent when slightly heated, we should say—in normal circumstances—that that made it *unusable.* But we could think of a situation in which this was just what was wanted. I am imagining that we perceive the expansion with the naked eye; and we ascribe the same numerical measure of length to bodies in rooms of different temperatures, if they measure the same by the ruler which to the eye is now longer, now shorter.

It can be said: What is here called 'measuring' and 'length' and 'equal length', is something different from what we call those things. The use of these words is different from ours; but it is *akin* to it; and we too use these words in a variety of ways.[53]

The alternative methods of measurement introduced in this passage are described very sketchily and it is not too easy to understand them. The difficulty starts as an expository one, because the strange methods have to be explained in a way that will make them intelligible to us. So we are asked to think of shopkeepers who use retractable rulers to give certain customers short measure, or of people who see that their rulers have extremely high coefficients of expansion but also know that the objects to be measured are made of the same substance, and so realize that their results will not be upset by variations in temperature between the rooms containing them. But these examples immediately introduce a real difficulty: if the people using these systems of measurement think of them in the ways in which we have to think of them in order to understand them, they will not be radically different from our system (the first horn of the dilemma). Therefore, we must suppose that they do not think of them as we do, because they do not start from our

[53] *RFV* I §§ 4–5.

system and modify it to suit special circumstances. On the contrary, what we regard as a modification of our method is their one and only method. But then we face the question on the other side of the dilemma: 'When we try to see what they are doing as a radically different system of measurement, do we really understand it?'

The second of the two illustrations given by Wittgenstein does not help us to answer the question, because the system that it introduces is not really a different one from ours. We deal with the problem of the coefficients of expansion of our measuring instruments by making them of materials that reduce it to a minimum. The proposed alternative—allowing maximal expansion but making sure that it is matched by the expansion of the objects to be measured—does not introduce any radical difference. Motorists check their tyre pressures hot and cold and it would be possible to invent a self-adjusting pressure-gauge.

The other illustration is more interesting, because the shopkeepers really could be measuring things in a way that was radically different from ours. But in order to get this into the example, we have to suppose that they *never* separated measurement as we practise it from what we would regard as other modes of assessment. So they would not consciously stretch the elastic ruler for a favoured customer but would automatically measure the amount that he deserved. Now there is nothing mysterious about lumping together considerations of fact and value—we often do it ourselves—but can we really understand people who *never* separated the two in a case like linear measurement and desert? A similar question could be posed about a colour-vocabulary which, from our point of view, made questions of hue and questions of taste inseparable. This is the other horn of the dilemma.

Wittgenstein, as usual, opposes the outright rejection of eccentric ways of measuring—'That isn't measuring at all!'—and counsels tolerance. Certainly, but we do need to understand what we are tolerating, and here he seems to leave us in the lurch. Apparently, he means us to take his strange cases as examples of radically different methods of measurement, but it is not easy to understand them in that way. No doubt, it would be wrong to assume that factual language must always be developed first, and that the contributions made to meaning by needs, feelings, and taste can only be added later, but it really is difficult to see how the measurement of objects—a purely factual matter for us—could be inseparable from the piece of favouritism that he describes. Measurement is such a widespread phenomenon that it would hardly be impossible for his shopkeepers to abstract it from the special performance that he attributes to them. Indeed, he even seems to suggest that they do abstract it and do know that they are cheating. But then their practice would not be radically different from ours.

What are we to make of this? It is unlikely that he is showing incompetence in the exposition of his ideas, and more likely that his apparent failure to make any headway is itself a demonstration of a point that strikes him as important. It was suggested above that what he is trying to show us is that we can never start by identifying a range of candidates for possibility completely different from the real possibilities that we recognize, and then go on to determine which of them actually achieves possibility, in the way in which we can identify a range of completely different possibilities—'That bird is a bittern, or a night-heron, or . . .'—and then go on to determine which of them is realized. The point can be generalized: we cannot start by identifying completely different systems, one of which is to be chosen as the system of interconnected possibilities presented by colour-classification, or by measurement. Candidates for possibility can never be lined up like candidates for actuality.[54] That does not mean that there are no alternative systems of colour-classification or measurement, but only that they must be introduced by gradual transformations of our systems. There is nothing here at all like the discovery of new species of bird in the antipodes.[55] Colour-classifications are not found but set up, and philosophers who imagine alternatives to ours can easily go too far and describe behaviour which we would not have sufficient reason to interpret as any kind of reaction to colours.[56]

If philosophers cannot explain our conceptual systems by lining up radically different alternatives and giving reasons for the particular choices that we might seem to have made, are they simply reduced to recording that people find it natural to continue a series or to group colours in the ways that they do? Most of us share the feelings of Wittgenstein's interlocutor in *Lectures on the Foundations of Mathematics*:[57] if we merely observe that we find a certain way of proceeding natural

---

[54] See above, p. 448 n. 46.

[55] His earliest version of this point is directed against Russell, who treated different logical forms like different species of animal. See *TLP* 5.553 ff., discussed in Vol. I p. 126, and Russell: *The Philosophy of Logical Atomism*, pp. 216 and 281.

[56] This is not the same as rejecting the interpretation merely because the system is not exactly the same as ours. See *Remarks on Colour*, §§ 86–8 on the difference between modifying our system and setting up what may not be a system of colours at all.

[57] *LFM* pp. 182–4, quoted above, pp. 444–6.

and leave it at that, the implication is that 'all this is arbitrary'. Wittgenstein's response is that he is not trying to explain the patterns traced by our minds but only to record them, and so he is not implying either that they are arbitrary or that they are not arbitrary. Philosophy is not another science, and philosophers must 'do away with all *explanation*, and description alone must take its place'.[58]

It is questionable whether he really does succeed in holding his philosophy to this austere ideal. Because philosophy is a critique of language expressed in language, he sees it as something to be attempted entirely from the inside. All that a philosopher can do is to work over language as we have it, seeking the kind of understanding that one might achieve if one were studying a style of painting. He must never allow himself to forget that there are alternatives, but he must not demand radically different alternatives to convince him that our way of construing the world is not the only way. It hardly needs to be added that Wittgenstein is not denying that language can be studied scientifically, but only trying to maintain a firm line between that way of studying it and philosophy.

But can he really hold this line? It is, of course, not enough for him to claim that 'we are not doing natural science; nor yet natural history— since we can also invent fictitious natural history for our purposes'.[59] That is not enough to establish his point, because the fictitious natural history has to make the adoption of the alternative language-games intelligible, just as our actual natural history makes our adherence to our actual language-games intelligible. But that means that the natural history has to *explain* the language-games. Now it would obviously be circular to say that our actual colour-vocabulary is explained by the natures of the colours that it discriminates. That would be an empty explanation, because it could have been used to explain any other way of dividing up the range of colours instead of the one that we have adopted, and it marks a point at which science peters out in metaphysics. However, it does not follow that our colour-vocabulary could not be explained in any way, and it would be quite natural to offer the kind of explanation based on our interests that was mentioned above. It is true that such explanations could not be extended to really bizarre variations or make them intelligible, but they do deal perfectly successfully with less extreme variations and, of course, they are scientific.

[58] i.e. 'do away with all explanation in philosophy'. See *PI* I § 109, quoted above, p. 200.   [59] *PI* II § xii, quoted above, p. 450.

The character of this kind of explanation of a language-game is even more obvious in a case like the ownership of experiences. The contingent layout of our personal lines yields a straightforward scientific explanation of the language-game of ascribing sensations to people.[60] True, he does concede that 'Our interest certainly includes the correspondence between concepts and very general facts of nature'[61] because they make the formation of concepts different from ours 'intelligible'. But he leaves the way in which they make it intelligible unexamined, and it must be scientific—what else could it be?

Wittgenstein could admit this but claim that explanations like these are scientific footnotes to philosophy and that it is perfectly clear where we cross the line between the two disciplines. There is, however, another point at which it is much more difficult to see how they can be neatly separated. Language is in many cases built on to a pre-linguistic system and so, in order to understand it, we must go beneath it and investigate its ancient foundations. He demonstrates this in the case of pain, but he could have extended his treatment of this case to much of descriptive language. If we want a really striking example of this order of development, we can find it in the ascription of spatial properties to objects in the visual field corresponding to objects in the cone of physical space ahead of us.[62] Now the private language argument of *Philosophical Investigations* provides him with a way of dealing with one aspect of this connection between position in the visual field and position in physical space ahead of us: if the connection were severed, we would not have any concept of position in the visual field. So he is not forced to fall back on the weak thesis, that a vocabulary which completely separated these two elements in our concept of spatial position would merely be unnatural, like a vocabulary which divided the visual field into four quadrants and put the descriptions 'upper left hand', 'lower right hand', etc. on a four-day cycle of rotation.

However, there is another aspect of the connection between the two elements in our concept of spatial position which he cannot deal with so easily. If language is a system built on older foundations, as it evidently is in this case, will that not reopen the door to the kind of scepticism that Kripke claims to find in Wittgenstein's presentation of the problem of rule-following? It will no longer seem to be sufficient for us to specify the criteria that we accept for following a rule correctly

---

[60] See *PR* § 63, discussed above in Ch. 10.
[61] *PI* II § xii.   [62] See above, pp. 400–6.

in everyday life. For when language is seen as a system built on pre-linguistic foundations, it seems to lose its autonomy because the question whether those criteria are strict enough will be unavoidable, just like the quesion whether its pre-linguistic basis was sufficiently well adapted to its environment. An instrument for measuring angles has to be accurate enough to keep a rocket on course, and, similarly, the measurement of the world by our regular linguistic reactions looks as if it ought to meet a definite standard of accuracy. But how do we know that it does? How do we even know what degree of regularity we actually achieve in our use of language? These questions cannot be blocked by a simple insistence that philosophy is not another science. If language is ever introduced as a substitute for natural reactions which carry an established 'hypothesis', its lofty refusal to be judged by any external standard will not be the end of the matter.

Here it is worth taking up the discussion of Kripke's interpretation of this part of *Philosophical Investigations* at the point where it was left.[63] Wittgenstein allows that at some point in the future eccentricities might begin to affect the practice even of an experienced user of a colour-vocabulary. The question is 'What does he take that possibility to show?' Kripke suggests that he takes it to show that language does not give us a fixed standard for measuring the world. Against this interpretation it was argued that Wittgenstein was not expressing any kind of scepticism about language. On the contrary, he believed that our language-games are self-correcting systems and, what is more, that they set the standard for correct measurement of the world. If this seems presumptuous, it may be mitigated by the fact that they often originate as systems of natural regularity, but there is a price to be paid for the mitigation—it may make it impossible to exclude external standards.

The alternative interpretation was put forward without much argument, but support can be found for it in two different areas. First, it can be shown that the passages in *Philosophical Investigations* which Kripke interprets as expressions of scepticism about rule-following are really nothing of the kind: they are part of a reductive argument directed against Platonizing theories of meaning.[64] This will be demonstrated in the next chapter. Second, Wittgenstein's whole treatment of language-games indicates that he did not regard them as precarious systems struggling to meet some external standard of

---

[63] See above, p. 443.
[64] *PI* I §§ 201–2. See above, pp. 440–1 and Vol. I pp. 10 and 59–60.

accuracy, but, rather, as self-correcting standard-setters. To put the point more concisely, he did not share Kripke's view that the way we go on in daily life is only a second-best substitute for genuine regularity.[65] However, if there is anything in the criticism of his account that was developed above, perhaps he ought to have shared it. For though language often enjoys the advantage of introduction as a substitute for natural reactions, there is also a hidden disadvantage: we can always question whether the standard of regularity achieved by those reactions was high enough.

Something has already been said about the non-sceptical character of Wittgenstein's treatment of language-games, but perhaps it would be worth trying to pull some of the threads together before this chapter is concluded. The first point that needs to be emphasized is that the two resources that stabilize our use of any descriptive word—agreement in judgements and calibration on standard objects—help to constitute the stability that they produce.[66] According to him, what we have here, at the base of any descriptive vocabulary, is an indissoluble partnership between language and the world: it is not the case that language has to meet some external standard of accuracy as an instrument of measurement, nor is it the case that its internal standard is independent of the world in which it originated.[67] We are all familiar with the rhetoric of the controversy between subjectivists and objectivists, but at this level he denies that any difference between the two theories can be made out.[68]

One way of appreciating his position is to ask how language-games operate as self-correcting systems. The obvious part of the answer is that we correct one another and conformity is enforced by the need to communicate. This is our first resource. But we also have a second resource: our shared language is itself continually but more unobtrusively tested against the world.[69] Naturally, all corrections are particular

---

[65] i.e. he is not doing what Kripke says that he is doing, offering a 'sceptical solution to a sceptical problem'. See Kripke: *Wittgenstein on Rules and Private Language*, p. 68.

[66] See above, pp. 434–5.

[67] This can be seen as an adaptation of an early thesis: 'And if this were not so, how could we apply logic? We might put it in this way: if there would be a logic even if there were no world, how could there be a logic given that there is a world?' *TLP* 5.5521. See above, p. 385 n. 61.

[68] Cf. *Zettel*, §§ 357–8: 'We have a colour system as we have a number system. Do the systems reside in *our* nature or in the nature of things? How are we to put it?—*Not* in the nature of numbers or colours. Then is there something aribtrary about this system? Yes and no. It is akin both to what is arbitrary and to what is non-arbitrary....' The passage was quoted with part of its sequel in vol. I p. 16.   [69] See above, Ch. 14.

corrections—what else could they be?—and the general post-dated suspicion, that there may always be some latent eccentricity which will only emerge in the future, ought not to generate scepticism. Why should I need to suppose that my use of a word is already on fixed rails laid with perfect accuracy into the future?[70] Isn't it enough that there will be opportunities to make corrections when they are needed?

He would not deny that doubts can be pushed beyond the point to which they have, at any time, been taken, but he would claim that they will then be automatically transformed into something else because there is no court of appeal beyond our ordinary criteria. If we are not satisfied by their satisfaction, we can only move into a philosophical investigation of rule-following, which will end by telling us that we ought to be satisfied. It is an illusion to suppose that there is a thin line of essential regularity running through each person's use of each word in his vocabulary like a steel wire which needs no strengthening because it cannot be snapped, or that there ought to be another language available for an independent assessment of all our language-games.[71] We study them as ordinary phenomena and we report our results in ordinary factual language used reflexively to describe itself.

We may agree with his rejection of the excessive intellectualization of the human predicament which is characteristic of so much of Western philosophy, and, like him, we may turn our backs on the two false ideals that it generates—language as a system of measurement which is completely independent of the world that it measures, and a world that in no way depends on the language that measures it. We may concede that these two ideals are not only unattainable but also lacking in any authority.[72] They hold up a picture to which there is no reason that the world and our record of it should conform. But beyond that point, agreement may not be so readily forthcoming. When language has been naturalized, how can it refuse to be judged by the same external standards as the natural reactions which it replaced?

---

[70] See *PI* I § 218–19.
[71] As J. Lear suggests in 'The Disappearing "We"'. See above, p. 429 n. 14.
[72] See Vol. I pp. 16–17.

I7
Rule-following: the Rejection of the Platonic Theory in Philosophical Investigations

PHILOSOPHY often produces a feeling of insecurity about our thought or our language very like the anxiety about claims to empirical knowledge that has haunted epistemology from Antiquity. Can we really rely on our words to measure the world accurately? Speech is, after all, only a system of rule-governed behaviour which we maintain by our own efforts. Is it not presumptuous to set up language as the measure of the world? This doubt is apt to develop into the familiar fugue of philosophical scepticism. One by one, we discount all our available resources and it does not occur to us that it is the legitimacy of our demands for something better that ought to be questioned.

Wittgenstein treated this feeling of insecurity sympathetically but firmly. It was understandable that a self-appointed measure of the world should have moments of self-doubt, but they need not lead either to general scepticism about the competence of language or to the kind of empty theory that is so often offered as the antidote to scepticism. The first thing that needs to be done—and it may turn out to be all that is needed—is to identify the ultimate criteria of correctness that we find acceptable when we are actually using language rather than theorizing about it.

People often find it incredible that this simple response to philosophical doubt could be sufficient. What they overlook is that, though the general principle of Wittgenstein's treatment of scepticism about the pretensions of language is simple, the details of it are complex and subtle. The colour-vision of the two eyes of a single person may differ slightly—so why should there not be a similar difference between the colour-vision of two people? Ruskin believed that the Industrial Revolution had faded all the colours that we see in nature, but that a corresponding adaptation in the use of our colour-words had concealed the change from us. In such a case we are not forced to make an immediate choice between accepting the theory of

Schlick and Carnap[1] and dismissing the speculation as senseless. We can treat these doubts more sympathetically, making them as concrete and definite as possible and then inquiring whether they could not, after all, be settled empirically by an appeal to our established criteria of correctness. Since they arise on the fringe of our system, it ought not to be surprising how often they become decidable when we make its boundary more precise.

Naturally, there are doubts that cannot be settled in this way and they have to be given a different treatment designed to show up their emptiness. But here too the response is subtle. Instead of relying on a pugilistic use of the verification principle, Wittgenstein always tries to demonstrate how easy it is for us to employ language in a way that deprives it of its sense without realizing that that is what we are doing. So his first move is often to nudge the use of language a little further out of orbit, so that the loss of sense becomes obvious, and then to go back and demonstrate the same loss of sense in the less extreme deviation of the sceptic.[2]

This method of dealing with doubts about constancy of meaning and about the reliability of language as a measure of things is not intended to prove that it is an absolute arbiter of reality deriving its authority from some other world. That would be the Platonic theory, as far removed as it could possibly be from Wittgenstein's way of thinking. He is not trying to produce any theory of language, especially not Platonism, which he elaborately rejects in the second main episode of *Philosophical Investigations*.[3] He is only trying to show that language has a limited degree of self-sufficiency derived from its application to the one and only world. If it were never checked against the objects that it measures, and if its results were always accepted with immediate trust, however wild they might be, it could not survive, and yet on each occasion of its application to objects by a proficient speaker, *it* measures *them*. It is tempting to suppose that in this partnership between language and the world, one of the two must be dominant in all transactions, but that is not so at all. When someone is still acquiring language, and especially in the early stages, the world is the dominant partner, but later, when proficiency has been attained, the weight shifts to the other side of the partnership. However, that is a shift that can never be total, because what makes a speaker a reliable

[1] See above, pp. 302–3, and Vol. I pp. 52–3.
[2] He makes the transition from hidden to patent nonsense. See *PI* I, § 464.
[3] *PI* I §§ 138–242.

:an never *simply* be his own spontaneity or even his agreement
pontaneous reactions of the rest of the community of users
ᴏ. ᴜᴇ language.[4] What we have here is a self-supporting circle: no
point on its circumference supports the others because no point on its
circumference rests on anything wholly outside it.

It is important to see that there are two distinct alternatives to
attributing this limited self-sufficiency to language. One possibility
would be to make the world the dominant patner in every transaction,
thus putting language in a position of absolute dependence on it. The
obvious objection to this is that it would be absurd to hold that every
time someone applies a word to something in the world all that is
happening is that his use of it is being calibrated by that thing. What
would be to make the world the dominant partner in every transaction,
never put to any practical use? If every time that a ruler was applied to
an object, all that was happening was that its length was being checked
against a known length, who would buy rulers?

The second alternative would be to make language the dominant
partner in every transaction. This idea is unconvincing by itself,
because it would give language a completely unexplained authority as
an instrument of measurement. So a supplement is always added at
this point: language derives its standards of measurement from
another world, or, at least, from another aspect of this one. The
resulting theories, which vary both in their account of the source of the
standards and of the way in which they are stamped on our minds, are
Platonic,[5] and it is against them that the argument of the second main
episode of *Philosophical Investigations* is directed. The first alternative
evidently did not merit serious consideration.

If Wittgenstein's defence of the limited self-sufficiency of language
is convincing, there is no need to seek reassurance in any Platonic
theory. In fact, the argument developed in this part of his book goes
further than this: Platonism is not only unnecessary but also
impossible. The argument is not an easy one to interpret and
throughout the examination of it in this chapter and the next it must
not be forgotten that it has a positive aspect as well as a negative one. In
its negative aspect it is a rejection by *reductio* of Platonism, which,
according to him, would destroy the distinction between following
rules and violating them instead of preserving it. But behind this attack
the positive account of language as a system with limited self-
sufficiency is lined up in reserve.

[4] See above, Ch. 14.   [5] See above, 440–1, and Vol. I pp. 10–11.

It is the negative side of his discussion that is difficult to interpret. Platonism is supposed to be reduced to absurdity and the absurdity is said to be its abolition of the very distinction that it was designed to preserve more securely than it could be preserved by the ordinary resources described by Wittgenstein. This is evidently a reductive argument with an unusual structure. The structure that one would expect to find would be something like this: 'Yes, the distinction between following and violating a rule would be preserved if the theory were true: but no, it cannot be true, because a contradiction is deducible from it.' However, that is not quite what we find, if the interpretation to be proposed in this chapter is correct. For, on this view of what he says, he is arguing that the Platonic alternative would do worse than fail to improve on the ordinary resources because of an internal incoherence: it would actually destroy the distinction that needed preservation.

There is another very different interpretation of this argument which has been put forward by S. A. Kripke,[6] and criticized by G. P. Baker and P. M. S. Hacker[7] and by C. McGinn.[8] Kripke does not construe it as any kind of reductive argument. He thinks that Wittgenstein is simply trying to demonstrate that language is much more precariously based than we take it to be when we use it so confidently in everyday life. So he reads this part of *Philosophical Investigations* as a dramatization of our insecurity intended to pose a sceptical problem, by making it look as if there is nothing between us and linguistic chaos. However, according to him, all is not lost, because Wittgenstein does find a resource to steady us, agreement in judgements with other members of our linguistic community. He calls this a 'sceptical solution', because it gives us much less than most of us demand. It is evidently a solution which would not have been available to speakers of a private language (if such a language could have been spoken). The whole movement of Wittgenstein's thought, when it is interpreted in this way, is very like Hume's thinking about causal necessity. For, as Kripke points out, Hume began with a demonstration that this concept is much less securely based than we take it to be when we use it so confidently in everyday life, and then proceeded to describe its actual basis, as he saw it, in terms which leave many people dissatisfied.

[6] S. A. Kripke: *Wittgenstein on Rules and Private Language.*
[7] G. P. Baker and P. M. S. Hacker: *Scepticism, Rules and Language.*
[8] C. McGinn: *Wittgenstein on Meaning.*

This interpretation of Wittgenstein's argument is very different from the one that will be proposed here, and the discussion would be too diffuse for clarity, if the texts were presented one by one and the two interpretations pitted against one another step by step. A different procedure is needed. First, the argument will simply be presented as a *reductio ad absurdum* of Platonism, and after that the evidence that might seem to support Kripke's rival interpretation will be examined and shown to be compatible with this one. In the exposition of the argument as a *reductio* the usual three questions will have to be answered. What are the premises? What absurdity is deduced from them? And which premiss is responsible for it?

The whole topic is complex as well as controversial and the treatment of it will be clearer if the answers to the three questions are given in two stages. First, they will be answered in a preliminary way without much citation of texts. Then the details will be added with full textual support. Finally, to round off the discussion of the controversy, there will be a brief review of evidence apparently favourable to Kripke's interpretation.

There is one more point that needs to be made about this programme before it is begun. It will not be necessary to direct as much attention to the positive side of Wittgenstein's discussion as to its negative side. There are three reasons for this. First, the constructive side of it has already been largely explained in Chapters 14 and 16, and what now needs to be interpreted is the central destructive argument (the 'sceptical solution to a sceptical problem', if Kripke were right). Second, on the positive side of the matter, the main difference between Kripke's view and the view to be defended here is that he puts all the weight of the 'sceptical solution', as he calls it, on one of the two resources used by Wittgenstein, agreement in judgements, and omits the other one, calibration on standard objects, but that part of his interpretation was disputed in Chapter 14. Third, apart from that important difference, Kripke's presentation of the constructive part of Wittgenstein's discussion does not differ greatly from its presentation here. The divergence on the positive side is not about the meaning of what Wittgenstein says but about the spirit in which he says it. If Kripke were right, the text should be read as a sceptical complaint that our predicament is so precarious without the extra resource of Platonism,[9] while, on the interpretation adopted here, he is merely

---

[9] In fact, Kripke's omission of the second of our two empirical resources makes our predicament look more precarious than it really is.

reminding us that our available resources are perfectly adequate, so that, even if Platonism did not make impossible demands on our credulity and understanding,[10] there is really no need for any such theory.

The first item on the programme set out above was the achievement of a general view of Wittgenstein's argument as a *reductio*. We need quick answers to the three questions that were posed and it is best to start with the last of them, 'What is the theory that generates the absurdity?'

Whence comes the idea that the beginning of a series is a visible section of rails invisibly laid to infinity? Well, we might imagine rails instead of a rule. And infinitely long rails correspond to the unlimited application of a rule.

'All the steps are really already taken' means: I no longer have any choice. The rule, once stamped with a particular meaning, traces the lines along which it is to be followed through the whole of space.—But if something of this sort really were the case, how would it help? . . .[11]

So Wittgenstein's target is the theory that the guidance given by a rule is complete, covering every possible case in advance and leaving nothing to be contributed to what counts as compliance by the mind of the person who is following it.

One of his ways of attacking this theory is to point out that nothing forces the rule-follower to make whatever move he makes next.[12] However, this is open to a common misunderstanding: it is often taken to mean that the rule-follower is only inclined to make the move, or merely feels a certain predisposition to make it.[13] But Wittgenstein is not downgrading the compulsion felt by the rule-follower or placing the necessity of its outcome low on any independently established scale of degrees of necessity. He is not denying that the compulsion may well be irresistible (just try to believe that this geranium is blue!), but only pointing out that it is not wholly external to the rule-follower. His target is a general misunderstanding of all degrees of necessity of this

[10] As usual, Wittgenstein says very little about the credibility of Platonism and concentrates on its intelligibility. In general, we get his discussion of his adversaries' theories out of focus if we take him to be arguing that we should not believe them. A scientific theory can be tested against the evidence, but Platonism, like other philosophical theories, avoids that risk, and so what he questions is its internal coherence. See above, Ch. 9.

[11] *PI* I §§ 218–19, first paragraph.

[12] *PI* I §§ 139–40, quoted and discussed below, pp. 472–3.

[13] A misunderstanding corrected by G. P. Baker and P. M. S. Hacker, *Scepticism, Rules and Language*, p. 39 n. 56.

kind, even the inexorability of logic, and he is not proposing a relative reassessment of particular cases of necessity. That is made very clear by the simile of the fixed rails. The point that he is making is not that some rules are more dictatorial than others, but, rather, that it is a general misrepresentation of all rules to assimilate them to rails laid down in advance. That view of them eliminates the contribution made by a rule-follower to what counts as following the rule, and makes him look like the 'driver' of some fully automated car of the future.

But where exactly is the absurdity supposed to be located? It is not immediately evident in this passage, which confines itself to two points; the fixed rails are an illusion and they would not help us even if they were really there, 'invisibly laid to infinity'. However, it may be that a closer scrutiny of the reason why Platonism is useless, will reveal some absurdity concealed in it. The best place to look is the relation between the rule-follower and his rule. Rails laid out to infinity would be useless unless the traveller were locked on to them, and, similarly, complete guidance by rules already laid down in reality would be useless unless there were something in the rule-follower's mind that latched him on to them infallibly. The need for such a locking device is obvious and one of the special features of Platonism is that it requires it to be maximally effective:

> 'It is as if we could grasp the whole use of the word in a flash.' Like *what* e.g.?—Can't the use—in a certain sense—be grasped in a flash? And in *what* sense can it not?—The point is, that it is as if we could 'grasp it in a flash' in yet another and much more direct sense than that.—But have you a model for this? No. It is just that this expression suggests itself to us. As the result of the crossing of different pictures.
>
> You have no model of this superlative fact, but you are seduced into using a super-expression. (It might be called a philosophical superlative.)[14]

If a rule-follower has an ordinary flash of understanding, what he has understood, as shown by what he does, may amount to very little. It is only in the mythology of rule-following that the flash of understanding locks him on to fixed rails laid to infinity.

But where is the absurdity?

> This was our paradox: no course of action could be determined by a rule, because every course of action can be made out to accord with the rule. The answer was: if everything can be made out to accord with the rule, then it can

[14] *PI* I § 191–2.

also be made out to conflict with it. And so there would be neither accord nor conflict here.[15]

So the absurdity is the abolition of the very distinction that the theory was designed to make more secure, the distinction between obeying and disobeying a rule. This is the special feature of the reductive argument which was explained above. What we would expect to find would be, first, the concession that the theory would indeed preserve the distinction, if it were true, and then the proof that it could not be true, because it is incoherent. However, what we actually find is the claim that the theory abolishes the distinction that was supposed to be its protégé, with the implication that this is where the absurdity lies.

But how does it abolish the distinction between obeying and disobeying a rule? The passage just quoted does not tell us, because it merely gives us the last line of Wittgenstein's *reductio*, and so we have to go back to the first of the three questions posed above, 'What are the premisses of this *reductio*?' The passage continues like this:

> It can be seen that there is a misunderstanding here from the mere fact that in the course of our argument we give one interpretation after another; as if each one contented us at least for a moment, until we thought of yet another standing behind it. What this shows is that there is a way of grasping a rule which is *not* an *interpretation*, but which is exhibited in what we call 'obeying the rule' and 'going against it' in actual cases.
>
> Hence there is an inclination to say: every action according to the rule is an interpretation. But we ought to restrict the term 'interpretation' to the substitution of one expression of the rule for another.[16]

The first sentence of this continuation makes it perfectly clear that the argument is a *reductio* and not the sceptical complaint that Kripke takes it to be.[17] For the idea that is being criticized is said to be the result of a misunderstanding. The meaning of a sentence can never be completely determined by another sentence which interprets it and this impossibility is misunderstood by those who hope to overcome it by interpreting the interpretation and continuing in this way until a complete verbal determination of the meaning of the original sentence has been achieved.[18]

---

[15] *PI* I § 201, first paragraph.   [16] *PI* I § 201, second and third paragraphs.
[17] See C. McGinn: *Wittgenstein on Meaning*, p. 68.
[18] An 'interpretation' is an analysis expressing the meaning of the original sentence in different words. In the second paragraph of the quoted passage Wittgenstein says that an action done according to a rule ought not to be called an 'interpretation' of a rule. This is a recantation of something that he himself had said in 1930. See *CLI* p. 24.

So Wittgenstein's *reductio* has to prove that this really is a misunderstanding. We may think that the fact, that a particular interpretation of a sentence always leaves something to be explained, only shows that the interpretation is not self-explanatory and, therefore, itself needs to be interpreted in a way that will be self-explanatory. But if we do think this, we are wrong. There is no way in which the meaning of a word can be completely determined by further words:

'But how can a rule show me what I have to do at *this* point? Whatever I do is, on some interpretation, in accord with the rule.'—That is not what we ought to say, but rather: any interpretation still hangs in the air along with what it interprets, and cannot give it any support. Interpretations by themselves do not determine meaning.

'Then can whatever I do be brought into accord with the rule?'—Let me ask this: what has the expression of a rule—say a sign-post—got to do with my actions? What sort of connection is there here?—Well, perhaps this one: I have been trained to react to this sign in a particular way, and now I do so react to it.

But that is only to give a causal connection; to tell how it has come about that we now go by the sign-post; not what this going-by-the-sign really consists in. On the contrary; I have further indicated that a person goes by a sign-post only in so far as there exists a regular use of sign-posts, a custom.[19]

No rule can be completely laid down in words and the complete expression of any rule must include its actual applications.[20] But how is this proved?

Wittgenstein argues for it by demonstrating the consequences of supposing it not to be so. If it were not so—if a rule governing the use of a word could be completely laid down in further words—those words would have to act as an infallible device in the rule-follower's mind, locking him on to the fixed rails of the correct application of the original word governed by the rule. Now it is obvious that the wording of the rule does not do this any more than the original word did it. That is why those who take this line immediately find themselves sliding down a regress of interpretations. So their only resource is to claim that there must be something else in the rule-follower's mind—something additional to any words—which latches him on to those

---

[19] *PI* I § 198. The answer to the objection made in the last paragraph is a further development of the discussion in *BLBK* pp. 12–14. See above, pp. 376–7.

[20] G. P. Baker and P. M. S. Hacker make this point by saying that there is an internal relation between a rule and its applications (*Scepticism, Rules and Language*, Ch. 3). This way of putting it shows how it is connected with the picture theory of sentences. See above, p. 494 n. 74.

rails. But what can this locking device possibly be? Is it a disposition to apply the original word correctly? Or will it be something that occurs at a definite moment of time?

It is, of course, essential to have the disposition to apply the word correctly, but a disposition is not the sort of thing to which a rule-follower can refer in order to read off what his next move ought to be. So all the weight of Wittgenstein's attack falls on the other suggestion that there is something that actually occurs in his mind and gives him infallible guidance. This thing, whatever it is, is supposed to lock him on to the fixed rails of correct use because its meaning is instantly self-intimating. It is the kind of thing that qualifies as an instant mental talisman.[21]

But what can it possibly be? As we have seen, mere words will not do the trick because any analytical formula will itself stand in just as much need of interpretation.[22] Is it, then, a mental image or picture? But though a picture may have a natural application, it will also have many other applications, any one of which could be chosen instead of the natural one. It soon becomes apparent that Wittgenstein has a general objection to any candidate for the post of instant mental talisman: nothing could possibly fill the post, because any single thing in anyone's mind would always be connectible with more than one set of applications. When this objection is directed against the mental image as an instant mental talisman it makes the point made long ago by Berkeley and endorsed by Hume.[23] However, Wittgenstein generalizes the point in two directions: he extends it to cover every possible type of mental occurrence and he makes it include formulae governing the construction of mathematical series as well as universals.

That completes the first stage of the interpretation of Wittgenstein's reductive argument. Its main lines have been sketched in and, though many details will have to be added, its general structure is clear. Platonism involves something more than an ontology, because it is not enough that the fixed rails should be laid to infinity, but also necessary that something in the rule-follower's mind should connect him with them. So there has to be an instant mental talisman. But Wittgenstein argues that this is a requirement that could never be satisfied. All that

[21] See above, pp. 208–9, and Vol. I pp. 58–60.

[22] A point directed against contemporary linguistic philosophers who exaggerated the powers of analysis.

[23] See Berkeley: *Principles of Human Knowledge*, Introduction, and Hume: *Treatise of Human Nature*, I. i. 7.

can possibly be found in this area is some inadequate approximation to what Platonism demands, an equivocal image or a formula that itself needs to be interpreted. This leaves a gap which can be filled only by the rule-follower's practice, which supplies the necessary further determination of what counts as following the rule. If his practice is overlooked, there will be a vacuum which no absolute Platonic rules can possibly fill, because they will always 'hang in the air', leaving the rule-follower with no way of telling the difference between obeying the rule next time he applies it and disobeying it.

The next thing to be done is to fill in the details of this argument. First, something more needs to be said about the surprising twist in its structure that was mentioned above: the deduced absurdity is the abolition of the very distinction that Platonism was designed to make more secure. This is because Wittgenstein's central thesis is that a rule-follower could not possibly have an instant mental talisman to guide his steps, and so Platonism, which makes his guidance by the rule depend on this unavailable piece of equipment, leaves him without any guidance at all. That is the absurdity. But what takes the place of the theory that it destroys? As usual, we must avoid the inference that, because what is rejected is a theory, therefore what is put in its place must also be a theory. Wittgenstein does give a positive account of what it is like to follow a rule, but he does not offer it as a theory. He merely reminds us of certain familiar facts about our use of language. This is characteristic of his treatment of philosophical theories.[24] He does not argue that Platonism is false, nor does he waste time showing how it protects itself from confrontation with any evidence. What he argues is that it could not be true, because certain familiar facts show that its superlatively strong explanation of rule-following destroys the essential link with what the rule-follower actually has to do.

There is another, very perspicuous way of presenting and explaining his contention, that Platonism is absurd because it abolishes the distinction that it was intended to preserve. Consider a rule-follower's almost irresistible tendency to continue a series in what we all regard as the right way. If we distinguish between the two ends of the transaction—the commanding end, which includes the formulation of the rule, and the obedience end, which includes what he actually does—where should we place his tendency to do what he does? Does it belong to the commanding end or to the obedience end? Now the

[24] See above, Ch. 9.

Platonist is a champion of law and order and so he would say that it must be placed at the obedience end. According to him, there would be chaos if rule-followers could justify their idiosyncratic applications of words by appealing to the ways in which they happened to find it natural to apply them.[25] Their tendencies to find certain continuations natural must themselves be moulded by the rule. A rule is sovereign and its authority is not derived from the minds of its subjects, as it might be in Rousseau's political theory.

Wittgenstein retorts that, on the contrary, law and order would break down if the natural tendencies of rule-followers did not also play a part at the commanding end of the transaction. It is important to appreciate that his point is that in that case they would break down in a different way: the distinction between obedience and disobedience would collapse because there is no course of action that cannot conceivably be taken to accord with a rule. It is, therefore, essential that our natural tendencies be allowed some say in what counts as following it. However, their contribution is not an example of spontaneous creativity *ex nihilo*, and so the champion of law and order did have a point. The trouble is that he exaggerated it when he refused to concede our natural tendencies any role at the commanding end. That really would abolish the distinction between obedience and disobedience. Now this is a catastrophe which is not obvious at first, because the immediate reaction to any naturalistic account of rule-following is usually that well-known feeling of giddiness which makes us exaggerate the claims of law and order. So what we must do is indulge the feeling and give full rein to the exaggeration, and then we shall see that Platonism, which is supposed to be the antidote, actually makes matters worse.[26]

Evidently, the burden of this reasoning is carried by the critique of the instant mental talisman. So most expositions of Wittgenstein's argument concentrate on this part of it and say less about the function that believers in the talisman expect it to perform. This creates the impression that Wittgenstein was attacking an adversary long since weakened by the arguments of Berkeley and Hume and of no contemporary importance. In order to correct this imbalance, the setting of this part of the controversy has been described in full detail

[25] This is, of course, a tendentious statement of Wittgenstein's view. He did not think that different people find different continuations natural or that nature gives them weak inclinations. See above, p. 465 n. 13.

[26] See above, pp. 440–1.

here. The function of the instant mental talisman was supposed to be to lock a rule-follower into the correct use of a word which, it was thought, was completely determined independently of him. If this function is omitted, the controversy about the talisman loses much of its point, because the discussion is then confined to the consistency of the speaker's practice, with nothing said about its correctness. But what someone who has just mastered the use of a word thinks is 'Now I've got it right', and his strong feeling that he is at last on fixed rails is not just a convinction about what he is going to do, right or wrong. The ontology of Platonism plays as large a part here as its epistemology, and Wittgenstein's critique is directed against something bigger than the theory of abstract general ideas attacked by Berkeley and Hume.

The critique of the instant mental talisman has a very wide scope. It is most easily appreciated in the special case where the talisman is a mental image. But it could be an analytical formula or even a flash of understanding—indeed, anything that might seem to concentrate in the moment of its mental occurrence the whole use of a word.[27] Here is Wittgenstein's argument against the suggestion that this magic feat might be performed by a mental image:

When someone says the word 'cube' to me, for example, I know what it means. But can the whole *use* of the word come before my mind, when I *understand* it in this way?

Well, but on the other hand isn't the meaning of the word also determined by this use? And can't these ways of determining meaning conflict? Can what we grasp *in a flash* accord with a use, fit or fail to fit it? And how can what is present to us in an instant, what comes before our mind in an instant, fit a *use*?

What really comes before our mind when we *understand* a word?—Isn't it something like a picture? Can't it *be* a picture?

Well, suppose that a picture does come before your mind when you hear the word 'cube', say the drawing of a cube. In what sense can this picture fit or fail to fit a use of the word 'cube'?—Perhaps you say: 'It's quite simple;—if that picture occurs to me and I point to a triangular prism for instance, and say it is a cube, then this use of the word doesn't fit the picture.'—But doesn't it fit? I have purposely so chosen the example that it is quite easy to imagine *a method of projection* according to which the picture does fit after all.

The picture of the cube did indeed *suggest* a certain use to us, but it was possible for me to use it differently.

Then what sort of mistake did I make; was it what we should like to express by saying: I should have thought the picture forced a particular use on me? How could I think that? What *did* I think? Is there such a thing as a picture, or

[27] See *BLBK* p. 42, quoted above, p. 210.

something like a picture, that forces a particular application on us; so that my mistake lay in confusing one case[28] with another?—For we might also be inclined to express ourselves like this: we are at most under a psychological, not a logical, compulsion. And now it looks quite as if we knew of two kinds of case.

What was the effect of my argument? It called our attention to (reminded us of) the fact that there are other processes, besides the one we originally thought of, which we should sometimes be prepared to call 'applying the picture of a cube'. So our 'belief that the picture forced a particular application upon us' consisted in the fact that only the one case and no other occurred to us. 'There is another solution as well' means: there is something else that I am also prepared to call a 'solution'; to which I am prepared to apply such-and-such a picture, such-and-such an analogy, and so on.

What is essential is to see that the same thing can come before our minds when we hear the word and the application still be different. Has it the *same* meaning both times? I think we shall say not.

Suppose, however, that not merely the picture of the cube, but also the method of projection comes before our mind?—How am I to imagine this?— Perhaps I see before me a schema showing the method of projection: say a picture of two cubes connected by lines of projection.—But does this really get me any further? Can't I now imagine different applications of this schema too?—Well, yes, but then can't an *application come before my mind*?—It can: only we need to get clearer about our application of *this* expression. Suppose I explain various methods of projection to someone so that he may go on to apply them; let us ask ourselves when we should say that *the* method that I intend comes before his mind.

Now clearly we accept two different kinds of criteria for this: on the one hand the picture (of whatever kind) that at some time or other comes before his mind; on the other, the application which—in the course of time—he makes of what he imagines. (And can't it be clearly seen here that it is absolutely inessential for the picture to exist in his imagination rather than as a drawing or model in front of him; or again as something that he himself constructs as a model?)

Can there be a collision between picture and application? There can, inasmuch as the picture makes us expect a different use, because people in general apply *this* picture like *this*.

I want to say: we have here a *normal* case, and abnormal cases.[29]

[28] G. E. M. Anscombe translates 'confusing one picture with another'. Although the word 'Bild' does not occur in the German, this translation certainly captures the sense (cf. *PI* I § 191). However, it is clumsy and potentially misleading to speak of 'confusing two pictures' of the way pictures operate. No doubt, this is why the word 'Bild' does not occur in the German.

[29] *PI* I § 139–41. In the middle of this passage there is a cryptic remark of great importance: '. . . we might also be inclined to express ourselves like this: we are at most

The critique of the instant mental talisman goes back a long way. It can be found in the lectures that he gave in Cambridge between 1930 and 1932[30] and, in its most accessible form, in *The Blue Book*.[31] It is not surprising that it occurs in the early lectures, because it is a development of the theory of meaning of the *Tractatus*, which he was explaining informally to his Cambridge audience.

In the *Tractatus* the central point of the picture theory is that the sense of a sentence is derived from the objects named in it and that it is impossible to say what its sense is, adopting some other standpoint than the one from which they were named, because there is nowhere else to go. The sense of a sentence can only be shown in its actual use.[32] It is a short step from this position to the position adopted in *Philosophical Investigations*, where continuous practice is substituted for pin-point naming, but the link between language and the world can still only be exhibited in the actual use of language. It is interesting that the negative aspect of this account of meaning developed so early, while its positive aspect established itself much more slowly.

There is another way of explaining the structure of Wittgenstein's reductive argument when it is interpreted in the way proposed here. This further explanation involves a complex analogy and it is not easy to follow, but it does throw a lot of light on his later ideas about meaning. So it will be presented in some detail—it is worth it—and then, to conclude this chapter, the evidence that seems to favour Kripke's very different interpretation of this part of *Philosophical Investigations* will be reviewed.

The analogy that can be used to present Wittgenstein's argument is an analogy between the state of a machine and the state of mind of a person who has developed a series up to a certain point and knows how to go on. The comparison is Wittgenstein's and, of course, there is no implication that people are machines or even that they are very like

---

under a psychological, not a logical compulsion. And now it looks quite as if we knew of two kinds of case.' His implication is that *all* 'logical compulsion' involves a psychological element—the contribution made by our own minds. Consequently, if someone is told that a particularly strong case of 'logical compulsion' depends on what we ourselves find it overwhelmingly natural to do, it would be a mistake for him to react by exclaiming, 'Oh, then this is only a case of psychological compulsion after all!' For that would imply that there are also cases of pure 'logical compulsion' without the admixture of any psychological element, which, according to Wittgenstein, is false. See above, pp. 465–6, and below, pp. 531–3.

[30] See *CLI* pp. 15, 31–2, and 67.   [31] *BLBK* pp. 34–6.

[32] See *TLP* 2.172–4, 3.262–3, and 4.12. See above, pp. 215–16, and Vol. I pp. 143–6.

them. The point is only that there is a certain parallelism between two illusions, one about machines and the other about people. Someone who was familiar with a certain machine might feel that he could actually see its future movements in the present arrangement of its working parts, not just in some extended use of 'see' but literally and directly, as if they were already occurring. The parallel illusion, which a person might harbour about himself when he contemplates a series, so far as he has developed it, and grasps the whole continuation in a flash, is described in a passage which has already been quoted from *Philosophical Investigations* but is worth quoting again:

'It is as if we could grasp the whole use of the word in a flash.' Like *what* e.g.?—Can't the use—in a certain sense—be grasped in a flash? And in *what* sense can it not?—The point is, that it is as if we could 'grasp it in a flash' in yet another and much more direct sense than that.—But have you a model for this? No. It is just that this expression suggests itself to us. As the result of the crossing of different pictures.

You have no model of this superlative fact, but you are seduced into using a super-expression. (It might be called a philosophical superlative.)[33]

He does not deny that we can 'grasp the whole use of a word in a flash'. His point is only that this description of something familiar that happens to us is not the 'philosophical superlative' that we take it to be when we think that we can actually see the whole future use of the word in the momentary flash. The illusion occurs because we combine two different pictures of meaning: 'On the one hand, we take as the criterion for meaning something which passes in our mind when we say it [sc. the word], or something to which we point when we explain it. On the other hand, we take as the criterion the use we make of the word or sentence as time goes on.'[34]

The passage cited from *Philosophical Investigations* continues:

The machine as symbolizing its action: the action of a machine—I might say at first—seems to be there in it from the start. What does that mean?—If we know the machine, everything else, that is its movement, seems to be already completely determined.

We talk as if these parts could only move in this way, as if they could not do anything else. How is this—do we forget the possibility of their bending, breaking off, melting, and so on? Yes; in many cases we don't think of that at all. We use a machine, or the drawing of a machine, to symbolize a particular action of the machine. For instance, we give someone such a drawing and assume that he will derive the movement of the parts from it. (Just as we can

---

[33] *PI* I §§ 191–2, quoted above, p. 466.
[34] *LFM* p. 182, quoted above, pp. 444–6.

give someone a number by telling him that it is the twenty-fifth in the series 1, 4, 9, 16, . . .

'The machine's action seems to be in it from the start' means: we are inclined to compare the future movements of the machine in their definiteness to objects which are already lying in a drawer and which we then take out.—But we do not say this kind of thing when we are concerned with predicting the actual behaviour of a machine. Then we do not in general forget the possibility of a distortion of the parts and so on.—We *do* talk like that, however, when we are wondering at the way we can use a machine to symbolize a given way of moving—since it can also move in quite *different* ways.

We might say that a machine, or the picture of it, is the first of a series of pictures which we have learnt to derive from this one.

But when we reflect that the machine could also have moved differently it may look as if the way it moves must be contained in the machine-as-symbol far more determinately than in the actual machine. As if it were not enough for the movements in question to be empirically determined in advance, but they had to be really—in a mysterious sense—already *present*. And it is quite true; the movement of the machine-as-symbol is predetermined in a different sense from that in which the movement of any given actual machine is predetermined.

When does one have the thought: the possible movements of a machine are already there in it in some mysterious way?—Well, when one is doing philosophy. And what leads us into thinking that? The kind of way in which we talk about machines. We say, for example, that a machine *has* (possesses) such-and-such possibilities of movement; we speak of the ideally rigid machine which *can* only move in such-and-such a way.—What is this *possibility* of movement? It is not the *movement*, but it does not seem to be the mere physical conditions for moving either—as, that there is play between socket and pin, the pin not fitting too tight in the socket. For while this is the empirical condition for movement, one could also imagine it to be otherwise. The possibility of a movement is, rather, supposed to be like a shadow of the movement itself. But do you know of such a shadow? And by a shadow I do not mean some picture of the movement—for such a picture would not have to be a picture of just *this* movement. But the possibility of this movement must be the possibility of just this movement. (See how high the seas of language run here!)

The waves subside as soon as we ask ourselves: how do we use the phrase 'possibility of movement' when we are talking about a given machine?—But then where did our queer ideas come from? Well, I show you the possibility of a movement, say by means of a *picture* of the movement: 'so possibility is something which is like reality'. We say: 'It isn't moving yet, but it already has the possibility of moving'—'so possibility is something very near reality'. Though we may doubt whether such-and-such physical conditions make this movement possible, we never discuss whether *this* is the possibility of this or of that movement: 'so the possibility of the movement stands in a unique relation to the movement itself; closer than that of a picture to its subject'; for it can be doubted whether a picture is the picture of this thing or that. We say 'Experience will show whether this gives the pin this possibility of movement', but we do not say 'Experience will show whether this is the possibility of this movement': 'so it is not an empirical fact that this possibility is the possibility of precisely this movement'.

We mind about the kind of expressions we use concerning these things: we do not understand them, however, but misinterpret them. When we do philosophy we are like savages, primitive people, who hear the expressions of civilized men, put a false interpretation on them, and then draw the queerest conclusions from it.[35]

The basic point that he makes in this text is straightforward—the future movements seem to be 'already *present*'—but he develops it in a subtle way that is not at all easy to understand.

The basic point of this text was made by Hume in his critique of the concept of 'power'. In certain familiar cases we cannot resist the temptation to smuggle our expectations into what we actually see. So we say that we see in the bent bow its future action when it is released, but perhaps we would not say that we saw the future explosion in the undetonated cartridge. Or, to take another pair of examples, familiarity and a certain empathy might make us say that we could see the future action of a water-wheel in its present predicament, but we might not have a similar reaction to the valve-mechanism of an internal combustion engine. Now nothing could be more familiar to us than our own minds and it would hardly make sense to suggest that we needed empathy to understand them. Consequently, the common tendency to say that we can see the future action in the present state is especially strong in cases like the flash of understanding. There is, of course, nothing wrong with saying it, provided that we do not mean it literally: 'When we do philosophy we are like savages, primitive people, who hear the expressions of civilized men, put a false interpretation on them, and then draw the queerest conclusions from it.'

Wittgenstein's development of this basic point is less easy to understand. He contrasts two ways of looking at a machine. We may wonder whether a particular machine, perhaps a second-hand car, will in fact continue to function as it should; or, we may use a particular machine to symbolize a certain mechanical action—for example, centrifugal scattering. It is the idea of using a machine as a symbol that is hard to understand. What exactly is the point of this use of a machine? And what light does it throw on following a linguistic rule?

[35] *PI* I §§ 193–4.

Suppose that someone hears that a milk-separator works by centrifugal force but does not understand what he is told, because he does not have that concept. So his informant puts objects of the same shape and size but of different weights on the turntable of a gramophone. Now he may not get the point immediately and it will probably be necessary to set the turntable in motion in order to demonstrate centrifugal force in action. But suppose that someone else is familiar with the mechanical effect. Is Wittgenstein's point that it does not matter to this person whether the turntable actually revolves, because he will see immediately that the heavier objects will tend to fly off tangentially with more force, and so in this case the apparatus can be used as a symbol of centrifugal scattering?

There is also another question raised by the way in which Wittgenstein develops his basic point. Machines are designed to function in specific ways and that immediately introduces normative considerations. When a person inspects a second-hand car, the question that he asks himself is 'Will it continue to work?' and that means 'Will it continue to function in the way in which it ought to function?' So we might say that a machine used as a symbol of its own future action is an idealized machine, because the future action that is meant is correct action. It does not follow that the person who is trying to introduce the concept of 'centrifugal force' into his explanation is obliged to believe that the gramophone will function perfectly and turn the table at a steady 78 revolutions per minute. That cannot be necessary, because Wittgenstein says that he could have used a drawing of the machine instead, and there would be no question of the drawing functioning perfectly. He even suggests the possibility of saying 'that a machine, or the picture of it, is the first of a series of pictures which we have learned to derive from this one'.[36] So it looks as if the idealization of the 'machine-as-symbol' is not a matter of belief but merely notional: that is how we think of a machine when we use it as a symbol, because it is a symbol of a machine of that type working perfectly. We, therefore, have to find a parallel way in which normative considerations come into the investigation of following linguistic rules.

This task is not entirely straightforward. A car is a machine built to perform a specific function, but the standard of correctness for language seems to be entirely internal and that threatens to upset any

---

[36] i.e. the first picture or model (see Vol. I p. 119) in a series which is then called, pleonastically, 'the series originating in it'.

parallelism. However, if there is anything in the line taken in the previous chapter, the internal standard of correctness of factual language is, in origin and essence, external, because its funcion is to discover and record regularities in nature. This function is, of course, less specific than that of a car, and our choice of the regularities that we impose on ourselves in order to perform it is not at all narrowly circumscribed. Nevertheless, there is some sort of limit to what would count as a self-imposed regularity used for this purpose, and, once we have set up regular forms of behaviour that meet this liberal external standard, they themselves set the internal standard of correctness.[37]

This has a bearing on Kripke's treatment of the scepticism that he claims to find in Wittgenstein's presentation of the problem of rule-following.[38] The sceptic, according to Kripke, tries to undermine the rule-follower's confidence that he is using a word correctly. The doubt that he instils is radical, because he tells the rule-follower that he does not even know how he himself is in fact interpreting the rule. He would know that only if there were some contemporary fact about himself, which was accessible to him, and which completely determined the way in which he was using the word. But there is no such talismanic fact. Next, Kripke envisages rule-followers trying to defend themselves against this sceptical attack by appealing to their dispositions to apply the word in a certain way. To this he makes two responses. First, he points out, as Wittgenstein does, that the phrase 'in a certain way' is empty until it is given a content by the development of the disposition, which will always be open-ended. Second, he observes that, in any case, the appeal to a dispositional fact is inappropriate, because it misses the point. The point is that rule-followers have to justify what they are doing, and, even if the question of fact were settled by their appeal to their disposition to call geraniums, blood, and rubies 'red', they would not have done anything to justify their practice.[39]

There is something seriously askew in this discussion. Quite apart from the interpretation of *Philosophical Investigations*, if the rule-

[37] Wittgenstein always turns the request for an external standard by remarking that we cannot get beyond the question whether we find a certain regular pattern of behaviour natural or not. But it is arguable that his own use of the pre-linguistic system on to which language is grafted forces his philosophy beyond the point at which he sees it as bound to halt—internal standards of correctness. See above, pp. 454–7, and below, pp. 513–16.

[38] Even if his claim to find this scepticism in Wittgenstein's *mise-en-scène* is mistaken, the line taken by his sceptic is interesting and worth considering in its own right. See above, p. 443 and below, p. 489.

[39] See Kripke: *Wittgenstein on Rules and Private Language*, p. 37.

follower is challenged to produce a fact about himself which
completely determines his use of the word 'red', it may well be that this
dispositional fact is the wrong kind of fact,[40] but it can hardly be
faulted merely because it is a fact and leaves all normative issues
untouched. If that response is appropriate, why was the original
request a request for a talismanic *fact*? And why does Kripke represent
Wittgenstein as satisfied with another fact, namely the fact that the
rule-follower is disposed to apply the word in the same way as other
members of his linguistic community?

Kripke has an answer to that last question: the only standard of
correctness recognized by Wittgenstein is internal. That may be so, but
it would not follow that agreement in judgements is, in his view, the
only stabilizer constituting correct usage, and it was argued in Chapter
14 that he allowed for another one.[41] But the point that now needs to
be made against Kripke is different: if in the end this dispositional fact
about the whole community is going to be allowed to meet the
challenge, then what is wrong with the dispositional fact about the
individual can not merely be that it is a fact, but must be that it is too
narrowly circumscribed. If all facts really were disallowed from the
beginning, it was a waste of time searching for the talismanic fact about
the individual.

Underlying this issue there is a formidable problem. Could
Wittgenstein really succeed in keeping the criterion of linguistic
correctness entirely internal to language?[42] Whatever the answer to
that question, the point that he makes about normativeness in his
discussion of 'the machine-as-symbol' is quite clear: when we use a
machine as a symbol of its own future action, what we have in mind is
its correct action, and so we idealize the machine and think of it as
functioning perfectly. We then have to take care not to 'cross two
different pictures': when we look at a machine for sale and ask
ourselves whether it is really going to function properly, we must not
idealize it in that way. If it looks unlikely that we would fall into that
confusion, it is worth recalling Hume's point: in certain cases familiarity
and empathy do their best to persuade us that we can literally see the
future performance in the present state. So Wittgenstein ends the
discussion by marking the differences between our idealized conception
of the machine-as-symbol and our less charitable attitude to particular
machines, and he shows how certain modal concepts, like possibility,

---

[40] See above, p. 469.
[41] Calibration on standard objects.   [42] See below, pp. 513–16.

and, Hume would have added, necessity, incite us to 'cross' the two pictures unwittingly.

That concludes the second stage of the interpretation of this passage. The first thing that it does is to draw attention to the fact that we can actually 'see' the future performance in the present state of a machine or in the present state of our own minds. Then it expatiates on the differences between two pictures—the idealized machine, used as a symbol of its own future performance, and the actual machine which may be faulty and so may not perform properly. These differences tend to be forgotten if we take our powers as 'seers' too literally. But is there a deeper level at which the passage can be understood, and a more profound meaning?

It is often worth asking this question about a text of Wittgenstein's, and in this particular case there is an important feature of meaning which has not yet been brought into play. When a person uses a word, he has not only his own past record, perhaps accompanied by a flash of understanding, but also his intentions for the future. A machine has to wait for its future performances to prove its value today, but a person can think ahead and react in advance to some (but not all) future predicaments. Now as Wittgenstein points out, there is no magic in advance reactions: like reactions at the time, they indicate what someone finds it natural—perhaps overwhelmingly natural—to say, and, what is more, when the time does arrive, advance reactions have to be remembered and interpreted.[43] Still, they are a fact of life for us, but not for machines, and this has an interesting effect on Wittgenstein's analogy.

He compares the present contents of my mind, when I am following a linguistic rule, with the present state of a machine. However, when I predict the performance of a machine I rely on my familiarity with it and sometimes, perhaps, on a kind of empathy, but I do not need these resources when I think about myself and about the way in which I am going to use the word 'red' in the future. This is not just because I have internalized the linguistic rule and so do not rely on the kind of familiarity that I need for something external. Even when we add that I could hardly need empathy with myself, the explanation is still not complete. We also have to add that I have something which the machine lacks, namely intentions. The state of a machine has no *direct* connection with its own future performance, and, when I use it as a

---

[43] See *RFM* I § 3, quoted and discussed above, pp. 438–441.

symbol, though it does then get a direct connection with it, it gets it through my intention, not its own, because it has no intentions, least of all the intention to take its present state as a symbol of its own future performance.

This is relevant to Wittgenstein's analogy, because the illusion that he is trying to diagnose and dispel is reinforced by the fact that meaning is backed up by intention. The meaning of a word, as I construe it, actually draws on the way in which I intend to use it in cases that I have not yet encountered, especially if I explore them in advance thought-experiments, because they strike me as critical cases that I may well encounter later. Now it is very easy to lump together intended future applications with applications that have actually been made. My intentions are going to be carried out, are they not? So here in the background of Wittgenstein's analogy we have another inducement to 'cross' the two pictures.[44]

It is, perhaps, the most important inducement of all, because it comes from the inside story of using a word with a meaning. Indeed, the image of the Platonic rails stretching ahead to infinity becomes far more persuasive when we contemplate it through our own intentions. The effect of adding this further level to Wittgenstein's discussion is interesting. It has already been pointed out that the Platonic rails would be no help to us unless we had some device which locked us on to them.[45] But the devices that we use in everyday life when we are contemplating the employment of a word are very different. They are such things as the formulation of the rule, mnemonic illustrations, and, perhaps, the conscious resolution to avoid certain common errors. Behind these devices the two resources examined by Wittgenstein are lined up in reserve—calibration on standard objects and agreement in judgements with others.

Now in any context in real life in which we might use the available devices, the idea that a word might draw its meaning partly from future applications would be an absurdity to be rejected almost before it is entertained. However, though this aspect of Platonism is, according to Wittgenstein, incoherent, it is very appealing to theorists. The meaning of a word is timeless and so we feel strongly inclined to imagine the

---

[44] This inducement is not another point of analogy. On the contrary, I merely project into the machine my intention to use it as a symbol in a particular way. Of course, I have already idealized the connection between the machine's present state and its future performance and that facilitates the projection. But no further point of analogy is involved.

[45] *PI* I § 219, quoted and discussed above, p. 465.

removal of the obstacle that stand in the way of our entertaining the attractive idea. If we think of our intended future applications of the word as somehow already present, the impossibility of drawing on future cases for its meaning seems to vanish, so that we are free to indulge the fantasy of anticipatory ostensive definition.

Even without this deeper level of interpretation, Wittgenstein's treatment of the 'machine-as-symbol' succeeds in throwing a bright light on his ideas about meaning. But the analogy becomes much more interesting when the extra level is included. For if, by whatever not really executable manœuvre, the meaning of a word, as used by me now, really were tied criterially to all its as yet unmade correct applications, then my present mental state would be very like the present state of a machine advertised as perfect, but with its perfection tied criterially to performances yet to come. The points of analogy are especially interesting in this case, and so too are the points of disanalogy.

The main point of analogy is, of course, that the present state is tied criterially to future performances. This has a curious effect on my application of the word. An ordinary description of the mental equipment backing up this performance would mention the devices listed above, adding, perhaps, that I make the best use that I can of them. But my mental equipment and my use of it are idealized if they are tied criterially to all my future applications of the word when these are assumed to be correct, as they are in the best outcome described in the Platonic theory.

The main point of disanalogy emerges when we note that a machine might really be bought with a guarantee and returned if it failed to live up to it. Indeed, we often use idealized descriptions which draw this kind of cheque on the future. For example, the criteria for 'I know that it is going to rain' are contemporary, but the criteria for 'I knew it would' are deferred. However, the Platonic fantasy goes one step further than this. For future rain serves as an accessible criterion, and, if it fails to occur, I admit that I did not know that it would occur. But there will never be an accessible deferred criterion for the Platonically idealized description of my mental states, because the picture of the fixed rails of my future correct use of the word has no application whatsoever. We do, of course, have ordinary deferred criteria and they are described by Wittgenstein in his account of teaching someone the meaning of a word, but the Platonic picture has nothing extra to which it might be attached. It simply floats above the action inapplicably. If a name is needed for this strange use of descriptions tied to the future—but to the etherealized future rather than the ordinary mundane future—it might be called 'super-idealization'.[46] We indulge in a limited kind of idealization when we use an ordinary deferred criterion for 'knowing': super-idealization puts the deferred criterion in the sky.

There is a passage in *Lectures on the Foundations of Mathematics* which explains the origin of these superlative Platonic illusions very clearly:

> I want to show that the inexorability or absolute hardness of logic is of just this kind. It seems as if we had got hold of a hardness which we have never experienced.
>
> In kinematics we talk of a connecting rod—not meaning a rod made of steel or brass or what-not. We use the word 'connecting rod' in ordinary life, but in kinematics we use it in quite a different way, although we say roughly the same things about it as we say about the real rod: that it goes forward and back, rotates, etc. But then the real rod contracts and expands, we say. What are we to say of this rod: does it contract and expand?—And so we say it *can't*. But the truth is that there is no question of it contracting or expanding. It is a *picture* of a connecting rod, a symbol used in this symbolism for a connecting rod. And in this symbolism there is nothing which corresponds to a contraction or expansion of the connecting rod.
>
> Similarly, if I say that there is no such thing as the super-rigidity of logic, the real point is to explain where this idea of super-rigidity comes from—to show that the idea of *super-rigidity* does *not* come from the same source which the idea of *rigidity* comes from. The idea of rigidity comes from comparing things like butter and elastic with things like iron and steel. But the idea of super-rigidity comes from the interference of two pictures—like the idea of the super-inexorability of the law. First we have: 'The law condemns', 'The judge condemns'. Then we are led by the parallel use of the pictures to a point where we are inclined to use a superlative. We have then to show the sources of this superlative, and that it doesn't come from the source the ordinary idea comes from.[47]

This important text treats rules governing logical inferences in the same way as rules governing the application of descriptive words to things, but that is a development beyond the scope of this book.

The explanation of the deeper level of the analogy between a state of mind and a state of a machine yields a new way of looking at the structure of Wittgenstein's argument against Platonism. As usual, he is trying to give a down-to-earth account of our linguistic practices, and,

[46] Cf. *PI* I § 192, quoted above, pp. 466 and 475.
[47] *LFM* pp. 198–9.

in particular, of the mental equipment of speakers at the moment when they apply words to things. So he mentions formulations of the rule that they are following, their illustrative images, their memories of their past applications of the words, and their acquired tendencies to continue in a certain way. These are the resources that we actually use at the moment of speaking and we manage quite well with them. His objection to Platonism is that it dreams up something which is supposed to be better, but which would, in fact, abolish the very distinction between obedience to a rule and disobedience that it was intended to preserve. It would abolish the distinction because it would deprive us of the guidance that we need, and in fact get from our shared tendencies to continue in certain ways. It takes these tendencies and places them entirely at the obedience end of the transaction, offering us, as a substitute at the commanding end something that is no use at all.

The Platonist would reply, 'You don't have to worry about the correctness of your practices in my theory, because, under certain conditions, it is guaranteed.' But the trouble is that the conditions are not ordinary, recognizable, conditions, and the guarantee is only given by a stroke of the philosopher's pen. The mental state and equipment of a rule-follower is simply tied criterially to future successes which are not presented in a way that makes them recognizable, but are merely pictured as already lined up in advance somewhere, somehow. The substitution of super-idealized description for down-to-earth description achieves absolutely nothing. It may promise to allay the anxieties of a self-doubting linguistic instrument of measurement, but all that it really does is to discount his actions by tying his resources and efforts criterially to their own future successes pictured metaphysically as already laid out ahead of him.

It will be evident that this is a further example of the structure found in the private language argument. Two things, which are necessarily attached to different criteria in real life, are clamped together in a philosophical theory. The point of the private language argument was that the correctness of a person's use of a word must not be tied criterially to what he has in his mind when he uses it, namely, his intention to use it in a certain way that strikes him as correct, and his impression that he is using it correctly. The argument against Platonism has the same structure but the opposite direction of fit. Instead of defining success in contemporary mental terms, the Platonist defines the contents of the speaker's mind in terms of success.[48] Either way, the speaker's action is discounted. To put the point in terms of Wittgenstein's other mechanical analogy, the necessary friction or give and take between the two surfaces, language and the world, has been lost.[49]

When we read one of Wittgenstein's discussions of philosophical illusions, there are two things which we may not find it easy to hold together in our minds simultaneously, his success in dispelling them and the depth and difficulty of the problems that produced them. It is not hard to appreciate the seriousness of the problems when they are presented in the traditional way, but when they are presented in his way, the success of his treatment—if, indeed, it does succeed in dissolving them—only seems to show that they must have been trivial. This, of course, does not follow, unless 'trivial' means 'non-scientific', and in fact his successes are often hard-won. But that is easily forgotten in the actual denouement. So in a case like Platonism, after we have appreciated its errors, it is a good idea to go back and gauge the depth of the problem that the erroneous theory was designed to solve.

The problem may be put like this: 'How does the measurement of the world by language actually work?' The difficulty that we experience when we try to answer this question has two main sources. First, we do not really know where to look for an answer. The question is clearly profound, but its profundity does not seem to extend in any particular direction that can be related to our ordinary investigations of the world. Evidently a scientific account of language is not what is required, because that would itself be an example of the kind of measurement that it was expected to explain. This, of course, is the second source of the difficulty of the problem and it was identified accurately in the *Tractatus*: we feel that we must have an answer which will not suffer from the apparently universal disadvantage that it is expressed in further factual sentences.

The classical reaction to these difficulties was to look for a special kind of theory, expressed, of course, in words, but without the usual commitments of factual language. The idea was that, if no such theory could be found, our linguistic practices would be left completely arbitrary, and that they would achieve unison—if indeed they did achieve unison—merely by judicious imitation, like the annual singing of Humpback Whales in Hawaiian waters. Now the only available

---

[48] See above, p. 422, and Vol. I pp. 59–60.
[49] See above, p. 421.

model for this kind of theorizing was science. So the suggestion was that there is a special harmony between language and the world, like empirical truth except that it is achieved at the deeper level of meaning. This was intended to forestall what was seen as the only other possibility, the possibility that our system of language is entirely arbitrary. It also intended to explain our feeling that, when we use language, we are compelled to go on in the way that we do.

Some of the details of this kind of theory of language have already been given.[50] Just as the contingent layout of the world determines which factual sentences are true, so too, according to these realists, there is a deeper level at which the essence of the world determines which factual sentences make sense. In the system of the *Tractatus* there were two points at which this sense-giving force made its impact on language. First, the general truth-functional structure of factual language was supposed to be stamped on to it by the basic grid of elementary possibilities, each of which must either be realized or not realized, with no third alternative.[51] Second, the combinatorial powers of names in elementary sentences were supposed to be projected into them by the objects that they designated.[52] But though Wittgenstein's critique of Platonism was a recantation of these earlier ideas, it was also much more than that. For the *Tractatus* was only one contribution to a long tradition of realism. The distinctive mark of all such theories is the claim that, in one way or another, the essential nature of the world is fixed independently of us and puts its imprint on any language that we are able to use to describe it. This is not a gratuitous fantasy. We only have to ask ourselves, 'Or are we free to invent what we like by way of language?' and the idea of those underlying metaphysical constraints begins to take shape in our minds as a counterweight to silliness.

If we are going to avoid these illusions, we have to refuse the dilemma, 'Either super-idealized[53] guidance or caprice'. Naturally, that is not like refusing both alternatives on a menu, because it takes a long and difficult philosophical investigation to show us that what we are being offered are not two self-contained alternatives, but two incomplete pictures.[54] The way we go on is neither capricious nor

---

[50] See above, pp. 206–11 and Vol. I Chs. 1 and 2.

[51] *TLP* 6.124, discussed in Vol. I pp. 23–5.   [52] See Vol. I pp. 116–22.

[53] See above, p. 484. Cf. Vol. I pp. 16–17.

[54] Just as the way to avoid the illusion of phenomenal properties that elude all criteria is to reject the dichotomy, 'Either intrinsic or extrinsic'. See above, pp. 406–13 and Vol. I p. 41.

locked on to fixed rails, but there is no third description of it which is more appropriate and equally brief. The only way to understand our linguistic practices is to describe them as they are in full detail. The simplifying question, 'Is it a case of complete guidance or of improvisation?' can be accepted and answered only when it is asked about a particular sequence of actions judged against the yardstick of a particular rule.[55] For in such cases we start from our shared assumption about what counts as 'doing the same again'. But when the same question is asked about the assumption itself, where can we go for an answer? We cannot opt for either alternative, and yet we do not have a third suggestion of equal brevity.

At this point we would be well advised to give up the idea that there must be a satisfactory theory to be found here—either one of the two on offer or some third possibility—and to look, instead, for a way of combining the two incomplete pictures in an accurate description of our actual practices. That is what Wittgenstein tries to do and there is no short way of presenting his investigation and appreciating it. The task itself is extraordinarily difficult, like picking up shafts of coloured light, which have been polarized by the prism of a false philosophy, and weaving them back into pure daylight. Even when we see it done, we are apt to complain, because the successful use of this method leaves us exactly where we were. It is difficult to assimilate the idea that an outcome which has nothing in it for a theorist may, nevertheless, yield understanding.

Even if we accept this point, we may fail to internalize it and make it part of our mentality. For there is in our culture a strong intellectual current set in the opposite direction. We assume that understanding can only come from the discovery of something new and never from a more penetrating and sympathetic description of the old. So when we examine our own linguistic practices, we feel obliged to accept the dilemma, 'Either super-idealized guidance or caprice', and only a few bold spirits choose the second option.

The first option was taken by Wittgenstein in the *Tractatus*. Later, in *Philosophical Investigations* he rejects his realism about the basic grid of factual possibilities. That is how the book begins, and it then moves on to a criticism of his realistic explanation of the combinatorial powers of names. These self-criticisms are also aimed at the endemic realism of Western philosophy, but not with a view to promoting conventionalism.

[55] See *RFM* I § 1.

He saw that, if we really did have to choose between those two alternatives, there would be much to be said for realism, but he rejected the dilemma.

Kripke's first reaction to Wittgenstein's so-called 'sceptical paradox' is an eloquent plea for realism. How can what I mean by a word be determinate if it is not completely fixed by something in my mind when I use it? As Kripke points out, the problem is not how I know what I mean but what constitutes my meaning.[56] Surely, it ought to be fixed by some contemporary fact about me. It has already been explained that Wittgenstein himself did not see this as a sceptical problem, but only as something which would be seen as a sceptical problem by the theorist against whom he was arguing.[57] So it really is one of the pieces of the jigsaw, but it does not belong where Kripke puts it. It has to be fitted in as part of the realist's complaint about the actual situation of a rule-follower when he compares it with the supposedly better situation that he has dreamed up for him. There is also another point that needs to be made about this complaint: as Wittgenstein hears it, it is not only that there is nothing in a speaker's mind to make the meaning with which he uses a word fully determinate, but also that there is no fixed point in the world outside his mind on to which such an instant talisman, if he could get one, might fasten. With this addition, Kripke's presentation of the so-called 'sceptical problem' is a plea for the realism which is one of the two theories rejected by Wittgenstein.

It is worth emphasizing that it is an essential feature of the rejected realism that the instant mental talisman is supposed to latch on to some fixed point outside our minds. So his argument is not only that there is nothing in a speaker's mind to make his meaning fully determinate, but also that the fixed rails of correct usage already laid out in reality on which that mental talisman would keep us if Platonism could be believed, are an illusion. That is why he asks:

> Whence comes the idea that the beginning of a series is a visible section of rails invisibly laid to infinity? Well, we might imagine rails instead of a rule. And infinitely long rails correspond to the unlimited application of a rule.

> 'All the steps are really already taken' means: I no longer have any choice.

[56] See Kripke: *Wittgenstein on Rules and Private Language*, p. 39. There is, of course, a normative supplement to this question. We need to know not only what constitutes my meaning, but also what makes it correct. See Kripke, ibid., pp. 24 and 37, discussed above, pp. 479–80.

[57] See above, pp. 441–3, 457–8, and 463–5.

The rule, once stamped with a particular meaning, traces the lines along which it is to be followed through the whole of space.—But if something of this sort really were the case, how would it help?

No; my description only made sense if it was to be understood symbolically.—I should have said: *This is how it strikes me.*

When I obey a rule, I do not choose.

I obey the rule *blindly*.[58]

The realist's 'infinitely long rails' would make no difference to a rule-follower if there were nothing in his mind to latch on to them, but equally, if there were an instant talisman in his mind, it would need to have something to latch on to.[59] The argument is that there could be no such thing in his mind.

Much of the evidence for this identification of the target of Wittgenstein's reductive argument has now been given. However there is also a group of early texts, yet to be mentioned, which offer a somewhat different version of the Platonism that is under attack. It is a variant of the version put forward in the *Tractatus*, and it is an easier version to understand, because it is formulated very explicitly. It makes its first appearance in the lectures given in Cambridge in 1931–2:

The grammatical rules applying to it determine the meaning of a word. Its meaning is not something else, some object to which it corresponds or does not correspond. The word carries its meaning with it; it has a grammatical body behind it, so to speak. Its meaning cannot be something else which may not be known. It does not carry its grammatical rules with it. They describe its usage subsequently.[60]

This is a particularly interesting version of Platonist realism. The meaning of a word is determined not by something remote, like the 'fixed rails' described in *Philosophical Investigations*. It is determined by something which the word carries along with it. However, this meaning-fixer is not on the list of familiar devices which we actually use when we apply the word to things: it is not, for example, the rule of application, because that is said to be a later derivative from it. The 'grammatical body', which fixes the meaning of the word, is something

---

[58] *PI* I §§ 218–19, quoted and discussed above, p. 441.

[59] C. McGinn makes this point in *Wittgenstein on Meaning*, pp. 98–102. However, he makes it not as part of Wittgenstein's argument, but as an extension of it. This robs Wittgenstein's discussion of much of its interest. Instead of spanning the controversy between classical realists and nominalists, it would confine itself to the mental side of the problem on the One and the Many, on which the British Empiricists concentrated.

[60] *CLI* p 59.

which we feel *behind* the word. So it has the independence that any Platonist meaning-fixer requires, but without the usual remoteness.

This ingenious theory, which tries to have the best of both worlds, is a development of the picture theory of sentences. According to the *Tractatus*, the meaning of a name[61] is the object designated by it and that object projects its combinatorial possibilities into the name. The first of these two theses then fades into the background, leaving the second one to be generalized to apply to all descriptive words, even when they are not construed as names: the 'grammatical body' behind a word determines not only its combinatorial properties with other similar words, but also every other feature of its use.

As often happens to Wittgenstein's early doctrines, this one is described most perspicuously later, when it is being rejected:

Consider the following analogy: between a cube or pyramid with one painted surface, behind which is an invisible body, and a word and the meaning behind it. Any position in which this surface could be placed will depend on the position of the solid body behind it. We are tempted to think that, if we know a cube is behind the painted surface, we can know the rules for arranging the surface with other surfaces. But this is not true. One cannot deduce the geometry of the cube from looking at the cube. Rules do not follow from an act of comprehension. Analogously, we are tempted to think we can deduce the rules for the use of a word from its meaning, which we supposedly grasp as a whole when we pronounce the word. This is the error I would eradicate. The difficulty is that inasmuch as we grasp the meaning without grasping all the rules, it seems as if the rules *could* be *developed* from the meaning.[62]

The same error in the theory is pointed out in a later text:

'The concept Scot is not a Scot.' Is this nonsense? Well, I do not know what anyone who says that is trying to say, that is, how he is intending to use this sentence. I can think out several uses for it, which are ready to hand. 'But you just *can't* use it, nor can you think it in such a way that the same thing is meant by the words "the concept Scot" and the second "Scot", as you *ordinarily* mean by these words.' Here is the mistake. Here one is thinking as if *this* comparison came into one's mind: words fit together in the sentence, i.e. senseless sequences of words may be written down; but the meaning of each word is an invisible *body*, and these meaning-bodies do *not* fit together. ('Meaning it gives the sentence a further dimension.')[63]

This mistake is connected with the illusion generated by 'the machine-as-symbol' and it is a source of much confusion in the theory of logic:

[61] Its *Bedeutung*. See Vol. I p. 75 n. 43.
[62] *CLII* pp. 50–1.   [63] *RPP* I § 42.

The statement 'This fits that', asserted of two bodies, may be either of two different kinds, a geometrical one or an experiential one. If the diameter of the tongue of the left-hand piece is 3 inches and of the corresponding depression of the other piece is 2 inches,[64] then to say they cannot be put together can mean either that the application of physical strength or of a machine cannot force them to fit (a clear empirical statement), or that they cannot fit so long as the one remains 3 inches and the other 2 inches. The differrence in the grammars of 'They can't be fitted' in these two cases is like that between 'This piece of chalk is longer than that' and 'A 3-inch piece of chalk is longer than a 2-inch piece.' It is a rule about the use of 'fitting' that it makes no sense to say 3 inches fits 2 inches. The difficulty is in using the word 'can' in different ways, as 'physically possible' and as 'making no[65] sense to say . . .'. The logical impossibility of fitting the two pieces seems of the same order as the physical impossibility, only more impossible! If one fixes the use of 'apple' so that it excludes the use of 'not' before it, then the impossibility of fitting the two is not like the impossibility of physical fitting.[66]

Here we have another example of Platonic super-idealization. But it is beyond the scope of this book to follow the line of thought leading from the diagnosis of the mistake in the realist's account of the meanings of descriptive words to the diagnosis of his related mistake in his account of the inexorability of logic. This group of texts has been cited only in order to make the limited point, that in 1929 Wittgenstein did not immediately abandon Platonic realism, but tried to devise a version of it which would give him the best of both worlds. So when he worked out the sophisticated treatment of rule-following which can be found in *Philosophical Investigations*, the version of Platonic realism that was offered in the *Tractatus* is not the only version that he was recanting. He was also recanting the theory of the meaning-body.

Two further matters remain to be investigated in this chapter. First, something more needs to be said about the origin and structure of Wittgenstein's critique of the instant mental talisman. Second, the evidence that seems to support Kripke's very different interpretation of this part of *Philosophical Investigations* must be assessed.

A particularly clear example of the argument against the instant mental talisman was cited above from *Philosophical Investigations*—the case of mental images—and it was pointed out that too many commentators are content to rehearse the argument without saying

---

[64] This is illustrated in the text by a picture of a tongue fitting into a groove, or, as he says, 'a depression'.

[65] The negative has insinuated itself prematurely.

[66] *CLII* pp. 145–6. Cf. *LFM* pp. 198–9, quoted above, p. 484, and *PI* I § 140.

anything about its anti-Platonic thrust.[67] That cannot be right, if only because Wittgenstein would not have mentioned the fixed rails 'laid to infinity' if he had merely been making the point made by the British Empiricists about the particularity of anything that occurs in a person's mind.

However, the misinterpretation which takes the part of Wittgenstein's argument for the whole is easily adopted, because he himself gives the part such prominence. This is not just an accident of exposition and there are several ways of explaining why the critique of the instant mental talisman bulks so large that it can seem to be the whole point. One explanation would be that this is where all the work of Wittgenstein's *reductio* is done,[68] and so this is the point that his readers take. But there is another, more interesting explanation to be derived from the way in which his ideas about Platonism and the instant mental talisman actually developed. They developed independently of one another, because he had other reasons for rejecting Platonism, and so the critique of the instant mental talisman was presented for many years as a separate argument.

If we go back to 1930, we find Wittgenstein's philosophy in a transitional phase. The basic grid of factual possibilities has been modified,[69] but it is still retained and given the same realist treatment that it had been given in the *Tractatus*:

... in order that propositions may be able to represent at all, something further is needed which is the same both in language and reality. For example, a picture can represent a scene rightly or wrongly; but both in picture and scene pictured there will be colour and light and shade.

Thought must have the logical form of reality if it is to be thought at all.[70]

At the deeper level of meaning reality is still the dominant partner. However, to offset this, another doctrine is still retained from the *Tractatus*: the pattern stamped onto language by reality can only be shown:

Grammar is not determined by facts. You can only get into conflict with reality by saying something which is not true. We cannot describe a paradigm for grammar, because we should have to use language to do it.[71]

This is the unstable position described above in Chapter 9. It is true

---

[67] See above, pp. 471–2 and 489–90.   [68] See above, pp. 466–9.
[69] By the relaxation of the criterion of simplicity. See Vol. I pp. 82–7.
[70] *CLI* p. 10. Cf. *TLP* 2.18.
[71] *CLI* p. 95. Cf. *PG* § 68, quoted above, p. 449 n. 48.

that at the deeper level of meaning reality is the dominant partner, but its influence on language is something which cannot be explained in detail. This is not a scientific theory and not really any kind of theory. It is vestigial realism, still hanging on but really on the way out as an independent philosophical theory. So in an earlier set of lectures in the same series we find him saying:

To a necessity in the world there corresponds an arbitrary rule in language.[72]

Later, in *Philosophical Grammar* this becomes:

'The only correlate in language to an intrinsic necessity is an arbitrary rule. It is the only thing which one can milk out of this intrinsic necessity into a proposition.'[73]

It is evident that realism, as an independent philosophical theory, was already disappearing before the critique of the instant mental talisman was brought to bear on it.

It is not too surprising that he should have other reasons for abandoning realism. But what is surprising is that he did not use the critique of the instant mental talisman to reinforce his rejection of realism, in spite of the fact that it was there in *Cambridge Lectures, 1930–32*, already worked out in considerable detail.[74] Why did he not use it against realism then in the way in which he used it later in *Philosophical Investigations*?

Before an answer is sought to this question, some evidence is needed. The main premiss of the argument against the instant mental talisman appears very early:

. . . In all language there is a bridge between the sign and its application. No one can make this for us; we have to bridge the gap ourselves. No explanation ever saves the jump, because any further explanation will itself need a jump. No reason compels us to learn language.[75]

---

[72] *CLI* p. 57 (1931).   [73] *PG* § 133.

[74] It, too, is a development of the doctrine of showing. According to *TLP*, it is impossible to say what the sense of any sentence is, because that is something which can only be shown by the use of the sentence. The other idea which came out of the doctrine of showing was that the constraints put on language by the structure of reality cannot be described in language. See Vol. I pp. 142–52.

[75] *CLI* p. 67 (1931–2). The last sentence reads like the result of hasty note-taking. The last sentence but one reappears in many texts, e.g. in *PR* § 26, 'Sooner or later there is a leap from the sign to what is signified', or in *BRBK* p. 143, 'We meet again and again with this curious superstition, as one might be inclined to call it, that the mental act is capable of crossing a bridge before we've got to it.' This formulation shows how the superstition exploits intention-based knowledge of the future (see above, pp. 481–3).

The inference, that a sentence can never contain a complete specification of its own sense, is drawn in an earlier set of lectures:

. . . Thinking means operating with plans. A thought is not the same thing as a plan because a thought needs no interpretation and a plan does. The plan (without its interpretation) corresponds to the particular sentence, the interpreted plan to the proposition. Proposition and judgment are the same thing, except that the proposition is the 'type' of which the judgment (made in a particular place by a particular person at a particular time) is the token: cf. a number of copies of a plan or of a photograph. How do we know that someone had understood a plan or order? He can only show his understanding by translating it into other symbols. He may understand without obeying. But if he obeys he is again translating—i.e. by co-ordinating his action with the symbols. So understanding is really translation, whether into other symbols or into action.

We cannot get the interpretation into the plan; the rules for interpreting a plan are not part of the plan.[76]

This passage marks a transitional stage in Wittgenstein's thoughts about meaning. Although he denies that we can get the interpretation into the plan or the sentence, he sanctions a use of the word 'translate' which might encourage the idea. He also allows that a thought needs no interpretation. It was not until later that he achieved complete liberation from the picture of meaning as 'the unambiguous shadow that admits of no further interpretation'.[77]

The best exorcism of this idea is to be found in *The Blue Book*:

. . . What one wishes to say is: 'Every sign is capable of interpretation; but the *meaning* mustn't be capable of interpretation. It is the last interpretation.' Now I assume that you take the meaning to be a process accompanying the saying, and that it is translatable into, and so far equivalent to, a further sign.

. . . let us imagine an instance in which it does happen. Supposing I had a habit of accompanying every English sentence which I said aloud by a German sentence spoken to myself inwardly. If then, for some reason or other, you call the silent sentence the meaning of the one spoken aloud, the process of

Cf. *PI* I § 197 on 'the super-strong connection between the act of intending and the thing intended'.

[76] *CLI* p. 24 (1930). Again there seems to be something wrong with the note-taking. Wittgenstein is unlikely to have said that the only way to show understanding of a plan is to translate it into other *symbols*. For he goes on to imply that it is possible to show understanding by translating into actions. It is certainly odd to call this 'translating', perhaps less odd to call it 'interpreting' (though this use of 'interpretation' is repudiated in *PI* I § 201: see above, p. 467 n. 18), but surely impossible to call the actions 'symbols'. Symbols of what?

[77] *PG* § 102.

meaning accompanying the process of saying would be one which could itself be translated into outward signs. Or, *before* any sentence which we say aloud we say its meaning (whatever it may be) to ourselves in a kind of aside. An example at least similar to the case we want would be saying one thing and at the same time seeing a picture before our mind's eye which is the meaning and agrees or disagrees with what we say. Such cases and similar ones exist, but they are not at all what happens as a rule when we say something and mean it, or mean something else. There are, of course, real cases in which what we call meaning is a definite conscious process accompanying, preceding, or following the verbal expression and itself a verbal expression of some sort or translatable into one. A typical example of this is the 'aside' on the stage.

. . . Let us revert to our question: 'What is the object of a thought?' (e.g. when we say, 'I think that King's College is on fire').

. . . One of the origins of our question is the twofold use of the propositional function 'I think *x*'. We say, 'I think that so-and-so will happen' or 'that so-and-so is the case', and also 'I think just the same *thing* as he'; and we say 'I expect him', and also 'I expect that he will come'. Compare 'I expect him' and 'I shoot him'. We can't shoot him if he isn't there. This is how the question arises: 'How can we expect something that is not the case?', 'How can we expect a fact which does not exist?'

. . . There are several origins to this idea of a shadow. One of them is this:

. . . We imagine the shadow to be a picture the intention of which *cannot be questioned*, that is, a picture which we don't interpret in order to understand it, but which we understand without interpreting it.

The shadow, as we think of it, is some sort of a picture; in fact, something very much like an image which comes before our mind's eye; and this again is something not unlike a painted representation in the ordinary sense. A source of the idea of the shadow certainly is the fact that in some cases saying, hearing, or reading a sentence brings images before our mind's eye, images which more or less strictly correspond to the sentence, and which are therefore, in a sense, translations of this sentence into a pictorial language.— But it is absolutely essential for the picture which we imagine the shadow to be that it is what I shall call a 'picture by similarity'. I don't mean by this that it is a picture similar to what it is intended to represent, but that it is a picture which is correct only when it is similar to what it represents.

If we keep in mind the possibility of a picture which, though correct, has no similarity with its object, the interpolation of a shadow between the sentence and reality loses all point. For now the sentence itself can serve as such a shadow. The sentence is just such a picture, which hasn't the slightest similarity with what it represents.

The idea that that which we wish to happen must be present as a shadow in our wish is deeply rooted in our forms of expression. But, in fact, we might say that it is only the next best absurdity to the one which we should really like to say. If it weren't too absurd we should say that the fact which we wish for must be present in our wish. For how can we wish *just this* to happen if just this isn't present in our wish? It is quite true to say: The mere shadow won't do; for it stops short before the object; and we want the wish to contain the object itself.—We want that the wish that Mr. Smith should come into this room should wish that just *Mr. Smith*, and no substitute, should do the *coming*, and no substitute for that, *into my room*, and no substitute for that. But this is exactly what we said.

Our confusion could be described in this way: Quite in accordance with our usual form of expression we think of the fact which we wish for as a thing which is not yet here, and to which, therefore, we cannot point. Now in order to understand the grammar of our expression 'object of our wish' let's just consider the answer which we give to the question: 'What is the object of your wish?' the answer to this question of course is 'I wish that so-and-so should happen'. Now what would the answer be if we went on asking 'And what is the object of this wish?' It could only consist in a repetition of our previous expression of the wish, or else in a translation into some other form of expression. We might, e.g., state what we wished in other words or illustrate it by a picture, etc., etc. Now when we are under the impression that what we call the object of our wish is, as it were, a man who has not yet entered our room, and therefore can't yet be seen, we imagine that any explanation of what it is we wish is only the next best thing to the explanation which would show *the actual fact*—which, we are afraid, can't yet be shown as it has not yet entered.— It is as though I said to some one 'I am expecting Mr. Smith', and he asked me 'Who is Mr. Smith?', and I answered, 'I can't show him to you now, as he isn't there. All I can show you is a picture of him.' It then seems as though I could never entirely explain what I wished until it had actually happened. But of course this is a delusion. The truth is that I needn't be able to give a better explanation of what I wished after the wish was fulfilled than before; for I might perfectly well have shown Mr. Smith to my friend, and have shown him what 'coming in' means, and have shown him what my room is, before Mr. Smith came into my room.[78]

The 'unambiguous shadow that admits of no further interpretation' is an illusion and the only way to get rid of it is to replace it with something substantial, about which you must then ask yourself how you would use it. Maybe you will replace it with another verbal formulation, or perhaps you will substitute a mental picture, but, whatever you put in its place, you will find that it too can be interpreted in more than one way, so that it too can serve to express more than one sense. Naturally, Wittgenstein is not denying that the wish has a definite sense. His point is only that its sense is not something which

[78] *BLBK* pp. 34–8.

stands behind the words and acts as a perfect guide to their correct application to things, but something that is constituted by their correct application. The illusion is produced by taking this achievement, imagining it happening earlier and treating it as an infallible guide to itself. This is a clear case of super-idealization, like the 'machine-as-symbol'.

Why then did he not connect the two developments of the doctrine of showing in 1930? Why did he not immediately use the critique of the instant mental talisman against realism in the way in which he used it later in *Philosophical Investigations*? We can only guess, and here is one possible answer.

His early interest in realism was focused on to the question 'How does reality put its stamp on factual language?' That is a very general question and it led to the ontology and semantic theory of the *Tractatus*. It is a question which is not closely connected with particular moves made in particular language-games. So in the lectures that he gave in Cambridge in 1930–2 his objection to Platonic answers to it is a very general one: they offer us a picture completely cut off from any application. Now there are various ways in which this kind of theory might be applied and one of them is to use it to explain what we actually do when we follow linguistic rules. It is from this point of view that Platonism is criticized in *Philosophical Investigations*: 'Even if something of this sort were the case, how would it help?'[79]

In the *Tractatus* almost nothing had been said about the identification of the things that we name.[80] Evidently, the assessment of a theory of language from this point of view would be made only when specific linguistic practices were under examination. Even in the lectures given in Cambridge in 1930–2 this condition is not really met. It is met in *The Blue Book* where the practices examined are making a wish and having a thought. Those are specific achievements where the need for guidance can be illustrated, and so the dilemma criticized in *Philosophical Investigations* begins to emerge: 'Either super-idealization or infinite latitude'. But the best opening for this critique of realism is provided by linguistic practices that patently involve repetition, like applying and reapplying the rule for the development of a mathematical series or naming a recurrent property. So it was only when these practices were investigated in depth that the two developments of the

---

[79] *PI* I § 218, quoted above, pp. 441 and 489–90.
[80] See above, p. 208, and Vol. I pp. 10–11.

doctrine of showing were brought together, and the critique of the
instant mental talisman was used against Platonic realism.

Here a point that was made in Chapter 9 is worth repeating.
Wittgenstein argues not only that realism is useless because it has no
application, but also that it is internally incoherent. That is characteristic
of the strategy that he adopts against his adversaries' theories. They
cannot be tested like scientific theories because they do not make that
kind of contact with the phenomena, but they can be tested for internal
coherence and the result is often negative.[81] The reductive argument
against Platonism can be seen from this point of view to be a special
case. The absurdity of the theory emerges only when it is offered as an
explanation of the way in which our application of words is guided by
linguistic rules, because when it is forced into contact with the
phenomena at this point, it abolishes the very distinction that it was
supposed to preserve.[82]

Finally, there is the question whether there is any evidence that
might support Kripke's alternative interpretation of this part of
Philosophical Investigations. There is, and if it is not going to be taken in
the way that he takes it, it must be explained in some other way.

The argument of § 201 of the book[83] has been interpreted here as a
reductio of Platonic realism: if the application of a word did have to be
completely determined by something wholly outside us, the distinction
between obeying and disobeying the rule for its use would be abolished.
Kripke takes this unacceptable outcome to be the consequence not of a
mistaken theory of language, but of an inherent weakness in language
itself: the uses of words are not stabilized by anything available to any
single speaker and so they can only be stabilized by agreement in
judgements between all the speakers of a language.[84] The question,
which of these two interpretations fits § 201 was dicussed above[85] and
it was argued that Kripke's interpretation does not fit this text. But
§ 201 is followed by this:

And hence also 'obeying a rule' is a practice. And to *think* one is obeying a
rule is not to obey a rule. Hence it is not possible to obey a rule 'privately':
otherwise thinking one was obeying a rule would be the same thing as obeying
it.

[81] See above, pp. 206–7.   [82] See above, pp. 462–3 and 466–7.
[83] Quoted above, pp. 466–7.
[84] See Kripke: *Wittgenstein on Rules and Private Language*, pp. 88–9. This part of
Kripke's interpretation was criticized above, in Ch. 14.
[85] See above, pp. 442–3, 463–4, and 489.

Language is a labyrinth of paths. You approach from *one* side and know your way about; you approach the same place from another side and no longer know your way about.[86]

Kripke takes the first of these two paragraphs, § 202, to contain the conclusion of the private language argument, which is, therefore, on his view, completed long before § 243, where, according to the prevalent interpretation, which was followed in Chapter 12, it is supposed to begin. [87] Does his view fit this text?

The investigation of rule-following which, according to Kripke, is, or at least contains, the private language argument, develops at § 138 out of the critique of the *Tractatus*. One of the main points is that following a rule is a practice. However, a practice is not necessarily communal[88] and in § 198 Wittgenstein avoids answering the question whether it would be possible for only one man to obey a rule.[89] So it would be surprising if he intended the chief conclusion of the argumentation running through these sections to be 'that it is not possible to obey a rule "privately" '. If that had been where he was heading, he would have had to say much more about privacy in these sections, and he would surely have given a direct negative answer to his question, whether it would be possible for only one man to obey a rule.

But what is the alternative to Kripke's interpretation of § 202? There is only one other possibility: if the preceding argument is a *reductio*, reaching its conclusion in § 201, the inferences added by Wittgenstein in § 202 can only be further consequences. If we look back at the last paragraph of § 201, we find the first of these further consequences, and like the two in § 202, it is introduced with the word 'Hence'. It is that, when people find that 'there is a way of grasping a rule . . . which is exhibited in what we call "obeying a rule" and "going against it" in actual cases', they feel inclined to extend the word 'interpretation' to these acts, but the inclination must be resisted.[90] The second further consequence ('Hence also . . .') is that ' "obeying a rule" is a practice'. This is not a big step, because it has already been called 'a custom', 'a use', and 'an institution'. The third further consequence, 'Hence it is not possible to obey a rule "privately" ', does not contain the word 'also', because it is deduced from the lemma 'And

---

[86] *PI* I §§ 202–3.   [87] S. A. Kripke: op. cit., p. 3.
[88] A point well made by G. P. Baker and P. M. S. Hacker, *Scepticism, Rules and Language*, pp. 20–1.
[89] See above, pp. 377–83.
[90] The inclination was indulged in *CLI* p. 24. See above, p. 467 n. 18.

to *think* one is obeying a rule is not to obey a rule.' These two lines of the argument, on the interpretation that is being defended here, take a big step forward. For though it follows from the fact that ' "obeying" a rule is a practice', it takes the whole of the private language argument, beginning at § 243, to show that it does follow. So how can Wittgenstein's claim, that it does follow, be made so prematurely?

The answer must be that he is inserting a signpost which points forward to the private language argument beginning at § 243. And why not? The interconnections between the problems discussed in the book are often too criss-cross to be indicated by the linear order of the remarks,[91] and the links between his two central arguments are certainly complex enough to make a forward reference necessary.[92] In fact, in two of the earlier drafts of this part of *Philosophical Investigations* the three sections, 201–3, were placed much later, after the private language argument, which starts at § 243, and in that position the statement that 'it is not possible to obey a rule "privately" ' really did make a backward reference.[93] If the forward reference in the text as we now have it strikes us as awkward, some excuse for its awkwardness is given in § 203.

---

[91] Cf. *PI*, Preface, p. ix, quoted above, p. 212 n. 21.

[92] See below, p. 518 for an example of the intersection of two different investigations.

[93] The history of these drafts and the vicissitudes of §§ 201–3 are explained very clearly by G. P. Baker and P. M. S. Hacker, *Scepticism, Rules and Meaning*, pp. 10–21.

18

The Next Problem

IT would be too much to expect that even the lines of Wittgenstein's thought that have been selected and traced in this book could all be pulled together now and presented as a single pattern. Excessive systematization is a common fault among philosophers, reducing their options by lumping them together in large packages tied up by theories instead of allowing each investigation to follow its natural course, and it can have the same effect on the interpretation of another philosopher's *œuvre*. It is a habit of thought that comes from science, because it is science that encourages the 'craving for generality' and 'the contemptuous attitude to the particular case'.[1]

However, anyone who begins to read Wittgenstein's philosophy, especially his later writings, will soon become aware of an underlying structure.[2] The solipsist ties the world as he finds it to his ego and then, instead of offering an independent identification of his ego, he tells us that it is the point of view from which the world as he finds it is seen. There is a circularity in this manœuvre which makes it indistinguishable from immobility. A person is, in fact, independent of the world at least to this extent: he is placed in it, moves around in it, explores it, and construes it as extending beyond the limits of his exploration at any given moment. Solipsism freezes this mobility by suppressing the very idea of anything below his horizon and offers, instead, a low-risk option: tie the world to your self and your self to nothing, and you will be safe within a limited system protected from all the hazards of ordinary interaction between subject and object. Wittgenstein severs the definitional connection which holds this system together and looks for more flexible links between the subject and the objective world which will preserve the limited independence of both partners.

The same logical structure reappears in his argument against the possibility of a private language. This is hardly surprising, because the

[1] *BLBK* p. 18, discussed above, pp. 202–3.
[2] See above, pp. 222 and 422.

argument is directed against another part of the same philosophical theory. His critique of solipsism dealt with the privatization of the subject, and this argument deals with the privatisation of objects presented to the subject. If they were sense-data introduced in complete detachment from the physical world, no language could record them. For in the detached world the would-be speaker of a language would have no criterion of truth independent of his impression that what he said was true, and that would not be enough, because speaking a language is an acquired skill, and before anyone can set out to acquire a skill, he must know how to tell when success crowns his efforts. This is a reductive argument, designed to show up the absurdity of another safe system. Language has to run the risk of discoverable falsehood and a theory which eliminates the risk by tying truth to the speaker's impression of truth, when that impression has never had any independent confirmation, simply makes language impossible. So here is another definitional connection which must be severed and replaced with something more flexible.

Wittgenstein's investigation of rule-following exhibits the same structure, but this time there is no special concern with reporting sensations. The problem is a general one about all uses of language: 'How can our words measure the world?' However, the answer to this question that he considers and rejects is an answer which misconstrues our relations with our environment in something like the way in which solipsism misconstrued them. The idea, that we measure the world by imposing regularities on ourselves, seems to leave too much to our independent judgements, and the Platonist's reaction to this apparently excessive liberalism is to offer another risk-minimizing theory: the regularities essential to language are automatically imposed on us by reality.

Wittgenstein objects that this too would make language impossible. For even if the correct uses of our words were already laid down ahead of us in reality, we would still need to pick them up, and nothing in our minds that helped us do that could possibly function automatically. An image, or a formula, would still have to be connected with the actual things to which the words were to be applied, and any theory which eliminated the contribution made by us at those points to what counted as correct application would abolish the distinction between truth and falsehood. It was argued in the previous chapter that here too Wittgenstein is severing a definitional connection and substituting something more flexible which will allow the familiar give and take between language and the world. But in this case it is much less easy to see that this is what is going on.

It is worth inquiring what makes it more difficult to see that this really is a case of a definitional connection set up in the wrong place by a philosophical theory. We need to go back to the earlier description of the flexible relations with the world on which language, as we speak it, depends.[3] On the one hand, we use factual language to make claims about the world, but, on the other hand, the meanings of those claims themselves result from the ways in which the two surfaces have previously been brought into relationship with one another. Now it is easy enough to appreciate, if not to agree with, the point made by Wittgenstein in the private language argument: the two surfaces would cease to be related to one another, if every factual claim were assessed for truth or falsity without any constraint being imposed from outside the speaker's mind. It is also fairly easy to understand why he treats the introduction of the instant mental talisman as a necessarily unsuccessful attempt to internalize the external conditions of meaning. But it is much harder to understand his treatment of the super-idealization of the speaker's mental state and equipment which he attributes to the Platonist. This is surprising, because it is closely connected with his criticism of the instant mental talisman—almost two sides of the same coin—and one would expect each to be as readily intelligible as the other. Why is this not the case?

Let us start at the point that is most easily grasped. The general effect of all these mistaken ways of thinking about meaning, which is to eliminate everything that happens at the interface between language and the world, is especially clear in the case of the instant mental talisman. The idea is that there must be a self-interpreting interpretation, which would allow us to fix the meanings of words from inside language without ever crossing the line that divides it from the world.[4] A related idea was brilliantly analysed in the passage quoted from *The Blue Book* in the previous chapter:[5] we feel that a wish should have all the advantages of internalizing its object without the final absurdity of actually doing so.

But how can the same elimination of movement at the interface between language and the world be effected by a theory like Platonism,

³ See above, pp. 461–2, and Vol. I pp. 58–60.

⁴ The necessary friction between the two surfaces is then lost. See *RPPI* § 397, quoted and discussed above, pp. 421–2.

⁵ *BLBK* pp. 34–8, discussed above, pp. 495–8.

which operates on the far side of the dividing line? That kind of realism starts by postulating that all the correct applications of a word are already laid out paradigmatically in reality. It then ties the mental state and equipment of a speaker by definition to this paradigm, because it assumes that he has already grasped it in its entirety. These are the two moves that produce the super-idealization described in the previous chapter.[6] Now if the arrangement of the working parts of a machine really were taken to symbolize its own correct performance, then, considered as a symbol, it would be defined in terms of its own future successes. It is in just this way that the Platonist defines the mental state and equipment of the speaker in terms of his hypothesized correct uses of the word in the future. The effect is the substitution of a super-idealized mental state for the ordinary one, and so the movement at the interface between language and the world is lost.

But why does Wittgenstein need to say anything about Platonism at this point? Would it not have been enough for him to stay on our side of the line dividing language from the world and to demonstrate that the theory of the instant mental talisman cannot possibly succeed in internalizing the conditions of meaning? But if he had drawn in his horns in this way, he would have left out something essential. Kripke emphasizes, surely rightly, that he was concerned with meaning as a normative concept and that he was investigating the correct use of a word rather than my use of it, whether it was correct or not.[7] It is this concern that brings Platonism into his discussion, because the ontology of Platonism promises us an external standard of correct use. But, Wittgenstein argues, even if the ontology were accepted, it would be no help to us without the impossible instant mental talisman.

Why, then, was anyone ever led into this mistaken way of thinking about meaning? The search for the better scheme of things, which, if Wittgenstein is right, is unattainable, starts when the relation between language and the world, as we actually experience it, is found wanting. This dissatisfaction with what appears to be the way in which the two

---

[6] See above, pp. 474–84.
[7] See S. A. Kripke: *Wittgenstein on Rules and Private Language*, p. 37. The 'machine-as-symbol' takes account of this important point. A machine is designed to function in a certain way and it is this function—its correct function—that would be symbolized by the arrangement of its working parts. See above, pp. 478–9. Naturally, behind the points of analogy exploited by Wittgenstein there are big differences between people and machines. People are not designed to use words in certain ways, their performances actually contribute to what counts as success, and a linguistic community enjoys a certain Rousseauesque autonomy. See above, p. 471.

surfaces are brought into contact with one another is not an ordinary case of scepticism. The complaint is not that, for all we know, particular claims to truth may fail, but, rather, that language may not be capable of measuring the world at all.[8] Does it set a real standard, and, if so, what makes the standard an appropriate one for the world?

What Platonism insinuates is that the standard would be a real one only if it were imposed on us by the world, which, of course, would automatically make it an appropriate one too. This theory takes science as its model, because its leading idea is that meaningful sentences are related to possibilities in something like the way in which true sentences are related to facts. But the trouble is that we have no way of identifying particular candidates for possibility, parallel to the way in which we identify particular candidates for actuality.[9] To put the criticism in less metaphysical terms, it is only against the background of a system of rules that the world can impose anything on us. So given our rules for the meanings of our words, the world forces us to hold certain sentences true. But what could possibly be the background against which it might force us to adopt one set of rules for the meanings of our words rather than another set? Nothing can be imposed on us until we ourselves have built the first bridge between language and the world, and then what is imposed on us will not be the adoption of a rule but the consequence of having adopted it, a truth.[10]

This puts the Platonist in a quandary. He wants to give us a theory about the deeper appropriateness to the world which confers meaning on our language. However, there is no extra material available for the construction of such a theory. So he is reduced to using the ordinary material in a new way. Everyone would agree that to understand a word is to be able to use it correctly. So the Platonist imagines all its correct applications laid out in advance paradigmatically. Now we who understand the word need to be related in some way to this extended paradigm. But out of what material is this special relationship to be constructed? All that we have in real life is knowledge of various

---

[8] 'Scepticism' can, of course, be extended, as Kripke extends it, to include these radical doubts about meaning. But it must be made clear that Wittgenstein does not share them, and that his 'paradox' is not intended to show up a weakness inherent in language, but, rather, something which would be a weakness only if Platonism were true.

[9] We have facts and possibilities surrounding them, but no outer circle of candidates for possibility. See above, p. 215–16 and Vol. I pp. 142–52.

[10] See *PR* § 47: 'Time and again the attempt is made to use language to limit the world and set it in relief—but it can't be done. . . .' The passage is quoted in full in Vol. I p. 95, and discussed above, pp. 276–8. Cf. *PG* § 68, quoted above, p. 449 n. 48.

ordinary kinds, and so the theorist's next step is to invent a superior kind of knowledge attached by definition to the paradigm. The poverty of the ideas that produce this super-idealization is shown up the moment that we ask 'How does this superior state of mind manifest itself?' For the only possible answer is 'By absenting itself if the speaker ever applies the word incorrectly'. But, quite apart from the emptiness of this answer—it is like saying 'If this machine breaks down, the guarantee is void'—it presupposes a fixed standard of correctness, which we have not yet been given.

The theory of the instant mental talisman comes in at this point and tries to give us the impression of having fixed the standard of correctness without crossing the line between language and the world,[11] or, to put it in another way, without *our doing anying*. However, the actual practice of applying the word is a necessary part of fixing the standard and the pretence of fixing it entirely from within language is easily unmasked. The best that we could ever achieve if we gave 'one interpretation after another, as if each one contented us at least for a moment, until we thought of yet another standing behind it',[12] would be an asymptotic approach to a standard, like Achilles' shortening of the tortoise's lead.

Platonism and the theory of the instant mental talisman play into each other's hands. Their aim is to allay the doubt that language might not set a real, or an appropriate, standard for measuring the world. Wittgenstein reacts to them in three complementary ways. He tries to reduce the theories themselves to absurdity, but he also offers a sympathetic treatment of the deflection into absurdity of the original attempt to understand the relation between language and the world,[13] and, finally, he tries to convince us that this understanding cannot be achieved by any theory, but only by a careful description of the interplay between language and the world without any attempt to get outside it all.[14]

This naturalism is not a new phenomenon in the history of ideas. True, Wittgenstein's development of it was original and until the last moment unpredictable, but it had a long ancestry. Several commentators have noted affinities between his appeal to the plain facts, which are all that nature seems to offer us, and Hume's appeal to them. There is, for example, a striking similarity between Hume's account of causal

---

[11] Cf. *CLI* p. 67 and p. 24, quoted above, p. 494 and p. 495.
[12] *PI* § 201, quoted in full above, p. 466–7.
[13] See above, pp. 219–22.   [14] Cf. *PI* I § 109, quoted above, p. 200.

inference and Wittgenstein's account of the moves that we make in logic. Now in *Philosophical Investigations* and *Remarks on the Foundations of Mathematics* logic is not set apart as a discipline concerned with an altogether different and much stronger form of necessity,[15] nor is it even restricted to the study of logical inference. The range of human activities covered by it includes developing a mathematical series and applying a descriptive word to things. The concept underpinning all these activities is the concept of 'doing the same again', and, according to Wittgenstein, if we 'do the same again' with a word like 'scarlet', we are merely doing what we find it natural to do when we impose regularity on ourselves at this point in our experience. According to Hume,

'To consider the matter aright, reason[16] is nothing but a wonderful and unintelligible instinct in our souls, which carries us along a certain train of ideas, and endows them with particular qualities, according to their particular situations and relations. This instinct, 'tis true, arises from past observation and experience; but can anyone give the ultimate reason why past experience and observation produces such an effect, any more than why nature alone should produce it? Nature may certainly produce whatever can arise from habit; nay, habit is nothing but one of the principles of nature, and it derives all its force from that origin.[17]

Although the field in which Hume draws attention to the working of nature is causal inference rather than logic, what he says about this kind of reasoning is very like what Wittgenstein says about following a linguistic rule.[18] There is, as will soon appear, a certain difference in emphasis between Hume's treatment and Wittgenstein's—the latter is more concerned with the speaker's identification of the next move to be made, while the former is more concerned with the thinker's impression of its inevitability—but the underlying naturalism is the same.

Kripke's interpretation of Wittgenstein's treatment of rule-following starts from the evidently Humean naturalism of *Philosophical Investigations* and *Remarks on the Foundations of Mathematics*. But he goes too far, if the criticisms developed above are correct. For he argues that Wittgenstein, like Hume, poses a sceptical problem and offers a

---

[15] See *PI* I § 140, quoted and discussed above, pp. 472–3.

[16] i.e. the 'reason' that manifests itself in inductive inference.

[17] Hume: *Treatise of Human Nature*, I. iii. 16.

[18] See my 'Hume's Empiricism and Modern Empiricism', in *David Hume: A Symposium*, ed. D. F. Pears, Macmillan, 1963, pp. 27–30.

sceptical solution to it.[19] He means that Hume started from doubts about the validity of causal inference and ended with a theory which did not give the sceptics all that they wanted to rid them of their doubts, and that Wittgenstein's investigation of the validity of our linguistic practices ran a parallel course. Against this it has been argued here that Wittgenstein was not drawing attention to something which he regarded as an inherent weakness of language, but, rather, showing up the absurdity of Platonic realism.

There are various ways in which this very different interpretation could now be reinforced. For example, Wittgenstein argues that the solution proposed by Platonism involves something inconceivable— an instant mental talisman—and he can hardly have regarded the unavailability of something inconceivable as a reasonable ground for scepticism.[20] In any case, it is, at least, confusing to speak of 'a sceptical solution to a sceptical problem'. For what is the base-line from which we are supposed to calculate that a certain way of thinking about our linguistic practices is sceptical? If it is the relation between language and the world, naturalistically described, Platonism would be judged hyper-credulous (if it were not, as Wittgenstein argues, incoherent). If, on the other hand, Platonism is chosen as the base-line, the naturalistic account would appear to be sceptical. It may not be easy to decide where the base-line for the use of the word 'sceptical' should run. For how could anyone claim to know in advance whether Wittgenstein's naturalism would succeed in making sense of our practices? But it is surely confusing to draw the line in two different places in the course of a single piece of exposition.

When this difference between Kripke's interpretation and the one proposed here has been put aside, the underlying point is much the same:[21] Wittgenstein's investigation of rule-following, like Hume's investigation of causal inference, reaches a naturalistic conclusion. There are, as already observed, differences of emphasis between the two investigations, but the fundamental idea is the same in both cases: the correctness of a practice can be judged only by its own internal standards. So Hume's response to the request for a justification of

[19] See Kripke: *Wittgenstein on Rules and Private Language*, pp. 60–70.

[20] Kripke draws attention to its inconceivability (ibid., p. 51) but appears not to see it as an obstacle to his interpretation.

[21] But not exactly the same, because Kripke thinks that when Wittgenstein was investigating the criteria of correctness used by us in real life, he found only one resource, agreement in judgement with others, but it has been argued here that he also appealed to a second resource, calibration on standard objects. See Ch. 14.

causal inference was to search the mind for the resources used in the original setting up of the practice, and Wittgenstein's response to the request for an explanation of linguistic rule-following which would show that we really were measuring the world was to draw attention to the resources available in everyday life for the establishment and maintenance of language. Where else could we go for answers?

It would hardly be an exaggeration to call this 'the central question of philosophy'. It is, of course, a methodological question, but that does not mean that the answer to it will be devoid of substantial implications. Philosophers who are dissatisfied with internal criteria of correctness usually run up a metaphysical scaffold to support the external criteria that seem to them to be necessary. Even those who are satisfied with internal criteria still feel the need to ask external questions, like 'What advantages do we get from our practices?' This pragmatic question is there to be asked, whether it belongs to philosophy or not. It is, of course, the kind of question that is excluded from philosophy by the line of demarcation that Wittgenstein drew around the subject. However, it may be that the exact scope of the discipline is not so important, provided that we realize that pragmatic questions about our internal criteria of correctness are quite different from the question what these criteria are. It is even arguable that the pure philosophy of Wittgenstein needs anthropology at least as an appendix. Certainly, it is not surprising that he found it hard to maintain the line between the two disciplines.[22]

There is also another discipline which Wittgenstein was especially concerned to exclude from philosophy, the physiology of the nervous system. He believed that it was for scientists to put forward and test hypotheses about the relation between mind and brain, and that there was no reason to favour any particular hypothesis a priori. That was, of course, part of his general view of the separateness of science and philosophy. If he held it with special fervour at this point,[23] the reason was not that he maintained that materialism is *false*. What he championed was the independence of the philosophical investigation of mind rather than the independence of mind that might be claimed by a believer in our ancestors' disembodied existence.[24]

Hume's line was similar. True, he did not have the post-Kantian idea that philosophy and science are separate disciplines. So from that later point of view his *Treatise* appears to mix philosophy with psychology.

---

[22] See above, pp. 455–7.
[23] See *Zettel*, §§ 608–13.   [24] See above, pp. 251–5.

However, he did steer his psychologico-philosophical investigation clear of neurology, except for one small excursion which he immediately cut short.[25] He wanted his study of mental phenomena to run parallel to the study of physical phenomena, but not to cross the line dividing the two. So he offered his discovery of the laws of the association of ideas as the counterpart of Newton's discovery of the laws governing the movements of stars,[26] but he made no attempt to gear psychological laws to physiological laws.

Wittgenstein had different reasons for defending the independence of the philosophical investigation of mind from neuro-physiology. He was acutely aware how easy it is to fail to see that the two disciplines ask, and try to answer, completely different questions. The philosopher of mind studies the moves that we make inside such language-games as ascribing sensations to people and explaining their behaviour. When he examines the justifications that we offer for things that we say as part of these practices, he realizes that they soon run out, because on the edge of language the speaker can only report his acquired tendency to apply his words to the world in one way rather than another. At this point the neurologist may be able to offer an explanation of this tendency, but, though he will use the same terminology as the speaker and the philosophical observer—'I do it because . . .', 'He does it because . . .'—he will be using it to make an entirely different point, and this crucial difference is easily overlooked.

It may be objected that it does not really matter if we change the subject without realizing that that is what we are doing. For if we take a broader view than Wittgenstein's of what philosophy includes, we shall still be operating inside philosophy. But that would miss his main point, which was that we may fail to realize that if we say, 'He did it because he lost his temper', we will be saying something of a completely different kind from 'He did it because such and such neurons fired.'

But who could fail to realize anything so obvious? This is the question that is always asked when a distinction has been drawn in a philosophical investigation of this kind. What Wittgenstein says is

[25] Cf. Hume: *Treatise of Human Nature*, I. ii. 5: ' 'Twou'd have been easy to make an imaginary dissection of the brain, and have shewn, why upon our conception of any idea, the animal spirits run into all the contiguous traces and rouze up the other ideas that are related to it.'

[26] Ibid., I. i. 5: 'Here is a kind of ATTRACTION, which in the mental world will be found to have as extraordinary effects as in the natural, and to shew itself in as many and as various forms.'

something that nobody would deny, a platitude.[27] But his point is not that people will openly reject the distinction that he is drawing and say, 'But I think these two uses of the word "because" really are the same.' What concerns him is their tendency to treat them as the same without realizing that they are doing so.

There are several ways of falling into this trap and the most insidious way, often described by him, is to let the possibility of a neural explanation of a move made in a language-game persuade us that there must also be a psychological explanation with the same kind of structure. That is to say, first, we see the possibility of an explanation that goes like this: 'We think in this way because our neurons fire in that way, and our neurons fire in that way because they have such and such properties', and there we have to stop; then, realizing that we also have to stop when we search a speaker's mind for his reasons for applying a word in this way rather than that, we imagine that there must be a similar terminus within his mind—something psychological with the same kind of structure and function as the neurons in his brain:

How does the philosophical problem about mental processes and states and about behaviourism arise?—The first step is the one that altogether escapes notice. We talk of processes and states and leave their nature undecided. Sometime perhaps we shall know more about them—we think. But that is just what commits us to a particular way of looking at the matter. For we have a definite concept of what it means to learn to know a process better. (The decisive movement in the conjuring trick has been made, and it was the very one that we thought quite innocent.)—And now the analogy which was to make us understand our thoughts falls to pieces. So we have to deny the yet uncomprehended process in the yet unexplored medium. And now it looks as if we had denied mental processes. And naturally we don't want to deny them.[28]

This adds yet another dimension to the 'machine-as-symbol'. So far, Wittgenstein's treatment of that complex topic has been interpreted as a step-wise development of an analogy between people and machines: first, the illusion that there is an instant talisman in the mind of a person using a descriptive word, a 'self-interpreting interpretation', was shown to be like the illusion that we can literally see the future correct performance of a machine in the present arrangement of its working parts; then this analogy was elaborated to cover the bizarre

---

[27] See above, pp. 219–24, and Vol. I pp. 17–18.
[28] *PI* I § 308, quoted above, pp. 212–13.

fantasy that the present mental state of the speaker might actually be defined in terms of his correct applications of the word in the future. We can now add a further point to the analogy. It is an evident fact that neural explanations terminate with descriptions of brain-states, and that is why we imagine that explanations of a speaker's practices must terminate with parallel descriptions of his mental states. Consequently, instead of resting content with his tendency to find it natural to go on in this way rather than that, we look for something in his mind that will make it inevitable. That is one way in which the fantasy of the instant mental talisman originates. It is a picture without any application, but it has a strong grip on our imaginations and so it diverts us from our mental lives as we actually live them and sends us off in pursuit of a will-o-the-wisp.

Wittgenstein turns his face against neurology not because speakers of a language might have sawdust in their heads, but because, from the point of view of a philosopher with his restricted conception of the subject, it would not matter what they had in their heads. Of course, we not only know that they do not have sawdust there, but also know something about the kind of explanation that would satisfy us in neurology. So quite disastrously, we transfer the ghost of that kind of explanation from brain to mind.

Wittgenstein's naturalism leaves many people dissatisfied. This may merely be because the habit of theorizing is so deeply rooted in their minds that they are more inclined to question the premisses of his critique of that kind of philosophy than to give it up. Or they may not see the point of his platitudes, because they fail to identify the targets at which they are aimed. Or perhaps they simply fail to respond to the way in which his imagination illuminates the drama of philosophy as he sees it—'He is just another positivist' etc.[29] But there is also a deeper reason for dissatisfaction. We may doubt whether he can really succeed in maintaining the purity of the subject as he conceives it.

The same doubt may be felt about Hume, who set himself a similar task when he undertook to discover from the inside how the mind works. He too was opposed to theorizing and believed that solutions to philosophical problems could be found only through an accurate description of what actually happens in our minds. True, he allowed a place for laws, unlike Wittgenstein, who excluded all explanation from philosophy,[30] but Hume's laws had to be laws that fitted the

[29] See Vol. I p. 18.
[30] See *PI* I § 109, quoted above, p. 200.

phenomena like gloves without the adjustments provided by speculative hypotheses.[31] That was why he avoided excursions into neurology. However, the pressure on him to deviate from his chosen psychological line was much less strong than the pressure on Wittgenstein to deviate from his purely linguistic line. For Hume was more concerned with facts than with standards and he says less about 'rules by which to judge of causes and effects'[32] than about the psychological mechanism that makes us judge them in the way that we do. His *Treatise* is a selection from the natural history of the human species and he had no strong inducement to enlarge its scope. In fact, he had a good reason for drawing the line where he did: the natural extension of the philosophy of the mind, conceived in his way, would have been into the physiology of the brain, a subject even more speculative in his day than in ours.

Wittgenstein's investigation is more subtle than Hume's but arguably more difficult to restrict in the way that he tried to restrict it. Superficially, of course, they are similar. They both maintain that our patterns of thought have no independent basis in reality but merely develop along the lines that we find natural to follow. In both cases there is no suggestion that the force exerted by our nature is weak. Hume did not think it really possible consciously to draw a conclusion that ran counter to an average collection of what we accept as strong evidence, but only logically possible; and Wittgenstein took the same line about the possibility that a competent user of a colour-word might apply it in good faith to something which, the rest of us would agree, had a different colour. The point of dramatizing bizarre deviations was the same in both cases—to show that there is no *intellectual* obstacle standing in their way. But beneath this similarity there is a big difference: Hume merely records what happens in people's minds, but Wittgenstein extracts an internal standard of correctness from their practices.

That is why neither Wittgenstein's presentation of the problem of

---

[31] Cf. *Treatise of Human Nature*, 'Introduction': 'And tho' we must endeavour to render all our principles as universal as possible, by tracing up our experiments to the outmost, and explaining all effects from the simplest and fewest causes, 'tis still certain we cannot go beyond experience; and any hypothesis, that pretends to discover the ultimate original qualities of human nature, ought at first to be rejected as presumptuous and chimerical.' Cf. Newton: *Principia*, General Scholium, 'Hitherto I have not been able to discover the cause of those properties of gravity from phenomena, and I frame no hypothesis, *hypotheses non fingo* . . .'

[32] The chapter heading of *Treatise of Human Nature*, I. iii. 15.

rule-following nor his treatment of it is sceptical. His point is that the standard of correctness for what we do can be discerned *in* what we do, and that it is the demand for a superior standard which produces scepticism when it is found that there is no way of meeting it. This is a more subtle form of naturalism. True, the philosopher is still confined to recording facts about human beings, but he records them with a view to eliciting what lies behind them, the actual standards of correctness implicit in our practices and the dreams of superior standards that march in the shadows and are always ready to delude us.[33]

However, the spirit in which Wittgenstein records the facts does make it difficult for him to maintain the purity of philosophy as he conceives it. His method is to describe our linguistic practices and their place in our lives, but without the pessimistic implication which is sometimes to be found in Hume's writings, that this is not a way of defeating scepticism, but only a second-best alternative to opposing it. On the contrary, the point of Wittgenstein's description of our linguistic practices is to demonstrate that their criteria of correctness are implicit in them and necessarily satisfiable because the practices could never have been set up without the successful use of them. The point at which there is pressure on him to expand the scope of his philosophy and include facts of a different kind has already been located.[34] It is the point at which the speaker's reasons for saying what he does say run out, and he can only tell us that this is the way in which he finds it natural to go on. Why not try to explain its naturalness instead of leaving it to the speaker to do the only thing that he can do, namely report it as a plain phenomenological fact?

No doubt, there are cases, in which the transition from things available to the speaker to some underlying structure that is not accessible to him can be misleading. Certainly, a version, usually speculative, of the underlying neural structure, is one of the sources of the illusion of the instant mental talisman. But there are other cases where there is no such risk of confusion. The evident fact, in no way speculative, that our nervous systems are independent of one another, explains several features of our concept of the ownership of sensations.

---

[33] See above, p. 222. Incidentally, the idea that scepticism is generated by pictures without any application can also be found in Hume's *Treatise*, but he lacked the confidence that allowed Wittgenstein to restructure the treatment of criteria in a way that would eliminate scepticism.

[34] See above, pp. 451–7.

Wittgenstein himself emphasizes the logical possibility that one person might feel a pain in another person's tooth. What risks of confusion are avoided by not mentioning the nervous system in this context?[35] He himself insists on the importance of the fact that the word 'pain' is inserted in a pre-linguistic structure of some complexity.[36]—indeed, the existence of that structure may well be essential to his private language argument.[37] In other cases, such as the ascription of spatial properties to things in the visual field, it is almost impossible to understand what is going on without transcending the resources available to someone engaged in the language-game,[38] so there is a strong case for extending the scope of his naturalism and including any facts about our lives that help us to understand our own systems of thought.

There is another point at which it is worth comparing Wittgenstein's naturalism with Hume's. Both philosophers write about the experience of following a rule. In Hume's case the rule governs a causal inference, while in Wittgenstein's case it is a logical rule governing the application of a descriptive word or the continuation of a mathematical series. But both are concerned with the phenomenology of rule-following, which raises several difficult questions. When a rule-follower makes a move, does it strike him as inevitable? Is it really inevitable, or were there alternatives? And what is it like for him at the time? Does the move simply force itself on him or is there something in his mind from which he reads it off as the right move? Or perhaps the inner prompting is more immediate, like a voice within, telling him what to do.

Hume claims that, when someone makes a causal inference, he gets an impression of necessitated transition from the sensory impression of the cause to the idea of the usual effect.[39] His inference and the feeling of its inevitability are the result of past experience which has conditioned him to think in that way. The feeling of inevitability, is, of course, an internal impression, unlike the sensory impression of the observed cause which starts the inference. The best analogy is the feeling of being physically pushed, but, of course, the thinker is supposed to be pushed psychologically along a track formed by the association of the idea of the cause with the idea of the effect.

---

[35] See above, p. 254 n. 51.   [36] Cf. *PI* I §§ 244–5 quoted above, pp. 261 and 331.
[37] See above, Ch. 15.   [38] See above, pp. 401–6.
[39] Hume: *Treatise*, I. iii. 14: 'For after a frequent repetition, I find that upon the appearance of one of the objects, the mind is determin'd by custom to consider its usual attendant, and to consider it in a stronger light upon account of its relation to the first object. 'Tis this impression, then, of *determination*, which affords me the idea of necessity.'

If Hume is asked why this thinker, like everyone else, finds it natural to make an inference in line with past observations, he has no answer except that it is human nature to go on in this way. He could, of course, seek an explanation in the physiology of the brain,[40] but, if he stays within his preferred mental system, there is nothing more for him to say and, as Wittgenstein would put it, he has reached bedrock.[41] Given that the subject has the general habit of forming associations of ideas that reflect the way things go in the world, the particular association that produces his inference is, of course, imposed on him by past evidence. What Hume denies is that the general habit of forming associations in this way is imposed on him by the world. It is just his own inner nature. Like Wittgenstein, he is making the point that, though we cannot deviate from the tracks laid down by normal thinking, what prevents us from deviating is nothing intellectual, or, at least, nothing ratiocinative.

So, though Hume concedes that the subject gets an impression of necessitated transition when he makes the inference, he never says that it makes the transition genuinely necessary. He does not even say that he is guided by this internal impression or reads off what he is to infer. The impression makes no substantial contribution to the actual mental process and it is emphasized by Hume only because it explains the subject's view of what is going on consistently with radical empiricism. In fact, nothing makes the transition genuinely necessary in Hume's system, because it is no more necessary than the transition from cause to effect in the physical world which it reflects in the observer's mind.[42] He is not worried by the objection that this is a circular account of causal necessity. For he has already given a non-circular account of everything that, according to him, really is involved in any causal sequence, physical or mental. If one of these sequences happens to be observed, that is something extra, because what occurs in the observer's mind contributes nothing to what happens, and would have happened without him, in his surroundings.[43]

[40] See *Treatise*, I. i. 5, quoted above, p. 511 n. 26.

[41] Cf. Wittgenstein: *PI* I § 217.

[42] If Hume had extended his treatment of causal necessity to logical necessity, he could have made his point in Wittgenstein's way: '. . . we might also be inclined to express ourselves like this: we are at most under a psychological, not a logical compulsion. . . .' (*PI* I § 140, quoted above, pp. 472–3).

[43] See *Treatise*, I. iii. 14: 'As to what may be said, that the operations of nature are independent of our thought and reasoning, I allow it; and accordingly have observ'd, that objects bear to each other the relations of contiguity and succession; that like objects may be observ'd in several instances to have like relations; and that all this is

Even such an innocent and ineffective impression of necessitated transition would be unacceptable to Wittgenstein. His objection to it would be that what we do in a case like this is bedrock. There is no need and no room for any further support or explanation of our practice. If anyone ever does have anything that would count as an impression of the inevitability of the conclusion of his causal inference, it is certainly not a feature of all such cases. Even if our general practice did stand in need of explanation, it could not get it from an impression with a description that is merely derived from the position in which it occurs, between the subject's observation of the cause and his inference of the effect. Anything invoked to explain a move ought to be describable in a way that leaves it a logically open question whether the move is ever actually made. The impression of being physically pushed may satisfy this condition, but it is certainly not met by the impression of being pushed psychologically. So from Wittgenstein's point of view, Hume's naturalistic treatment of causal inference spoils a good idea by adding a piece of mythology inspired by radical empricism.

At this point the investigation of what occurs in the mind of a person following a rule intersects with the investigation of the possibility of a private language. For an internal impression which did satisfy the requirement of independent describability would come under fire from the position examined in Chapter 14. However, there is no need to explore that avenue again and we may ask, instead, what, according to Wittgenstein, really would occur in the mind of a person applying the word 'scarlet' to a geranium or continuing a straightforward mathematical series.

It is interesting to observe how his answer to this question changed in the 1930s. In an early remark on the phenomenology of following a mathematical rule he says that each application requires a separate insight:

> . . . Supposing there to be a certain general rule (therefore one containing a variable), I must recognize each time afresh that this rule may be applied *here*. No act of *foresight* can absolve me from this act of *insight*. Since the form to which the rule is applied is in fact different at every step.[44]

> independent of, and antecedent to the operations of the understanding. But if we go any further, and ascribe a power or necessary connexion to those objects; this is what we can never observe in them, but must draw the idea of it from what we feel internally in contemplating them. And this I carry so far, that I am ready to convert my present reasoning into an instance of it by a subtility which it will not be difficult to comprehend.'

[44] *PR* § 149.

This is corrected in a later marginal note, 'Act of *decision*, not *insight*', and when the passage recurs in *Philosophical Grammar*, the correction is added at the end of it:

... But it is not a matter of an act of *insight*, but of an act of *decision*.[45]

However, both suggestions are rejected in *Lectures on the Foundations of Mathematics*:

Intuitionism comes to saying that you can make a new rule at each point. It requires that we have an intuition at each step in calculation, at each application of a rule; for how can we tell how a rule which has been used for fourteen steps applies at the fifteenth?—And they go on to say that the series of cardinal numbers is known to us by a ground-intuition—that is, we know at each step what the operation of adding 1 will give. We might as well say that we need, not an intuition at each step, but a *decision*.—Actually there is neither. You don't make a decision: you simply do a certain thing. It is a question of a certain practice.

Intuitionism is all bosh—entirely. Unless it means an inspiration.[46]

If 'you simply do a certain thing', there is no phenomenological accompaniment of your doing it, not even an unannounced decision or choice. You just do it. That is the implication of the passage quoted earlier from *Philosophical Investigations*:

'All the steps are really already taken' means: I no longer have any choice. The rule, once stamped with a particular meaning, traces the lines along which it is to be followed through the whole of space.—But if something of this sort really were the case, how would it help?

No; my description only made sense if it was to be understood symbolically.—I should have said: *This is how it strikes me.*

When I obey a rule, I do not choose.

I obey, the rule *blindly*.[47]

I do not make a choice because it is by now my second nature to obey the rule. However, my reaction is not like that of the soldiers who did not 'reason why' before they obeyed the order to charge. They could have questioned the order, but they had been trained not to do so and their implicit obedience was the effect of military discipline. But if I questioned the authority that makes me call this flower 'scarlet', there would be nowhere for me to go inside the language-game of describing

---

[45] *PG* p. 301. Cf. *CLII* pp. 133–4.
[46] *LFM* p. 237 (1939).
[47] *PI* I § 219. Quoted above, p. 465.

the colours of things.[48] I would have reached bedrock and there would be nothing more to be done with words, because I would have got down to the pre-linguistic structure which lies beneath the language-game:

> . . . For instance you say to someone 'This is red' (pointing); then you tell him 'Fetch me a red book'—and he will behave in a particular way. This is an immensely important fact about us human beings. . . . The point is that one only has to point to something and say, 'This is so-and-so', and everyone who has been through a certain preliminary training will react in the same way. . . .[49]

The pre-linguistic structure is already in place before language is learned, and that is why the lesson can be so impressively brief and so lastingly effective.[50]

So far, Wittgenstein's account of rule-following has been pitted against Platonism, because that is the centre of the dispute between naturalists and anti-naturalists. But when we are investigating the peripheral question, what, according to Wittgenstein, occurs in the mind of a rule-follower, we encounter another rival. The new rival is the theory of inspiration mentioned in the last paragraph of the passage quoted on page 519 from *Lectures on the Foundations of Mathematics*.[51] According to that theory, whenever I have to apply a rule, a voice within me tells me what to do. This is the linguistic counterpart of one of the theories avoided by Hume, the theory that someone who makes a causal inference reads off what he must do from his internal impression. Now one way of objecting to the theory of the ever-ready inner voice would be to argue that, though Socrates and Joan of Arc may have heard such voices occasionally, in a straightforward matter, like following a linguistic rule, we neither have this resource nor need it. But this is how Wittgenstein argues against it:

> Let us imagine a rule intimating to me which way I am to obey it; that is, as my eye travels along the line, a voice within me says: '*This* way!'—What is the difference between this process of obeying a kind of inspiration and that of

---

[48] So Hume might have said that we form particular associations of ideas in the light of what we observe happening in the world, but when we make causal inferences we follow these associational tracks blindly.

[49] *LFM* p. 182, quoted in full above, pp. 444–6. This is another example of the role played by the pre-linguistic structure. See above, Ch. 15, for a discussion of its contribution to the private language argument.

[50] It is only when we are able to find the obvious surprising that the importance of a simple but deep fact, like this one, becomes clear. See Vol. I pp. 17–18.

[51] *LFM* p. 237.

obeying a rule? For they are surely not the same. In the case of inspiration I *await* direction. I shall not be able to teach anyone else my 'technique' of following the line. Unless, indeed, I teach him some way of hearkening, some kind of receptivity. But then, of course, I cannot require him to follow the line in the same way as I do.

These are not my experiences of acting from inspiration and according to a rule; they are grammatical notes.

It would also be possible to imagine such a training in a sort of arithmetic. Children could calculate, each in his own way—as long as they listened to their inner voice and obeyed it. Calculating in this way would be like a sort of composing.

Would it not be possible for us, however, to calculate as we actually do (all agreeing, and so on), and still at every step to have a feeling of being guided by the rules as by a spell, feeling astonishment at the fact that we agreed? (We might give thanks to the Deity for our agreement.)

This merely shows what goes to make up what we call 'obeying a rule' in everyday life.

Calculating prodigies who get the right answer but cannot say how. Are we to say that they do not calculate? (A family of cases.)

Imagine someone using a line as a rule in the following way: he holds a pair of compasses, and carries one of its points along the line that is the 'rule', while the other one draws the line that follows the rule. And while he moves along the ruling line he alters the opening of the compasses, apparently with great precision, looking at the rule the whole time as if it determined what he did. And watching him we see no kind of regularity in this opening and shutting of the compasses. We cannot learn his way of following the line from it. Here perhaps one really would say: 'The original seems to *intimate* to him which way he is to go. But it is not a rule.'

The rule can only seem to me to produce all its consequences in advance if I draw them as a *matter of course*. As much as it is a matter of course for me to call this colour 'blue'. (Criteria for the fact that something is 'a matter of course' for me.)[52]

The point that is easily overlooked comes near the beginning: 'These are not my experiences of acting from inspiration and according to a rule; they are grammatical notes.' It is interesting that he says this just after he has argued that, if obeying a rule were inspiration, speaking a language would not be an acquired skill, or, if it were one, it would merely consist in each person listening carefully to his own inner voice, and the exercise of this minimal skill would not produce agreement in judgements between members of the same community. So the point is not just that we do not have these inner voices, but that, if we did have

[52] *PI* I §§ 232–8.

them and did listen to them, an important feature of language would be lost—it could no longer be used as a means of communication.[53] It follows that it would be impossible to use agreement in judgements in order to set up such a language, if indeed it would still be a language. As usual, the argument is reductive.

But would it be a language? The answer appears to be negative. For this particular reductive argument adds a further point to the discussion of reidentifying types of thing: if the key to the connection between stimulus and response is internalized, and if there is nothing to distinguish this key from a randomizer, then the vocalizations of these people would not count as a language. This might be called 'the third private language argument'.[54]

It is worth observing that he could have used a different argument against the theory of the inner voice. He could have argued that anyone who *always* relied on an inner voice would simply be repeating what it said without understanding it; but though that might seem to explain how he 'recognized' things, it would not really explain it, because he would still need to 'recognize' the pronouncements of his inner voice, and it would be no good postulating a second inner voice to help him with that problem. Wittgenstein does not use this argument, but he does develop a similar argument in the remark that immediately follows the passage just quoted from *Philosophical Investigations*:

> How is he to know what colour he is to pick out when he hears 'red'?—Quite simple: he is to take the colour whose image occurs to him when he hears the word.—But how is he to know which colour it is 'whose image occurs to him'? Is a further criterion needed for that? (There is indeed such a procedure as choosing the colour which occurs to one when one hears the word '. . .'.)
>
> ' "Red" means the colour that occurs to me when I hear the word "red" '—would be a *definition*. Not an explanation of *what it is* to use a word as a name.[55]

This argument is set out more fully in *The Blue Book*:

> If I give someone the order 'fetch me a red flower from that meadow', how is he to know what sort of flower to bring, as I have only given him a *word*?
>
> Now the answer one might suggest first is that he went to look for a red

---

[53] See above, pp. 382–4.

[54] Maybe it would be better to stop using the name 'private language argument'. Wittgenstein never used it, and it has been used here mainly because it is now traditional to call the argument beginning at *PI* I § 243 by that name. The case for not using it would be that, however carefully we distribute the title among Wittgenstein's arguments, it has an extraordinary power to blind us to their actual structures and interrelations.

[55] *PI* I § 239.

flower carrying a red image in his mind, and comparing it with the flowers to see which of them had the colour of the image. Now there is such a way of searching, and it is not at all essential that the image we use should be a mental one. In fact the process may be this: I carry a chart co-ordinating names and coloured squares. When I hear the order 'fetch me etc.' I draw my finger across the chart from the word 'red' to a certain square, and I go and look for a flower which has the same colour as the square. But this is not the only way of searching and it isn't the usual way. We go, look about us, walk up to a flower and pick it, without comparing it to anything. To see that the process of obeying the order can be of this kind, consider the order '*imagine* a red patch'. You are not tempted in this case to think that *before* obeying you must have imagined a red patch to serve you as a pattern for the red patch which you were ordered to imagine.[56]

However, in *Philosophical Investigations* the objection made against the theory of the inner voice is not that it generates an infinite regress, but that it goes against an essential feature of any language—speaking it is an acquired skill. This provides further confirmation for the interpretation of the private language argument proposed in Chapter 14: the reason why there could not possibly be such a language was not the difficulty of setting it up, but, rather, that whatever anyone did privately would not count as speaking a language, because it would not meet the central requirement for an acquired skill, which is that there must be a viable, independent criterion which distinguishes getting it right from getting it wrong.[57]

It may be found surprising that in this passage in *Philosophical Investigations* nothing is said about the second of the two resources which yield an independent criterion for this distinction. Why does Wittgenstein here confine himself to saying, 'I shall not be able to teach anyone else my "technique" of following the line' except by telling him to listen to his own inner voice, but 'then, of course, I cannot require him to follow the line in the same way that I do'? The impossibility of reaching agreement in judgements is important, but so too is the impossibility of calibration on standard objects. So why not mention that too? But his silence here on the further point can hardly be used to start an objection to the interpretation proposed in Chapter 14. For the point that Wittgenstein is making here against the theory of the inner voice is that the vocalizations of a speaker relying on it would not count as a language, because there would be nothing to distinguish the key to the connection between stimulus and response from a

---

[56] *BLBK* p. 3.   [57] See above, p. 329.

randomizer. This would have the obvious consequence that teaching this 'technique' to another person would not yield agreement in judgements and so neither the teacher nor the pupil would have any way of telling when the lesson had been learned. It would also have the further consequence that someone trying to set up such a practice on his own would not have any expectations about the way in which his inner voice would react to a standard object. For if he got the hang of what his inner voice was doing, he would not need to listen to it, and so the theory is either a wheel spinning idly or incoherent. Wittgenstein did not feel any need to mention this second consequence, because it is equally obvious and produced in the same way as the first one.

His reason for considering the theory of the inner voice is not that it is a plausible theory. In fact, there are several obvious things wrong with it which he does not mention in this passage. Here he focuses very sharply on the two features of the theory that he finds interesting. The theory is intended to explain the important fact that, when I have learned a rule, I apply it as a matter of course—'As much as it is a matter of course for me to call this colour "blue" '.[58] However, the explanation is mistaken, because it assimilates the ordinary case of applying a rule to the rare and quite different case of genuinely inspirational application.

He brings out the ordinariness of the ordinary case by imagining a different reaction to the achievement of agreement in judgements: people reach agreement in their judgements just as we do, but feel spellbound and marvel at their achievement.[59] If we are going to succeed in imagining this, we shall have to credit them with a religious attitude to the 'daily round'. Without such an attitude, they would find the rule governing the word 'blue' irresistible but totally undramatic in its operation, because it would operate through them rather than on them, just as it does with us. Indeed, when I reflect on what happens so smoothly and quietly in my own case, I almost feel that I could have called this harebell 'red', but that is an illusion. The truth is that it is because the inner compulsion to call it 'blue' is irresistible that it does not need to manifest itself in anything more than my just calling it 'blue'. To put the point in another way, as far as anything ratiocinative goes I *could* have called it 'red', but that does not mean that I could really have called it 'red'.

Incidentally, it is worth noting what he says about the inspirational

[58] *PI* I § 238.
[59] Ibid., § 234.

theory of arithmetic. Each child would be taught to listen to his own inner voice and 'calculating in this way would be like a sort of composing'.[60] Here, as at so many other points, the attempt to strengthen the structure of a language-game in a way in which it does not need to be strengthened immediately turns it into another, quite different kind of performance. It is interesting that the deviation in the direction of art occurs in this case because the children do not aim at agreement in their calculations. A similar deviation was noted earlier, but it had the opposite cause: exclusive concentration on agreement in judgements turned factual language into a kind of choral improvisation.[61] There is no mystery in the fact that two opposite deviations lead the would-be scientist or mathematician towards artistic performance. In one case inspired reactions produce a scattered pattern of results, while in the other case the results are held together in a tight pattern, but this is achieved in the wrong way, by direct imitation instead of by the same trained response to the same objects.

As usual, it is important to appreciate exactly what it is that Wittgenstein finds unacceptable. He is not rejecting the idea that I have to call this harebell 'blue', and it is no good sifting his accounts of bizarre deviations for some feature that will make their occurrence intelligible to us, any more than we should sift his account of what happens in our own case for some feature which will explain why we go on as we do. For his point is that there are no such features, and he is trying to make us stop looking for what is not there to be found. He is rejecting the idea that somewhere in my mental life, as I live it, I can identify something that forces me to call the flower 'blue'. This idea is very like the theory rejected by Hume after he has taken his investigation of causation back into the mind. However, Wittgenstein is not arguing in any sceptical spirit. He is certainly not suggesting that, because no such inner authority is to be found, there is a risk of a breakdown of law and order in our mental lives. His point is only that the authority is supplied not by any single item, but by the whole language-game with all its complicated attachments to the world.

Imagine a large and complex scaffolding erected over a piece of ground. The poles and struts run in all directions and the interlocking structure is hard to understand as we move around within it. Because it has not been put together in a perspicuous way, we have a certain feeling of insecurity. Are we adequately supported? Are we supported

---

[60] Ibid., § 233.
[61] See above, pp. 387–8.

at all? These questions are suppressed in daily life but released by philosophy and, once out, they have to be answered. The answer opposed by Wittgenstein is that there are special points inside the system at which all the required support is concentrated. Not only is that not so, but really it could not be so, and here his usual reductive arguments are brought to bear. The support is spread throughout the structure, eventually reaching the ground at many different points each of which makes its contribution to the stability of the whole.

The critique of the theory of the inner voice is a particularly clear example of this line of thought. We simply do not need to have all the support that stabilizes a particular language-game concentrated at a single point. So, not surprisingly, we do not have inner voices to play this unnecessary role. But the really telling point is that, if we did have them, they would immediately deprive the language-game of its essential features: it would be turned into a different language-game, or, perhaps, into something that would not count as language at all.

The same line of thought can be discerned in his treatment of the case of a teacher who tells a pupil to continue the series '2, 4, 6 . . .'. The teacher might say,

> 'But I already knew, at the time when I gave the order, that he ought to write 1002 after 1000.'—Certainly; and you can also say you *meant* it then; only you should not let yourself be misled by the grammar of the words 'know' and 'mean'. For you don't want to say that you thought of the step from 1000 to 1002 at that time—and even if you did think of this step, still you did not think of other ones. When you said 'I already knew at the time . . .' that meant something like: 'If I had then been asked what number should be written after 1000, I should have replied "1002".' And that I don't doubt. This assumption is rather of the same kind as: 'If he had fallen into the water then, I should have jumped in after him'.—Now, what was wrong with your idea?[62]

What is wrong with the idea is that this piece of knowledge, based on the speaker's intention, is not a peculiarly powerful stabilizer. Its formulation in advance is merely another manifestation of the internalized rule which is going to make the teacher say '1002' when he reaches that point in the series. There is no more support for his performance concentrated at this point in it than there is at any other point. As Wittgenstein observes in *Remarks on the Foundations of Mathematics*, if he uses this piece of knowledge later, he will have to apply it, and then his application of it will be yet another manifestation of the internalized rule.[63]

[62] *PI* I § 187, quoted above, p. 444.   [63] *RFM* I § 3, quoted above, p. 438.

It would be easy to collect from Wittgenstein's writings other examples of the illusion that he is trying to neutralize here. There is the talismanic image that is supposed to occur in the mind of someone who understands the order, 'Choose a yellow ball out of this bag':[64] or the mental aiming which is supposed to guarantee that I mean this face that I am drawing to be my friend's face;[65] or the queer way in which the future applications of a word are taken to be already present in my mind when I suddenly catch on to its meaning.[66] These are all ways of mythologizing the high-wire act of a speaker who moves around so faultlessly and so confidently inside his own language. Either an ordinary aid, like a mental image, is credited with miraculous powers and treated as the universal key to understanding, or a mythical aid, like the inner voice, is invented; or else, perhaps, we gesture in the direction of a mental act which we leave unspecified, so that its magic power of reaching into the future and anticipating all the correct applications of a rule is protected from falsification by its convenient indefiniteness.[67]

The system of support that allows speakers to make their moves inside their language involves their previous training and their continuing relations with the world around them and with one another. These props can all be investigated and described in factual language. What Wittgenstein opposes here is a pair of connected ideas. First, there is the idea that this external support can be internalized and used by speakers in the same way that they use the considerations that figure in whatever language-game they are playing. That, he thinks, cannot be right. The appeal to the logistics of a language-game is quite different from the appeal to considerations that figure inside it.[68] A speaker cannot mix the presuppositions of what he says with his reasons for saying it. His reasons are concentrated at the moment of speaking, but that is not true of the presuppositions.[69]

Here the second idea opposed by Wittgenstein comes in. Because the presuppositions are diffuse and internal considerations have to be neatly packaged, the internalization of presuppositions cannot be carried out so long as they are treated realistically. So they have to be transformed into something compact and identifiable in the speaker's

---

[64] See *BLBK* pp. 11–12. Cf. *BLBK* p. 3, quoted above, pp. 522–3.
[65] See *PI* I §§ 683–9.   [66] Ibid., I § 195.
[67] See above, pp. 205–7.
[68] This point is connected with the earlier doctrine of showing. See above, pp. 000–0
[69] The distinction between what is said in language and what is presupposed by it was introduced above, pp. 251–3.

stream of consciousness. Or perhaps we should say that the role of presuppositions is taken over in these theories by some definite identifiable mental item. How else can we explain the confidence with which he makes his move? That is how the myth of the instant mental talisman and all those other illusions are born. The real external connections of language are replaced by fictitious internal gadgets.

There is no single key to Wittgenstein's later philosophy. However, much of it really is generated out of three ideas examined in these concluding chapters. One is the idea that the moves available to a speaker in any given language-game are limited. For example, he cannot go on giving reasons for something that he has said, but must in the end rest it on the fact that he has been adequately trained in the use of the words that he has used. To put the point in Wittgenstein's favourite way, he has reached bedrock in the language-game.[70] The second idea is a development of the early doctrine of showing. In the *Tractatus* the relations between language and the world could not be described but only shown, and so a philosopher who tried to describe them in factual language could only produce comments which were inappropriately expressed and, therefore, extremely marginal and precarious. What developed out of this very restrictive view of philosophy was a more liberal, empirical treatment of language: naturally, the presuppositions of any language-game lie outside it, but that does not mean that they cannot be presented in other language-games, and much of his later work is a demonstration of the possibiity of such presentations and their power to loosen the knots that philosophers tie in their own thinking.[71] The third idea is that the main source of illusions in the philosophy of mind is the assumption that the external supports on which a language-game rests must somehow be pulled into it and made to function inside it. Instead of being left where they belong, outside it, and treated holistically, they are concentrated at definite points within the system where they generate a whole mythology of displaced devices.

If we are tempted to treat this as a summary of Wittgenstein's later philosophy, the omissions will make themselves felt immediately. For example, among the presuppositions of a simple language-game like describing the colours of objects there is one particularly important group of facts: we have natural tendencies, antedating language, to sort out colours in definite ways. In this study of the development of

---

[70] Cf. *PI* I § 217.
[71] See above, pp. 429–30 and 457–9.

Wittgenstein's philosophy the importance of natural tendencies of that kind first became apparent in the investigation of private language. His argument against the possibility of such a language relied on the idea that it would be impossible to explain our descriptions of perceived objects without them. The clearest illustration of this dependence of phenomenological description on natural tendencies was provided by the spatial properties of things in the visual field.[72] Those were all cases of descriptive words and of the rules to be followed when we apply them to things. But our natural tendencies also underlie our adherence to mathematical and logical rules:

... For instance, you say to someone 'This is red' (pointing); then you tell him 'Fetch me a red book'—and he will behave in a particular way. This is an immensely important fact about us human beings. And it goes together with all sorts of other facts of equal importance, like the fact that in all the languages we know the meanings of words don't change with the days of the week.

Another such fact is that pointing is used and understood in a particular way—people react to it in a particular way.

This hangs together with the question of how to continue the series of cardinal numbers. Is there a criterion for the continuation—for a right and a wrong way—except that we do in fact continue them in that way, apart from a few cranks who can be neglected?

This has often been said before. And it has often been put in the form of an assertion that the truths of logic are determined by a consensus of opinions. Is this what I am saying? No. There is no *opinion* at all; it is not a question of *opinion*. They are determined by a consensus of *action*: a consensus of doing the same thing, reacting in the same way. There is a consensus but it is not a consensus of opinion. We all act the same way, walk the same way, count the same way.

In counting we do not express opinions at all. There is no opinion that 25 follows 24—nor intuition. We express opinions by means of counting.[73]

It would be hard to exaggerate the importance of the role played in Wittgenstein's later philosophy by the pre-linguistic structure on which language supervened.

It certainly shapes the constellation of three ideas attributed to him above. The mistaken internalization of the external supports of language produces a whole mythology of magic mental aids and

---

[72] See above, pp. 331–2 and pp. 401–6.

[73] *LFM* pp. 182–4, quoted in full above, pp. 444–6. The point made by the last sentence must be that we count objects and arrive at opinions like the opinion that I passed five turnings to the left on my way down this street.

mechanisms. Instead of just going ahead and naming a colour, you are supposed to appeal to an instant mental talisman which takes the responsibility off your shoulders; even if meaning is doing, you are an agent who is not even minimally free—and so on. This erroneous internalization then leads to another equally serious fault, the false intellectualization of our mental lives. Something was said about this fault in the earlier discussion of the private language argument:[74] it is, for example, the source of the extraordinary idea that, if there were an original position in which language was set up, in it each subject would be faced by the purely intellectual task of naming his own sense-data. So in our case, it is as if our sense-data had never previously played any part in our lives but appeared on our horizon for the first time as a problem for our intellects. There is at this point a hard dilemma for Cartesian philosophers: on the one hand, if these pre-linguistic tendencies are ignored, the result is palpable absurdity, but on the other hand, there is no way in which they can be dressed up as items in the subject's stream of consciousness. They are not available to the subject in that way, because his thinking is not directed on to them but rather, exemplifies them. This is a partial vindication of the early doctrine of showing.

It is not too difficult for Wittgenstein to persuade us to reject the over-intellectualization of our practice of applying descriptive words to things. We can see that he is not minimizing the force of our natural tendencies to go on in the ways that we do, but only insisting that they are just ours, and that their contribution to our systems of classification is essential. We can also see that he is not denying the objectivity of the distinctions that we mark between different types of things, but only arguing that it is not an objectivity that is independent of our systems and, therefore, that it cannot be invoked to explain them.[75] But the passage just quoted from *Lectures on the Foundations of Mathematics* extends the same treatment to logical and mathematical rules. They too cannot be explained as reflections of the objective structure of reality, because they too rest on our pre-linguistic tendencies. It is at this point that the next problem surfaces. Did Wittgenstein really think that this treatment could be extended to logic and mathematics?[76] And if so, was he right?

These are questions beyond the scope of this book, but something

[74] See above, pp. 395–6.
[75] See above, Ch. 9, and Vol. I pp. 16–17 and 149.
[76] See Vol. I pp. 28–33.

can be said about their connection with some of the questions that have been discussed here. Both in *Philosophical Investigations* and in *Remarks on the Foundations of Mathematics* he connects his anti-Platonic treatment of mathematical and logical rules with his anti-Platonic treatment of rules for the use of descriptive words. This opens up a new avenue which cannot be explored here, but we can, at least, turn the corner and see what lies ahead.

In the previous chapter the argument against the Platonic theory of rule-following was formulated like this: 'Even if the correct applications of a descriptive word were all laid out in advance, it would not help a speaker to apply it correctly. For he would still need something in his mind to reflect that paradigmatic sequence, and he would have to understand whatever mental item played that role because he would have to apply it case by case. When he did this, the essential contribution made by him at the interface between language and the world could not be discounted, because, if it were discounted, the difference between obeying and disobeying the rule would vanish.'

The idea is that the Platonic paradigm is inadequate by itself, and, when the essential contribution made by the speaker has been added, superfluous. Why then did anyone ever find it plausible? Wittgenstein's diagnosis is that it seems plausible only when the speaker's state of mind has been idealized in something like the way in which a familiar machine is idealized when it is treated as a symbol of its own correct performance. He was well aware that the two idealizations do not work in exactly the same way, because there is an important difference between them: we do have an independent criterion for the correct performance of a machine, but we do not have any criterion of linguistic correctness that is completely independent of actual linguistic practices. In order to mark this difference, the speaker's state of mind was said to have been 'super-idealized'. That is to say, it had been detached from its contemporary setting and its origin in his past history, and attached by definition to a fantasized, and forever inaccessible, paradigmatic sequence of correct applications.[77]

That was where the matter was left, but if the discussion were abandoned at that point, it might well give the impression that Wittgenstein was distinguishing the mere psychological compulsion to continue the series of applications of a descriptive word in a certain

[77] A footnote can now be added to this argument: the suggestion, that what occurred in his mind might be an inner voice prompting him, is an attractive one, but, for the reasons given above (pp. 520–5), it is unacceptable.

way and another, stronger kind of compulsion guaranteed by a definition.[78] That would make his treatment of linguistic rules very like Hume's treatment of causal inference, because Hume made no attempt to extend his naturalistic account of causal inference to logical inference.[79] However, that would be a false impression. A definition yields a logical rule licensing the substitution of one phrase for another, and Wittgenstein explicitly extends his naturalistic account to logic. So, according to him, there is nothing sacrosanct about a move guaranteed by a definition, and even if there were other faults in the Platonic account of the use of descriptive words, it would fail at this point to give them the independent basis in reality which was its goal. The human contribution to what counts as the correct application of a descriptive word is matched by a similar human contribution to what counts as the correct development of a mathematical series or the correct use of a logical word[80] This is the part of his philosophy that strikes most people as paradoxical. How can logic and mathematics be 'psychologized'?

Those who find this paradoxical are usually less reluctant to accept his naturalistic treatment of rules governing our descriptive vocabulary. But according to him, these too are meaning-rules, and so, given his conception of logic, they too belong to it—on the edge, perhaps, but still part of it.[81] So his view was that it is no more paradoxical to treat the central rules of logic naturalistically than it is treat its peripheral rules naturalistically.

It is not surprising that not everyone finds this convincing. The doubters are ready to concede the point about rules for the use of descriptive words, because they recognize the flimsiness of Platonism when it is brought in to explain the grip that these rules have on our minds. We obviously achieve nothing if we project our use of the word 'red' on to the world, and then invoke the projection to explain our use of the word. The point, of course, is not that colours are the mere shadows of our reactions to them (whatever that would mean), but that no non-circular explanation of our colour-classification can be extracted from the colours we classify them.[82] Similarly, we achieve nothing if we attribute the incompatibility of 'red' and 'green' to the

[78] He rejects this account he is doing in *PI* I § 139. See above, p. 517 n. 42.
[79] See above, p. 508.
[80] See *PI* I § 187, quoted above, p. 444, §§ 288–9, quoted above, pp. 439–40, and *RFM* I § 3, quoted above, p. 438.
[81] Cf. *PI* I § 242, discussed above, pp. 382–3.
[82] See Vol. I pp. 16–17.

natures of the two colours.[83] But people are more impressed by the other side of Platonism, its explanation of the grip that logic has on our minds. It is easier to believe that the truths of logic owe nothing to us, and that logical rules, unlike rules governing the use of descriptive words, are completely independnt of our practices.

However paradoxical it may be to deny this, Wittgenstein does deny it. Maybe the paradox is reduced when we realize that he is not loosening the grip that logical rules have on our minds, but only reversing the relationship—the grip is ours, because it is we who will not let logic go. But though this is an important point, often underestimated in the rhetoric of the controversy, it is not enough to make the paradox acceptable to everyone. However, paradoxical or not, that is Wittgenstein's view, and so in the earlier discussion of his argument against Platonism it was an understatement to say that he took his adversary to task for using a definition to super-idealize the state of mind of a person applying a descriptive word to a series of things. The fact is that he treated the rule yielded by the definition in exactly the same way as the rule for the use of the word 'red'. So by a characteristically subtle twist, he extended his naturalism to the very thing that seemed to his adversary to be protected from it.

If we want to get the full force of his naturalism in these two connected fields, we should reconsider this:

> Then what sort of mistake did I make; was it what we should like to express by saying: I should have thought the picture forced a particular use on me? How could I think that? What *did* I think? Is there such a thing as a picture, or something like a picture, that forces a particular application on us; so that my mistake lay in confusing one thing with another?—For we might also be inclined to express ourselves like this: we are at most under a psychological, not a logical, compulsion. And now it looks quite as if we knew of two kinds of case.

> What was the effect of my argument? It called our attention to (reminded us of) the fact that there are other processes, besides the one we originally thought of, which we should sometimes be prepared to call 'applying the picture of a cube'. So our 'belief that the picture forced a particular application upon us' consisted in the fact that only the one case and no other occurred to us. 'There is another solution as well' means: there is something else that I am also prepared to call a 'solution'; to which I am prepared to apply such-and-such a picture, such-and-such an analogy, and so on.

---

[83] See my article, 'Incompatibilities of Colours', in *Logic and Language, Second Series*, ed. A. Flew, Blackwell, 1953.

What is essential is to see that the same thing can come before our minds when we hear the word and the application still be different. Has it the *same* meaning both times? I think we shall say not.[84]

Or this:

'But then what does the peculiar inexorability of mathematics consist in?'—Would not the inexorability with which two follows one and three two be a good example?—But presumably this means: follows in the *series of cardinal numbers*; for in a different series something different follows. And isn't *this* series just *defined* by this sequence?—'Is that supposed to mean that it is equally correct whichever way a person counts, and that anyone can count as he pleases?'—We should presumably not call it 'counting' if everyone said the numbers one after the other *anyhow*; but of course it is not simply a question of a name. For what we call 'counting' is an important part of our life's activities. Counting and calculating are not—e.g.—simply a pastime. Counting (and that means: counting like *this*) is a technique that is employed daily in the most various operations of our lives. And that is why we learn to count as we do: with endless practice, with merciless exactitude; that is why it is inexorably insisted that we shall say 'two' after 'one', 'three' after 'two', and so on.—'But is this counting only a *use*, then; isn't there also some truth corresponding to this sequence?' The *truth* is that counting has proved to pay.—'Then do you want to say that "being true" means: being usable (or useful)?'—No, not that; but that it can't be said of the series of natural numbers—that it is true, but: that it is usable, and, above all, *it is used*.[85]

---

[84] *PI* I § 140.   [85] *RFM* I § 4.

BIBLIOGRAPHY

A. *Works by, or originating from (*) Wittgenstein which are the most frequently cited sources*

* *Ludwig Wittgenstein and the Vienna Circle: Conversations Recorded by Friedrich Waismann*, ed. B. McGuinness, tr. J. Schulte and B. McGuinness, Blackwell, 1979. [*LWVC*]

Notebooks 1914–1916, ed. G. H. von Wright and G. E. M. Anscombe, tr. G. E. M. Anscombe, Blackwell, 1961. [*NB*]

'Notes for Lectures on "Private Experience" and "Sense Data" ', *Philosophical Review*, Vol. 77, No. 3, 1968. [*NLPESD*]

Philosophical Grammar, ed. R. Rhees, tr. A. Kenny, Blackwell, 1974. [*PG*]

Philosophical Investigations, tr. G. E. M. Anscombe, Blackwell, 1953; 3rd edn, Macmillan, 1958. [*PI*]

Philosophical Remarks, ed. R. Rhees, tr. R. Hargreaves and R. White, Blackwell, 1975. [*PR*]

Remarks on the Foundations of Mathematics, ed. G. H. von Wright, R. Rhees, and G. E. M. Anscombe, tr. G. E. M. Anscombe, Blackwell, 3rd edn., 1978. [*RFM*]

Remarks on the Philosophy of Psychology, Vol. I, ed. G. E. M. Anscombe and G. H. von Wright, tr. G. E. M. Anscombe, Blackwell, 1980. [*RPPI*]

Remarks on the Philosophy of Psychology, Vol. II, ed. G. H. von Wright and Heikki Nyman, tr. C. G. Luckhardt and M. A. E. Aue, Blackwell, 1980. [*RPPII*]

* *The Blue Book*, in L. Wittgenstein: *The Blue and Brown Books*, Blackwell, 1958. [*BLBK*]

* *The Brown Book*, in L. Wittgenstein: *The Blue and Brown Books*, Blackwell, 1958. [*BRBK*]

Tractatus Logico-Philosophicus, tr. C. K. Ogden, Routledge, 1922, and tr. D. F. Pears and B. McGuinness, Routledge, 1961. [*TLP*]

* *Wittgenstein's Lectures, Cambridge, 1930–32*, ed. D. Lee, Blackwell, 1980. [*CLI*]

* *Wittgenstein's Lectures, Cambridge, 1932–35*, ed. Alice Ambrose, Blackwell, 1979. [*CLII*]

Wittgenstein's Lectures on the Foundations of Mathematics, ed. C. Diamond, Harvester Press, 1975. [*LFM*]

B. *Other Works by, or originating from (*) Wittgenstein, infrequently cited*

Notes Dictated to G. E. Moore in Norway, in *Notebooks 1914–16* (q.v.).
On Certainty, ed. G. E. M. Anscombe and G. H. von Wright, tr. D. Paul and G. E. M. Anscombe, Blackwell, 1969.
Remarks on Colour, ed. G. E. M. Anscombe, tr. L. McAlister and M. Schättle, Blackwell, 1977.
The Big Typescript, unpublished. Item 213 in G. H. von Wright's list, *Philosophical Review*, Vol. 78, Oct. 1969, Special Supplement.
* 'The Language of Sense Data and Private Experience', notes taken by R. Rhees of Wittgenstein's Lectures, 1936, in *Philosophical Investigations* (the periodical), Vol. 7, Nos. 1 and 2, January and April 1984.
* 'Wittgenstein's Lectures in 1930–33', notes taken by G. E. Moore, in *Mind*, Vol. 63, No. 249 and No. 251, and Vol. 64, No. 253, January and July 1954 and January 1955.
Zettel, ed. G. E. M. Anscombe and G. H. von Wright, tr. G. E. M. Anscombe, Blackwell, 1967.

C. *Books and Articles on Wittgenstein*

BAKER, G. AND HACKER, P. M. S.: *Scepticism, Rules and Meaning*, Blackwell, 1984.
DONAGAN, A.: 'Wittgenstein on Sensation', in *Wittgenstein, the* Philosophical Investigations, ed. G. Pitcher, Doubleday, 1966.
HINTIKKA, J. and M.: *Investigating Wittgenstein*, Blackwell, 1986.
KRIPKE, S. A.: *Wittgenstein on Rules and Private Language*, Blackwell, 1982.
LEAR, J.: 'The Disappearing We', *Proceedings of the Aristotelian Society*, Supp. Vol. 58, 1984.
MALCOLM, N.: *Nothing is Hidden*, Blackwell, 1986.
McGINN, C.: *Wittgenstein on Meaning*, Blackwell, 1984.
PASCALL, F.: 'Wittgenstein, A Personal Memoir', in *Recollections of Wittgenstein*, ed. R. Rhees, Oxford, 1984.
THOMSON, J. J.: 'Private Languages', in *American Philosophical Quarterly*, Vol. I, No. 1, Jan. 1964.

D. *Other Books and Articles*

AUSTIN, J. L.: *Philosophical Papers*, Oxford, 1961.
BERKELEY, G.: *Principles of Human Knowledge*.
CARNAP, R.: 'Die physikalische Sprache als Universalsprache der Wissenschaft', *Erkenntnis*, Vol. 2, Nos. 5 and 6 (1932).
—— *The Logical Structure of the World*, tr. R. A. George, Routledge, 1967.
—— *The Unity of Science*, tr. M. Black, Kegan Paul, 1934.

COLERIDGE, S. T.: *Biographia Literaria*, in *The Collected Works of Samuel Taylor Coleridge*, Princeton, 1983.

EVANS, G.: 'Things without the Mind', in *Philosophical Subjects, Essays Presented to P. F. Strawson*, ed. Z. van Straaten, Oxford, 1980: reprinted in G. Evans: *Collected Papers*, Oxford, 1985.

HUME D.: *Treatise of Human Nature*.

MERLEAU-PONTY, M.: *Phénomenologie de la Perception*, Gallimard, 1945.

NEWTON, I.: *Principia*.

PUTNAM, H.: 'The Meaning of Meaning', in *Collected Papers*, Vol. 2, Cambridge, 1981.

PEARS, D. F.: 'Hume's Empiricism and Modern Empiricism', in *David Hume*, Macmillan, 1963.

—— 'Incompatibilities of Colours', in *Logic and Language, Second Series*, ed. A. Flew, Blackwell, 1953.

RUSSELL, B.: 'The Philosophy of Logical Atomism', in *Essays in Logic and Knowledge*, ed. R. C. Marsh, Allen and Unwin, 1956.

—— *The Problems of Philosophy*, Oxford, 1911.

SCHLICK, M.: 'Meaning and Verification', *Philosophical Review*, Vol. 45, 1936, reprinted in *Readings in Philosophical Analysis*, ed. H. Feigl and W. Sellars, Appleton-Century-Crofts, 1949.

STRAWSON, P. F.: *Individuals: an Essay in Descriptive Metaphysics*, Methuen, 1959.

INDEX

acquired skill, 333, 342, 344–5, 362–88
  acquisition of, 366–7, 375–7, 381
agreement in judgements, 339, 368–71,
  383–6, 434, 463, 480
Anscombe, G. E. M., 473 n. 28
Aristotle, 302 n. 13
atomism, logical, 203–4, 206, 256–7
Austin, J. L., 346 n. 33, 347 n. 34

Baker, G. P., 362 n. 3, 366 n. 14, 373 nn.
  29 and 31, 374 nn. 32 and 33, 463 n.
  7, 465 n. 13, 468 n. 20, 500 n. 88,
  501 n. 93
behaviourism, 212, 224, 228, 270, 309,
  312–13, 321, 349 n. 38, 351–3, 414,
  427, 512
Berkeley, G., 244, 469, 471–2
British Empiricism, 235, 278, 288, 315,
  493

calculus, 210, 279
Carnap, R., 204, 302–9, 316, 325–6, 405,
  461
Coleridge, S. T., 329
content, incommunicability of, 303, 306

Darwin, C., 450
decision, 519
definitions, immobilizing, 227, 229, 231,
  250, 361, 421–2, 483–6, 502–4
dispositions, 469, 480
dogmatism, 203–4, 206
doing (intentional action), 329, 333, 420,
  431–59, 507
Donagan, A., 342 n. 25

ego (or subject), 228–69, 297, 299, 301,
  308, 313–14, 327, 502
egocentrism, sliding-peg, 233, 276–7,
  290
Einstein, A., 203
Evans, G., 332 n. 9, 401 n. 21, 403, 405 n.
  32
explanation, 202–3, 206, 211–12, 216,
  455

expression, 347 n. 14
  natural, 309, 331, 339, 348, 399
eye, geometrical, 241–3, 245, 293, 322,
  325

Ficker, L., 302 n. 12

generality, the craving for, 201–2, 220,
  502

Hacker, P. M. S., 362 n. 3, 366 n. 14, 373
  nn. 29 and 31, 374 nn. 32 and 33,
  463 n. 7, 465 n. 13, 468 n. 20, 500 n.
  88, 501 n. 93
Hintikka, J. and M., 316 n. 33
holiday, language on, 217–18, 232
holism, 256, 271, 528
Hume, D., 237 n. 22, 242, 245 n. 37, 265,
  358, 380 n. 47, 427, 437 n. 27, 442
  n. 34, 463, 469, 471–2, 477, 480–1,
  507–11, 513–17, 525, 532

idealism, 233, 267 n. 81, 268
identity, criteria of,
  for the ego, 229, 267
  for particular sensations, 231–2,
    415–16
  for sensation-types, 213, 231, 267, 292,
    298, 321, 326, 415–16, 418–20,
    428–9, 439
idle cogs, 350–2, 430
incorrigibility, 257–9, 343–8, 350,
  359–60, 439
inner, as the characterization of the
  mental, 211–14, 325, 340, 350–7,
  400, 408–9, 411, 428–9
interpretation, verbal, 467, 505
intuition (inspiration), 519–25

Kant, I., 289, 317, 397, 510
knowledge, cases that are too good to
  count as, 259, 314
  of my future application of a rule, 444,
    481, 482, 494 n. 75, 526
Kripke, S. A., 226 n. 1, 358 n. 58, 362 n.
  2, 374 n. 33, 388 n. 65, 433 n. 20,

Kripke, S. A. (*cont.*):
  442–3, 447 n. 44, 456–8, 463 n. 6,
  464, 467, 474, 479–80, 489,
  499–500, 505, 506 n. 8, 508–9

language, as an instrument of
    measurement, 436, 458–9, 486–7
  limit of, 220, 234, 255, 276–7,
    299–300, 330, 336, 389–90
  limited self-sufficiency of, 461–2
  prelinguistic framework of, 260–1, 309,
    331–2, 358, 365, 396–406, 414,
    451, 456, 520, 528–30
  primary or phenomenological, 273–95
  scientific, 308–14, 321
  the solitary speaker of, 334–5, 338–9,
    362–88
  stabilization of, 434–5, 441–2
language-game, 206, 271, 279–80, 424
Lear, J., 268 n. 85, 429 n. 14, 459 n. 71
limbo, quasi-scientific, 206–7, 209, 221,
    337, 393 n. 6, 400 n. 15
line, personal, 252–66, 309, 345, 348–9,
    426–7
  type-, 309, 340, 345, 348–9, 404,
    426–8
Locke, J., 332
logic, 215, 383–5, 436

machine, as a symbol of its own action,
    475–86
Malcolm, N., 362 nn. 2 and 5, 365 n. 11,
    380 n. 48, 382
mathematics, 436–7, 438–40, 443–6,
    530–4
McGinn, C., 362 nn. 3 and 5, 378 n. 43,
    380 n. 48, 383 n. 57, 386 n. 62, 463
    n. 8, 467 n. 17, 490 n. 59
McGuinness, B., 273
measurement, alternative systems of,
    445–54
Merleau-Ponty, M., 332 n. 9, 405 n. 32
Möbius ring, 430

names, their attachment to objects, 207
naturalism, 437, 442, 451, 507, 510–20
necessity, 465–6, 473 n. 29, 508, 517–18,
    531–3
Newton, I., 203, 266, 511
no-ownership theory, 238, 249, 261–6

other minds, 274–5, 297–327

paradigm, for determining all the correct
    applications of a word, 208–11, 227
Pascal, Fania, 222 n. 41
Pears, D. F., 358 n. 58, 533 n. 83.
phenomenalism, classical, 235, 275, 277,
    282–3, 289–95, 297, 338 n. 17,
    341–2, 363, 389–406
  sliding-peg, 235, 277, 282–4, 287,
    289–95, 299, 301, 304, 320
Platonism, 206, 363, 385, 440, 465,
    483–8, 503–8, 531–3
  the meaning-body version of, 490–2
  Wittgenstein's reductive argument
    against, 457, 460–99
possibility, no identifiable candidates for,
    215–16, 356, 412, 448–9
practice, 363, 379, 420, 441, 499–501
presuppositions, 252, 257, 349, 415,
    425–7, 506
private language, the argument against,
    214, 227–8, 231, 235, 240 n. 32, 244
    n. 36, 249, 286, 298, 328–422
  the disabling defect of, 333, 339 n. 19
psychology, hypotheses of, 365–6
psychotherapy, 216, 218, 236–7
Putnam, H., 367 n. 16
Pythagoras, 211

Quine, W. V., 240

reading-machines, 379–81
reference to sensation-types, direct and
    independent of context, 298, 303–5,
    307, 317
Rousseau, J.-J., 471, 505 n. 7
rule-following, 205, 208, 371, 387, 431,
    441
Russell, B., 226 n. 2, 250 n. 46, 278, 281,
    288–9, 315, 373, 454 n. 55

scepticism, 259, 276, 282, 311, 425–6,
    430–1, 433, 441–2, 457–8, 460–1
Schlick, M., 273, 279–80, 284, 302–9,
    316–17, 325–6, 404, 461
science, 199–205, 220, 253–4, 424,
    435–6, 451–7, 487, 510–13
sensations, bodily, 284, 287
  ownership of, 237–69, 480
sensation-types, 213, 231, 267, 292, 298,
    300, 305, 313–14, 320, 328, 330,
    430
sense-data, 273, 277, 282–3, 286, 293–4,
    304, 391–406

sensory content, incommunicability of, 303, 306
  'intrinsic change' of, 357–8, 372, 402, 406–13, 417
shown, what can only be, 216, 299, 425, 474
solipsism, ego-based, 228–69, 291, 295, 318–19, 323–4
  the early argument against, 228, 233–5, 330, 362
  the later argument against, 230, 232, 235–6, 242–8, 319, 323–4, 330, 355, 362, 390
Strawson, Sir Peter, 238, 249, 261–6, 332 n. 9

super-idealization, 483–5, 487, 498, 504–5

talisman, instant mental, 209–10, 223, 469, 504, 507, 525, 527
  mental picture, used as, 471–4, 492–9
  verbal interpretation, used as, 433, 467–9
theories, 199–201, 206–7, 211, 214, 219, 222–4, 352–3, 488
Thomson, J. J., 342 n. 26
truth as hitting a target, 333–5, 392, 395, 405–6

verification principle, 342, 411, 461

Witty paper —
reaction agst
W → M Platonism &
W ← M agst autonomy of
mental —

how ther   can we
get connection +
if mistake?
→ global - local
Destin.

connect of
linear / coherentist?
how reflexivity   destin,
scope etc.